Lin MacDonald
Set Decorator

Street Furniture

Chris van Uffelen

Street Furniture

BRAUN

CONTENTS

8 Preface

Bike and Play

12 **Great Street Games**
KMA Creative Technology Ltd

13 **NiDondolo**
Mitzi Bollani

14 **VD 003**
Rovero Adrien Studio

15 **Park Games Science Park**
ZonaUno

16 **PIT IN**
STORE MUU design studio

18 **Flood Mitigation Measures**
Grimshaw

20 **Vélib and Mupi**
Agence Patrick Jouin

24 **Shelter Imperia**
RASTI GmbH

28 **Marguerite Bike Rack**
YHY design international

30 **Radhaus – Bicycle Station**
Osterwold & Schmidt – Exp!ander Architekten

34 **Cyclo Bicycle Stand**
díez+díez diseño

36 **Velo Bicycle Stand**
mmcité a.s.

Boundary

40 **Pilarete Bollard**
Pedro Silva Dias

41 **Haiku Bollard**
díez+díez diseño

42 **Heaven is a Place on Earth**
d e signstudio regina dahmen-ingenhoven

46 **Fence as Meetingpoint**
Tejo Remy & Rene Veenhuizen

48 **Bollard Elias**
mmcité a.s.

50 **Domplein**
OKRA landschapsarchitecten bv

52 **The Community Chalkboard**
Siteworks-Studio

56 **Platform House**
Ryo Yamada

57 **Lace Garden**
Anouk Vogel landscape architecture

58 **Allermöhe Wall**
Matthias Berthold, Andreas Schön

60 **Our Lights will lead the Way**
Sungi Kim & Hozin Song

61 **Animal Wall**
Gitta Gschwendtner

62 **Green Trap**
Adrien Rovero with Christophe Ponceau

Ensemble

66 **140 Boomerangs**
Studio Weave

70 **Center square, Rakvere**
KOSMOS

72 **Helga Eng Square, University of Oslo**
Bjarne Aasen Landskapsarkitekt MNLA

74 **Strossmayer Park**
Atelier Boris Podrecca

78 **National Harbor**
Sasaki Associates

82 **Benches at Elwood Foreshore**
ASPECT Studios

86 **City Center, Zutphen**
OKRA landschapsarchitecten bv

87 **Gran Vía de Llevant**
Arriola & Fiol arquitectes

88 **Storaa stream**
OKRA landschapsarchitecten bv

89 **Central Park of Nou Barris**
Arriola & Fiol arquitectes

90 **Sea Organ and Greeting to the Sun**
Marinaprojekt d.o.o.

94 **Chess Park**
Rios Clementi Hale Studios

98 **Quincy Court**
Rios Clementi Hale Studios

102 **Station square, Apeldoorn**
LODEWIJK BALJON landscape architects

104 **Bohaterów Getta Square (Zgody Square)**
Biuro Projektów Lewicki Łatak

108 **Książąt Czartoryskich Square**
Biuro Projektów Lewicki Łatak

110 **General Maister Memorial Park**
BRUTO d.o.o.

114 **Wellness Orhidelia**
BRUTO d.o.o.

116 **In Factory**
3GATTI

118 **Kic Village**
3GATTI

120 **Lazona Kawasaki Plaza**
Earthscape

122 **City Heart, Palmerston North**
CCM Architects, Ralph Johns & John Powell Landscape Architects

126 **Sylvia Park**
Isthmus

130 **Kumutoto**
Isthmus & Studio Pacific Architecture

134 **South Boston Maritime Park**
Machado and Silvetti Associates

136 **West Los Angeles City College, Pedestrian Promenade**
SQLA inc. LA

138 **HtO – Urban Beach**
Janet Rosenberg & Associates,
Claude Cormier architectes paysagistes inc.

140 **VivoCity**
Sitetectonix Private Limited

144 **Fountain Promenade at Chapultepec Park**
Grupo de Diseño Urbano

146 **Horizons**
Will Nettleship

147 **Under Road**
Vulcanica Architettura

148 **Riva Split Waterfront**
3LHD architects with Irena Mazer

Plants and Water

154 **Godot**
díez+díez diseño

156 **Thousand Year Forest**
Earthscape

158 **A Tree that will grow Dreams**
Earthscape

160 **Chafariz Drinking Fountain**
Estudio Cabeza

161 **One North Wacker Drive**
PWP Landscape Architecture, Inc.

162 **30 Adelaide Street East**
Janet Rosenberg + Associates

164 **Minato-Mirai Business Square**
Earthscape

166 **Reflecting Pools**
OLIN

168 **De Inktpot**
OKRA landschapsarchitecten bv

169 **Fountain Cameon**
Rainer Schmidt Landschaftsarchitekten
with GTL Landschaftsarchitekten

Garbage

172 **Garbage Can Senior 954**
Caesarea Landscape Design Ltd.

173 **Garbage Can Kiryat Uno**
Caesarea Landscape Design Ltd.

174 **Envac Disposal Chute**
EBD architects ApS

176 **Cylinder Waste Container**
mmcité a.s.

178 **BINA**
Gonzalo Milà Valcárcel

Light and Sign

182 **Wayfinding and Interpretive Graphics**
Sasaki Associates

186 **Signpost**
Despang Architekten

188 **Bargteheide Voice Shower**
Matthias Berthold, Andreas Schön

189 **York University Coordinated Signage and Wayfinding Program**
Kramer Design Associates (KDA)

190 **Welcome!**
Rainer Schmidt Landschaftsarchitekten

191 **Avenue Honore-Mercier**
Michel Dallaire Design Industriel – MDDI

192 **OliviO**
West 8 urban design & landscape architecture

194 **Dragonlight**
West 8 urban design & landscape architecture

195 **Weidenprinz Light Tree**
Freitag Weidenart, Bureau Baubotanik

196 **LITA**
Gonzalo Milà Valcárcel

197 **Peak**
West 8 urban design & landscape architecture

198 **Miguel Dasso Boulevard**
Artadi Arquitectos

200 **Linea**
töpfer.bertuleit.architekten

Pavement

204 **Nowy Square, Krakow**
Biuro Projektów Lewicki Łatak

206 **Centuries in turn**
Will Nettleship

207 **Wolnica Square, Krakow**
Biuro Projektów Lewicki Łatak

208 **Arizona Canal at Scottsdale Waterfront**
JJR|Floor

212 **Watermap**
Stacy Levy

216 **Ridge and Valley**
Stacy Levy

218 **Solarium, Parc des Prés de Lyon**
BASE

CONTENTS

220 Shanghai Carpet
Tom Leader Studio

221 Place Aristide Briand
Agence APS, paysagistes dplg associés

222 ITE College East
Sitetectonix Private Limited

Product Line

226 Burleigh – Surfboard Series
Street and Garden Furniture Company

228 Luxtram
Lifschutz Davidson Sandilands

230 Geo
Lifschutz Davidson Sandilands

232 City of Toronto coordinated Street Furniture Program
Kramer Design Associates (KDA)

236 Mobilia
EBD architects ApS

238 Zen
díez+díez diseño

240 Park Bench Radium
mmcité a.s.

242 Tramway de Bordeaux
Agence Elizabeth de Portzamparc

Seating

246 Finferlo
Mitzi Bollani

247 Vondel Verses
Anouk Vogel landscape architecture

248 Tokyo City Bench
Studio Makkink & Bey BV

249 Streetscape Furniture
sandellsandberg

250 The Big Bench
Buro Poppinga

252 Boom Bench
NL Architects

254 Topografico Bench
Estudio Cabeza

256 Patrimonial Bench
Estudio Cabeza

258 Encuentros
Estudio Cabeza

259 Miriápodo
díez+díez diseño

260 Solar Bench
Owen Song

261 cuc
Foreign Office Architects (FOA)

262 Bird Bed
Nea Studio

264 Park Bench Swinger
Architektin Mag. arch. Silja Tillner

266 Bench Castle 717
Caesarea Landscape Design Ltd.

267 SOL and NET
Diego Fortunato

268 Benches Martelo
Caesarea Landscape Design Ltd.

269 Alfil Set
Estudio Cabeza

270 West 8 Timber Seat
West 8 urban design & landscape architecture

272 West 8 Swirl Bench
West 8 urban design & landscape architecture

274 Benches at Pirrama Park
ASPECT Studios

276 Wirl
Zaha Hadid Architects

278 Leopold Square, Sheffield
Broadbent

280 The Wave
Street and Garden Furniture Company

282 Mollymook
Street and Garden Furniture Company

284 Twig
Street and Garden Furniture Company

286 QIM
Michel Dallaire Design Industriel – MDDI

288 Soft Bench
Lucile Soufflet

290 Bancs Circulaires
Lucile Soufflet

292 Union Bench Collection
Jangir Maddadi Design Bureau AB

294 Tree Guard Bench
Benjamin Mills

296 Pleamar Bench
díez+díez diseño

298 Ponte
díez+díez diseño

300 Dove
díez+díez diseño

302 SIT Collection
Diego Fortunato

304 LINK
nahtrang

308 SILLARGA / SICURTA
Juan Carlos Ines Bertolin, Gonzalo Milà Valcárcel

310 Botanic Bench
Street and Park Furniture

312 Tea Tree Gully Seat
Street and Park Furniture

314 SO-FFA
Baena Casamor Arquitectes BCQ S.L.P.

316	**Modular Bench Naguisa** Toyo Ito and Associates, Architects	
318	**Y** Alexandre Moronnoz	
320	**Interferences** Alexandre Moronnoz	
322	**Muscle** Alexandre Moronnoz	
324	**Trottola Spinning Top** Mitzi Bollani	
326	**liquirizia** Aziz Sariyer	
328	**mariù** Aziz Sariyer	
330	**Nido Bench** Esrawe Studio	
332	**Reverb Chair** Brodie Neill	
334	**Regency Benches** Julian Mayor	
336	**Bag Stools** Gitta Gschwendtner	
337	**Chair that disappears in the Rain** Tokujin Yoshioka Design	
338	**Šentvid Urban Park** BRUTO d.o.o.	
340	**Marunouchi Oazo North Building** Earthscape	
342	**Two generations of Cherry Blossoms** Earthscape	
344	**Nature and City Bench** Earthscape	
346	**Earth Thermometer** Earthscape	
348	**Memory Chair** Earthscape	

350	**Fukuoka Bank** Earthscape	
352	**City Mall, Christchurch** City Mall Alliance – Isthmus, Reset, Christchurch City Council and Downer EDI	
356	**Boat Seat, North Shore City** Isthmus	
358	**Pier Place Square, Cape Town** Earthworks Landscape Architects	
360	**Pedestrian Zone Sala** PLEIDEL ARCHITEKTI s.r.o.	
362	**Benches at Indre Kai** Smedsvig Landskapsarkitekter AS	
364	**The Red Ribbon** Turenscape, Kongjian Yu	
368	**Nakasato Juji Project** Ryo Yamada & Ayako Yamada	
369	**Benches and Seats Rhodes** Caesarea Landscape Design Ltd.	
370	**Anonymous Garden** Ryo Yamada & Ayako Yamada	
372	**Bubble Bench** OLIN	
374	**Glass Bench** OLIN	
376	**Concrete Things** KOMPLOT Design	

Shelter

382	**Veil Solar Shade** Buro North
386	**Street Furniture Franchise** Grimshaw
390	**Nicho PT** Pedro Silva Dias

392	**Cabine PT** Pedro Silva Dias
394	**Newspaper Kiosks** Heatherwick studio
398	**Urban Furniture and Equipment, Buenos Aires** Estudio Cabeza
400	**Kubus EXPORT – The transparent Room** Architektin Mag. arch. Silja Tillner, Prof. Valie Export
404	**Regio Shelters** mmcité a.s.
406	**Transfer Stations, São Paulo** Bacco Arquitetos Associados
408	**Texas Cowboys Pavilion** Miró Rivera Architects
410	**Central Park, Parkstadt Schwabing** Rainer Schmidt Landschaftsarchitekten
414	**Pavilions for Smokers** BRUTO d.o.o. with Urban Švegl
418	**Hortus urbanus** Corbeil + Bertrand Architecture de paysage
420	**Butterfly Pavilion** Della Valle + Bernheimer Design, LLP
422	**The Amazing Whale Jaw** NIO architecten
424	**Pergola, Le Havre** Claude Cormier architectes paysagistes inc.
426	**City Toilet** Brähmig, Ströer
430	**Trail Restroom** Miró Rivera Architects

432	Architects Index
447	Picture Credits
448	Imprint

PREFACE

Street Furniture
by Chris van Uffelen

Street furniture is a rarely observed topic and an apparently absurd combination of words. The term furniture is usually associated with the private sphere, while the street is a public space. The combination is even more bizarre in those Latin languages in which the word furniture derives from the word "mobile," i.e. something movable, whereas street furniture is extremely unmovable, as it is usually bolted or fixed to the floor. However, the derivation of "furniture" from the French "fournir," i.e. "to provide," precisely describes its function: street furniture provides us with comfort in public spaces, giving us information, seating, light, and protection. It thus serves similar purposes as the regular furniture within the home, rendering urban spaces livable.

↖↖ | **Pieter Lucas Marnette,** electrical distribution box in the style of the Amsterdam school, Amsterdam 1928
↖ | **Norman Foster and Partners,** serial product "Abribus" bus stop for JCDecaux, Paris 1994
← | **Santiago Calatrava architect and engineer,** individual designed bus stop at the Satolas Station, Lyon 2002

However, it not only creates the setting of our public life between the "wallpaper" of the building façades, but actually constitutes a substantial part of urban identity. Usually unnoticed, manhole covers and street signs are repeated elements that create a typical network for each city across its various districts or streets, connecting the individual buildings to a conglomerate with common features. This was most obviously and publicly successfully implemented in the Metro stations by Hector Guimard in Paris around 1900. If only parts of the greenish, plant-like metal shapes or maybe even the lettering "Metropolitain" are glimpsed on a picture, it is immediately apparent that the setting is the French capital near the Seine. Just as typical, but less renown are the paddle-shaped signs describing the "Histoire de Paris" (history of Paris), which were designed by Phillippe Starck for JCDecaux and set up around the city in 1998. Jean-Claude Decaux revolutionized street furniture by relieving cities from the high costs of furnishing their streets by marketing the elements as advertising space (bus stops) or making their use chargeable, such as the fully automated toilets, the Sanisettes, designed by him. Even though most street furniture is produced in series, unique designs are the second pillar of the genre. The unique pieces are usually much more conspicuous and intended to highlight a specific location within the city, or match a specific setting. Usually they do not consist of single items of a specific type of street furniture, but of ensembles including benches, planters, bollards or pavement that are analogous to the product lines of serial productions. These ensembles create entire environments and become self-serving; an individual location – a setting that requires its own space. Just like a bench with a roof, the city square brings people together and offers a communicative island in the flow of passers-by. Thus, in the times of "unprivate" living, perhaps street furniture is the most contemporary and topical type of furnishing.

BIKE AND PLAY

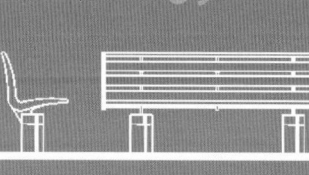

LIGHT AND SIGN

GARBAGE

BOUNDARY

SEATING

ENSEMBLE   PAVEMENT   PRODUCT LINE   PLANTS AND WATER   SHELTER

BIKE AND PLAY | KMA Creative Technology Ltd

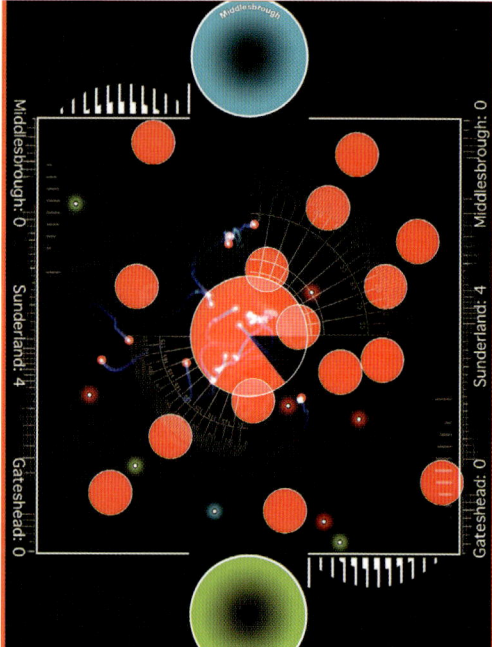

Great Street Games

↖↖ | Arena in Gateshead
↑↑ | Screen capture, from a game
↖ | Playing on the interactive light installation
↑ | Arena in Sunderland

The series of outdoor games used light projection and thermal-imaging technology to create jaw-dropping interactive playing arenas in which human movement triggered spectacular light effects. The games took place simultaneously in large urban spaces of three north-eastern UK locations. Participants in Gateshead, Sunderland and Middlesbrough competed against each other with no previous preparation. The scale of the arenas created a vast aesthetic impact on the urban environments in which they were placed, drawing audiences quite often by chance as people went about their daily lives. Curiosity drew people in, but it was the intelligence of the language within these games that held the public's attention and engaged them in problem solving, play and social engagement.

PROJECT FACTS
Client: The Great North Run Cultural Programme. **Completion:** 2009. **Production:** single piece. **Design:** individual design. **Functions:** playing, interactive light installation. **Main materials:** projected light, sound.

Mitzi Bollani

↑↑ | **Game in action,** Parco Galleana
↑ | **A soft nest for playing**
↗ | **Sketch**

NiDondolo

NiDondolo looks like a big nest and begins to rotate, twist and turn, and swing with any slight movement when in use. Children enter it crawling on all fours and safely play in it lying down or sitting up. Its name comes from a combination of two Italian words: Nido (nest) and Dondolo (swing). NiDondolo allows children to develop their sense of balance, coordination and creativity. The game offers extra interest and excitement for children with mental, physical or multiple impairments too. The robustness of NiDondolo also allows its use by adults to meet the needs of those parents who wish to share the fun with their very small infant children, or with their older daughters and sons.

PROJECT FACTS
Client: LEURA srl. Completion: 2009. Production: serial production. Design: individual design. Functions: playing. Main materials: steel, soft material.

BIKE AND PLAY | Rovero Adrien Studio

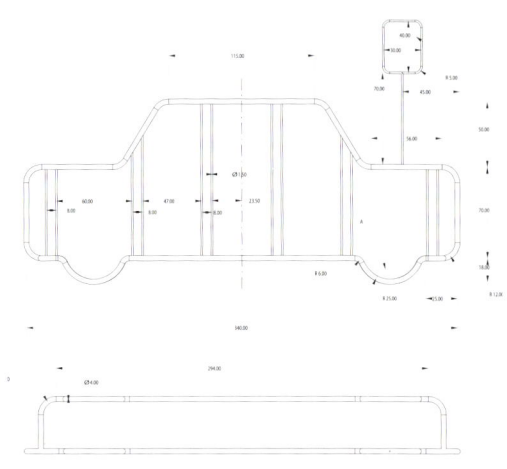

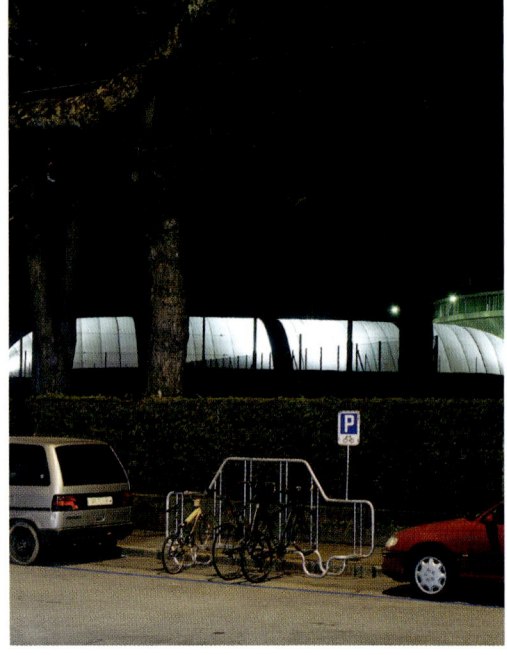

↖ | Bicycle stand
↑↑ | Elevation and plan
↑ | Street view

VD 003
Lausanne

This bike rack can be described as a six bikes vs. one car. The rack uses one parking lot to accommodate six bicycles and draws attention to the additional space that is required for car traffic. It has the silhouette of a car.

PROJECT FACTS
Address: Place de la Cathédrale, 1000 Lausanne, Switzerland. **Planning partner:** Inout / Frank Torres. **Client:** Inout. **Completion:** 2006. **Production:** single piece. **Design:** individual design. **Functions:** bicycle stand. **Main materials:** galvanised steel.

ZonaUno / Tobia Repossi

15

↑↑ | Rotating See Saw
↗↗ | Semiball
↑ | Speak into the tube
↗ | Spinning top

Park Games Science Park

Consisting of a series of devices to be positioned outdoors, the Science Park provides an interesting and enjoyable way of communicating concepts and principles on subjects including the natural sciences to art, music, architecture, and others. The connection between the park's interactive structures is their highly playful nature. They stimulate playing as an intimate process of growth based on learning and experimentation in a stimulating environment where natural and artificial elements interact and become one. The powerful intrinsic capacity of games to impart knowledge is used to discover science in everyday life.

PROJECT FACTS
Client: MODO srl. **Completion:** 2009. **Production:** serial production. **Design:** product line. **Functions:** playing. **Main materials:** inbox.

BIKE AND PLAY | STORE MUU design studio

↑ | **PIT IN,** bicycle stand and seating unit in one

PIT IN

PIT IN is a street object that fulfills several functions that are useful in everyday life in the city. For pedestrians it is a pleasant bistro-table offering a practicable opportunity for a short stop. However the target group for this design table are cyclists. They can easily dock with their bikes while the saddles of their own bikes turn into seats. Several problems faced by cyclists nowadays will be solved at one go. For instance, it won't be necessary to carry a bike lock while going to lunch, because one does not need to leave one's bike. The search for free seats in crowded areas won't be necessary either, as the own seat is mounted to the bike.

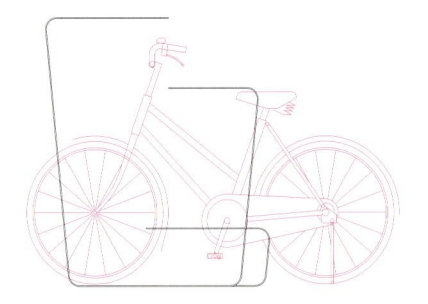

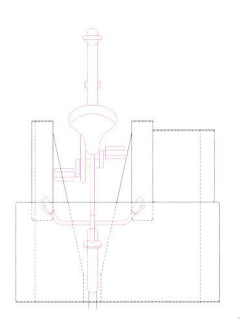

PROJECT FACTS **Completion:** 2009. **Production:** serial production. **Design:** individual design. **Functions:** seating, bicycle stand. **Main materials:** steel, plywood.

↑ | **Seating position,** feet and arms resting on the structure
↙ | **Plan and section**

↑ | **Side elevation,** used as simple bike stand
↓ | **Elevation,** pedestrians and cyclists can use the object

BIKE AND PLAY | Grimshaw / Casimir Zdanius

↑ | **Bicycle stand,** detail of eight meter option

Flood Mitigation Measures

New York City

Preventing excess storm water from entering the subway system was the primary objective of this project. The designs are located above existing subway vents that in the past were not exactly pedestrian traffic friendly due to their often deteriorated condition hovering above a significant void beneath. Designing elements that function as bicycle racks and benches added additional public value. Each unit is modular up to 1.5 meter increments and extendable to match the tunnels beneath. The elements have enough transparency to have a street presence even when not in use. Each bench seats up to three people and each module holds up to eight bicycles.

PROJECT FACTS **Address:** West Broadway between Chambers and Worth Streets, New York City, NY, USA. **Planning partner:** Grimshaw Industrial Design, Billlings Jackson Design, HNTB, Systra, Scape. **Client:** The Metropolitan Transit Authority of New York. **Completion:** 2009. **Production:** serial production. **Design:** product line. **Functions:** seating, bicycle stand, raised grille to prevent stormwater from entering subway system. **Main materials:** stainless steel, galvanized steel frame, recycled regalvanized bar grating.

↑ | View of eight meter design
↓ | Part Elevation

↑↑ | Bicycle stand and seating
↑ | Isometry

BIKE AND PLAY | Agence Patrick Jouin / Patrick Jouin

↑ | **Bicycle station**
↗ | **Attachment points**
→ | **Information point MUPI** (Mobilier urbain pour l'information)

Vélib and Mupi
Paris

The set of urban furniture for the city of Paris was commissioned by JCDecaux. 1,400 stations of Vélib, a contraction of the French words for velo – bicycle, and liberté – freedom, were installed throughout Paris at a rate of one approximately every 300 meters, offering over 20,000 bicycles to the public. The success of these pieces of urban furniture is due in part to the plant metaphor that inspires them. The soft curve of the attachment points evokes the form of grass, while the arch of the terminals resembles the shape of trees. The vegetal reference, combined with the exclusivity of this series to the city of Paris, pays subtle tribute to the farnaus urban contributions of Hector Guimard during the Art Nouveau era.

PROJECT FACTS **Address:** Paris, France. **Client:** JCDecaux SA. **Completion:** 2007. **Production:** serial production. **Design:** individual design. **Functions:** bicycle stand. **Main materials:** cast aluminum.

BIKE AND PLAY   AGENCE PATRICK JOUIN

↑ | **Attachment point,** with bike-locking mechanism
← | **Sketch**

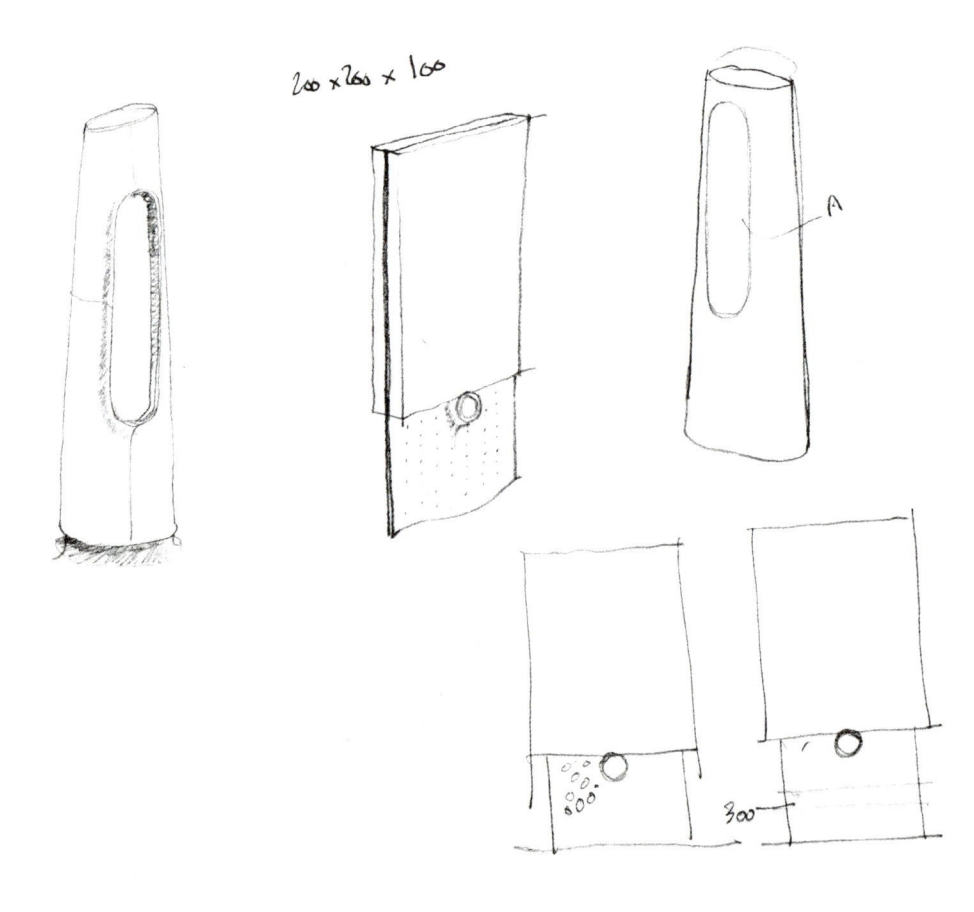

VÉLIB AND MUPI

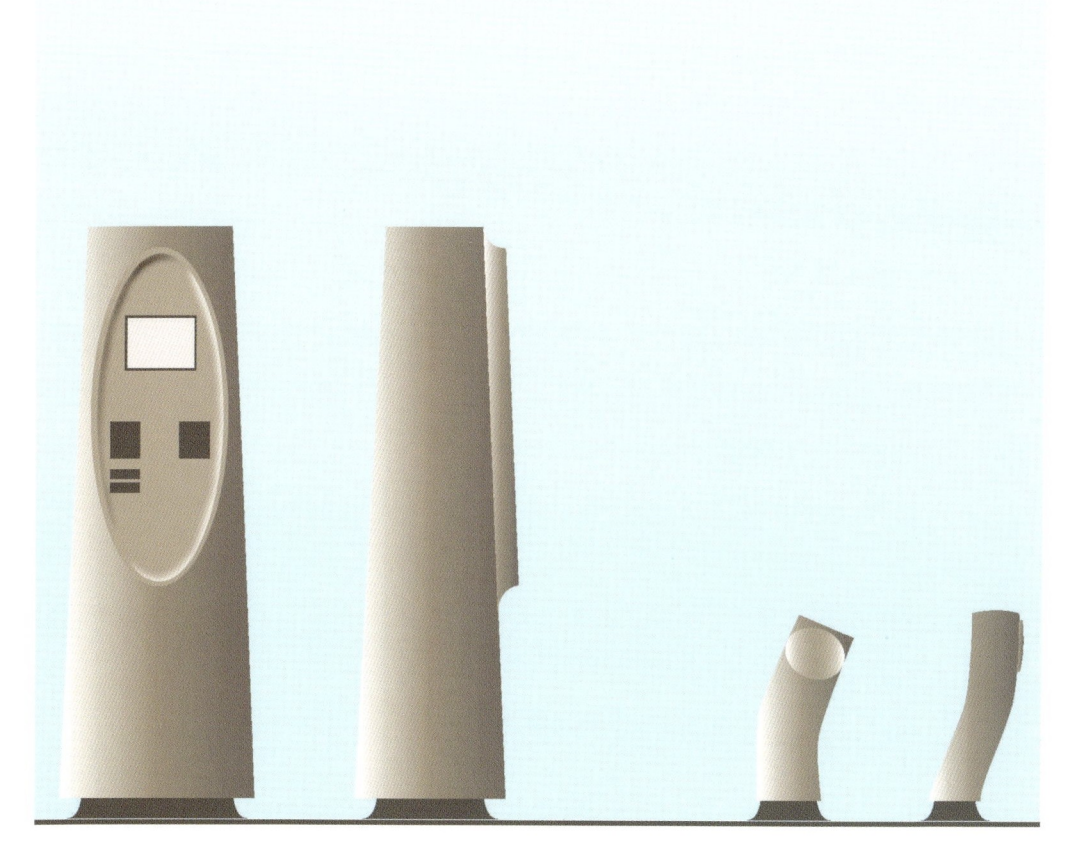

← | **MUPI and attachment points**
↓ | **Bicycle station,** MUPI and attachment points

BIKE AND PLAY | RASTI GmbH / Klaus Bergmann

↑ | **Basic construction,** made of heat-galvanized steel and profiled sheeting roof cover
→ | **Filigree shelter,** with transparent roofing

Shelter Imperia
Haren

The Imperia roofing system is a good opportunity for companies and cities to stylishly present themselves. The patented „Made in Germany" design can be produced in various sizes and colors. The core construction is made of hot-dip galvanized steel and a roofing made of galvanized and grey-white coated trapezoidal sheet metal. Imperia can be used as a personal shelter or multi-purpose roofing. It offers bicyclists a comfortable and secure parking and locking area. All variations can be adjusted to the respective urban design and fit harmoniously into the existing setting.

PROJECT FACTS **Address:** An der Mühle 21, 49733 Haren, Germany. **Client:** Rasti GmbH. **Completion:** 2005. **Production:** serial production. **Design:** individual design. **Functions:** shelters. **Main materials:** steel.

BIKE AND PLAY   RASTI GMBH

↑ | Lattice-style version in grey
← | Imperia as a one-sided bicycle shelter

SHELTER IMPERIA

← | Protective roof for bicycles, motorcycles, etc.
↓ | Timeless and classic design

BIKE AND PLAY

YHY design international /
Yoann Henry Yvon

↑ | Bike rack in use

Marguerite Bike Rack

The concept of the Marguerite bike rack seeks to motivate city dwellers to use the bike as an eco-friendly means of transport and is distinguished by a fresh and appealing design. Its compact mechanism offers enough parking space for numerous bikes in a limited space. Moreover, the innovative parking devices are very flexible as they can be placed in any part of the city, depending on the requirement of the users and the space. The stand has rows of bike holders which are shaped like petals coming out of a centerpiece. Manual movement of its petals allows to easily park and lock your bike. The Marguerite bike rack offers a combination of vivid colors, a deliberate mechanism, and eye-catching shapes.

PROJECT FACTS	

Completion: 2008. **Production:** single piece. **Design:** individual design. **Functions:** bicycle stand. **Main materials:** polythene, stainless steel.

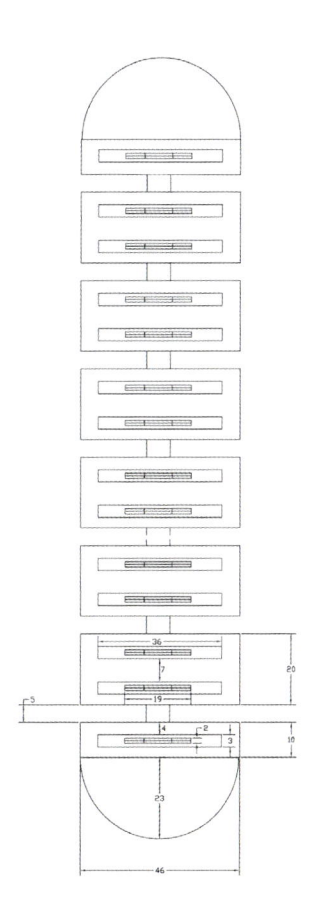

↑ | **Plan**
↓ | **Beautiful appearance** in the cityscape

↑ | **Detail of the centerpiece**

BIKE AND PLAY

Osterwold & Schmidt –
Exp!ander Architekten

↑ | **Attractive façade** of the new bicycle station
→ | **Building front,** illuminated at twilight

Radhaus – Bicycle Station
Erfurt

The theme of a bicycle station promises mobility and dynamism in contrast with a fixed position. Based on this concept, a slim structure was developed and placed on a wedge-shaped plot of land. The bicycle parking station is the first of its kind offering this particular application combination in eastern Germany. A total of 270 parking places and 32 boxes are located underneath its roof. The translucent façade of the building measuring approx. 70 meters was made of highly-insulated 8-chamber polycarbonate sheets, complemented by foil ornaments in shades of gold and silver. In addition to its function as a bicycle parking station, the building also functions as an "illuminated shed" to secure a previously unused residual area.

PROJECT FACTS **Address:** Bahnhofstraße 22, 99084 Erfurt, Germany. **Planning partner:** Torsten Braun (light design), Hennicke+Dr.Kusch (structural engineering), IBP Erfurt (building electronics). **Client:** City of Erfurt. **Completion:** 2009. **Production:** single piece. **Design:** individual design. **Functions:** shelter, bicycle stand, office, workshop, rental. **Main materials:** polycarbonate panels, steel, ornament film.

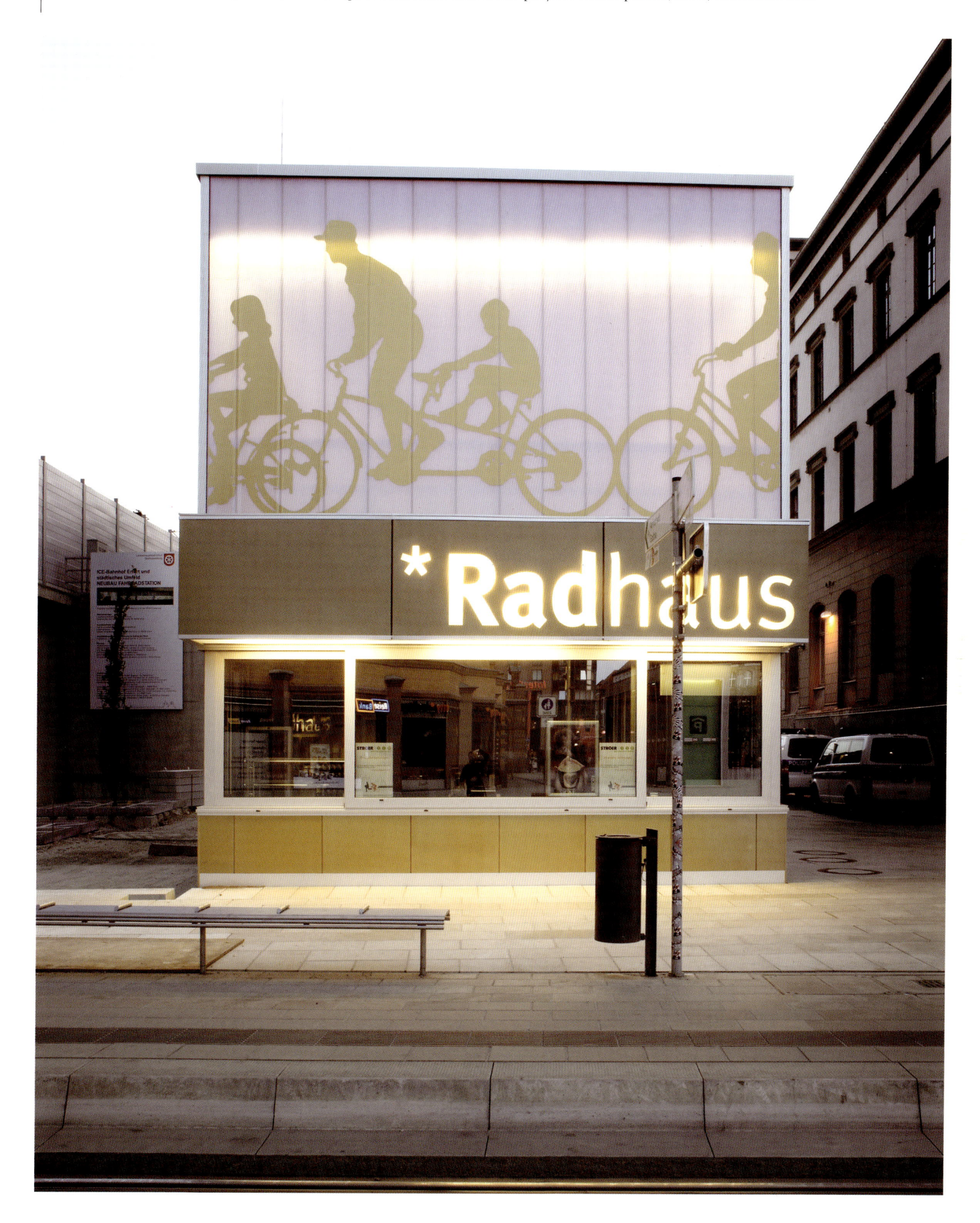

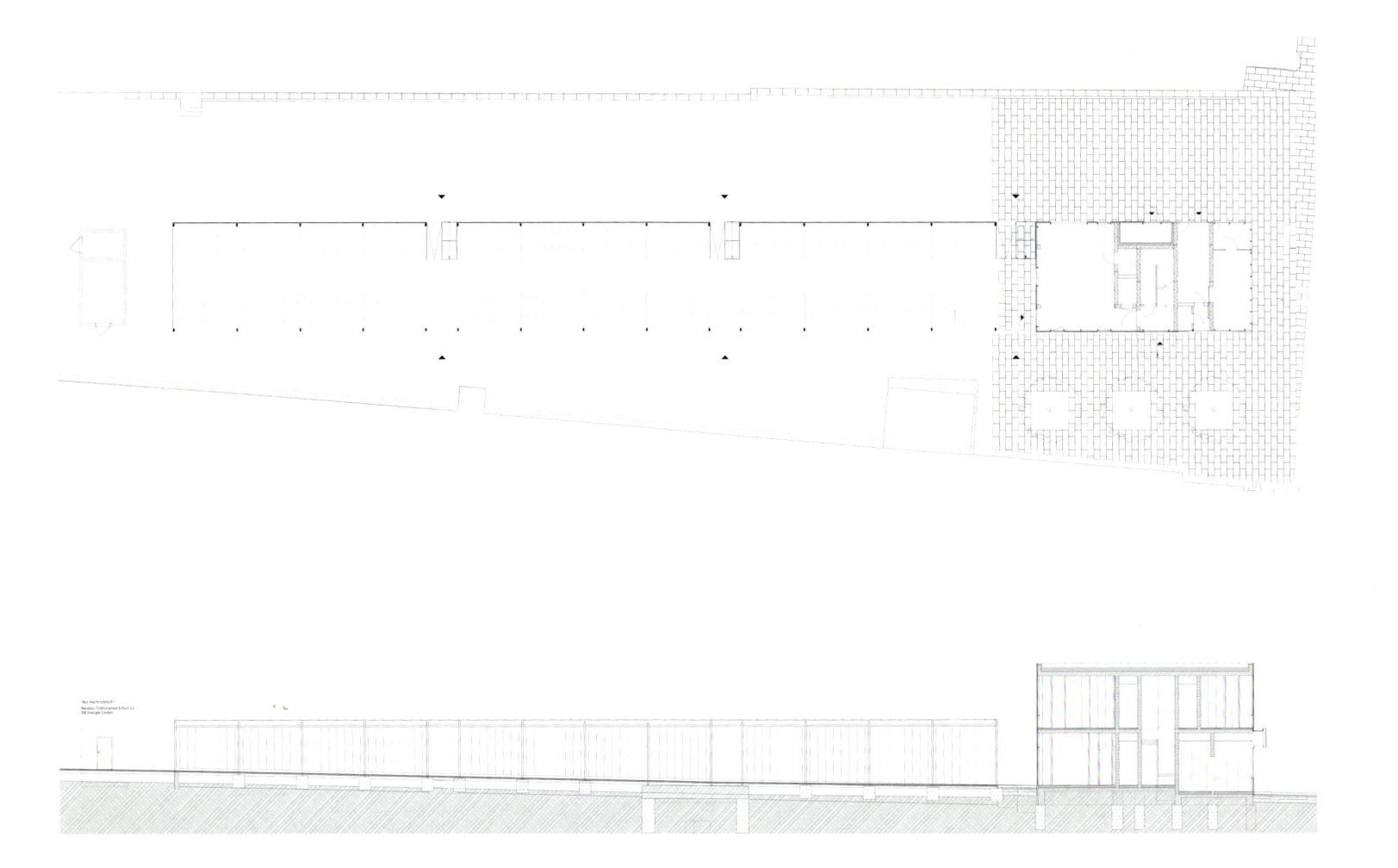

BIKE AND PLAY OSTERWOLD & SCHMIDT – EXP!ANDER ARCHITEKTEN

↑ | **Plan and section**
← | **Detail view**, related ornaments at the façade

RADHAUS – BICYCLE STATION

← | **Inside the shelter,** up to 270 bicycles can be accomodated here
↓ | **Bicycle station,** with Erfurt main station in the background

BIKE AND PLAY

díez+díez diseño

↑ | Cyclo in use

Cyclo Bicycle Stand

Cyclo combines two essential features of street furniture – it has an appealing design thanks to its rounded forms and is robust thanks to its concrete construction. It is thus a useful street element, able to resist the elements and vandalism. A main goal of the designers in developing the bicycle stand was to honor and support the cyclists, who make the cities and towns more livable with the simple gesture of their daily pedaling. With two versions, on drums for broad locations, or freestanding designed especially for small spaces, Cyclo covers all the needs that any municipality, private developer or private citizen can have when parking their bicycles.

PROJECT FACTS **Client:** Paviments MATA. **Completion:** 2009. **Production:** serial production. **Design:** product line. **Functions:** bicycle stand. **Main materials:** concrete.

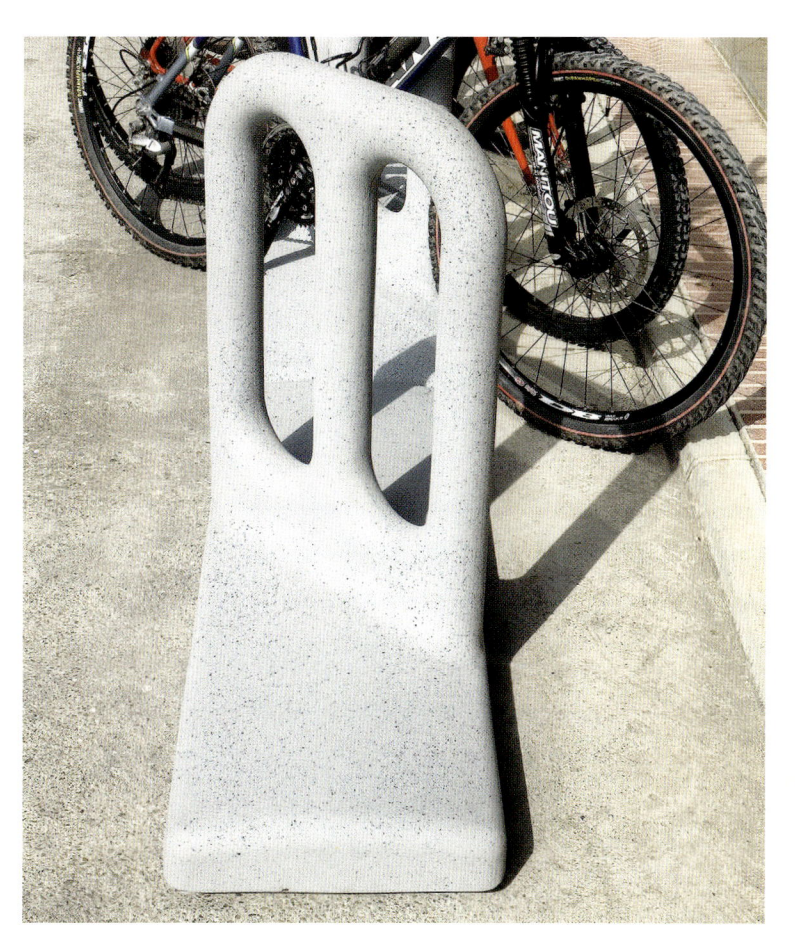

↑ | **Schemes of different models**
↓ | **Cyclo in use**

↑ | **Detail view**

BIKE AND PLAY | mmcité a.s. / David Karásek, Radek Hegmon

↑ | Side Elevation

Velo Bicycle Stand

This design consists of a curved sheet of steel with support legs and spaces for the bicycle tires between two forked gussets that are connected via a pipe at the highest point. The structure of the Velo bicycle stand is simple and sturdy. Of course, there is a wide range of models available in various colors and shapes that not only accommodate different numbers of parked bicycles, but also allow its use on one or two sides. Velo is a bicycle stand with a modern look and a great degree of practicality.

PROJECT FACTS
Client: mmcité a.s., City of Belfast. **Completion:** 2000. **Production:** serial production. **Design:** individual design. **Functions:** bicyle stand. **Main materials:** galvanized steel.

↑ | **Detail view**
↓ | **Plans**

↑ | **Velo model VL140**

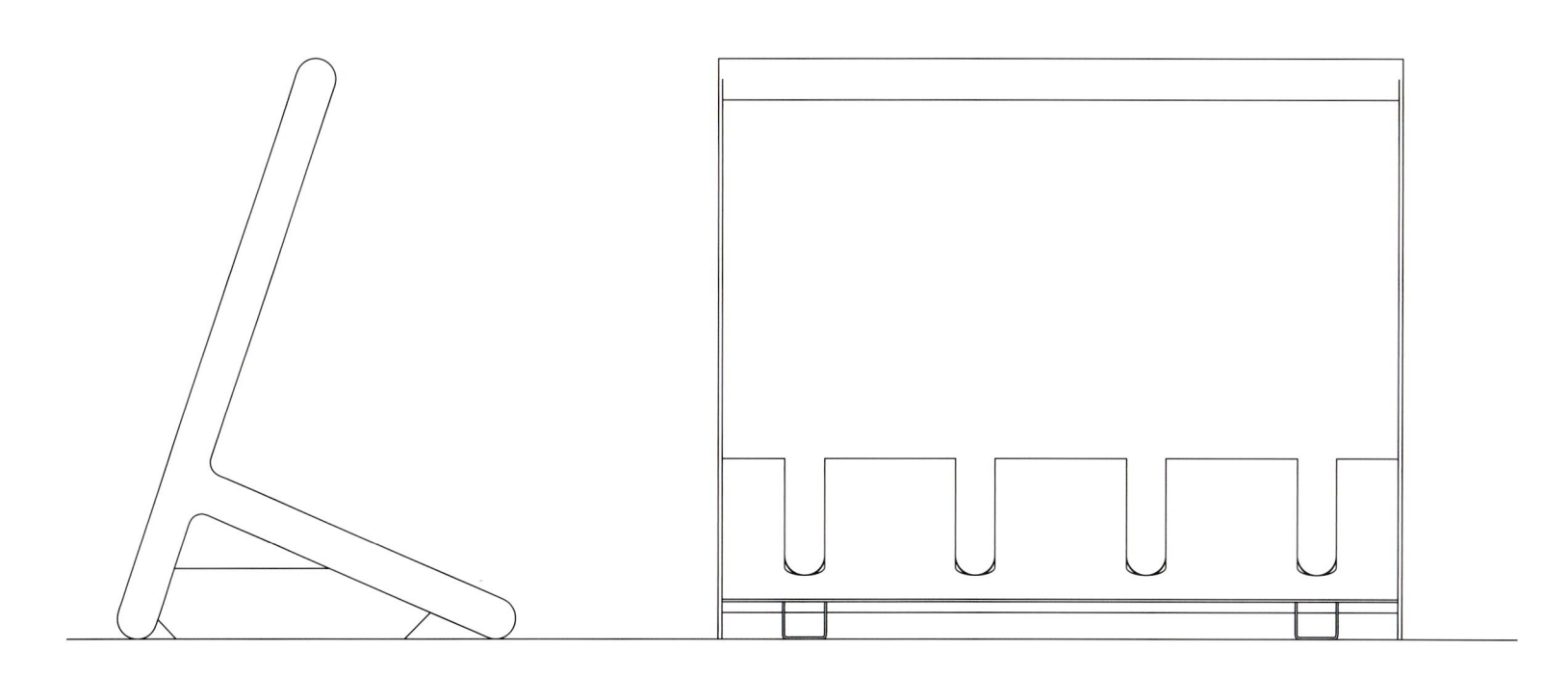

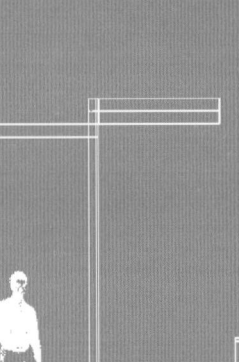

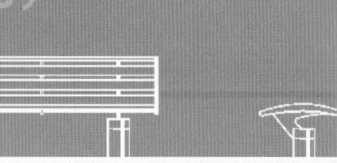

LIGHT AND SIGN · GARBAGE · **BOUNDARY** · BIKE AND PLAY · SEATING

ENSEMBLE

PAVEMENT

PRODUCT LINE

PLANTS AND WATER

SHELTER

BOUNDARY | Pedro Silva Dias

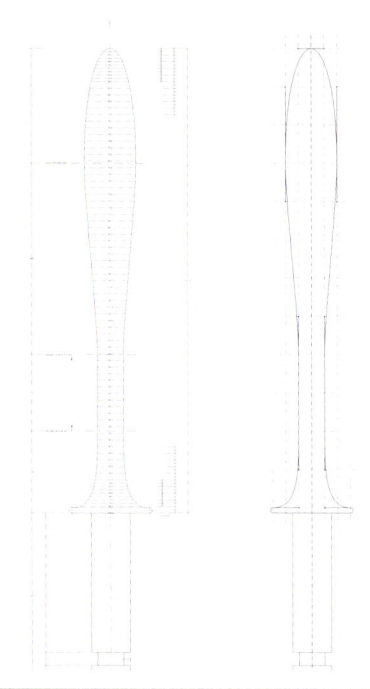

↖ | General view
↑↑ | Geometric construction
↑ | Detail

Pilarete Bollard
Sintra

The cast iron bollard was commissioned by the City Council of Sintra, a World Heritage town. The main idea of this project was to design an object without faces or edges. It has an organic shape, some kind of bubble, which emerges from the ground until it reaches its final functional height. Its base plate ensures solid attachment to the pavement and gives the false impression that the object is standing on the ground, rather than buried in it.

PROJECT FACTS
Address: Sintra, Portugal. **Client:** City of Sintra. **Completion:** 2001. **Production:** serial production. **Design:** individual design. **Functions:** bollard. **Main materials:** cast iron.

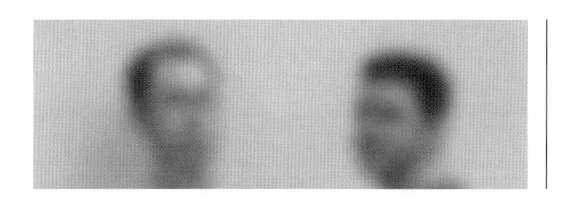

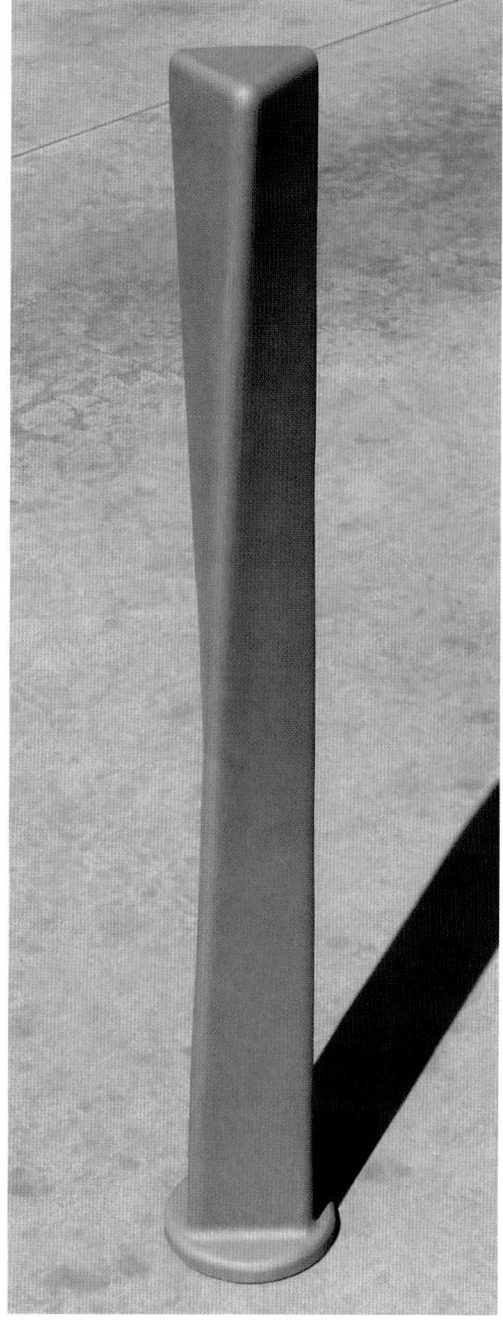

díez+díez diseño

↑ | Bollards
↗ | Singel bollard
↓ | Rendering

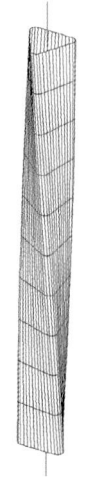

Haiku Bollard

Haiku has been created to give some connotations of fluency and naturalness to a usually rigid and monolithic element like the bollard, to facilitate its integration into public space. The slight ascendant twisting of its triangular section creates a nice sensation of movement, similar to the one a light breeze would cause on a smoke column. Haiku is meant to be a piece that in its repetition becomes a kind of installation in the style of those made by Christo and Jeanne-Claude.

PROJECT FACTS
Client: Tecnología & Diseño Cabanes. **Completion:** 2008. **Production:** serial production. **Design:** individual design. **Functions:** bollard. **Main materials:** cast aluminum.

BOUNDARY | d e signstudio regina dahmen-ingenhoven

↑ | **View along the Swarovskistraße** at night
↗ | **Veil and enclosed area** illuminated
→ | **Semi-transparent metal mesh**

Heaven is a Place on Earth
Wattens

This fantastic veil has just been completed for the Swarovski works in Wattens, Austria. It embraces the entire premises so that the entire entrance area becomes a "landmark" and a synthesis of the arts. It not only veils, but also functions as a gate. The semi-transparent material does not disclose the Swarovski secret. Instead, it allows the onlooker to surmise it. Even the opposite side of the street is incorporated in the shape of a grove lined with silver limes. This creates a fluid transition to the public space. Veil, landscaping, illumination and the design of the space merge to become a breathtaking backdrop. The veil is made of corrosion- and weather-resistant stainless steel mesh.

PROJECT FACTS **Address:** Swarovskistraße, 6112 Wattens, Austria. **Planning partner:** Baubüro Swarovski, 4to1 Lichtdesign. **Client:** D. Swarovski & Co., Wattens. **Completion:** 2008. **Production:** single piece. **Design:** individual design. **Functions:** fence, urban curtain. **Main materials:** metal mesh, stainless steel.

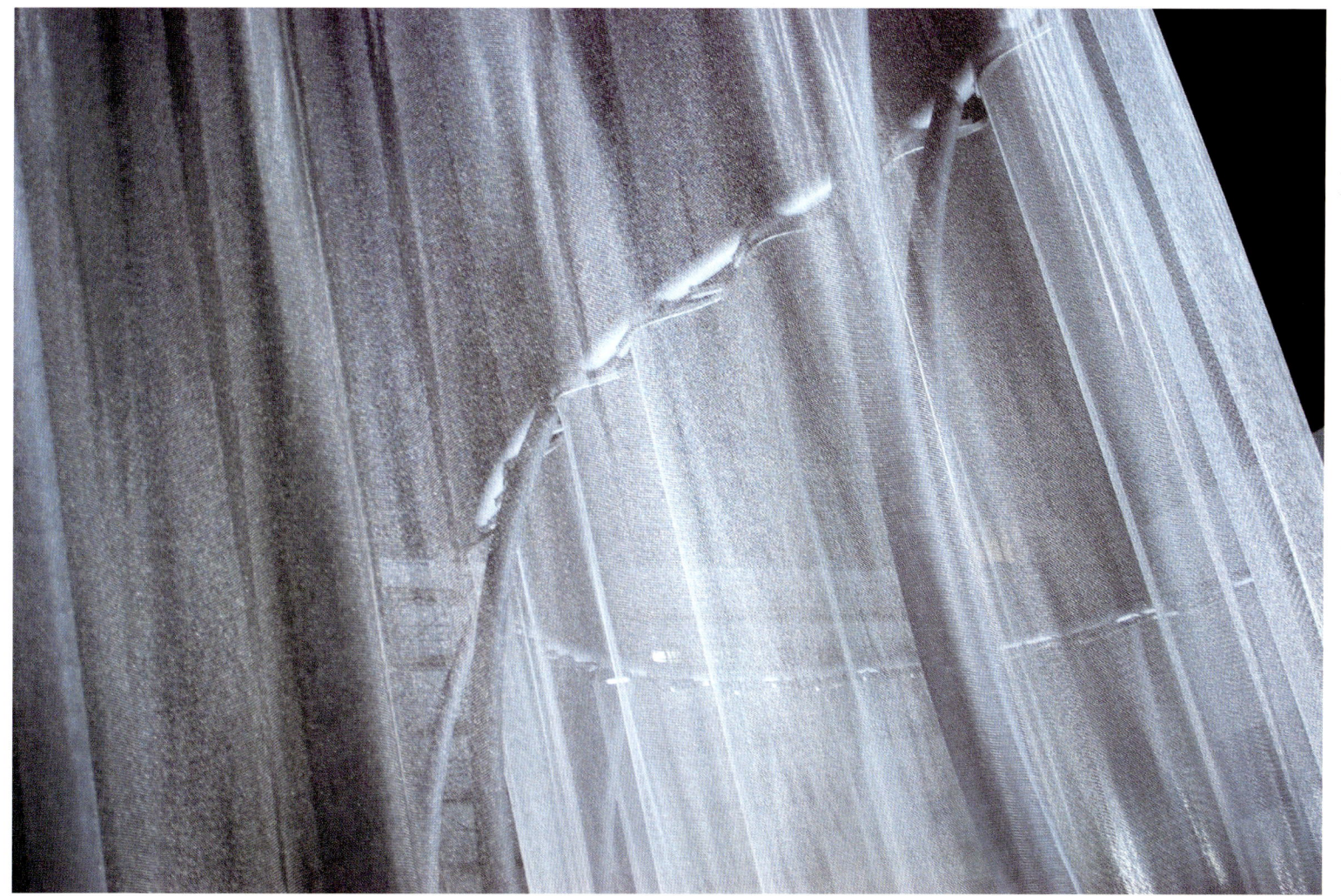

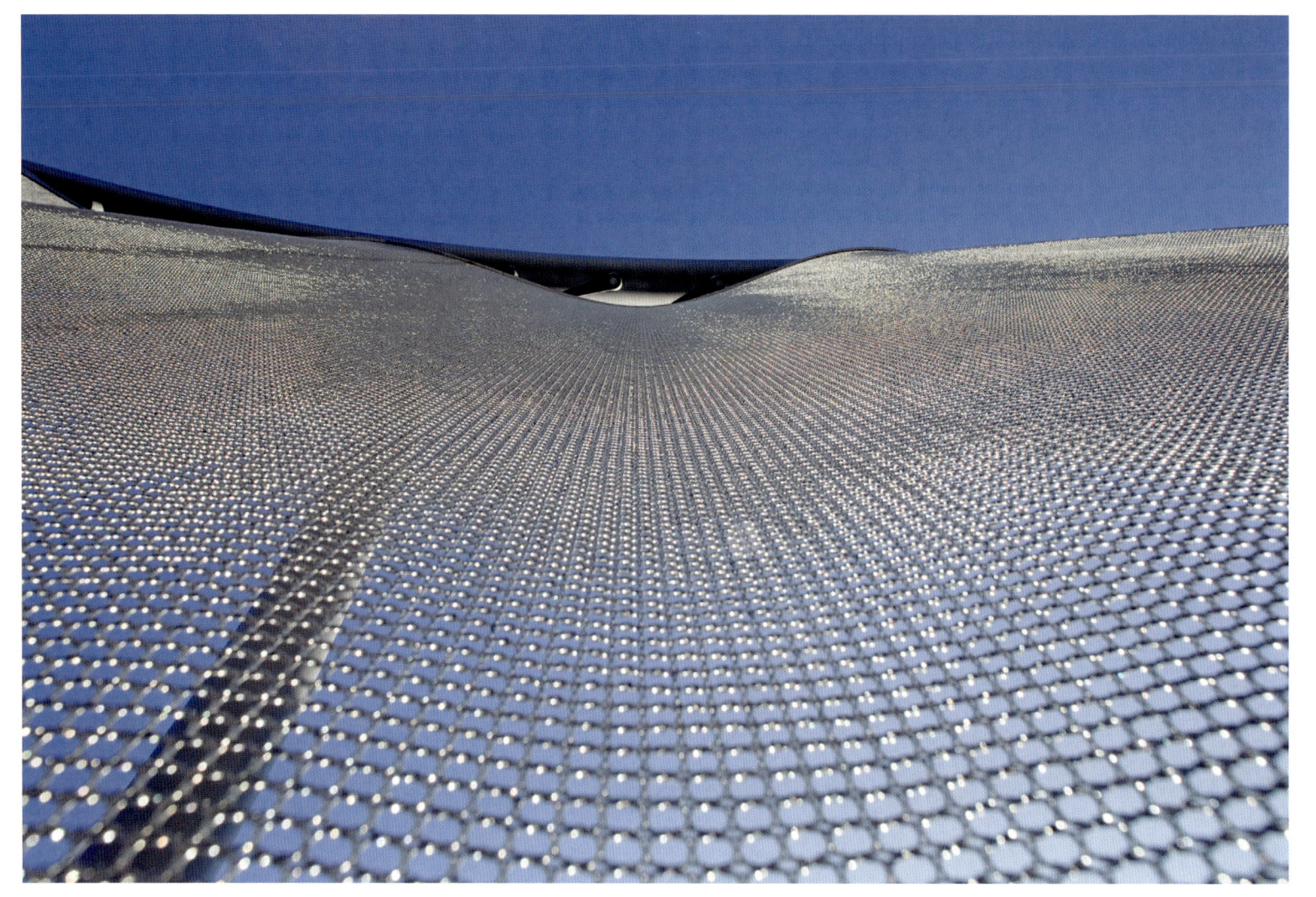

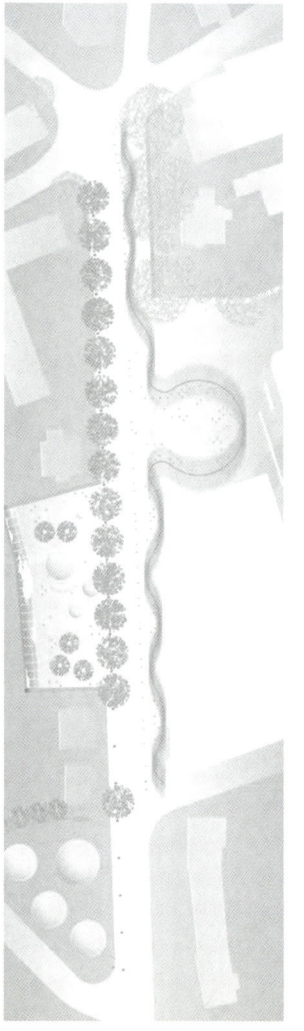

BOUNDARY   D E SIGNSTUDIO REGINA DAHMEN-INGENHOVEN

↑ | **View upwards**
← | **Situation**
→ | **Veil** mounted to sinuous steel tube

HEAVEN IS A PLACE ON EARTH

BOUNDARY | Tejo Remy & Rene Veenhuizen

↑ | **Seating platform**, in the fence

Fence as Meetingpoint
Dordrecht

Not only are the protrusions and recessions of the playground fence eye-catching, but they also allow for more interaction between those on either side of the fence, providing seats, nooks and play areas for children. Instead of the initial concept of adding nothing to the schoolyard, an existing element was used and converted. Part of the fence was transformed into lounge- and sitting spots for the students in order to create meeting places. A distortion of the existing rhythm creates these meeting places on both sides of the fence. The work, which covers five fence parts, replicates the measurements and color of the existing Heras fence.

PROJECT FACTS

Address: Willem de Zwijgerlaan 2, 3314 NX Dordrecht, The Netherlands. **Client:** Primary school "Het Noorderlicht", Dordrecht. **Completion:** 2005. **Production:** single piece. **Design:** individual design. **Functions:** seating, boundary. **Main materials:** steel, powder-coating.

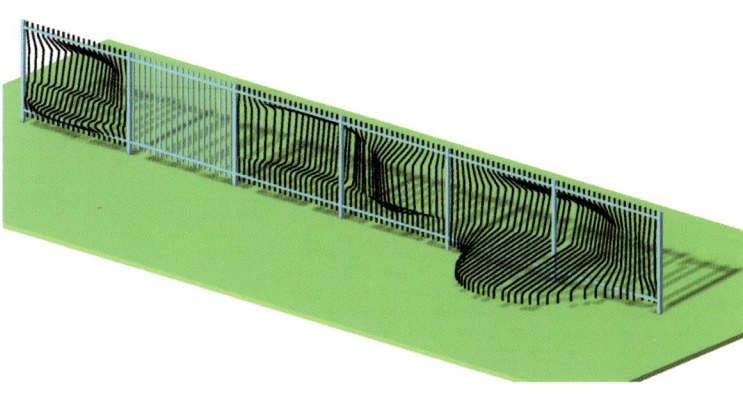

↑ | Seatings in use
↓ | Fence

↑ | Perspective

BOUNDARY | mmcité a.s. / David Karásek, Radek Hegmon

↑ | **Detail view**, bollard with city arms

Bollard Elias

They are rarely noticed, the silent guards in urban areas that control driveways and define the borders of specific areas. This is because they belong to the class of urban furniture that should not be too prominently seen. The bollard Elias, however, combines its watch function with a street illumination function and its time to shine is during dusk. It is structured as a rectangular steel pipe equipped with regular slots. This is where the fluorescent tubes are placed in the illuminated models of the series. Elias is a guard that modestly holds back during the day only to shine at night.

PROJECT FACTS **Client:** mmcité a.s., City of Prague. **Completion:** 2009. **Production:** serial production. **Design:** individual design. **Functions:** bollard, lighting. **Main materials:** steel.

↑ | Plans
↓ | Illuminated bollard

↑ | Illuminated bollard

BOUNDARY

OKRA landschapsarchitecten bv / Christ-Jan van Rooij, Hans Oerlemans, Martin Knuijt, Wim Voogt, Boudewijn Almekinders

↑ | **Fog and light line** in a museum

Domplein
Utrecht

The heart of the city of Utrecht is built on top of a castellum. The potential of the Domplein is to revitalize the significance of the origin of the city. The Castellum wall, at four meters underground, acquires a reference in the street and on the square. The dramatic potential of the Domplein is intensified with a clearly recognisable and mysterious dividing line. The marking is just as silent as the quiet archaeological witness underground. The line of light is only interrupted at the Castellum gates. Fragments of smoke come out of the gutter in the metal plates and reveal the presence of the ray of light. The line is even more visible during rain or mist and after darkness has set in.

PROJECT FACTS

Address: Domplein, 3512JE Utrecht, The Netherlands. **Construction:** Rots Maatwerk. **Client:** Stichting Domplein 2013. **Completion:** 2010. **Production:** single piece. **Design:** individual design. **Functions:** fog and light line. **Main materials:** corten steel, LED lighting.

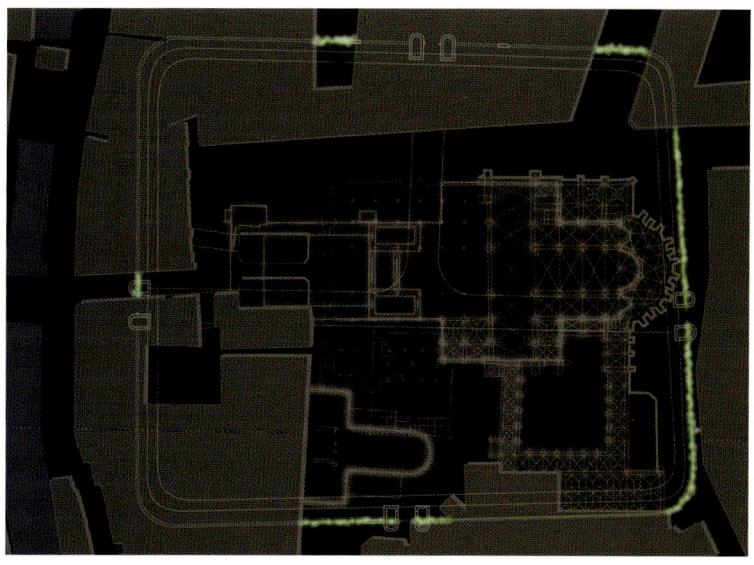

↑ | **Line** in front of the church
↓ | **Marking** by day

↑↑ | **Plan**
↑ | **Example machine** producing fog
↓ | **Fog and light line** in a street

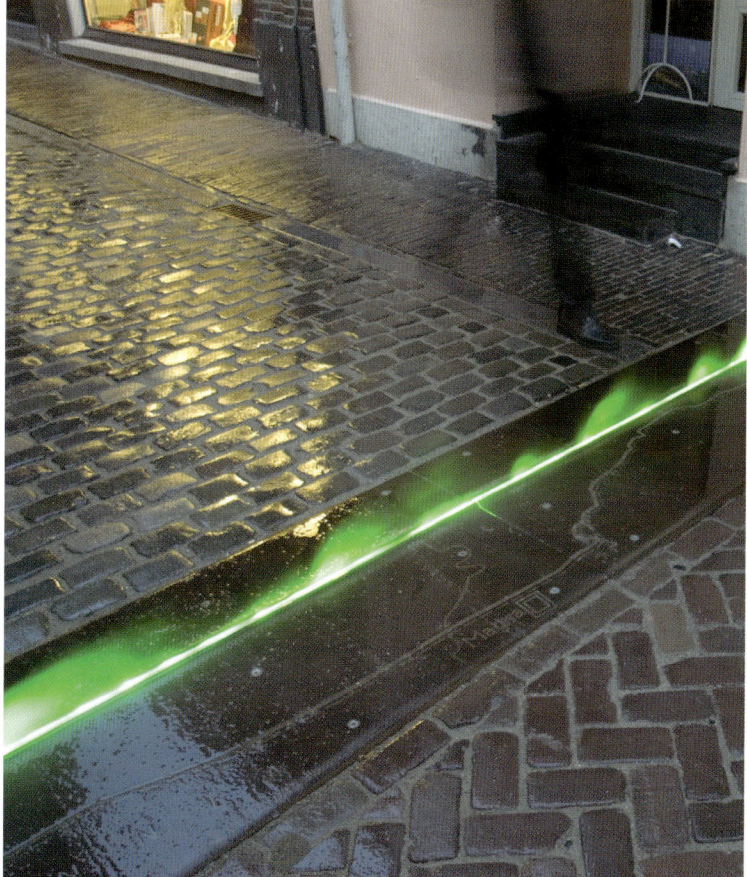

BOUNDARY

Siteworks-Studio / Pete O'Shea

↑ | General view
→ | Children writing on the board

The Community Chalkboard
Charlottesville, VA

A simple wall of black slate extends from Charlottesville's pedestrian mall toward a public amphitheater while forming a series of spaces between the street and city hall. Winner of a Thomas Jefferson Center for Free Speech competition, the monument celebrates the first amendment with a public chalkboard: a place for uninhibited expression and discourse. The wall is joined by a podium set in a gathering area below sculptures of the First Amendment's authors. Facing Thomas Jefferson's home, Monticello, the monument recognizes history while challenging us to move forward as a nation.

PROJECT FACTS

Address: City Hall, Charlottesville, VA 22901 USA. **Co-designer:** Robert Winstead. **Client:** Thomas Jefferson Center for the Protection of Free Expression. **Completion:** 2006. **Production:** single piece. **Design:** individual design. **Functions:** monument. **Main materials:** natural cleft Buckingham black slate, stainless steel, fiber optic lighting.

BOUNDARY   SITEWORKS-STUDIO

↑ | **Engraved text**
← | **An artist's drawing** of Lady Liberty

THE COMMUNITY CHALKBOARD

55

← | **Detail of chalk tray,** with young painters
↓ | **Perspective sketch**

BOUNDARY | Ryo Yamada

↖ | **Platform house,** wooden side
↑↑ | **Perspective**
↑ | **Detail**

Platform House
Sapporo city

This project, set up at a tram terminal, acts as a curtain to visually partition the terminal into two areas, the sidewalk and the terminal as such. Anyone can freely access the railroad at the tram terminal, yet Platform House visually helps people in safely getting into the railroad. It also serves as a sign to alert passengers they have arrived at the terminal. The conspicuous-looking lattice design made of thin yand long timbers softly and naturally partitions the space without impeding the visibility of each area. The design is inspired by the construction style of Japanese shrines in a method that allows people to subconsciously have a sense of attachment to a nearby local shrine.

PROJECT FACTS
Address: Sapporo, Hokkaido, Japan. **Planning partner:** Sapporo City University Yamada Studio. **Client:** Sapporo City. **Completion:** 2008. **Production:** single piece. **Design:** individual design. **Functions:** boards, signs, partition. **Main materials:** woods.

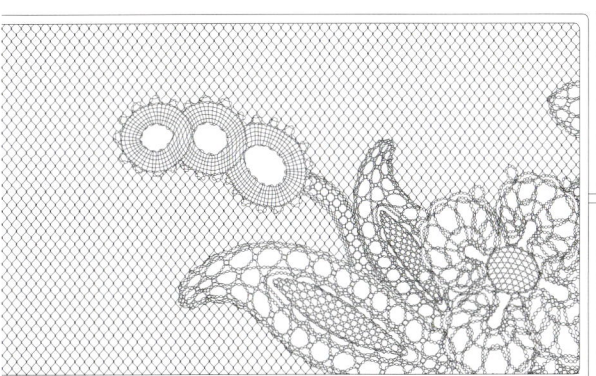

Anouk Vogel landscape architecture

↑↑ | **Lace Fence,** from Demakersvan
↑ | **Design sketch**
↗ | **Echinops sphaerocephalus**

Lace Garden
Amsterdam

The Lace Garden is the enclosed garden of an existing social housing block. It is planted with a collection of white-flowering shrubs, perennials and bulbs that are interlaced between the existing and new trees. Along three of its edges the garden is defined by a hedge separating it from the surrounding private gardens. From the south, the garden is publicly visible through a standard metal wire mesh fence with a lacy twist. The fence is inspired by traditional lace expressed in modern forms.

PROJECT FACTS
Address: Van Speijkstraat 67, 1057 GN Amsterdam, The Netherlands. **Planning partner:** Demakersvan. **Client:** Ymere. **Completion:** 2009. **Production:** serial production. **Design:** individual design. **Functions:** fence. **Main materials:** coated metal wire mesh.

BOUNDARY | Matthias Berthold, Andreas Schön

↑ | Individual designed fotoceramic

Allermöhe Wall
Hamburg

This project was launched to fix the destroyed wall, improve the quality of the building, and increase the deterrent to a repetition of the applied violence. It was implemented with a personal touch, emotions, creativity and in close contact to the local region. For this purpose, the destroyed glass panes were replaced by individually designed tiles. The residents were asked in a competition to paint, draw, photograph to write entries on the topic of "what or who I love". The entries were technically transferred onto tiles, giving every resident the opportunity to easily participate in the project and contribute to the renovation.

PROJECT FACTS **Address:** Railway station Allermöhe, Fleetplatz 1a, 21035 Hamburg, Germany. **Client:** KOKUS Kommunikations- und Kunstverein Allermöhe e.V. **Completion:** 2007. **Production:** single piece. **Design:** individual design. **Functions:** wall, art work. **Main materials:** fotoceramics.

↑ | Design sketch
↓ | Wall with fotoceramics

↑ | Way through the wall

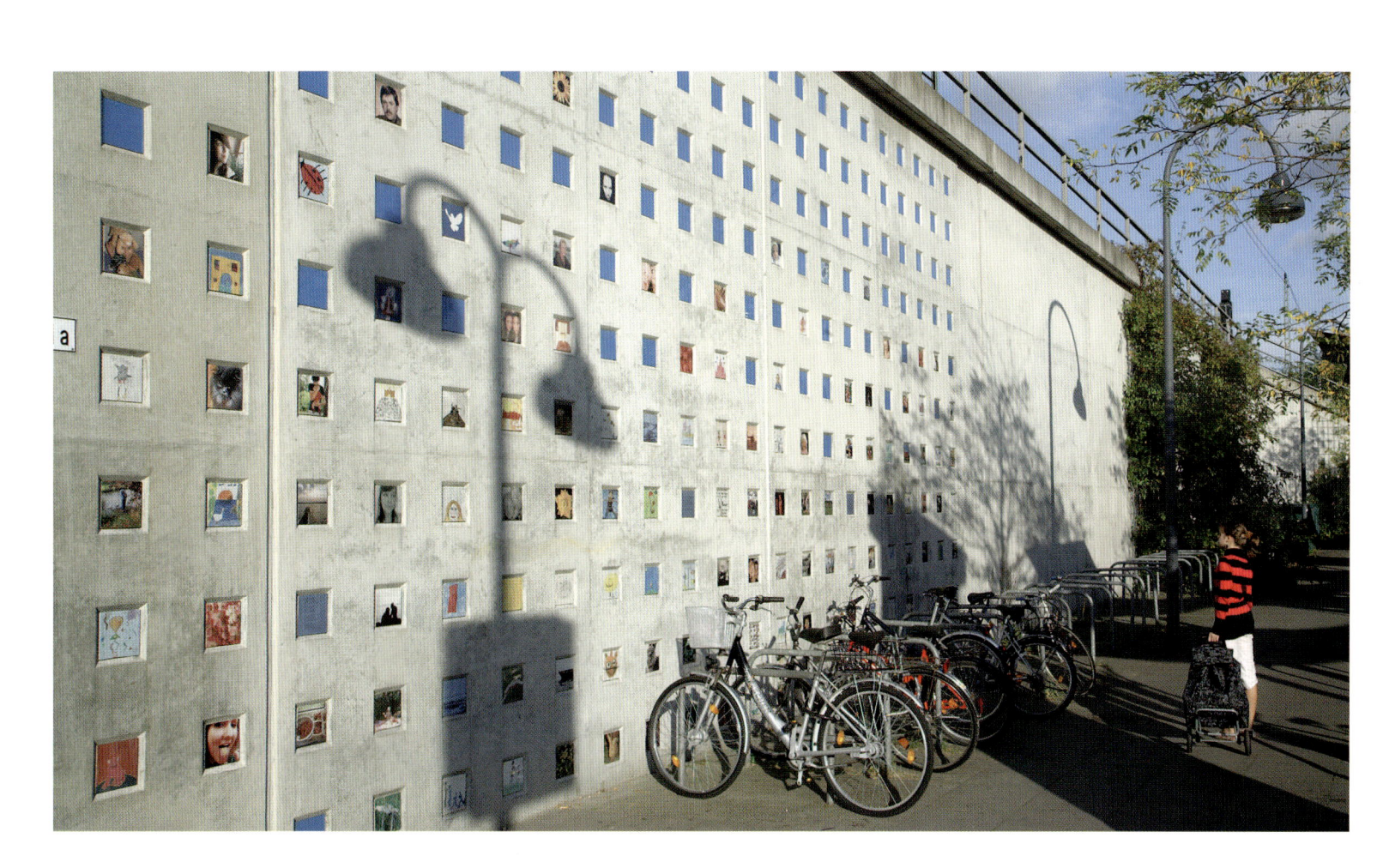

BOUNDARY | Sungi Kim & Hozin Song

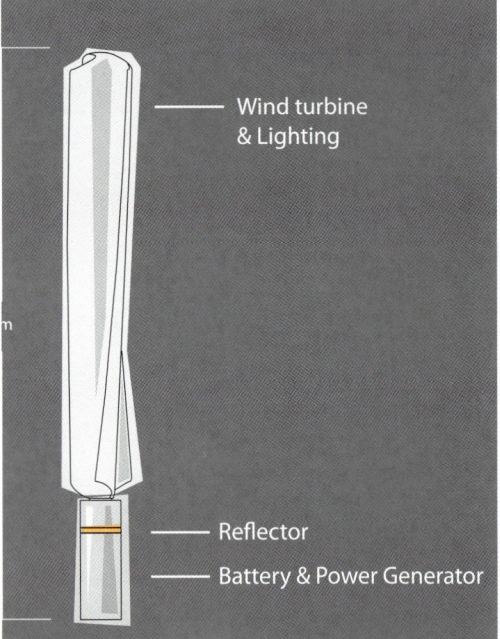

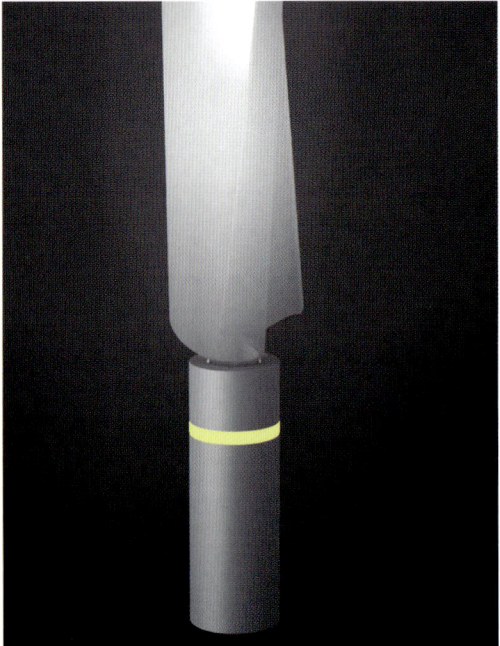

↖ | Bollards on the road
↑↑ | Technical sketch
↑ | Detail

Our Lights will lead the Way

The eco-friendly road lights for the countryside will run on wind-generated electricity created by the passing traffic. As a car passes by, the strong gush of wind it creates propels electric turbines that power the highway illumination system and load batteries that store the electricity for use in nights without wind. Wireless data link sensors turn on the lighting of the roadway 50 to 100 meters ahead of an oncoming automobile.

PROJECT FACTS
Completion: 2009. **Production:** serial production. **Design:** individual design. **Functions:** illumination, bollard. **Main materials:** polycarbonate.

Gitta Gschwendtner

↑↑ | Close up
↗ | Overview
↑ | Front view

Animal Wall
Century Wharf

The environmental impact of Cardiff Bay's extensive development is an ongoing concern and various measures have been taken to mitigate this. The approach taken for this artwork was to assist wildlife and encourage further habitation. The new housing development of Century Wharf will provide 1000 new apartments; and the 'Animal Wall' will match this with about 1000 nest boxes for different bird and bat species, integrated into the wall. Through consultation with an ecologist, four different sized animal homes were developed, which have been integrated in the custom-made Woodcrete cladding to provide an architecturally stunning and environmentally sensitive wall for Century Wharf.

PROJECT FACTS
Address: Century Wharf, Cardiff Bay, United Kingdom. **Architects for housing development:** WYG. **Client:** WYG. **Completion:** 2009. **Production:** single piece. **Design:** individual design. **Functions:** nest boxes for birds and bats. **Main materials:** woodcrete.

BOUNDARY | Adrien Rovero with Christophe Ponceau

↑ | **Pont Bessièrs**, with the Green Trap

Green Trap
Lausanne

Green Trap was implemented for the Lausanne Jardins festival by Christophe Ponceau and Adrien Rovero. It is a giant net suspended under the Pont Bessières. Throughout the festival, people could see the center of the net growing and going through all the cables. Green Trap is a different way of thinking of the green wall: not planted but growing according to the given condition like spiders building their nets in line with their specific locations.

PROJECT FACTS

Address: Pont Bessières, 1003 Lausanne, Switzerland. **Client:** Lausanne Jardins 2009. **Completion:** 2009. **Production:** single piece. **Design:** individual design. **Functions:** fence. **Main materials:** stainless steel.

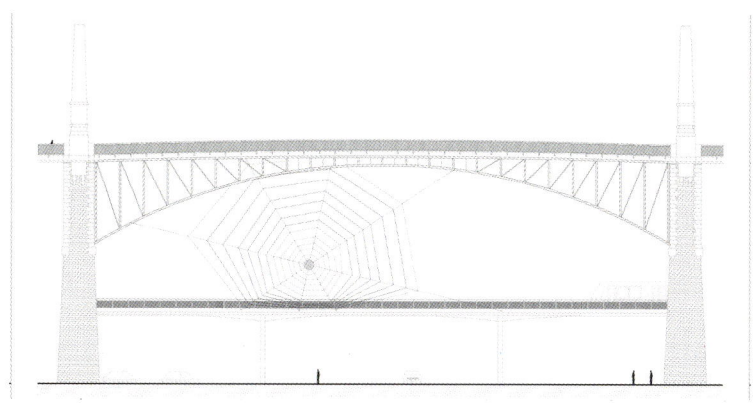

↑ | **Net**, detail
↓ | **View through the net**

↑↑ | **Pont Bessiers**
↑ | **Elevation**

LIGHT AND SIGN

GARBAGE

BOUNDARY

BIKE AND PLAY

SEATING

ENSEMBLE

PAVEMENT

PRODUCT LINE

PLANTS AND WATER

SHELTER

ENSEMBLE | Studio Weave

↑ | Boomerangs in West Smithfield
→ | Bird's-eye view

140 Boomerangs

140 Boomerangs is a project made up of modular Boomerang elements which may be assembled in various permutations. It is able to create site-specific, fluid, playful forms from a simple element that is easy to assemble and reassemble. The first home of the Boomerangs was a helical timber structure, inhabited by children's clay sculptures, which wrapped the Peace fountain at the center of West Smithfield during the London Architecture Biennale 2006. The second homes of the Boomerangs were as play-furniture in the City of London and in the playgrounds of each of the three local schools that took part in the workshops. Instead of creating one large body, the Boomerangs were used here in smaller units.

PROJECT FACTS **Client:** London Architecture Biennale '06, City of London. **Completion:** 2006. **Production:** single piece. **Design:** individual design. **Functions:** seating, exhibition space. **Main materials:** laminated veneer lumber.

ENSEMBLE   STUDIO WEAVE

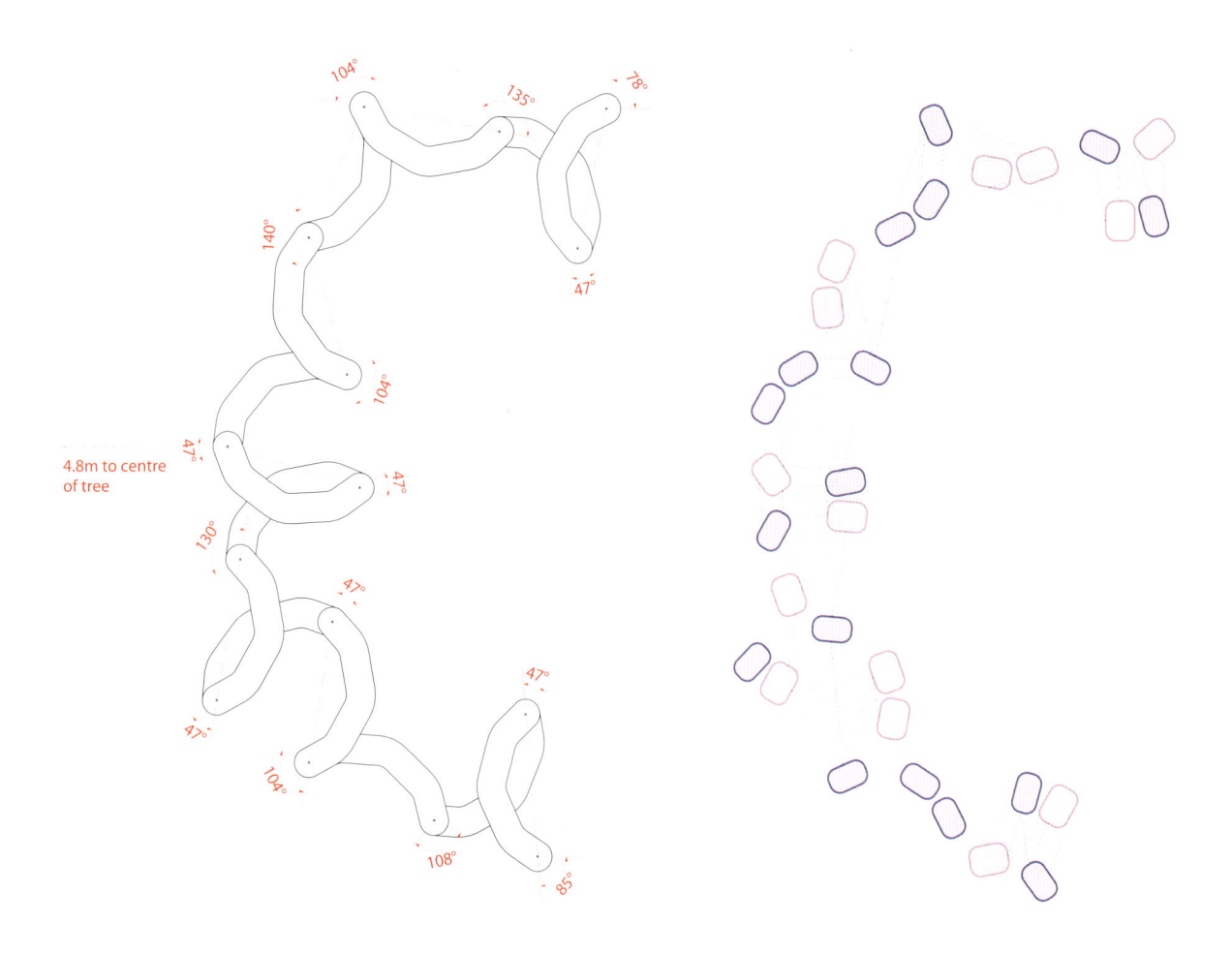

↑ | **Plans** for the use as benches
← | **Seating furniture,** during the London Architecture Biennale

← | **Modular arrangement of the Boomerangs** resulting in diverse forms
↓ | **Seating furniture,** during the London Architecture Biennale

ENSEMBLE

KOSMOS / Ott Kadarik, Villem Tomiste, Mihkel Tüür

↑ | Lanterns

Center square
Rakvere

Cobblestone circles divide the area of the square into different sections. A large lantern hanging over each section provides illumination. The squares vary in size and morphology. A large concave rock-circle functions as a fountain, while a circle in the center of the square functions as a mounded playing area for children. The rest of the square is covered with cubical stones of different tones constituting a gray and black lively zigzag pattern. On one side the square is adjoined by a long halyard marking the position of a perspective flanking building with preferably a public function. It serves as a recreational space as well as the main venue for parades and other large-scale events.

PROJECT FACTS

Address: Rakvere central square, 44306 Rakvere, Estonia. **Client:** City of Rakvere. **Completion:** 2004. **Production:** single piece. **Design:** individual design. **Functions:** seating, illumination, pavement, playing, fountain. **Main materials:** basalt, granite, cobblestone.

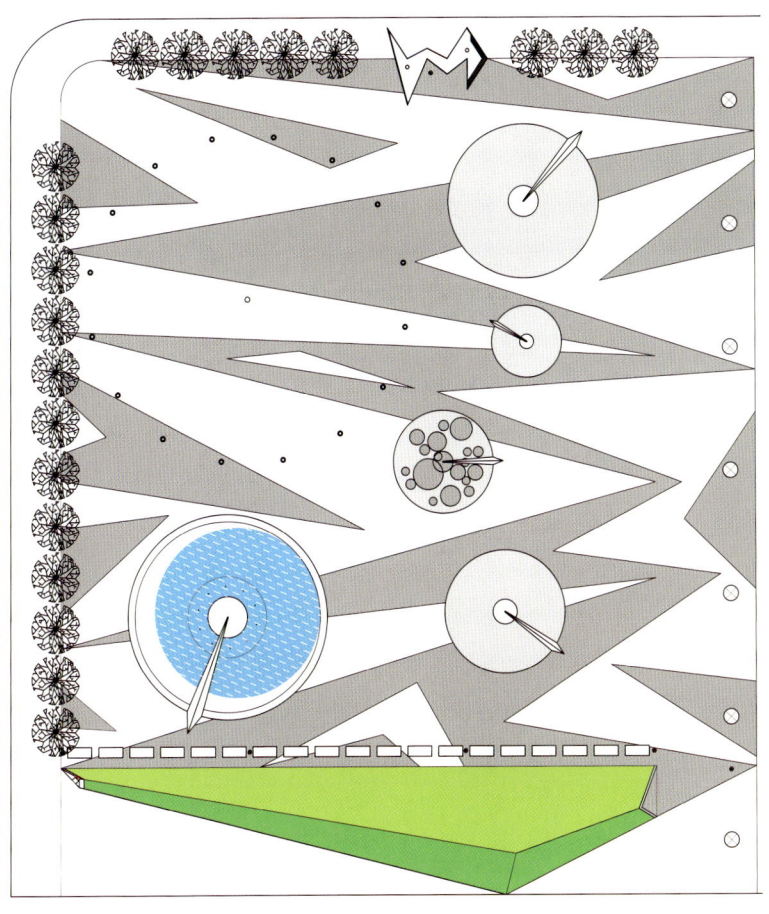

↑ | **Plan**
↓ | **Cobblestone circles,** dividing the square into different spaces

↑ | **Seatings**

ENSEMBLE

Bjarne Aasen
Landskapsarkitekt MNLA

↑ | **View of the campus during winter,** richly illuminated

Helga Eng Square, University of Oslo

Oslo

The central part of the library complex at Blindern campus forms one large plan, from which the buildings shoot up. The area forms a terrace from the north to the south. The new library square and the Helga Eng Square are connected to the terrace at the southern part of the University Square. The external spaces at Blindern are grandiose and uniform in terms of both form and material. This is reflected and emphasized in the design of the new spacious squares with gathering spaces, seating areas and bicycle parking. Granite from the old complex was reused as pavers on paths and squares around the new library.

PROJECT FACTS **Address:** Blindernveien, 0316 Oslo, Norway. **Planning partner:** Erik Ruud, Peter Aasen. **Client:** Statsbygg. **Completion:** 2000. **Production:** single piece. **Design:** individual design. **Functions:** seating, illumination, bicycle stand, sign, fountain. **Main materials:** granite, wood.

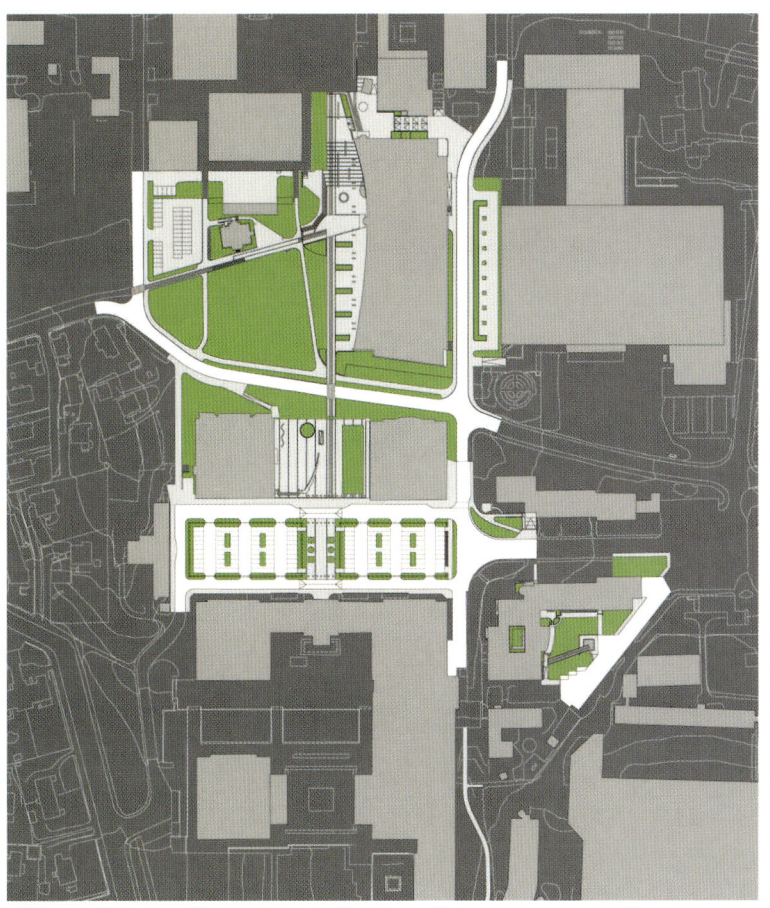

↑ | Site plan
↓ | Bicycle stands

↑ | **Sinuous bench,** made of natural stone and wood

ENSEMBLE | Atelier Boris Podrecca

↑ | Fountain
↗ | Waterfall
→ | Detail

Strossmayer Park
Split

The palace of the Roman emperor Diocletian is one of the most famous model examples of the adaptation and transformation of a historical structure by subsequent user generations. The palace was turned into a city district and its rooms into homes. In the 19th century, a city park was created along the northern wall, which increasingly deteriorated and was occupied by fringe groups. The redesign of the park with green islands that frame the preserved trees includes extensive new furnishings with various street furniture elements. Furniture such as stone benches and improved and newly designed elements such as fountains and light poles additionally enhance the setting.

PROJECT FACTS **Address:** 21 000 Split, Croatia. **Client:** City of Split. **Completion:** 2002. **Production:** single piece. **Design:** individual design. **Functions:** fountain, seating, lighting. **Main materials:** Dalmatian stone, metal.

ENSEMBLE ATELIER BORIS PODRECCA

↑ | Benches
← | Seating area

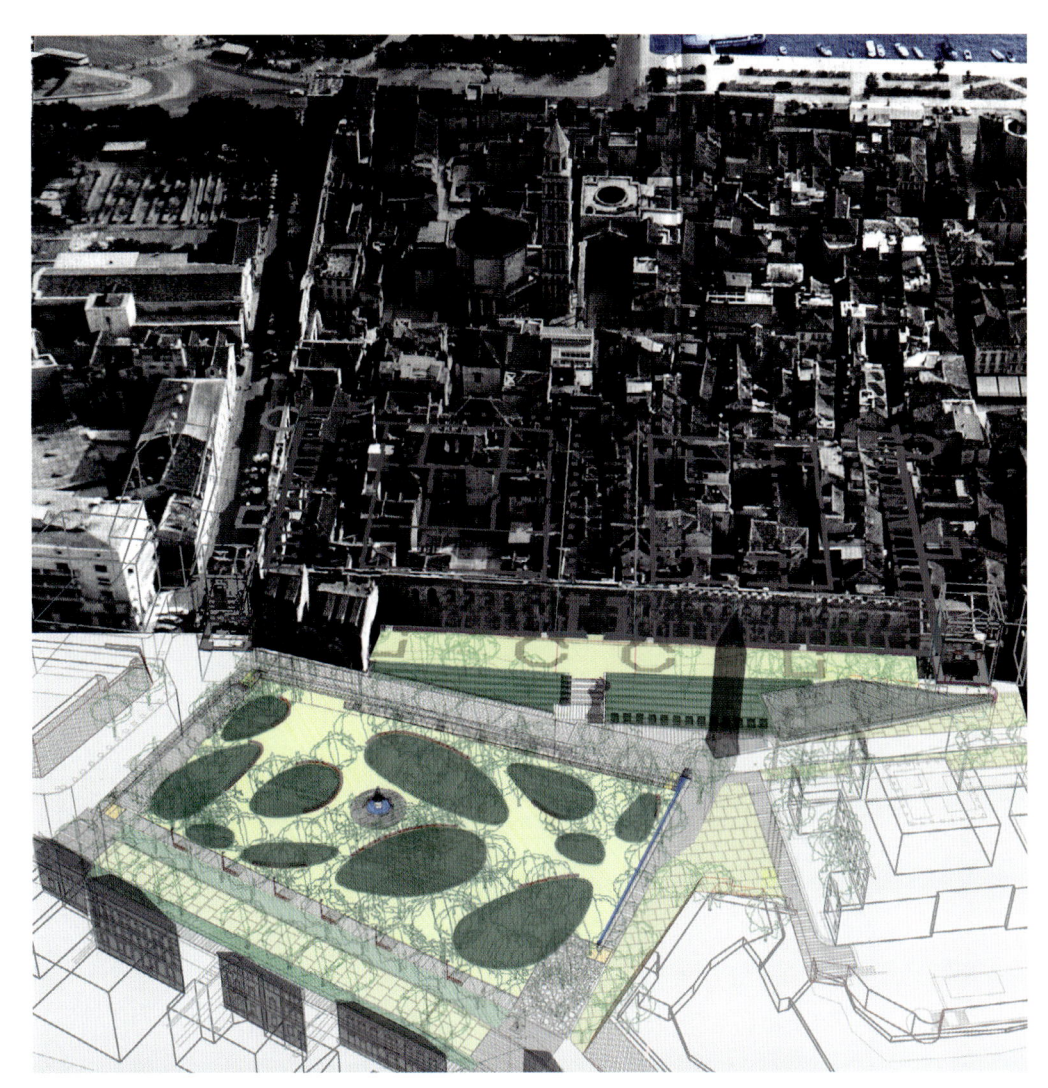

STROSSMAYER PARK

← | Site plan
↓ | Park view

ENSEMBLE | Sasaki Associates

↑ | **Integrated seatwall**
→ | **Granite fountain** and furnishings

National Harbor
National Harbor

National Harbor is a mixed-use community on the Potomac River near Washington, DC. The pedestrian spine, Grand Avenue, is inspired by Barcelona's famed Las Ramblas and showcases fountains, public art, vendor kiosks and retail storefronts. The Sasaki designed wayfinding system is unique, drawing from the context of the site. Colors reflect the national pride imbued in the site. Details make abstract reference to nautical themes, in keeping with the waterfront location. National Harbor's graphic identity is a combination of historic typography paired with a contemporary boat icon which gives this new destination a sense of belonging to its surroundings.

PROJECT FACTS **Address:** National Harbor, MD 20745, USA. **Client:** The Peterson Companies. **Completion:** 2008. **Production:** single piece. **Design:** individual design. **Functions:** seating, plant tub, sign, fountain. **Main materials:** granite, aluminum, Teak wood, glass, stainless steel.

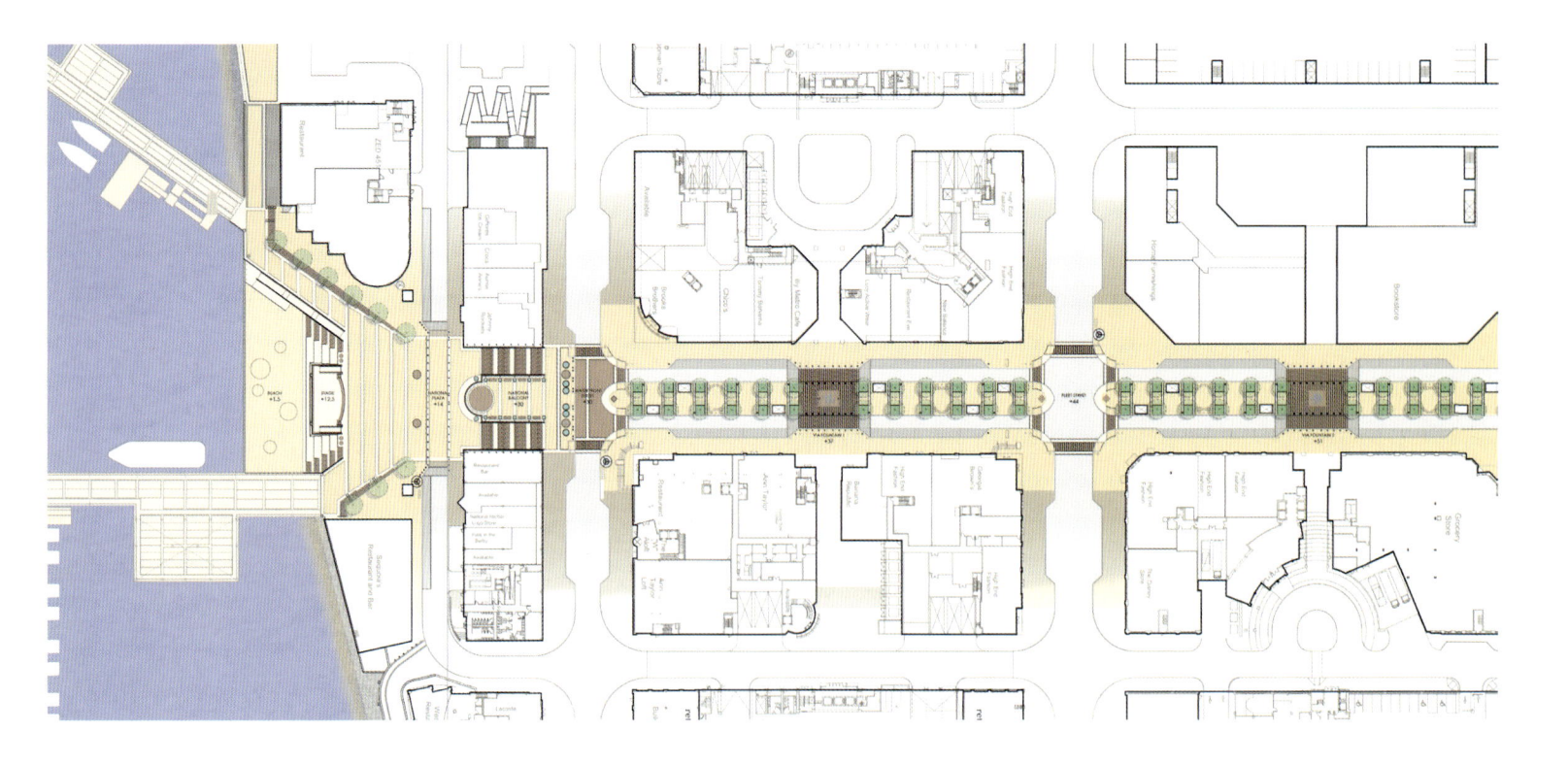

ENSEMBLE SASAKI ASSOCIATES

↑ | **Plaza Plan** for National Harbor
← | **Streetscape elements** emphasize linear plaza
→ | **Benches** at Harbor overlook

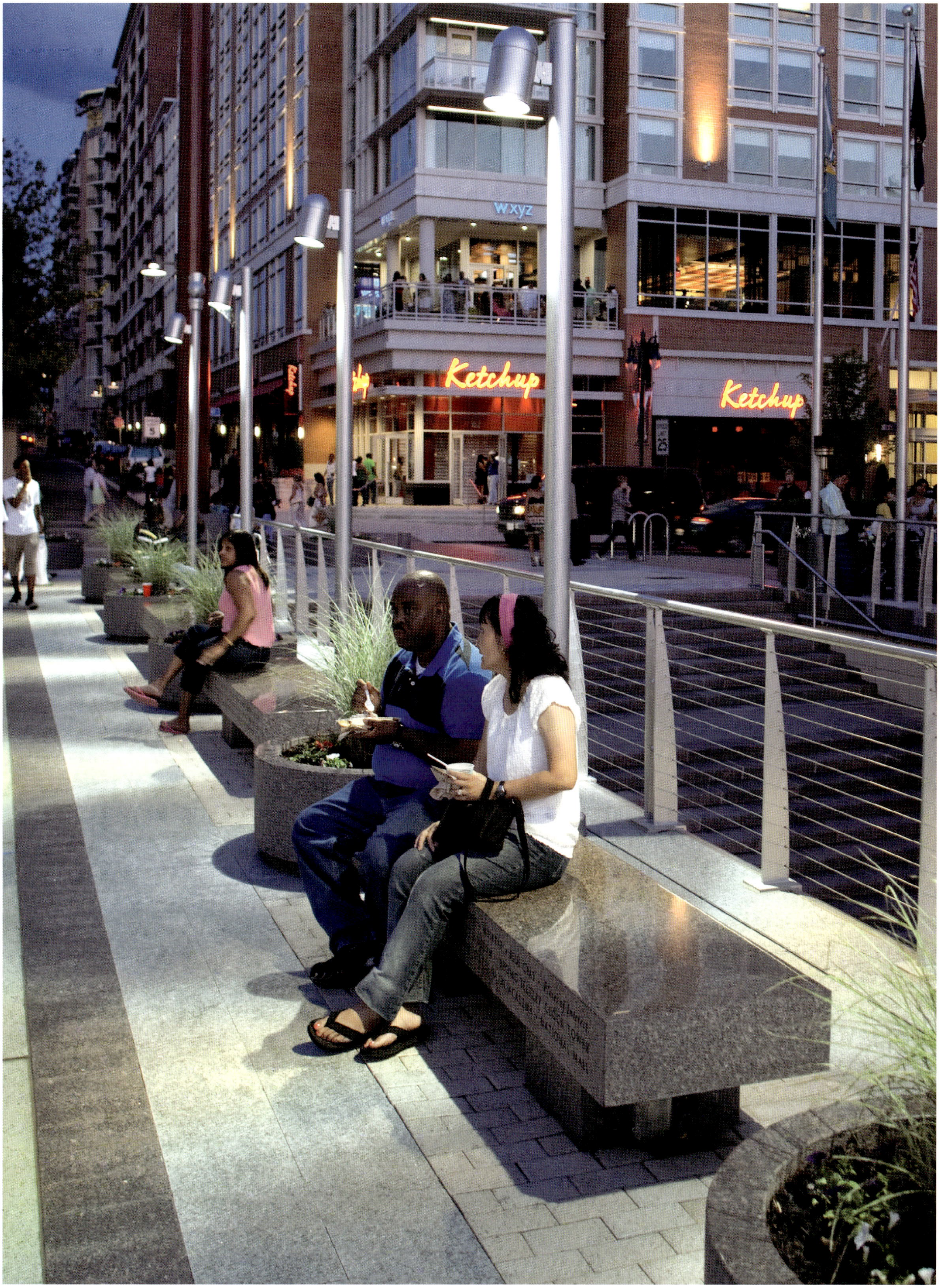
w xyz
Ketchup
Ketchup

ENSEMBLE

ASPECT Studios
(Melbourne Office)

↑ | **Bird's-eye view**
↗ | **Benches,** serving as seating furniture and delineation
→ | **Benches,** different perspective

Benches at Elwood Foreshore
Elwood, VIC

The Elwood Foreshore is the focus of the beach activity in the Elwood area. The benches serve a dual purpose of delineating the foreshore space from the car park entry and shared path exit. This border reinterprets the historical blue stone walls that have defined the vernacular of the suburban interface with Port Phillip Bay for more than 100 years. Illumination of the foreshore space was a primary concern and was incorporated into the benches, protected by a stainless steel screen. The construction method for the benches was developed in cooperation with the contractor to incorporate the steel structure as shapes that include fixing locations for lighting and steel panels to minimize wastage of materials.

PROJECT FACTS **Address:** Elwood Foreshore, Elwood, VIC 3184, Australia. **Planning partner:** Martin Butcher Lighting Design. **Client:** City of Port Phillip. **Completion:** 2009. **Production:** single piece. **Design:** individual design. **Functions:** seating, illumination. **Main materials:** in-situ concrete, stainless steel.

83

ENSEMBLE　　　　　　　　　　　ASPECT STUDIOS (MELBOURNE OFFICE)

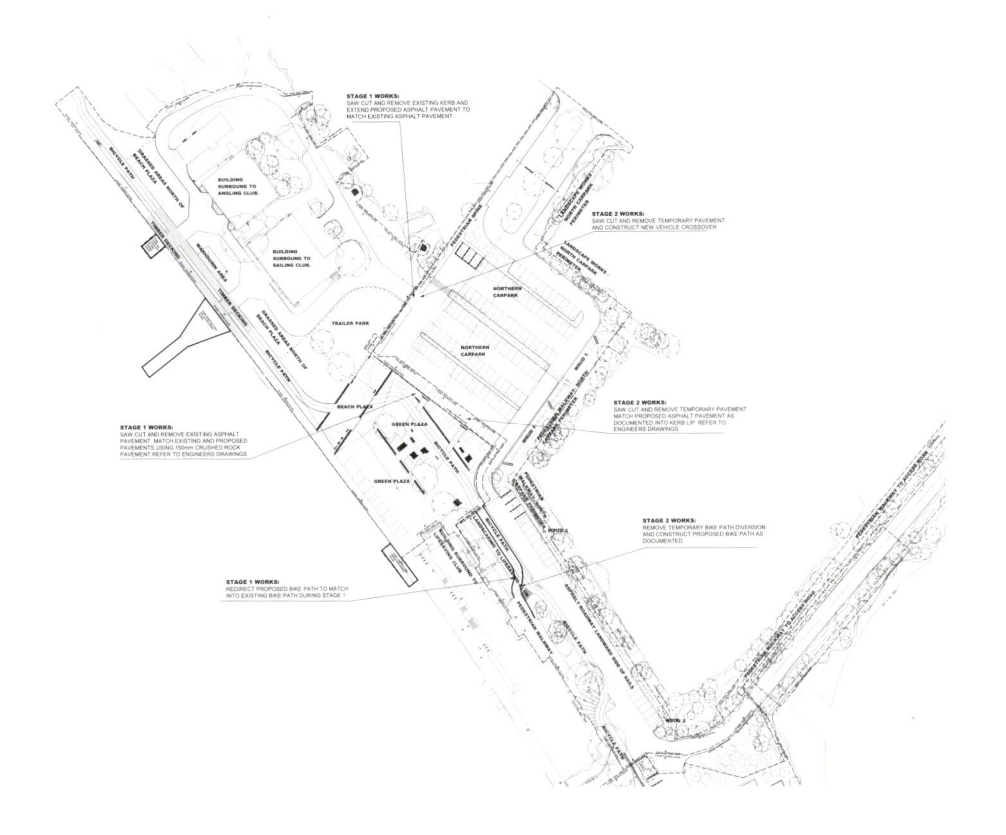

← | **Situation plan**
↓ | **Benches,** illuminated at night
→ | **Night view**

BENCHES AT ELWOOD FORESHORE

ENSEMBLE

OKRA landschapsarchitecten bv / Christ-Jan van Rooij, Hans Oerlemans, Martin Knuijt, Wim Voogt, Boudewijn Almekinders

↖ | **Ziezo**, a special developed seat
↑↑ | **Illumination**
↑ | **Street**, detail

City Center
Zutphen

The old Hanseatic city of Zutphen has a beautiful medieval city center with narrow streets, patios and beautifully shaped squares. Today, the city-center is increasingly turning into an attractive, lively place, and accordingly there is a growing need for high quality space. While the design of public realm reinterprets the history of the ancient hanseatic city, the used furniture has a contemporary design. The small seating elements, which are just meant for short breaks, are the monuments of the future. When empty, they capture the light in the dark streets. The choice of indirect lighting gives a fairytale-like effect and more even diffusion of the light in the street.

PROJECT FACTS
Address: Gemeente Zutphen, 7201 DN Zutphen, The Netherlands. **Client:** City of Zutphen. **Completion:** 2005. **Production:** serial production. **Design:** product line. **Functions:** seating, illumination, pavement. **Main materials:** stainless steel, red brick and bluestone.

Arriola & Fiol arquitectes /
Andreu Arriola, Carmen Fiol

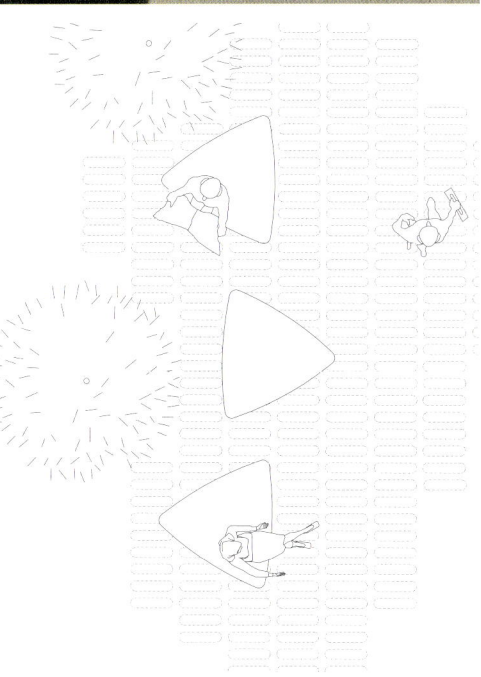

↑↑ | **Fountain Gran Via**
↗↗ | **Bird's-eye view Boomerang**, urban fossils
↑ | **Boomerang**, urban fossils
↗ | **Detail**
↓ | **Detail**, Extasi

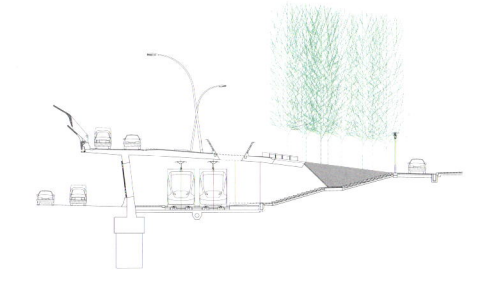

Gran Vía de Llevant
Barcelona

This urban furniture is part of a set of multiple seating or table series that can be used for everything from sitting down to doing homework, putting down backpacks or shopping bags. At the same time, they refer to the dimension of ancestral nature, the world of fossils and shells. Due to their shape, dimensions and materials, these elements, which are used to furnish squares like outdoor rooms, feature themes from the animal world, mineral references, and flying objects.

PROJECT FACTS
Address: Gran Vía Corts Catalanes, 08020 Barcelona, Spain. **Client:** Generalitat de Catalunya, Ajuntament de Barcelona. **Completion:** 2007. **Production:** serial production. **Design:** product line. **Functions:** seating, illumination, shelters, fountain, garbage can, drinking fountain, acustic screens. **Main materials:** wood, cast stone, anodized steel, stainless steel, brick.

ENSEMBLE

OKRA landschapsarchitecten bv / Christ-Jan van Rooij, Hans Oerlemans, Martin Knuijt, Wim Voogt, Boudewijn Almekinders

↖ | **Seatings,** next to a fountain
↑↑ | **Outdoor stage**
↑ | **Bench**

Storaa stream
Holstebro

For the municipality of Holstebro, the construction of a new cultural center served as the inspiration to give a new impulse to the structure of its public spaces. By being transformed into an outdoor stage, the public spaces around the cultural buildings, like cinema and dance theatre, provide the city with a new élan. The attractive public space acts as a catalyst for further development.

PROJECT FACTS
Address: Rådhuset, Kirkestræde 11, 7500 Holstebro, Denmark. **Planning partner:** Schul & CO Landskabsarkitekter, Light- and Theatre Consultant Åsa Frankenberg. **Client:** Holstebro city council. **Completion:** 2006. **Production:** single piece. **Design:** product line. **Functions:** seating. **Main materials:** concrete, wood.

Arriola & Fiol arquitectes /
Andreu Arriola, Carmen Fiol

↑↑ | **Chair "G"**
↗↗ | **Lampagena,** Magic Flute series
↑ | **Magic Flute series**
↗ | **Lamp Trivoli**

Central Park of Nou Barris
Barcelona

Palms and turning forks were placed as abstract shapes playing with light, wind and sound. They are graphic signs placed in high topographical distant points to act as guides through the wide open spaces. Used as protection shelters and called 'peinetas,' they have become the symbol of Nou Barris. The Magic Flute series of urban furniture is inspired by the characters from Mozart's opera.

PROJECT FACTS
Address: Parc Central de Nou Barris, 08042 Barcelona, Spain. **Client:** Pro Nou Barris S.A. **Completion:** 2007. **Production:** serial production. **Design:** product line. **Functions:** seating, illumination, shelters, garbage can, drinking fountain. **Main materials:** wood, precast concrete, anodized aluminium, stainless steel, brick, tiles.

ENSEMBLE | Marinaprojekt d.o.o. / Nikola Bašić

↑ | **Sea organ**
↗ | **Circular glazed surface**, Greeting to the sun
→ | **Greeting to the sun**

Sea Organ and Greeting to the Sun

Zadar

Sea organ and Greeting to the sun are parts of a comprehensive project of reshaping the promontory of the Zadar region. Sea organ is designed in the form of stairs, inducing people to stop and come down to the sea. The stone staircase is divided into seven sections containing polyurethane tubes of different diameters underneath in which the air is pushed and accelerated by the waves. Finally the air produces sounds, which come out through mystic apertures. Greeting to the sun is a circular glazed surface of 22 meters diameter which, by means of built-in photovoltaic cells, changes solar energy into lighting spectacle and turns the sound of the Sea organ into light sensations.

PROJECT FACTS

Address: Obala Petra Krešimira IV, 23210 Zadar, Croatia. **Sound sea organ:** Ivan Stamać. **Client:** City of Zadar. **Completion:** 2008. **Production:** single piece. **Design:** individual design. **Functions:** urban installations, production of electric energy. **Main materials:** stone, glass, photovoltaic cells.

ENSEMBLE MARINAPROJECT D.O.O.

↑ | Greeting to the sun
← | Sea organ and Greeting to the sun

SEA ORGAN AND GREETING TO THE SUN

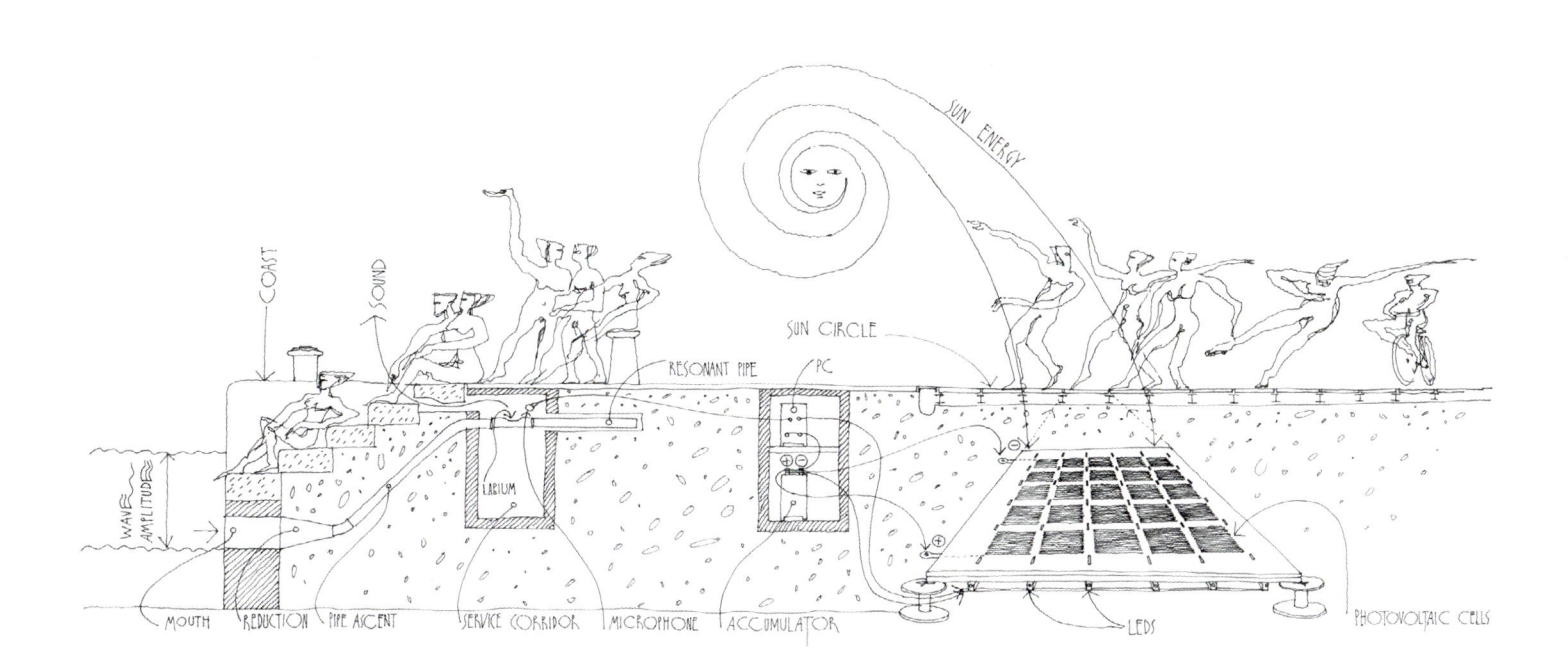

← | Sea organ
↓ | Sketch

ENSEMBLE

Rios Clementi Hale Studios /
Julie Smith-Clementi,
Mark Rios, Frank Clementi,
Bob Hale

↑ | **Chess tables**
→ | **16 regulation-sized chess boards,** sitting among the light towers

Chess Park
Glendale

To transform this rectangular space – once an unused pathway – into a chess park, the designers researched the game's history and based the design on its playing rituals, strategies and lore. Five playful light towers made from recycled plastic-and-wood lumber are topped with white synthetic canvas formed in the shape of an abstracted chess piece. The architects reinterpreted the shapes to represent the evolution of the ancient figurines, finding inspiration in Isamu Noguchi's famous lamps and the abstract sculptures of Constantin Brancusi. The light towers emit a warm glow and are strategically placed around the park, inspiring creativity and intellectual challenge.

PROJECT FACTS **Address:** 227 N. Brand Boulevard, Glendale, CA 91203, USA. **Client:** City of Glendale. **Completion:** 2004. **Production:** single piece. **Design:** product line. **Functions:** seating, illumination, chess tables, low platform stage. **Main materials:** trex (a recycled plastic and wood lumber product), canvas, concrete.

ENSEMBLE   RIOS CLEMENTI HALE STUDIOS

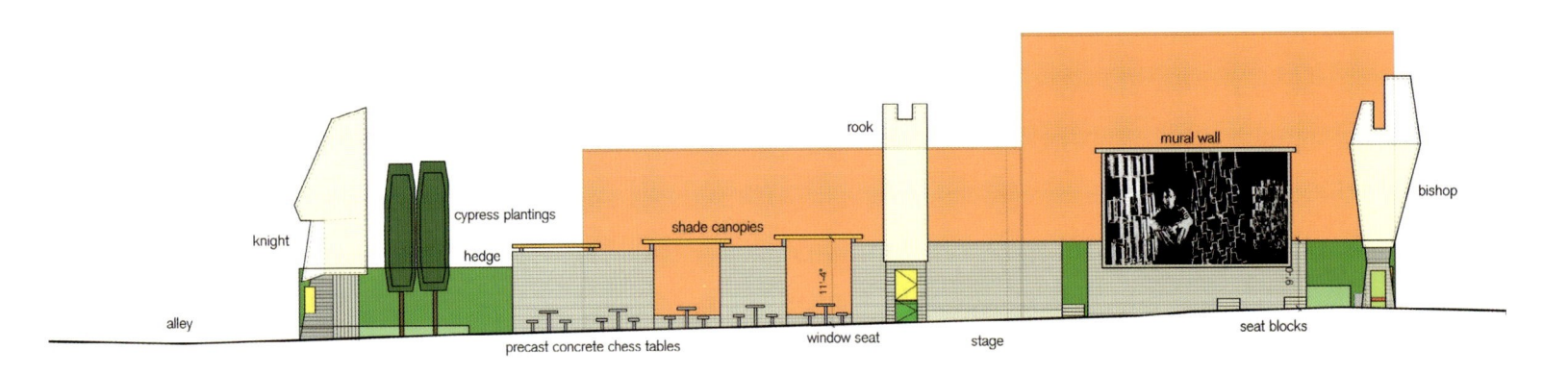

Labels on elevation: alley · knight · cypress plantings · hedge · shade canopies · rook · mural wall · bishop · precast concrete chess tables · window seat · stage · seat blocks · 11'-4"

↑ | **South elevation**
← | **King Tower's throne** to welcome storytelling performances

CHESS PARK

← | **Lighting** is integrated into the towers and structures
↓ | **Site plan**

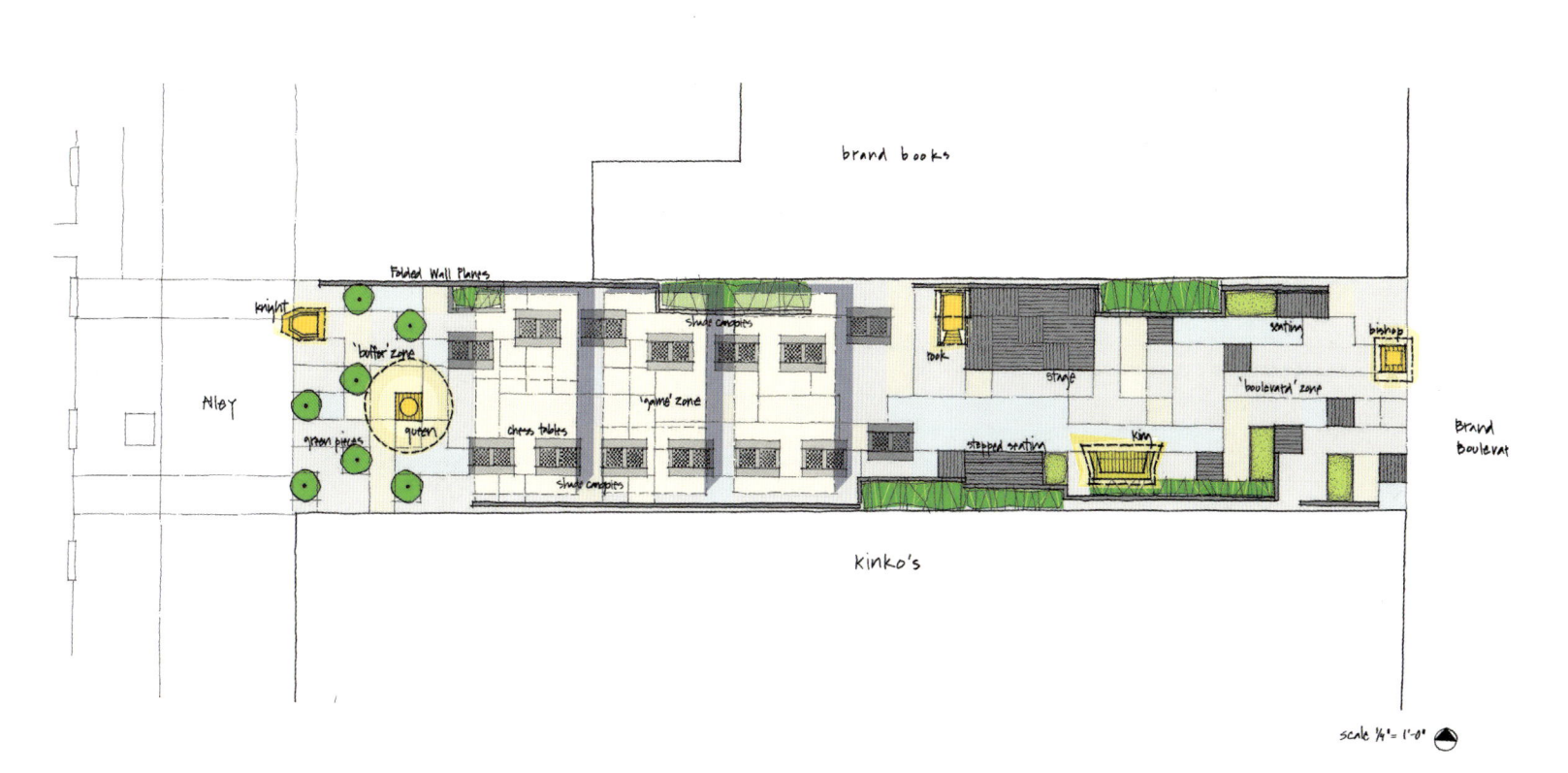

ENSEMBLE

Rios Clementi Hale Studios /
Julie Smith-Clementi,
Mark Rios, Frank Clementi,
Bob Hale

↑ | **Concrete benches and glowing resin tables**
→ | **Steel bases** with vibrant green translucent panels

Quincy Court
Chicago

Quincy Court, a remnant of an old downtown street, was transformed into an engaging, spring-like sculptural gathering place. The new plaza features seven tree-like canopy elements made of steel and three tones of translucent acrylic panels that are lit from above after dark. The "trees" are rooted by sandblasted concrete in an abstracted leaf pattern. New granite benches and pavers join existing seating and hardscape materials; while a new site furniture language is introduced using concrete benches and translucent resin tables glowing with inner lighting. Four large leaves are situated on the ground, seemingly scattered on the pavement, the "result" of a strong gust well known to the Windy City.

PROJECT FACTS **Address:** Federal Plaza, Chicago, IL 60610, USA. **Client:** General Services Administration (GSA). **Completion:** 2009. **Production:** single piece. **Design:** product line. **Functions:** seating, illumination, tables, sculptural forms. **Main materials:** steel, translucent acrylic panels, white granite.

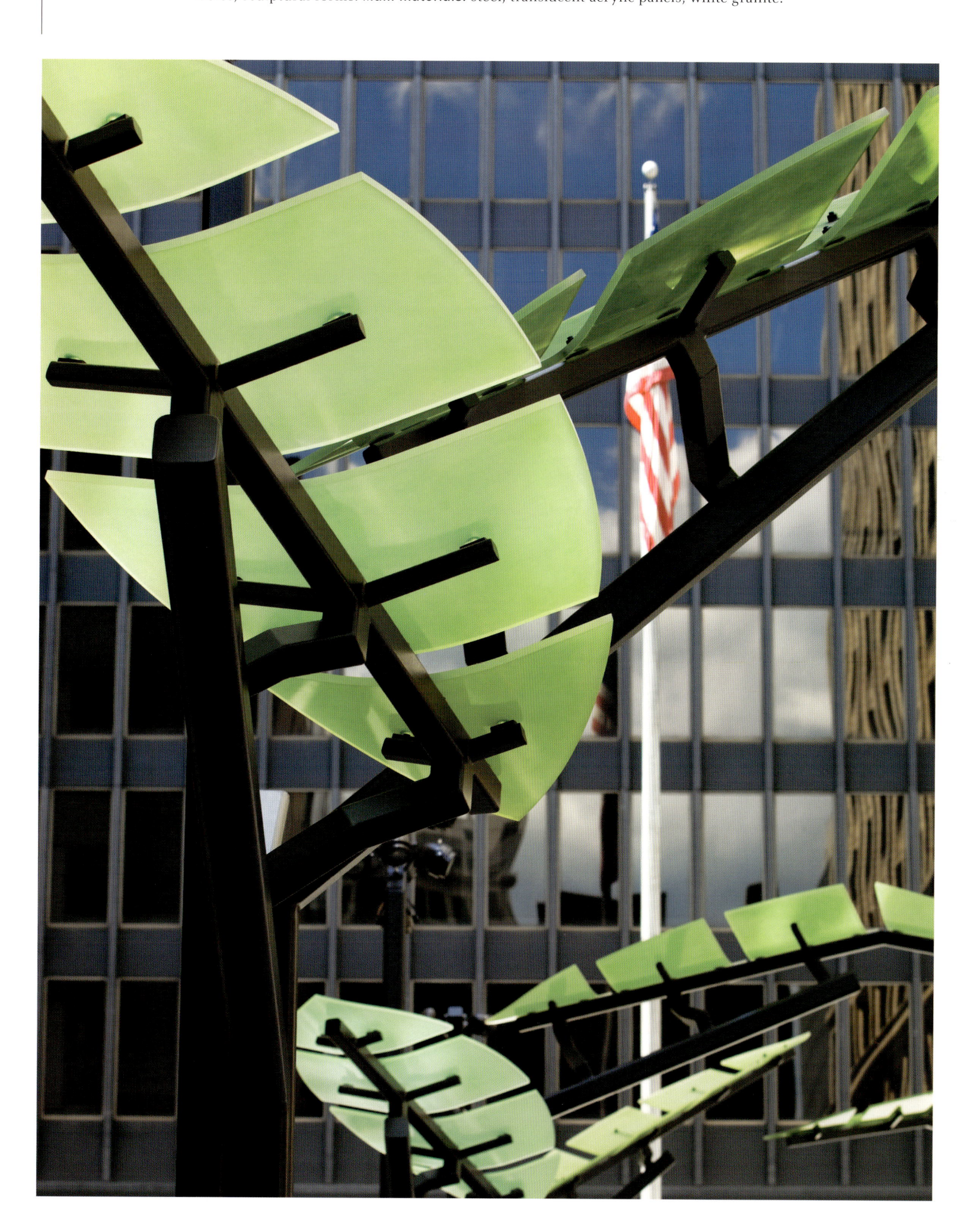

ENSEMBLE RIOS CLEMENTI HALE STUDIOS

↑ | **Integrated lighting** illuminates a canopy of leaves at night
← | **Fallen leaf forms** bringing an additional graphic element to cement pavers

QUINCY COURT

← | **A playfully placed leaf** that the "Windy City" has blown from the branches above
↓ | **Court plan**

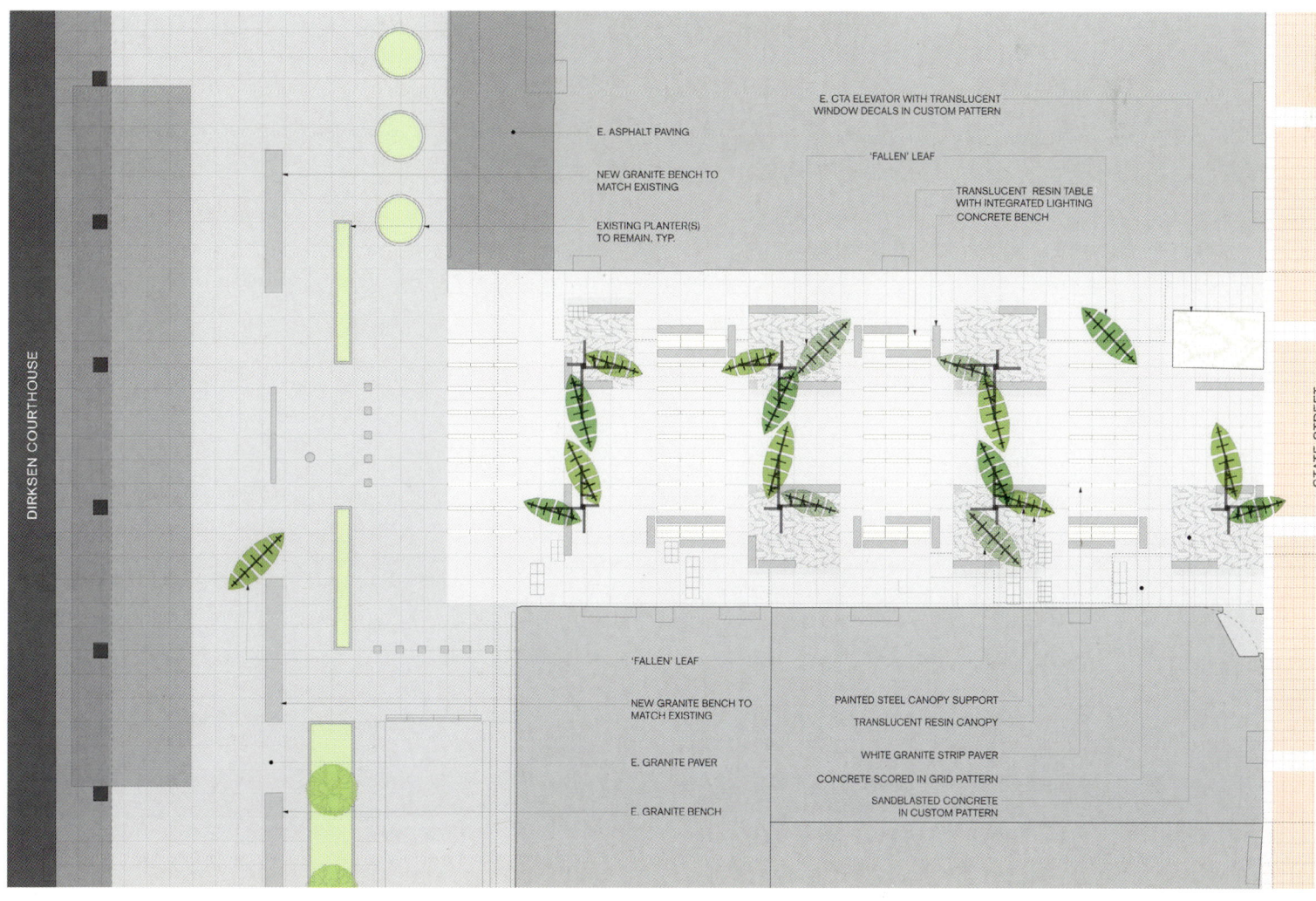

ENSEMBLE | LODEWIJK BALJON landscape architects

↑ | Water feature

Station square
Apeldoorn

The sand-colored paving and the pine trees in this shell-shaped space directly refer to the landscape of the region. The elegant surface radiates quietness and exclusive simplicity. The paving of yellow Portuguese granite runs up unto the tree trunks. Line drains, tree grids and lighting poles are integrated in a craquelure-like pattern. A series of elements further enlivens the space. A young crowd is attracted by a dry pool for skaters. Another attractive object is a water table made of blue-gray granite. A red steel provision for the roots defines an oversized tree grid and a number of robust seating elements are placed like crystals in the polygon cracks.

PROJECT FACTS **Address:** Stationsplein, 7311 Apeldoorn, The Netherlands. **Client:** City of Apeldoorn, Heijmans Vastgoed, BAM Vastgoed. **Completion:** 2008. **Production:** single piece. **Design:** individual design. **Functions:** water feature, skate pool, tree grid. **Main materials:** granite.

↑ | Water feature
↓ | Tree grid

↑↑ | Plan
↑ | Seating varieties

ENSEMBLE

Biuro Projektów Lewicki Łatak / Piotr Lewicki, Kazimierz Łatak

↑ | **Night view**
↗ | **Foggy athmosphere**
→ | **Tram stop shelters** with chairs

Bohaterów Getta Square (Zgody Square)
Krakow

In 1943, after the Nazis had liquidated the ghetto area, Zgody Square was full of useless things – a meaningful trace of the absence of their owners. Innumerable wardrobes, tables, sideboards and other furniture items had been abandoned there, which had been moved from one place to another no one knows how many times. By using the whole area of the square, the story of this place is now told. The remembrance of those who are no longer with us is expressed by an accumulation of ordinary objects. Chairs, a well with a pump, rubbish bins, tram stop shelters, bicycle stands and even traffic signs, stripped of their everyday practical functions, have acquired a symbolical aspect.

PROJECT FACTS

Address: pl. Bohaterów Getta, 30-547 Krakow, Poland. **Client:** City of Krakow. **Completion:** 2005. **Production:** single piece. **Design:** individual design. **Functions:** seatings, illumination, shelters, plant tubs, bicycle stands, garbage cans, signs, pavement, memory hall, shops. **Main materials:** syenite, basalt, porphyre and granite cobblestones, bronze, galvanized steel, concrete.

ENSEMBLE BIURO PROJEKTÓW LEWICKI ŁATAK

↑ | In the wintertime
← | Tree tub

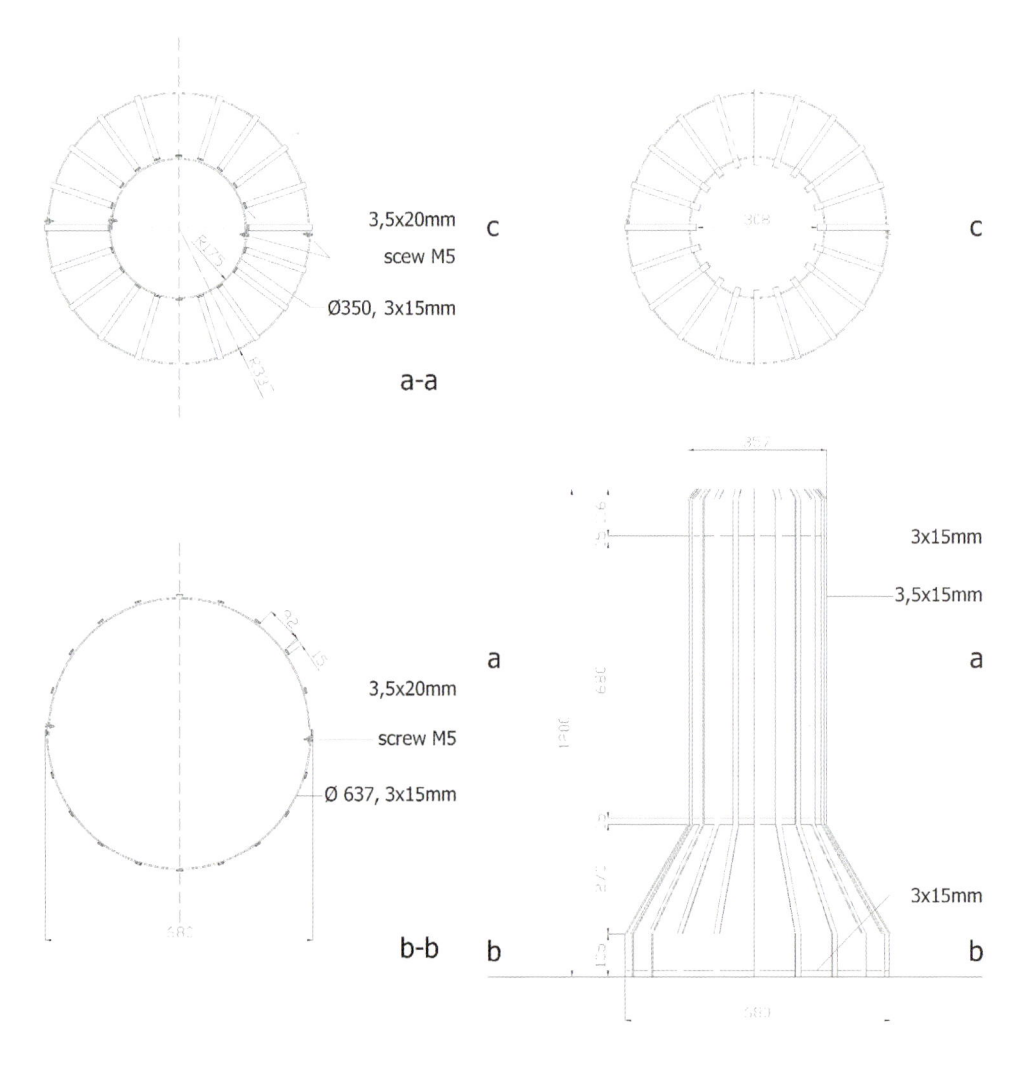

3,5x20mm
scew M5
Ø350, 3x15mm

a-a

c

c

3x15mm
3,5x15mm

3,5x20mm
scew M5
Ø 637, 3x15mm

3x15mm

a

a

b-b   b

b

BOHATERÓW GETTA SQUARE (ZGODY SQUARE)

← | During the Jewish Culture Festival
↙ | A monument, a sculpture, a piece of urban furniture

ENSEMBLE | Biuro Projektów Lewicki Łatak / Piotr Lewicki, Kazimierz Łatak

↑ | **Benches,** with litter baskets

Książąt Czartoryskich Square
Krakow

The new square was completely created from stone. The differentiation of the floor levels separates various functional areas. The introduced stairs prevent cars from blocking the space in front of the museum buildings. Stone urban furniture like benches with litter baskets, were created. The material of the relief is a porphyry road cube originating from Miekinia near Krakow. The deposit was used up long ago. An appropriately chosen granite and delicate graining was used as an addition to the porphyry surface. The richness of shapes provided by a single material and the possibilities of its dressing were used – from a block, via a cut, to flamed, bush hammered and polished surfaces.

| **PROJECT FACTS**   **Address:** pl. Książąt Czartoryskich, 31-015 Krakow, Poland. **Client:** City of Krakow. **Completion:** 2006. **Production:** single piece. **Design:** individual design. **Functions:** seatings, illumination, garbage cans, pavement. **Main materials:** bohus granite, strzegom granite, old porphyre cobblestones, bronze.

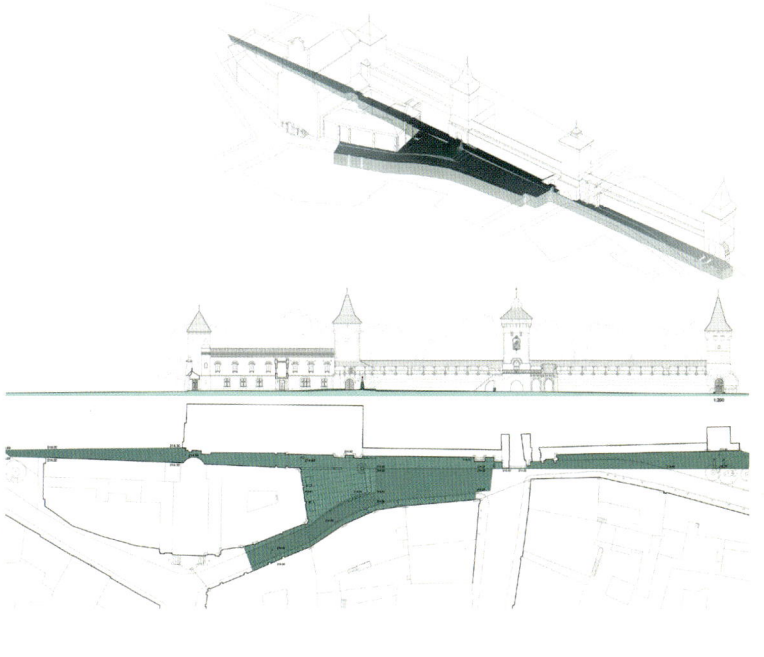

↑ | **Pavement**, old porphyre cobblestones and the new granite ones

↑ | **Plan, section, axonometric view**
↓ | **Bench with a garbage can**

ENSEMBLE | BRUTO d.o.o. / Matej Kučina

↑ | **Bench,** at water access
→ | **Park on the riverbank**

General Maister Memorial Park
Ljubno ob Savinji

The memorial park is designed as an abstract three-dimensional spatial illustration of the northern border mountain ridges, which Maister's soldiers fought for in 1918. The main space-defining elements are reinforced concrete prefabricates. They separate single triangular areas, framing the terrain as retaining walls. The whole embankment is secured against inundation with solid stone blocks, protecting the park like a stone shield. Elevated parts of walls are transformed into benches, incorporating litter bins and lights. Made out of welded metal rods, the sculpture represents a stylized image of General Maister followed by his horse and soldiers.

PROJECT FACTS **Address:** Ljubno ob Savinji 3333, Slovenia. **Sculptures:** Primož Pugelj. **Client:** General Maister society. **Completion:** 2007. **Production:** single piece. **Design:** individual design. **Functions:** seating. **Main materials:** stone, concrete, metal.

ENSEMBLE   BRUTO D.O.O.

↑ | **Sculpture,** with front wall
← | **Illuminated sculpture**

GENERAL MAISTER MEMORIAL PARK

← | **Night view**, from the bank
↓ | **Cross section**

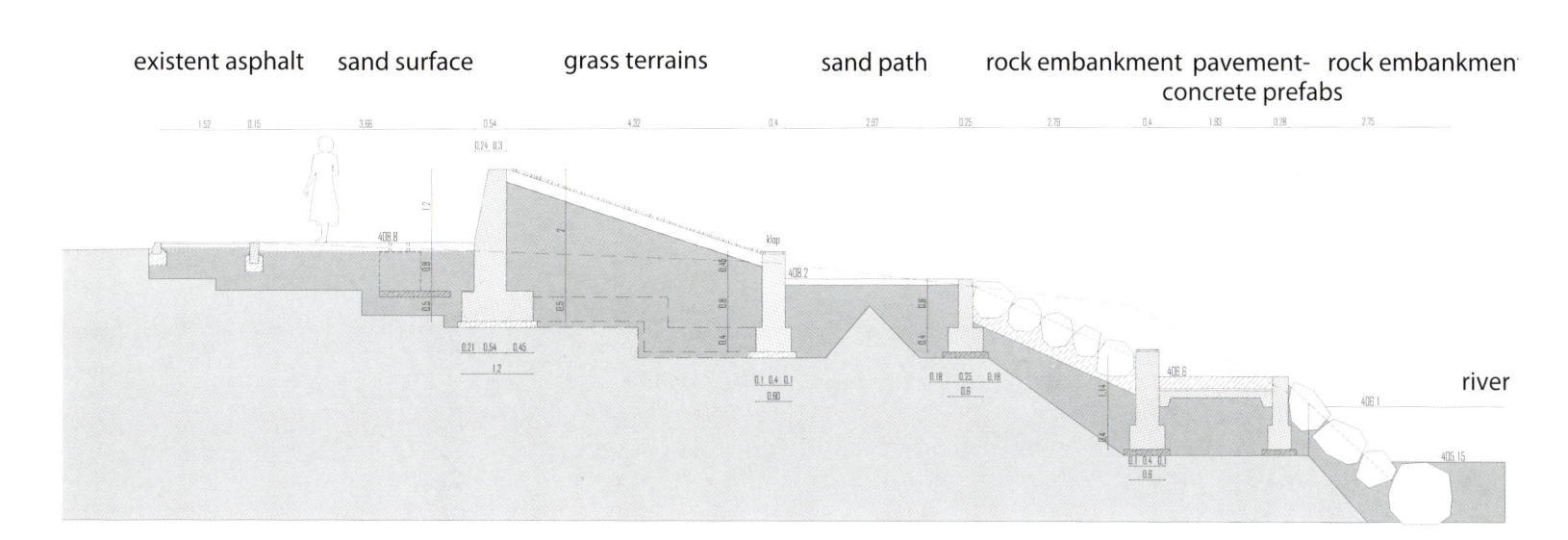

existent asphalt | sand surface | grass terrains | sand path | rock embankment | pavement-concrete prefabs | rock embankment

river

ENSEMBLE | BRUTO d.o.o. / Matej Kučina

↑ | Roof promenade

Wellness Orhidelia
Podčetrtek

The new wellness center is situated in the densely built-up area of the health resort and hotel complex Olimia. The colossal facility is entirely built below ground; therefore the whole area of the new complex is designed as an urban park. The luxuriant facility efficiently defines the space, which is linked to the surrounding area of other hotels and baths through slopes, stairs and terraces. The main elements are the paved entrance squares, the lush pathway that leads across the roof of the underground building, the wooden terraces that sweep gently to the open-air pools, and the green areas of the roof complex.

PROJECT FACTS **Address:** Zdraviliška cesta 24, 3254 Podcetřtek, Slovenija. **Planning partner:** ENOTA architecture. **Client:** Terme Olimia d.d. **Completion:** 2009. **Production:** single piece. **Design:** individual design. **Functions:** seating, illumination, protecting fence. **Main materials:** wood (bench), steel poles (fence).

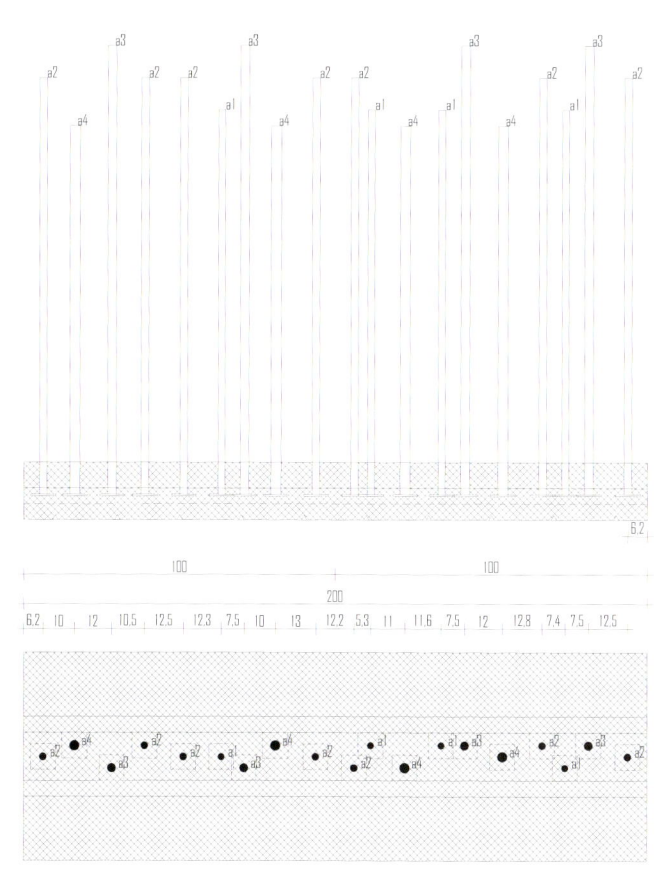

↑ | Fence
↓ | Bollards, benches and fence on the promenade

↑ | Illumination bollards

ENSEMBLE | 3GATTI

↑ | Mirror stainless steel benches

In Factory
Shanghai

In Factory is a redevelopment project for an abandoned industrial area in the center of a Chinese megalopolis. The surfaces lie vertically and horizontally; they are opaque, transparent (the effect of the "walls" created by a succession of metal rods), changeable (the American vine varies its aspect every season), but above all they reflect the light (like the treated steel of the benches and the horizontal surfaces of the "ceiling"). The result is a space which interacts with the density of the environment, particularly in the main courtyard, where a touch of the rods can generate a vibrating sound, and where the lamps, hanging at different levels, swing with the wind.

PROJECT FACTS

Address: 1147 Kangding Rd, 200042 Shanghai, China. **Client:** Shanghai Shang 'an Development and Administration Ltd. **Completion:** 2006. **Production:** single piece. **Design:** individual design. **Functions:** seating, lightning. **Main materials:** corten coated with epoxy.

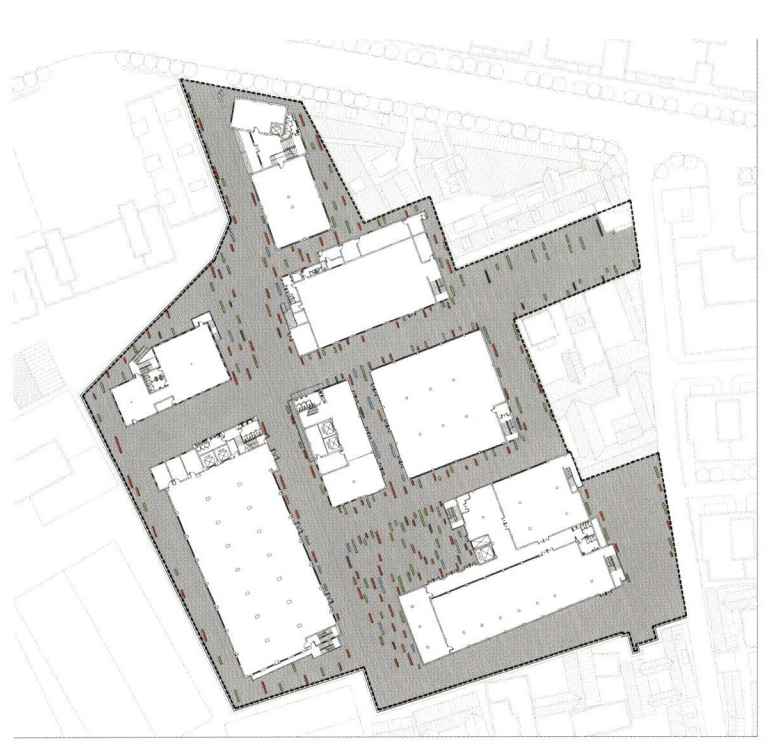

↑ | Site plan
↓ | Bird's-eye view

↑ | **Benches, water bassins and plant tubs**
creating horizontally aspects

ENSEMBLE 3GATTI

↑ | Mansard wooden furniture

Kic Village
Shanghai

The objective of this project was to redesign an angle of urban landscape in Shanghai. Surfaces and solids are fitted together. The surfaces consist of folded slips of paper which then materialize into wooden footboards, and the solids are advertising light boxes. These strips create the spatial and functional wealth of the project, as they could form ramps, benches, lounging chairs, traps, flower vases, roofing, luminous totems and even hazards and traps. The objective was to provide a certain danger element for the users of the area to jerk them awake from the usual urban monotony and to stimulate them mentally and physically by making them interact consciously with their surroundings.

PROJECT FACTS

Address: Block 8-2, Zhengmin Road, Yangpu District, 200433 Shanghai, China. **Client:** Shui On Development Limited. **Completion:** 2009. **Production:** single piece. **Design:** individual design. **Functions:** seating, illumination, shelters, plant tub, boards, signs, hazards and traps. **Main materials:** wooden deck, acrylic board, steel structure.

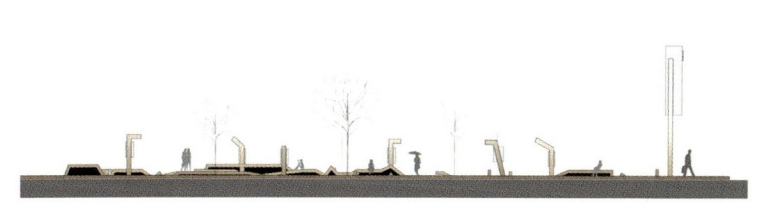

↑↑ | North elevation
↑ | Master plan

↑ | Wooden deck
↓ | Bird's-eye view

ENSEMBLE | Earthscape

↑ | **Streets on the plaza,** flanked by white seats

Lazona Kawasaki Plaza
Kawasaki

This shopping mall, which celebrated its opening in September 2006, is located next to the central station and constitutes the center of the business district of the city of Kawasaki. Alternating pavement patterns are used to create a vivid and colorful setting, underlined by artistic fittings placed at several locations. Among the most remarkable features of the setting and constituting a kind of signature of the designer are the white concrete paths cutting through the different layers of pavement. This way, the concrete pathways dominate the structure of the area and establish its optical focus.

PROJECT FACTS

Address: 72-1 Horikawa-cho Saiwai-ku Kawasaki city Kanagawa, Japan 212-0013. **Architect:** Ricardo Bofill Leví and Yamashita Sekkei Inc. **Client:** Toshiba / Mitsui Fudosan Group Ltd. **Completion:** 2006. **Production:** single piece. **Design:** individual design. **Functions:** seating. **Main materials:** concrete.

↑ | **Entering the plaza**
↓ | **Bird's-eye view**

↑ | **Perspective view**, Lazona Kawasaki Plaza

ENSEMBLE | CCM Architects, Ralph Johns & John Powell Landscape Architects / Guy Cleverley, Ralph Johns

↑ | Bird's-eye view
→ | Combination of seating elements and lighting

City Heart
Palmerston North

The master plan for the regeneration of the city's central park was implemented in stages. A palette of seating, lighting and structural furniture elements celebrates the unique historical, spatial and experiential characteristics of each section. The main pedestrian thoroughfare features contemporary lighting that references the line of the railway that used to run through the city. At the core of the area the clock tower was fully restored, increased in height and creatively illuminated to reinforce its role as an urban monument. Lighting was integrated into the seating elements, tree guards and the ground plane as well as customized vertical elements to support a high level of amenity and after dark use. The Coronation Garden provides generous seating, with the geometry focused on the relocated and restored stone fountain.

PROJECT FACTS **Address:** Palmerston North, 4410 New Zealand. **Client:** Palmerston North City Council. **Completion:** 2007. **Production:** single piece. **Design:** individual design. **Functions:** seating, illumination, fountain, tree guards. **Main materials:** hardwood timber, stainless steel, granite, concrete.

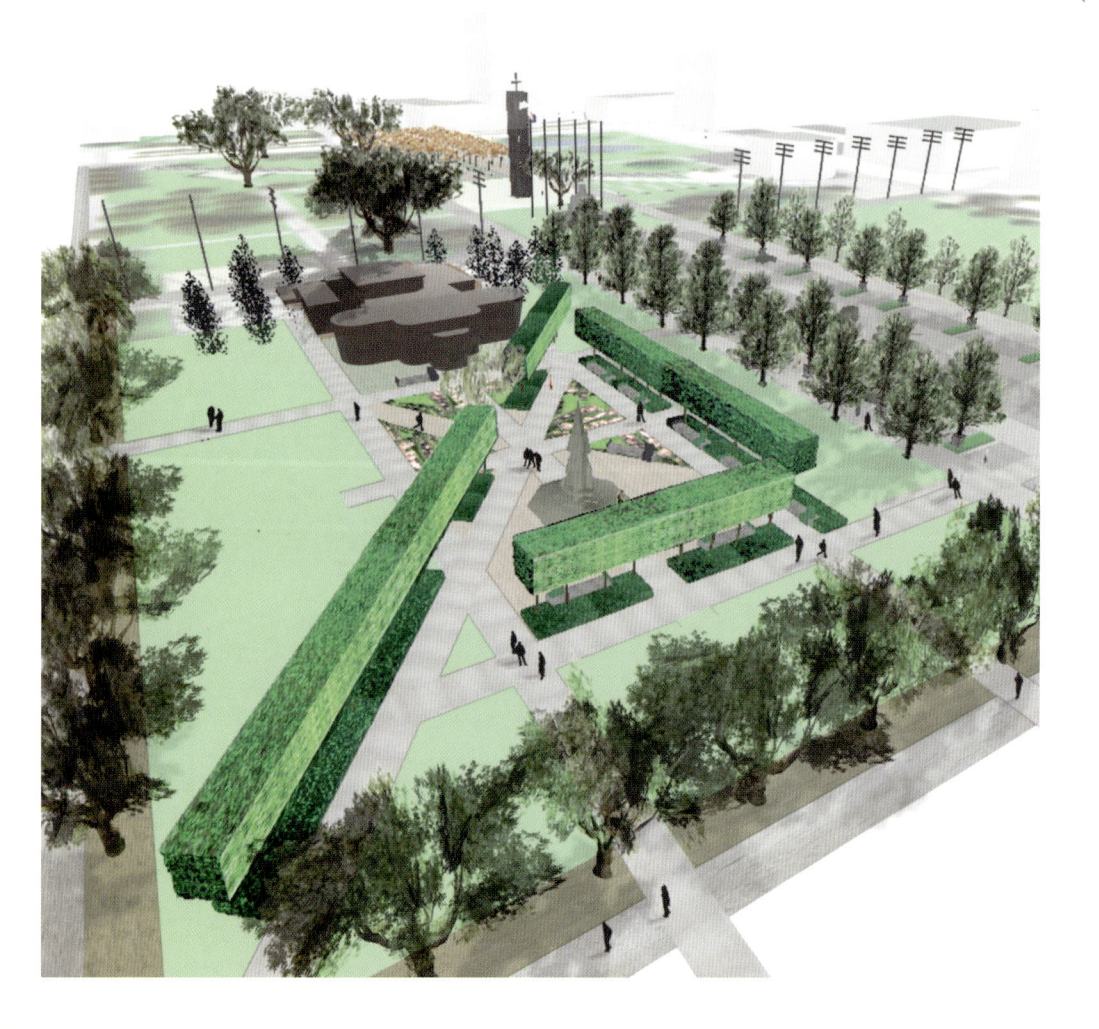

ENSEMBLE

CCM ARCHITECTS, RALPH JOHNS & JOHN POWELL LANDSCAPE ARCHITECTS

↑ | Group of public seats
← | Coronation Garden

CITY HEART

125

← | **Feature lights**
↓ | **Row of benches,** at the edge of Events Lawn

ENSEMBLE

Isthmus / David Irwin, Tim Fitzpatrick, Grant Bailey, Yoko Tanaka

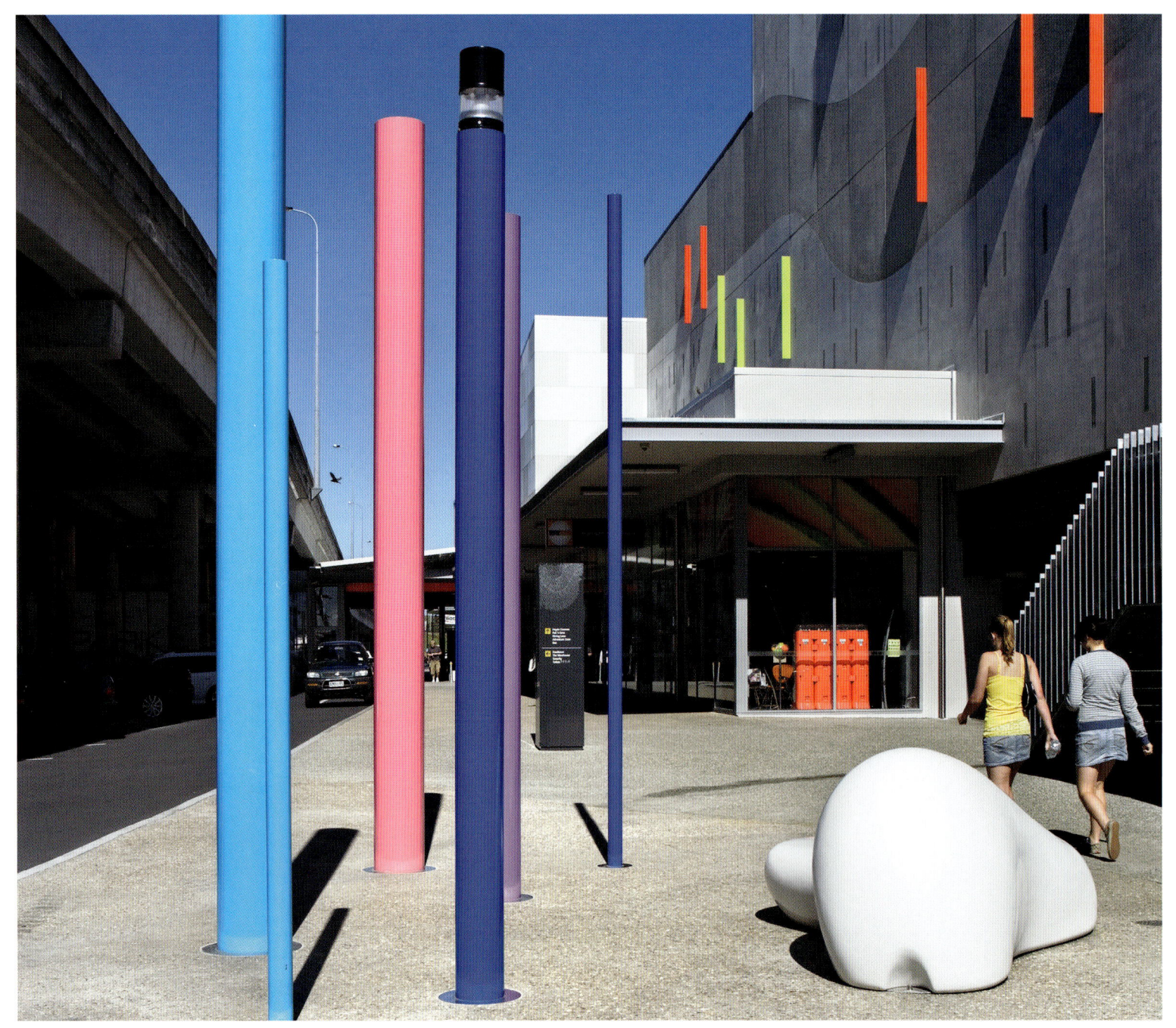

↑ | Seats and colored poles
↗ | Pathway to the shopping center
→ | Below the south-eastern arterial road overpass

Sylvia Park
Auckland

The main design elements are simple vertical steel poles, painted with vibrant colors that add life and excitement to the space. These poles are populated randomly (like trees in a forest) with different heights and colors. Informal gathering spaces are interspersed within the poles to provide opportunities for weekend markets, arts, performance and product displays. Organically shaped seats are also provided to further contrast with the built bridge structure. The seating is hollow and made from fiberglass and using a two-part mould. The Isthmus concept was designed and manufactured by Valentin Design.

PROJECT FACTS **Address:** 286 MT Wellington Highway, MT Wellington, Auckland, New Zealand. **Manufacturers:** CSP Pacific, Valentin Design. **Client:** Kiwi Income Property Trust (KIPT). **Completion:** 2008. **Production:** single piece. **Design:** individual design. **Functions:** seating, ilumination, vertical steel poles. **Main materials:** fiberglass, steel.

ENSEMBLE   ISTHMUS

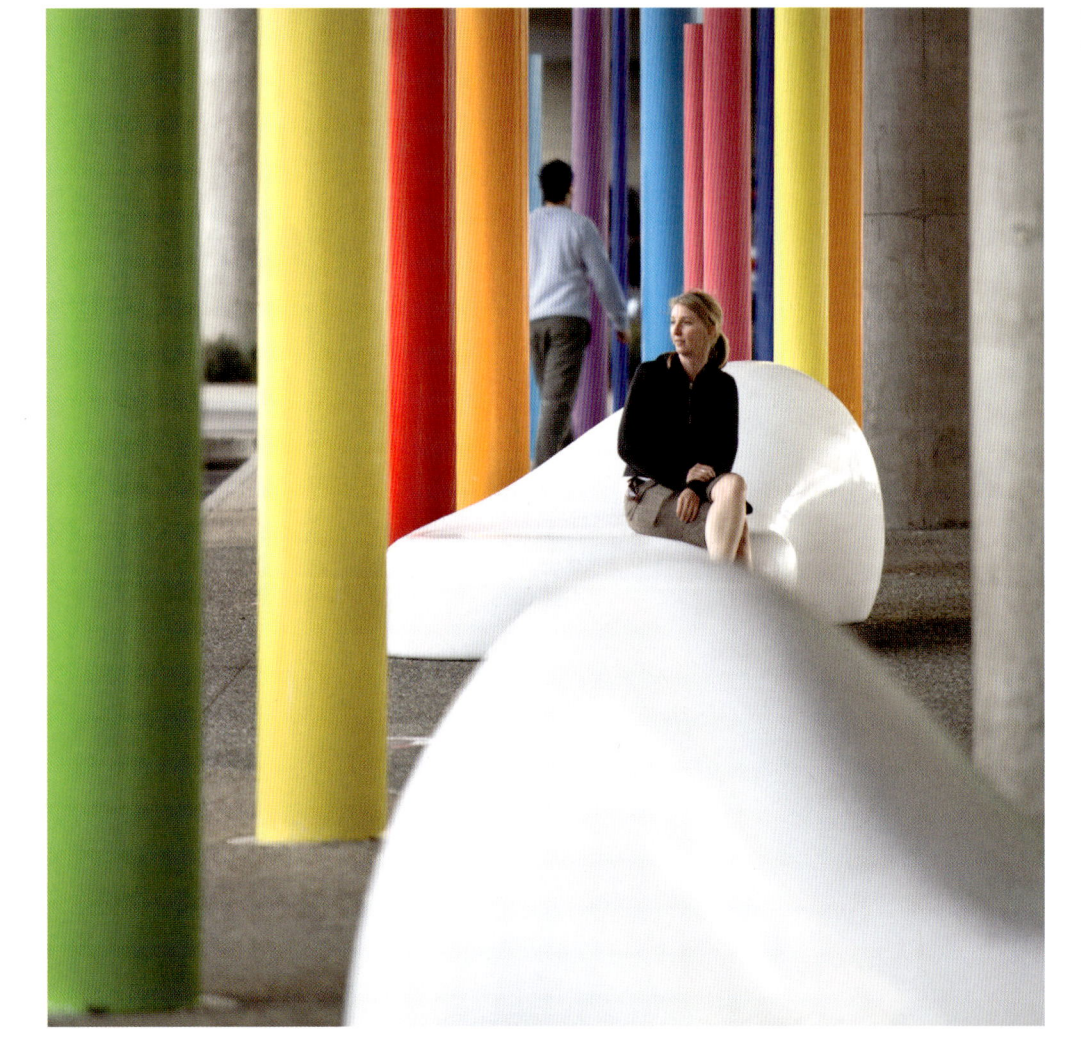

↑ | Vertical steel poles
← | Seat and colored poles

SYLVIA PARK

← | **Lighting** incorporated in selected steel poles
↓ | **Concept model**

Feature Seat
(Organic form, glowing at night)

Red Granite Paving Band

Blue Stone Paving Band

Clear pedestrian path

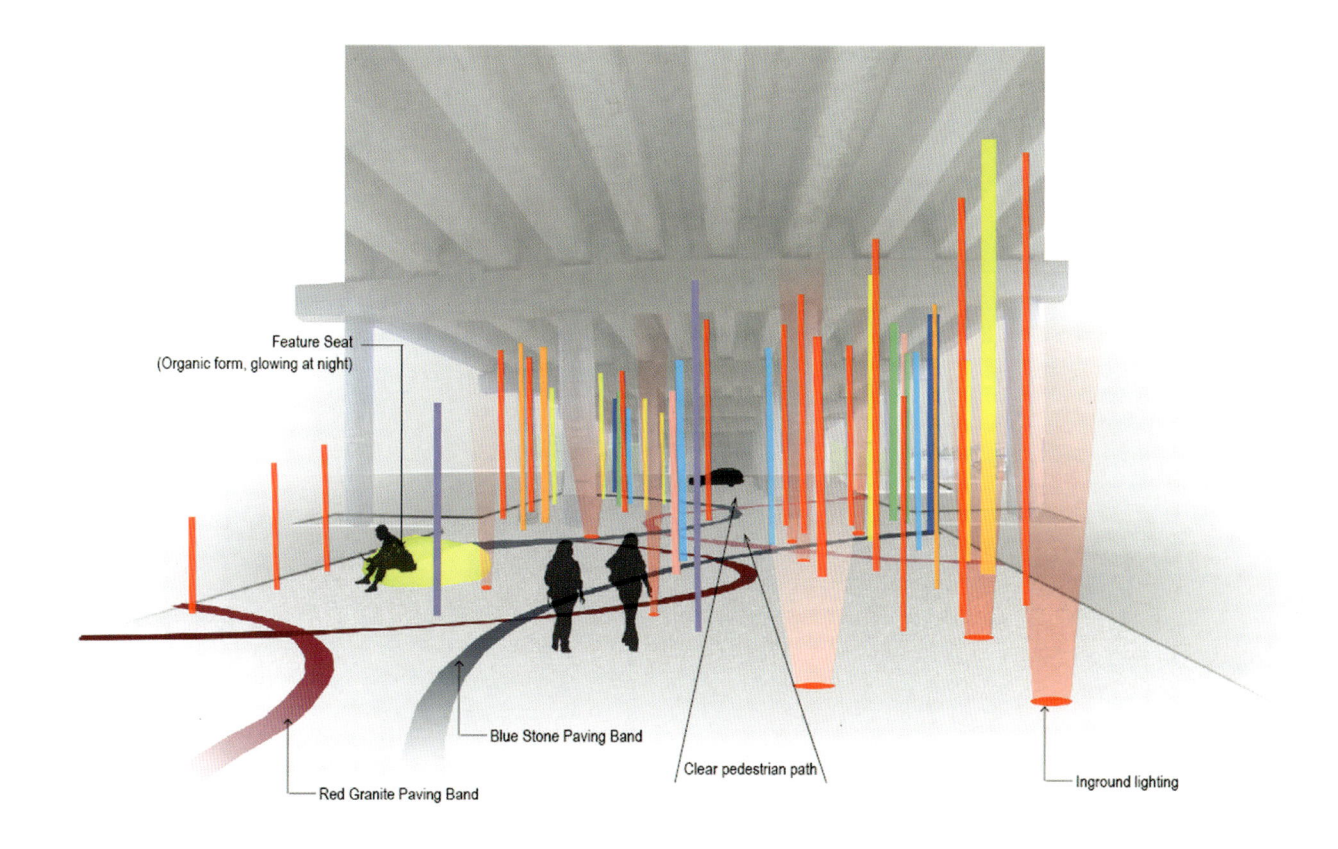

Inground lighting

ENSEMBLE

Isthmus & Studio Pacific Architecture / D. Irwin, S. McDougall, E. Williams, G. Marriage, D. Males, P. Mitchell

↑ | **Lighting and raft seats,** Wharf Plaza
→ | **Laneway lighting cubes**

Kumutoto
Wellington

Kumutoto reconnects Wellington with its harbor, extending the cities urban grid to meet the water. Traces of the past are preserved through robust furniture and a landscape aesthetic that echoes the maritime nature of Wellingtons waterfront. At the Kumutoto Stream mouth new pedestrian bridge strengthens the connection between the forgotten watercourse and the harbor and acts as an anchor point along the waterfront promenade. A sequence of seating terraces spills down to the water's edge allowing people to interact directly with the water or seek shelter from the wind. In the more sheltered urban spaces a procession of lighting towers overlook large floating timber and concrete raft seats designed to accommodate multiple groups and uses.

PROJECT FACTS **Address:** Kumutoto, Wellington Waterfront, Wellington, New Zealand. **Client:** Wellington Waterfront Ltd. **Completion:** 2008. **Production:** single piece. **Design:** individual design. **Functions:** seating, illumination, shelters, bridge. **Main materials:** timber, concrete, steel.

ENSEMBLE ISTHMUS & STUDIO PACIFIC ARCHITECTURE

↑ | **Kumutoto bridge and terraces**
← | **Kumutoto Stream mouth**

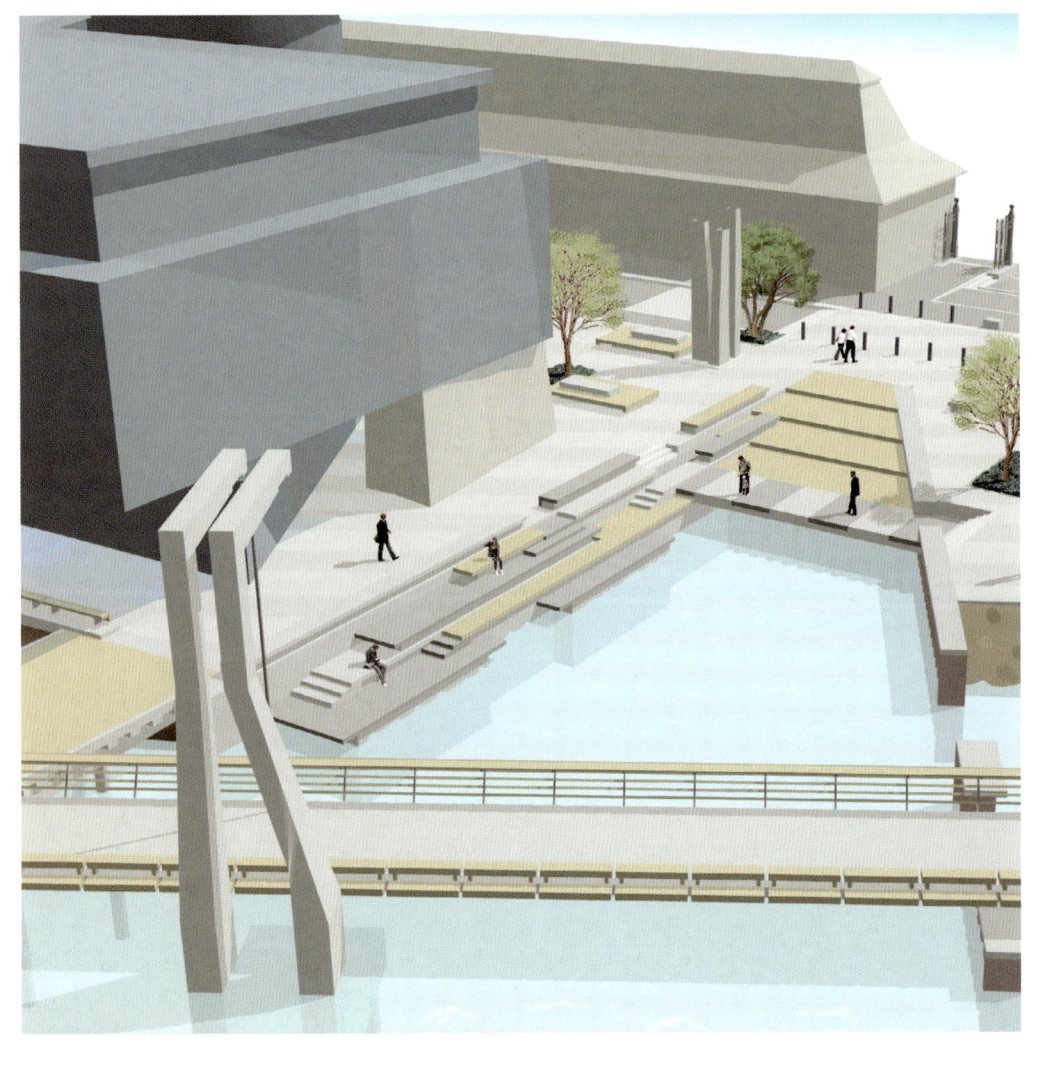

KUMUTOTO

← | **Kumutoto Plaza pallet seats**
↓ | **Kumutoto Bridge,** seats and balustrade

ENSEMBLE | Machado and Silvetti Associates

↑ | Seating area with artwork

South Boston Maritime Park
Boston

Resulting from collaboration with a local landscape architecture firm, the landscape and architectural elements create a seamless and fully integrated overall design. The park is conceived as a single design with three distinct zones unified through a consistent material palette and design methodology. The largest zone at the northern end of the park provides a raised lawn panel with a continuous staircase lining Northern Avenue. Two large pergolas mark the transition to the central zone. The middle zone contains a low café structure and outdoor seating areas, while the southern end of the park is conceived as a more intimate area of benches and densely planted shade trees.

PROJECT FACTS **Address:** "D" Street and Northern Avenue, Boston, MA 02210, USA. **Landscape architect:** The Halvorson Design Partnership. **Interpretive graphics:** Flanders + Associates. **Artists:** Ellen Driscoll in collaboration with Make Architectural Metalworking ("Aqueous Humor"), Carlos Dorrien ("The Waves" and "Passage from the sea"). **Client:** Massachusetts Port Authority. **Completion:** 2004. **Production:** single piece. **Design:** individual design. **Functions:** seating, pergola, café. **Main materials:** granite, teak, ipe wood, copper.

↑ | **Pergola and café**
↓ | **Elevation,** café with pergola

↑ | **Café detail**

ENSEMBLE SQLA inc. LA / Samuel Kim

↑ | **Sketch north view,** across Arts Walk to Arts/Tech Patio
→ | **Sketch areial view** of Arts Walk, Sculpture Lawn to Arts/Tech Patio

West Los Angeles City College, Pedestrian Promenade

Culver City, CA

This project represents the first phase of a 300 meter-long pedestrian promenade designed in conjunction with the new Science and Math buildings in the college. Most of the phase one portion consists of one portion of the promenade traverses in front of the Fine Arts Complex Buildings, thus the names "Arts Walk", "Sculpture Lawn", and "Arts/Tech Patio". The boardwalk concrete paving pattern is bordered by concrete banding along the building façades and provides modulation for the spacing of trees, pole lights, bollard lights and benches. The sunken "Arts/Tech Patio" paved in decomposed granite will facilitate for Café Bar, planned for second phase. The site furnishings include benches, litter receptacles, as well as patio tables with carousel seats and umbrellas.

PROJECT FACTS

Address: 10100 Jefferson Boulevard, Culver City, CA 90230, USA. **Architect:** ACSA inc. **Client:** West Los Angeles City College. **Completion:** 2010. **Production:** serial production. **Design:** product line. **Functions:** seating, illumination, garbage can, patio tables, umbrellas. **Main materials:** metal.

↑↑ | **Arts/Tech Patio,** table, chair and umbrella
↑ | **Benches,** at inside parameter

↑↑ | **Sculpture Lawn**
↑ | **Arts Walk,** from south

ENSEMBLE | Janet Rosenberg & Associates, Claude Cormier architectes paysagistes inc. / Janet Rosenberg, Claude Cormier

↑ | Adirondak chair

HtO – Urban Beach
Toronto

HtO succeeds in bringing people to the water's edge while providing a space for different types of activities. It quickly became Toronto's icon, giving an identity to Toronto from the water's edge with its multiple yellow umbrellas. The name is a play on the formula for water, H_2O, as it brings water and the city together, eliminating any barriers between Lake Ontario and the downtown area. As visitors enter HtO, they walk uphill through green dunes planted with willow trees and silver maples, then they descend down towards an expanse of sand peppered with tall yellow umbrellas, and a wooden boardwalk literally at the water's edge to experience the connection to the water.

PROJECT FACTS Address: Queens Quay blvd, Toronto M5J2G8, Canada. **Collaborator:** Hariri Pontarini Architects. **Client:** City of Toronto. **Completion:** 2007. **Production:** single piece. **Design:** individual design. **Functions:** seating, sun shades. **Main materials:** wood, perforated steel and stainless steel pole, concrete.

↑ | View to lake
↓ | HtO Plan

↑ | Promenade

ENSEMBLE | Sitetectonix Private Limited

↑ | **Wave pattern promenade,** planting and integrated seating
→ | **Seating planters,** planted with Dalbergia trees

VivoCity
Singapore

The VivoCity development consists of an integrated mega-mall. The landscape concept integrated site furniture like seating into the hardscape and softscape design. Along the street front, the North Plaza was conceptualized as a series of ground "waves" of earth-formed lawn mounds that recall the sea by rhythmic ups and downs. The stone walls become informal seating while the lawn itself constitutes a welcoming surface for relaxation. At the waterfront promenade a series of amoebas ramble along the timber decking, providing planting and seating opportunities. The amoeba-shaped planters contain earth mounds to separate the busy stone through-fare on the promenade from the tranquil atmosphere on the timber decking.

PROJECT FACTS

Address: 1 Harbour Front Walk, Singapore, Republic of Singapore. **Architects:** Toyo Ito Architects. **Client:** Mapletree Investments Pte Ltd. **Completion:** 2006. **Production:** single piece. **Design:** product line. **Functions:** seating, plant tub, paving. **Main materials:** natural stones, granites, pebbles, timber, stainless steel.

ENSEMBLE   SITETECTONIX PRIVATE LIMITED

② **ELEVATION 'A'**
Scale : 1:200

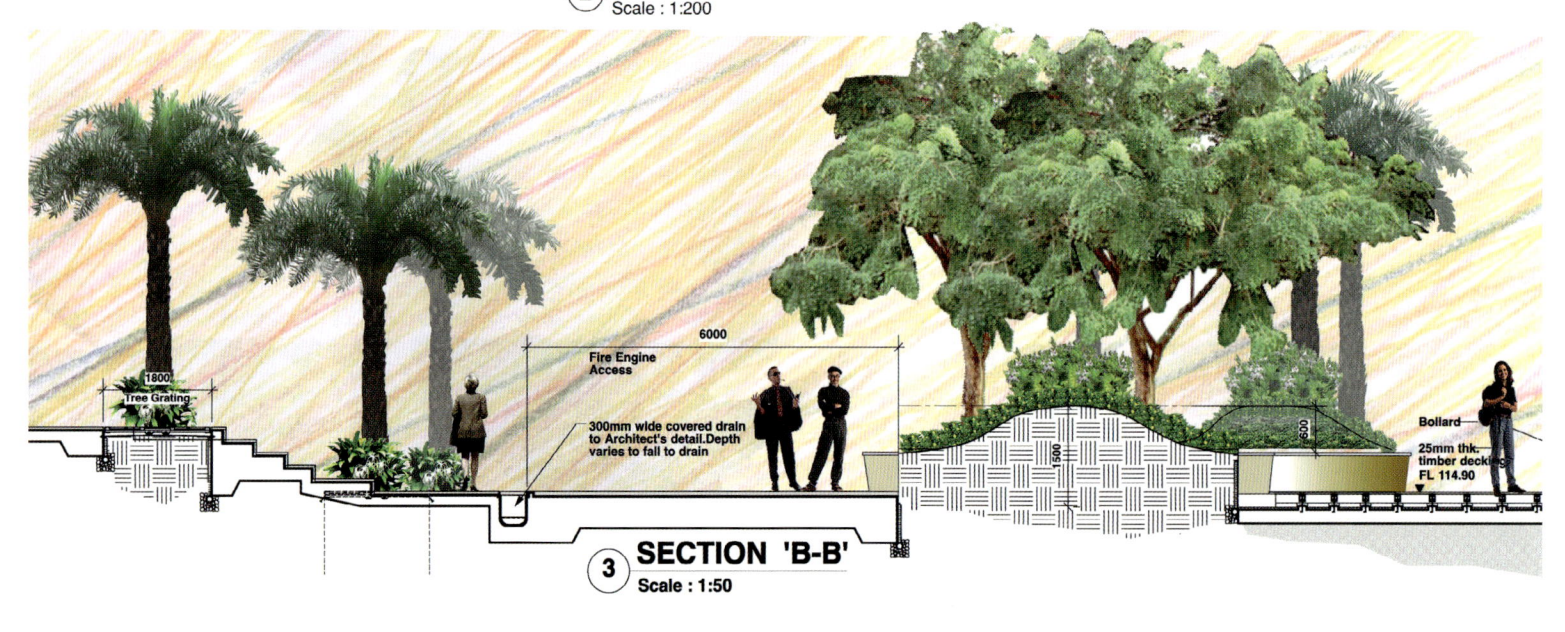

③ **SECTION 'B-B'**
Scale : 1:50

↑ | **Section and elevation,** showing integration of planting, planters and seating along promenade
← | **Aerial of North Plaza,** with earth-form lawn mounds

← | **Amoeba-shaped planters,** along promenade timber decking
↓ | **Lawn mounds,** used as casual seating and lounging

ENSEMBLE

Grupo de Diseño Urbano / Mario Schjetnan

↑ | **Furniture detail and fountain,** next to Tamayo Contemporary Art Museum Plaza

Fountain Promenade at Chapultepec Park

Mexico City

As part of a second phase of its restoration, an entirely new element has been added to the Chapultepec Park at Mexico City. A fountain promenade forms a line from the Museum of Anthropology to the Tamayo Museum. Formerly, there had been no link between these two important institutions. Grupo de Diseño Urbano created a striking visual and pedestrian connection with a 250 meter grade change and basins that float independently to minimize earthquake damage. Between the basins are beds of blue agapanthus and blue vinca planted among preexisting junipers, Aleppo pines, eucalyptus, and casuarinas. The project features black concrete and basalt pavers; cobblestones are placed around trees to permit infiltration.

PROJECT FACTS **Address:** Av. Reforma, Chapultepec Park, C.P. 11560 Mexico City, Mexico. **Planning partner:** Marco Arturo González. **Client:** Mexico City Government, Citizen's Regent Group and Revive Chapultepec Board of Donors. **Completion:** 2007. **Production:** single piece. **Design:** individual design. **Functions:** seating. **Main materials:** painted steel.

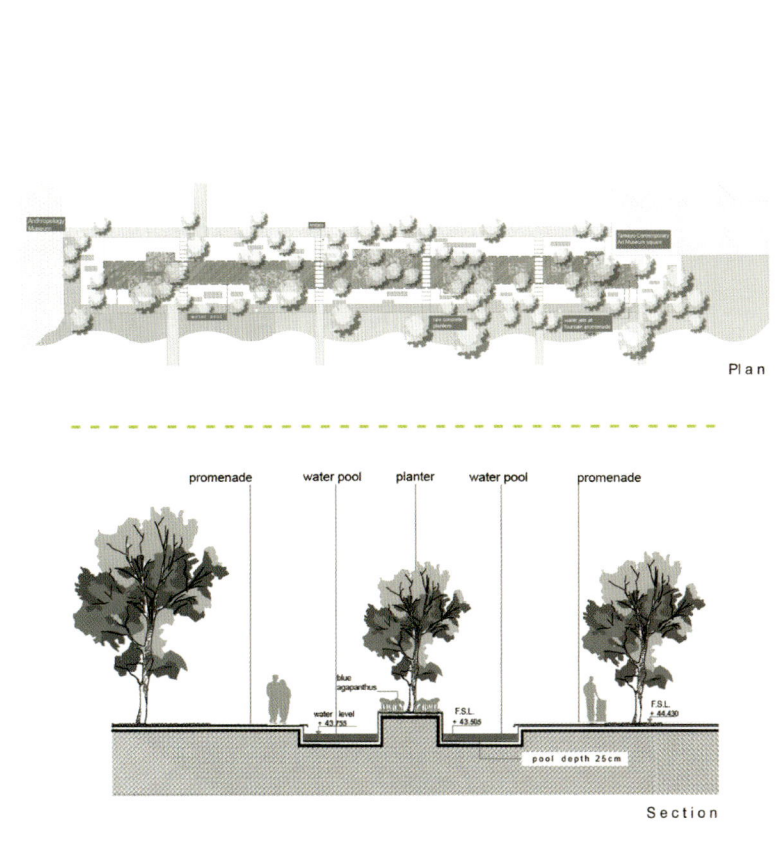

↑ | **Plan and section** of fountain promenade
↓ | **Fountain promenade**

↑ | **Furniture,** cascade detail

ENSEMBLE

Will Nettleship

↙↙ | **Cloud gate**, detail
↑↑ | **Pavement**, detail
↖ | **Cloud gate**
↑ | **Detail**

Horizons
Dayton

This project creates a gateway to a university campus on the pedestrian walkway from the main parking lot to the center of the campus. Located in Dayton, Ohio, the home of Orville and Wilbur Wright, the university is also the site of the Wright archives. In addition, the area around Dayton was an important center of Native American culture. The project has two subjects: first the imagination of the Wright brothers who aspired to look over the horizon, and second, the history of Native Americans in the lower Miami River Valley.

PROJECT FACTS
Address: Wright State University, Dayton, OH, 45435, USA. **Client:** Ohio Arts Council and Wright State University. **Completion:** 2002. **Production:** single piece. **Design:** individual design. **Functions:** pavement, gateway and connects to the campus. **Main materials:** brick, concrete, glass block, glazed concrete block.

Vulcanica Architettura / Eduardo Borrelli, Aldo di Chio, Marina Borrelli

↑↑ | **Model**
↑ | **Pier under construction**
↗ | **Rendering,** view from the square
↓ | **Elevations**

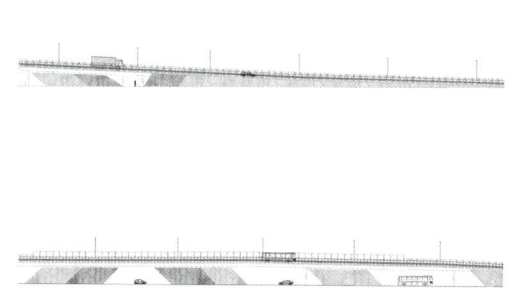

Under Road
Naples

Under Road is a project to complement the existing bridge that was interrupted over the square in Capodichino-Naples. It is designed like a singular powerful piece of street furniture matching the existing historical square at its feet. Today, the life of the square is totally chaotic: too much traffic, parking everywhere, a bus terminal and subway under construction. While any new urban furniture project is useless at this location, the bridge junction itself can be the shaping element of the urban context. The dynamism of the site is intensified by the design of the new bridge piers like modern obelisks bent by the speed, or rhomboidal monoliths with a strong inclination enhancing the view of the historical square.

PROJECT FACTS
Address: Piazza Di Vittorio, Naples, Italy. **Client:** City of Naples. **Completion:** ongoing. **Production:** single piece. **Design:** individual design. **Functions:** shelter, illumination. **Main materials:** concrete, steel.

ENSEMBLE | 3LHD architects with Irena Mazer / Tanja Grozdanic, Silvijc Novak, Marko Dabrovic, Sasa Begovic

↑ | **Benches**
↗ | **Sunshades** with integrated illumination
→ | **Riva promenade**

Riva Split Waterfront
Split

The city of Split and its Riva waterfront promenade, the paradigm of its history and character, are among the most interesting and most unique sites in the Mediterranean – an urbanized, public, open space, 1700 years old, situated in front of Diocletian's Palace. The modular Roman form of the palace became the framework that shaped the city. Similarly, dimensions, materials and the modularity of concrete elements in Riva directed the positions of all other elements of the public space. A total of 250 meters long and 55 meters wide, the Riva waterfront is the main public square, the venue for all kinds of social events, a promenade by day and a parade by night, the site of sport events, religious processions, festivals and celebrations.

PROJECT FACTS

Address: Obala Hrvatskog Narodnog Preporoda, 21000, Split, Croatia. **Urban elements:** Numen / For Use. **Light design:** Novalux. **Client:** City of Split. **Completion:** 2007. **Production:** individual design. **Design:** product line. **Functions:** seating, illumination, garbage can, drinking fountain, sunshades. **Main materials:** concrete, wood, steel.

ENSEMBLE   3LHD ARCHITECTS WITH IRENA MAZER

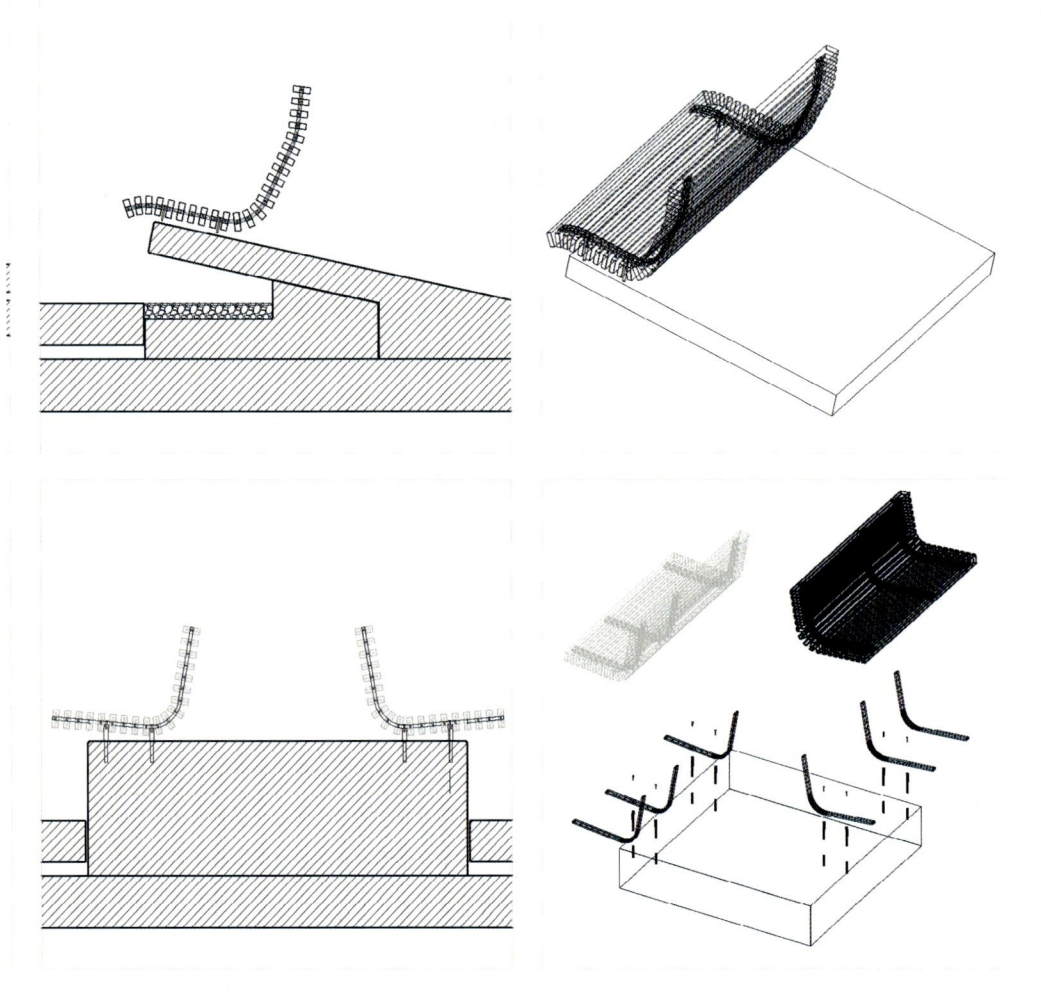

↑ | **Bird's-eye view**
← | **Drawings** of the benches

RIVA SPLIT WATERFRONT

← | **Benches,** detail
↓ | **Bird's eye-view,** with closed sunshades

LIGHT AND SIGHT

GARBAGE

BOUNDARY

BIKE AND PLAY

SEATING

PLANTS AND WATER

ENSEMBLE · PAVEMENT · PRODUCT LINE · SHELTER

PLANTS AND WATER | díez+díez diseño

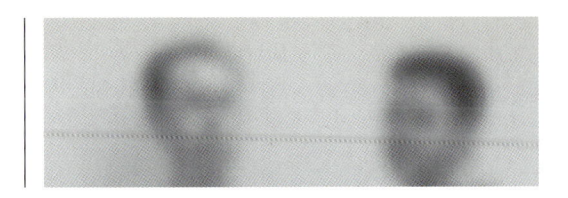

↑ | Row of seatings

Godot

We see the urban area as a place for casual meetings, expected dates and unexpected hazards; a space for looking at both the past and the present, or for projecting dreams onto the horizon; a place for sharing our solitude or exploring pleasurable discoveries; an environment with tranquil isles offering rest to the stroller or reader and any other traveler. The aim of this project was to create squares where those who have recently arrived can meet, and streets where those who are already here can discover other worlds. Therefore, the designers created Godot, a sedate bench, intimately associated with timeless elements and the surrounding trees.

PROJECT FACTS Client: ESCOFET 1886. Completion: 2005. Production: serial production. Design: individual design. Functions: seating. Main materials: concrete.

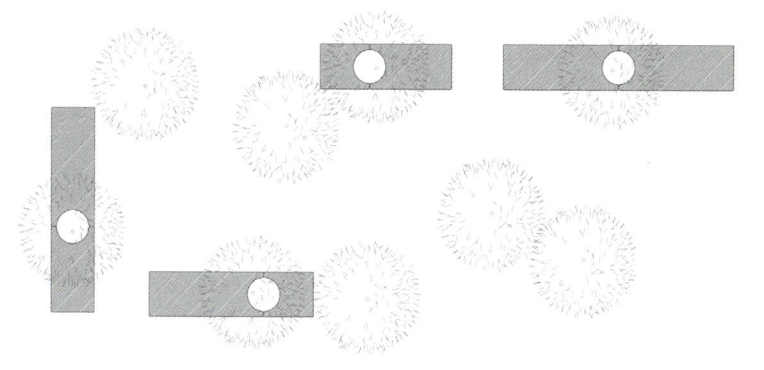

155

↑ | Detail
↓ | Seatings

↑↑ | Details of the internal anchor
↑ | Placement scheme

PLANTS AND WATER | Earthscape

↑ | Side elevation

Thousand Year Forest

Kawasaki

On the car park of the Lanzona development in Kawasaki's redevelopment project, trees have been planted into decorative modified cars whose light turns on when someone approaches. Over time, the trees will grow bigger, and the cars will be covered in greenery. Using the symbol of single plants, the message that "a forest can begin here" is transported.

PROJECT FACTS **Address:** Lazona Kawasaki, 72-1 Horikawa-cho Saiwai-ku Kawasaki city Kanagawa, Japan 212-0013. **Client:** Toshiba / Mitsui Fudosan Group Ltd. **Completion:** 2006. **Production:** single piece. **Design:** individual design. **Functions:** plant tub. **Main materials:** reinforcing bar.

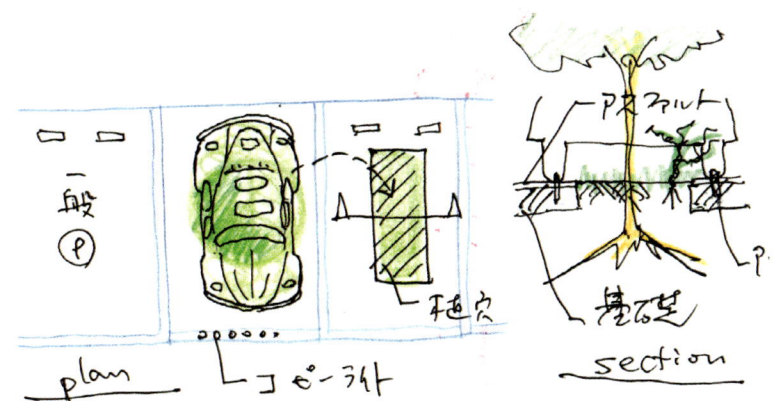

↑ | Sketch
↓ | The light turns on when someone approaches

↑ | Detail car front

PLANTS AND WATER   Earthscape

↑ | Bird's-eye view

A Tree that will grow Dreams
Kawasaki

An olive tree was chosen as a symbol for the rebirth of Kawasaki city. It carries the message of the whole Lanzona project. A few dozen locks hang on the tree branches while the keys to these locks were buried in the surrounding lakes. Maybe you will be the one to find the key (to the future), and unlock them! Inside the tree frame, hollowed out in the shape of a dove, cards in egg-shaped capsules with the wishes and messages of the staff members who worked on the Lazona Kawasaki project were buried. The positive thoughts within these capsules will provide nourishment for the olive tree to grow and support Kawasaki city's rebirth.

PROJECT FACTS **Address:** Lazona Kawasaki, 72-1 Horikawa-cho Saiwai-ku Kawasaki city Kanagawa, Japan 212-0013. **Client:** Toshiba / Mitsui Fudosan Group Ltd. **Completion:** 2006. **Production:** single piece. **Design:** individual design. **Functions:** plant tub. **Main materials:** white marble.

↑ | **Plant tup,** with olive tree
↓ | **Hollowed out in the shape of a dove**

↑ | **Locks in the tree,** the keys are buried in the surrounding lakes

PLANTS AND WATER | Estudio Cabeza / Diana Cabeza

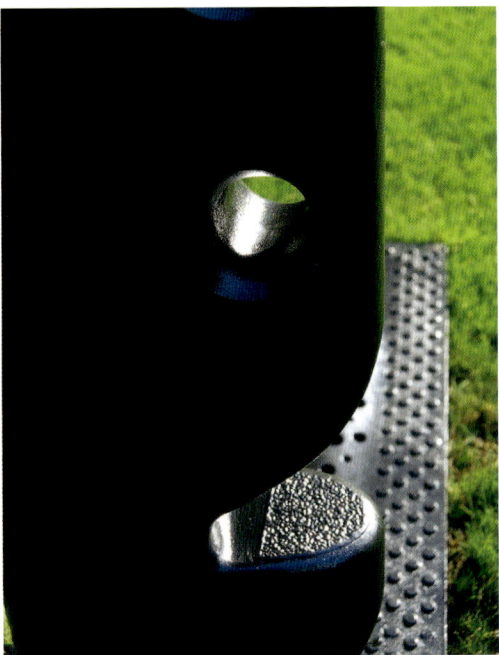

↖ | **Use situation**
↑↑ | **Paseo del Buen Pastor,** Córdoba, Argentina
↑ | **Close up**

Chafariz Drinking Fountain

As a rendering of the traditional neighborhood water spout, this dispenser solves the issue of providing drinking water in public spaces. Ideal for refreshment after park games or cycling, or during summer walks, the Chafariz stands proud waiting for thirsty adults and children. A totem and a user-friendly play object, its steps and grab holes on the sides allow children to safely climb up and drink.

PROJECT FACTS
Client: public and private clients. **Development team:** Diana Cabeza, Leandro Heine, Diego Jarczak. **Completion:** 2001. **Production:** serial production. **Design:** product line. **Functions:** drinking fountain. **Main materials:** cast iron, grit blastined and color polyester thermosetting powder coating.

PWP Landscape Architecture, Inc.

↑↑ | **"Floating bench"**, serving as a raised-tree planter
↗↗ | **Underground vaults**, required the creation of a sophisticated system of raised soil and irrigation systems to support the trees.
↑ | **Section**, through raised hemispherical planters
↗ | **Planters**, which seem to float above the cobble paving

One North Wacker Drive
Chicago, IL

The landscape for an office tower in downtown Chicago is a block-long 12 meter-wide pedestrian passage which is visible through the glazed wall of the building's lobby. Vaults running just below the sidewalk precluded conventional tree wells – a problem solved by special hemispherical armatures that sustain ground-covers and allow the root balls of the street trees to remain above ground. The raised tree wells – placed nine meter apart – carved stone benches, and the flat flamed-granite cobbles of the pavement serve to reinforce a human scale. The terrace at the North Franklin Street entrance contains three large bench planters, each with a treeless hemisphere floating in a pool of water.

PROJECT FACTS
Address: 1 North Wacker Drive, Chicago, Il 60606, USA. **Architects:** Lohan Caprille Goettsch Architects. **Client:** John Buck Company. **Completion:** 2002. **Production:** single piece. **Design:** individual design. **Functions:** Seating, plant tub, fountain. **Main materials:** stone, granite.

PLANTS AND WATER

Janet Rosenberg + Associates / Janet Rosenberg

↑ | **View into the courtyard** from the street

30 Adelaide Street East
Toronto

Dominated by two majestic Gingko trees, this courtyard offers an intriguing counterpoint to the geometry of the surrounding architecture. A bold sweeping granite arc, flanked by elegant stainless steel walls, directs visitors to the main entrance of the building. Sawn Ontario Limestone cubes, scattered along the water's edge, are both a sculptural presence for all seasons and an ideal place to sit, meet, and people-watch. A simple water fountain screens out the noise of the surrounding city, while the monochromatic planted dark green yews provide a strong contrast to the building. The highly detailed stainless steel site furnishings and planters were all custom-designed for this project.

PROJECT FACTS

Address: 30 Adelaide Street East, Toronto, ON, Canada. **Planning partner:** Quadrangle Architects. **Client:** Dundee Realty Management Corporation. **Completion:** 2002. **Production:** single piece. **Design:** individual design. **Functions:** seating, fountain, plant tub, public plaza. **Main materials:** sawn limestone, stainless steel.

↑ | Custom designed planter
↓ | Layout plan

↑ | Fountain

PLANTS AND WATER | Earthscape

↑ | Bird's-eye view

Minato-Mirai Business Square
Yokohama

Yokohama grew up with the sea. These days, it is still growing towards the sky through the construction of high rise buildings on landfills. This pond exists on the boundary between the sea and the sky. On the pond, the words relating to the sky will appear, reflected in the water's mirror surface, and disappear. The words relating to the sea will appear from the bottom after the water has gone. This way, people can rethink their own existence by reminding themselves of their origins – people originate from the sea and grow up on land.

PROJECT FACTS **Address:** 3-6 Minato-Mirai Nishi ward Yokohama city Kanagawa, Japan. **Planning partner:** Mitsubishi Estate. **Client:** Tokio Marine & Nichido Fire Insurance Co., Ltd. **Completion:** 2004. **Production:** single piece. **Design:** individual design. **Functions:** fountain. **Main materials:** stone, concrete.

↑ | **Pathway,** crossing the water bassin
↓ | **General view**

↑ | **Floor plan**

PLANTS AND WATER | OLIN / Lucinda R. Sanders

↑ | **Reflecting Pools** at Battery Place

Reflecting Pools
New York City

The Museum of Jewish Heritage was in need of a new landscape to connect the East Wing expansion to its surroundings. OLIN's design creates a place unique to the Museum yet reflective of the larger Hudson River landscape. At the front entrance, reflective pools of polished black granite set a contemplative mood. Water slowly rises from open joints in the granite ten centimeters below the surface. As the water flows over, it clings to the sides of the fountain and runs through a custom-made stainless steel trough where the water is captured and recycled below ground. The reflecting pools offer an attractive and engaging amenity while also serving as an inconspicuous vehicular barrier to meet the museum's security needs.

PROJECT FACTS **Address:** 36 Battery Place, New York, NY 10280, USA. **Planning partner:** R.J. Van Seters. **Client:** Museum of Jewish Heritage. **Completion:** 2007. **Production:** single piece. **Design:** individual design. **Functions:** fountain, vehicular barrier. **Main materials:** polished granite, stainless steel, concrete.

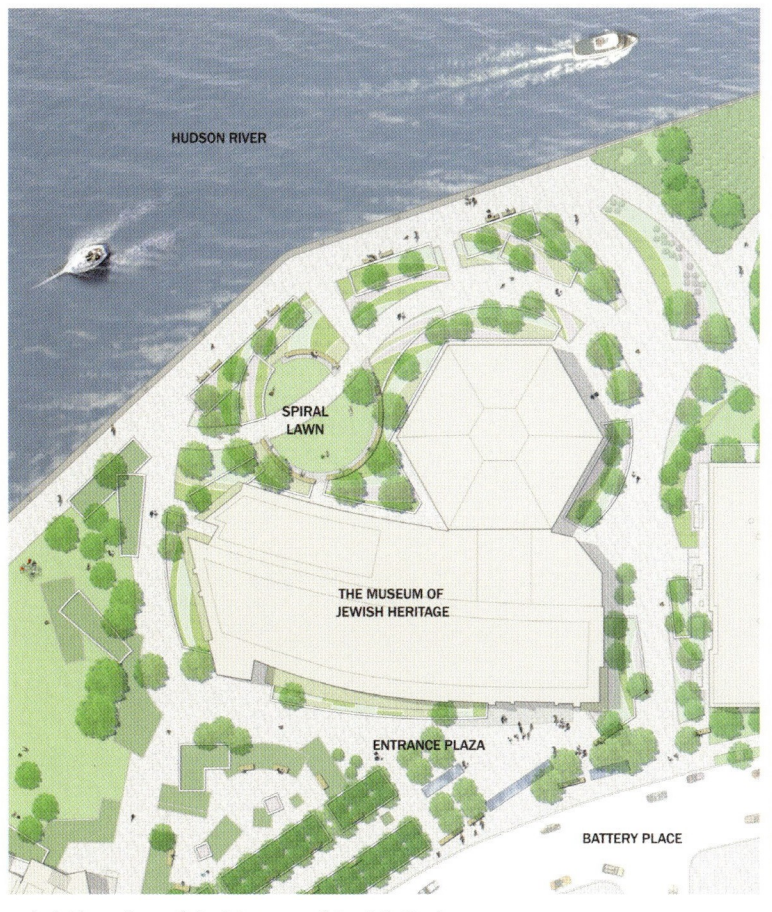

↑ | **Site plan** of the Museum of Jewish Heritage
↓ | **Elevation** showing how the water flows over the pools

↑ | **Cyclist** cooling off with one of the pools

PLANTS AND WATER

OKRA landschapsarchitecten bv / Christ-Jan van Rooij, Hans Oerlemans, Martin Knuijt, Wim Voogt, Boudewijn Almekinders

↖↖ | **Fountain and plant tub**
↑↑ | **View over fountain and plant tub**
↖ | **Bird's-eye-view**
↑ | **Movable plant bins**

De Inktpot
Utrecht

A highly frequented area, the use of the railway grounds, and the desire to create a leisure area came together in this project, starting with the modular floor. It offers a variety of uses in an area with limited space and lighting. Movable furnishings, such as mobile planters on rails and loose patio chairs, create a dynamic setting. Whenever more seating is required or more privacy is needed, the furnishings can be moved accordingly. If the hoist vehicle requires more space, everything can be simply pushed aside. In addition, extra objects, such as a patio floor with movable chairs and parasols, enhance the flexibility of the space.

PROJECT FACTS
Address: Gebouw De Inktpot, Moreelsepark 3, 3511 EP, Utrecht, The Netherlands. **Client:** Prorail. **Completion:** 2004. **Production:** single piece. **Design:** product line. **Functions:** seating, plant tub, fountain. **Main materials:** concrete, granite.

Rainer Schmidt Landschaftsarchitekten with GTL Landschaftsarchitekten

169

↑↑ | **Bench**, detail
↑ | **Pool with benches**
↗ | **Campeon pool**

Fountain Cameon
Neubiberg

Within the scope of the general planning of Campeon, the new headquarters of Infineon in the Unterhaching district of Munich, a roofed café area was created for visitors and employees within the site's green space. A reduced water pool serves as a large seating area as well as a contemplative design element. The water table is framed by an embrasure made of Corten steel. Linear seating elements along the length of the pool invite visitors to linger near the water.

PROJECT FACTS
Address: Am Campeon 1–12, 85579 Neubiberg, Germany. **Planning partner:** TEC PCM LA, USA. **Client:** Mo To Projektmanagement GmbH. **Completion:** 2006. **Production:** single piece. **Design:** individual design. **Functions:** seating, water bassin. **Main materials:** Cortensteel, wood.

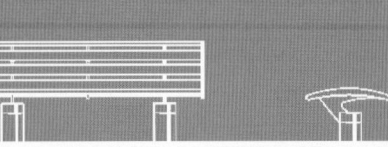

LIGHT AND SIGN GARBAGE BOUNDARY BIKE AND PLAY SEATING

ENSEMBLE PAVEMENT PRODUCT LINE PLANTS AND WATER SHELTER

GARBAGE | Caesarea Landscape Design Ltd.

↖ | **Garbage can,** with ashtray
↑↑ | **Situated next to a wall**
↑ | **Next to a bench**

Garbage Can Senior 954

The square-shaped garbage can with stainless steel cover fits best in modern orthogonal environments. It has a square casing holes pattern that reveals its metal thickness of just two millimeters, while the upper reinforcement inner ring and the rounded lower base are made of metal that is four millimeters thick. Concealed legs in rubber finish and a galvanized, oven-painted, 0.5 millimeters thick, inner container in pure polyester complete the design.

PROJECT FACTS
Client: "G" Kfar Saba-shopping center. **Completion:** 2009. **Production:** serial production. **Design:** product line. **Functions:** design solutions for collection of garbage. **Main materials:** perforated metal, stainless steel.

Caesarea Landscape Design Ltd.

↑ | **Caesarion 948LK,** detail
↗ | **View of garbage can** in a shopping mall

Garbage Can Kiryat Uno

The decorative wastebasket has a unique design pattern with a cylindrical volume. The metal cover is galvanized and enameled. There are versions with rubber footings or a cement base.

PROJECT FACTS
Client: Prestigious Mall in the city Kiryat Uno. **Completion:** 2008. **Production:** serial production. **Design:** product line. **Functions:** design solutions for collection of garbage. **Main materials:** laser-processed casing metal.

GARBAGE | EBD architects ApS

↑ | View of the urban model

Envac Disposal Chute

Envac's disposal chute for mobile suction was designed for the disposal of household waste and of waste in urban spaces. It is both physically smaller ApS much simpler to operate than previous solutions. The chute is one small part of the extensive mobile suction installation. The hatch is easy to open and enables two-handed delivery, while the size of the opening minimizes the risk of accidentally entering garbage that is too large. The product is easy to match with the given surroundings. The curved horizontal bars in sturdy steel serve the dual purpose of giving the product an architectural identity and warding off vandalism without appearing aggressive.

PROJECT FACTS

Client: ENVAC Denmark A/S. **Completion:** 2008. **Production:** serial production. **Design:** product line. **Functions:** garbage can. **Main materials:** painted steel, stainless steel.

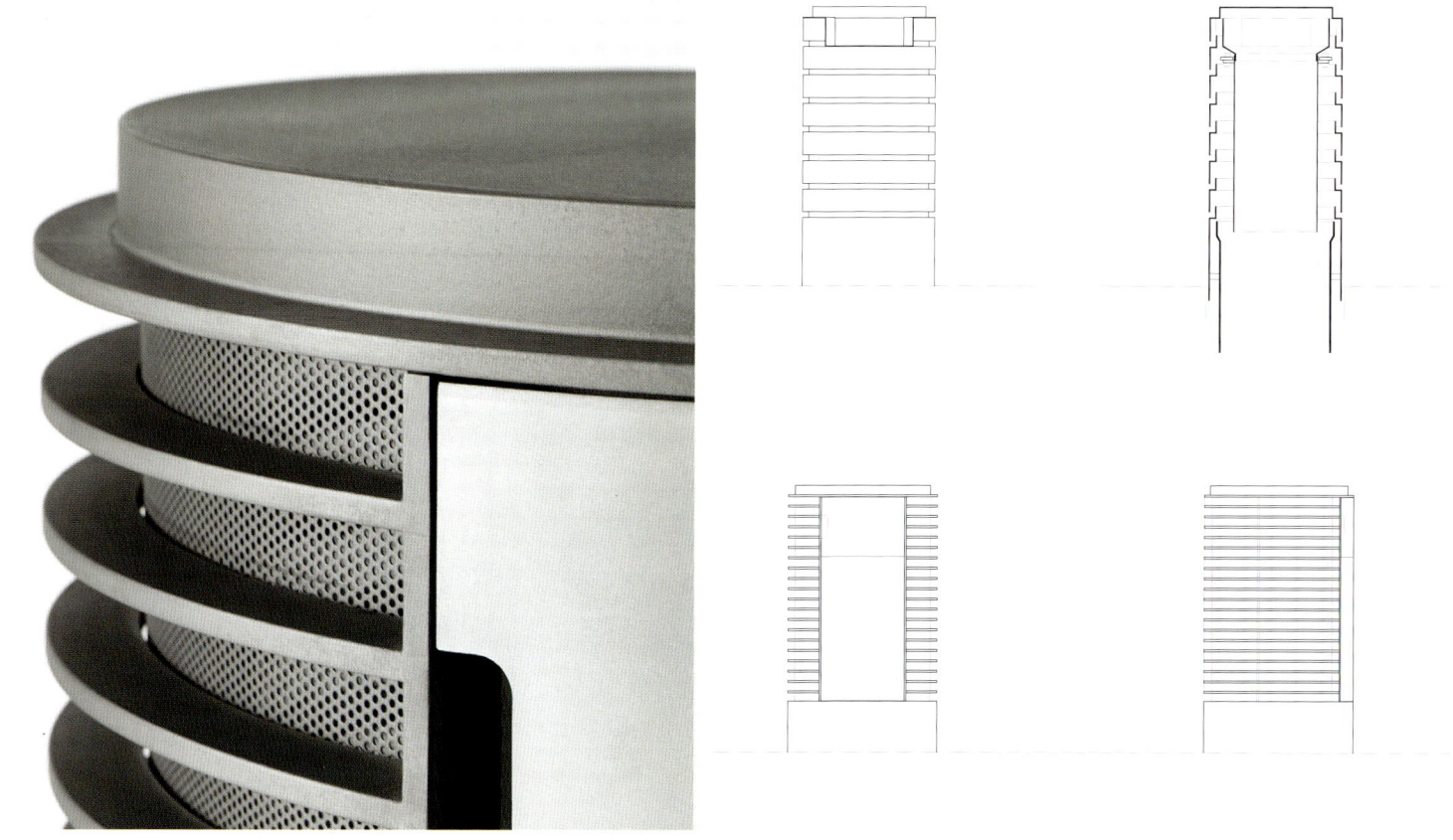

175

↑ | **Detail,** protection bars and opening
↓ | **Street model,** view with context

↑ | **Plans** "street" and "urban" version

GARBAGE | mmcité a.s. / David Karásek, Radek Hegmon

↑ | Cylinder in a park area

Cylinder Waste Container

Resembling an oversized layered cake or bobbin, the exterior of the Cylinder waste container is a pleasant alternative to its more bulky counterparts. Its ribbed outer casing is made of black polyethylene. The waste container hidden inside is made of sturdy steel and has a smooth surface for easy cleaning. A concrete base or steel feet can be attached to the container body. In addition, the container body can also be attached to a steel pipe. Cylinder is available in two diameters.

PROJECT FACTS **Client:** mmcité a.s., Santa y Cole. **Completion:** 2000. **Production:** serial production. **Design:** individual design. **Functions:** garbage can. **Main materials:** black polyethylene, concrete, galvanized steel.

177

↑ | Model with concrete foot
↓ | Plans

↑ | Model with larger diameter

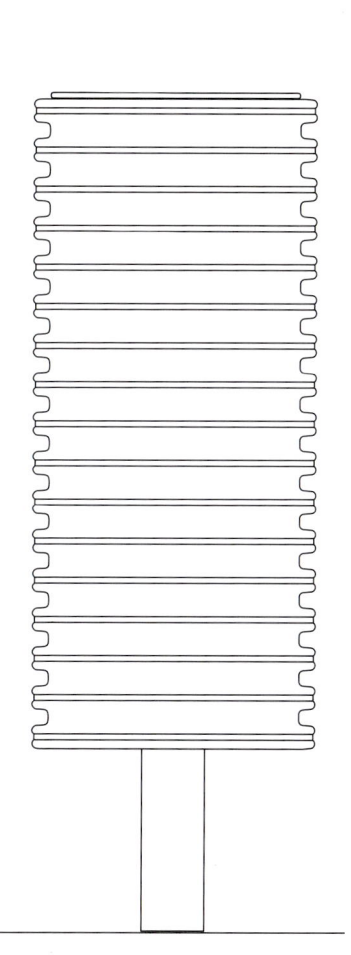

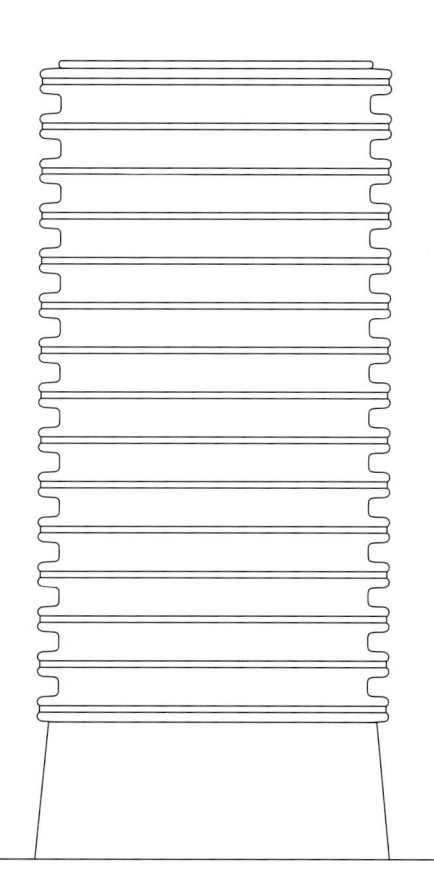

GARBAGE

Gonzalo Milà Valcárcel / Martina Zink, Gonzalo Milà Valcárcel

↑ | **Bird's-eye view,** Barceloneta beach, Barcelona

BINA

The main part of this two-piece polyethylene garbage bin is a container which holds the garbage bag pinned to a safe fastening device. The lid is locked by means of a metal peg and bayonet fitting, which prevents unauthorized manipulation. The article's functional value resides mainly on this lid since it prevents the waste from spilling and reduces the negative visual impact of a container filled to the brim. There are two different models – the original model is designed for beach installation and features a tapering body and ballast-filled bottom that guarantees stability when buried in the sand; the second model is designed to be directly fastened to the ground.

PROJECT FACTS

Client: Santa & Cole. **Completion:** 2004. **Production:** serial production. **Design:** individual design. **Functions:** garbage can. **Main materials:** polyethylene.

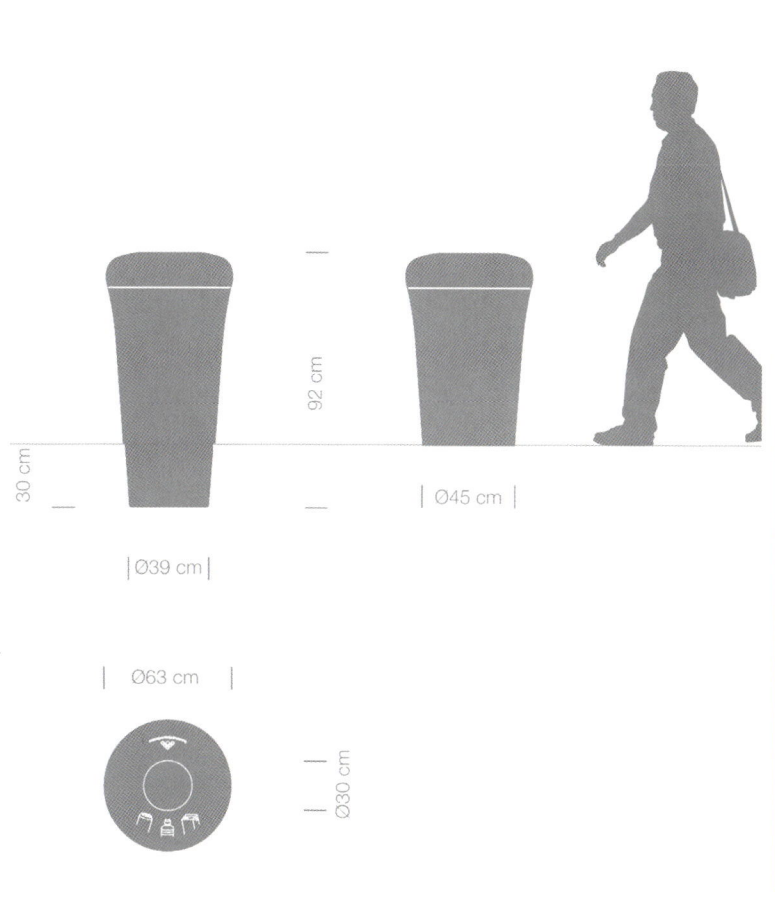

↑ | Sketch plan
↓ | Garbage cans on Barceloneta beach, Barcelona

↑ | Detail

LIGHT AND SIGN

GARBAGE

BOUNDARY

BIKE AND PLAY

SEATING

ENSEMBLE PAVEMENT PRODUCT LINE PLANTS AND WATER SHELTER

LIGHT AND SIGN | Sasaki Associates

↑ | **Kiosk,** the design is adapted to the context
→ | **Signage detail,** information is given about the history of Baton Rouge

Wayfinding and Interpretive Graphics
Baton Rouge

For the City of Baton Rouge, Sasaki created the program, design, and implementation of a downtown wayfinding system to better serve visitors. Imbued with a rich heritage stemming from a succession of French, English and Spanish rule and Native American culture, the designers drew from the city's rich visual vocabulary. District identity icons were designed as well as information kiosks, street name signs, and interpretive graphics with fresh contemporary interpretations of the city's history and culture. More than simply wayfinding, the elements, shapes, patterns, and details offer a visual display of the city's history. Heritage trail markers with historic commentary add additional depth to the system.

PROJECT FACTS **Address:** Baton Rouge, LA, USA. **Planning partner:** Washer-Hill Lipscomb Architects, Covalent Logic, Inc. **Client:** City of Baton Rouge. **Completion:** 2007. **Design:** product line. **Design:** individual design. **Functions:** sign. **Main materials:** aluminum, glass.

LIGHT AND SIGN

Rainer Schmidt
Landschaftsarchitekten

↖ | **Side view**, welcome sign in springtime
↑↑ | **Chinese photo session**
↑ | **School excursion**, the large seating area
↓ | **Photo montage**, design sketch

Welcome!
Munich

An exhibition sign was conceived within short notice for the exhibition of the Bayerisches Nationalmuseum entitled "The House of Wittelsbach and the Middle Kingdom – 400 years of China and Bavaria". It consists of the word "Welcome!" in Chinese characters. The oversized characters were erected on the lawn-covered ground floor of the museum's front yard, which was also designed by Rainer Schmidt Landschaftsarchitekten and completed in 2005. The characters consist of 3-dimensional wooden elements mounted on a steel base. In addition to its use as a popular photo motif for Chinese visitors, the construct is popular among children and adolescents who enjoy playing and sitting on it.

PROJECT FACTS
Address: Prinzregentenstraße 3, 80538 Munich, Germany. **Planning partner:** Atelier Seitz. **Client:** Bayerisches Nationalmuseum. **Completion:** 2009. **Production:** single piece. **Design:** individual design. **Functions:** sign. **Main materials:** steel, wood.

PROJECT FACTS **Address:** Baton Rouge, LA, USA. **Planning partner:** Washer-Hill Lipscomb Architects, Covalent Logic, Inc. **Client:** City of Baton Rouge. **Completion:** 2007. **Design:** product line. **Design:** individual design. **Functions:** sign. **Main materials:** aluminum, glass.

LIGHT AND SIGN   SASAKI ASSOCIATES

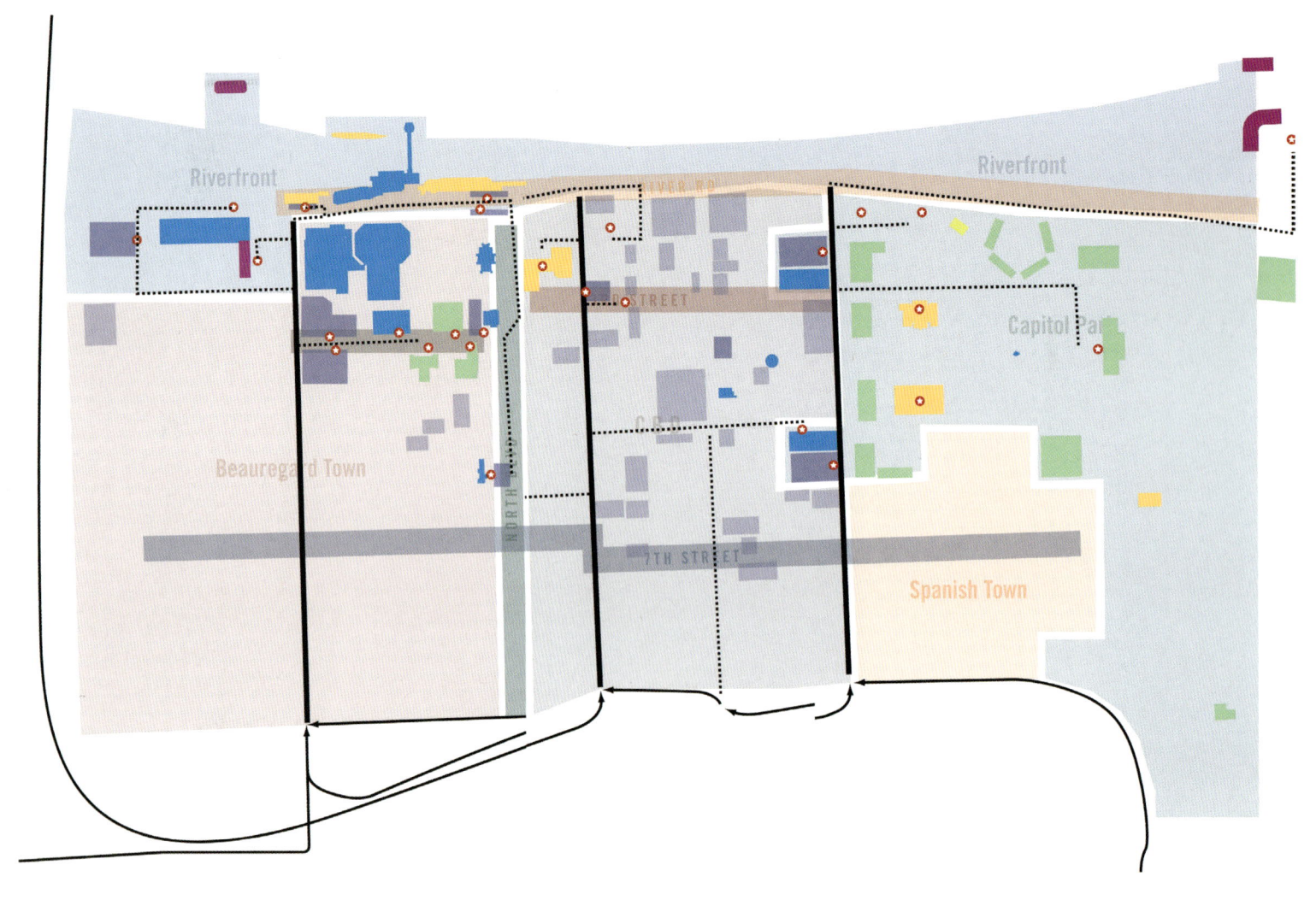

↑ | Arrival circulation diagram
← | Sign detail
→ | Fingerpost

WAYFINDING AND INTERPRETIVE GRAPHICS

LIGHT AND SIGN   Despang Architekten

↑ | Station square

Signpost
Karsruhe

The public realm with its sensory overload is subject to increasingly new demands. The need for comfort and orientation of the modern mobile society take their toll. A small object, which is found repeatedly in the city of Karlsruhe, emerged from the complexity of simplicity. A hard outer casing of made of U-300 structural steel with a flexible functional core encompasses the installation. The visualization of the tectonic principle is implemented through the materialization of the surface properties. The outer casing consists of a rough micaceous iron ore coating and the filling of processed brass, which increases the comfort of the venue through the application of LED light technology.

PROJECT FACTS

187

Address: City, 31275 Karlsruhe, Germany. **Client:** Karlsruher Verkehrsbetriebe. **Completion:** 2002. **Production:** serial production. **Design:** individual design. **Functions:** sign. **Main materials:** steel, brass, stainless steel, LED.

↑ | Sketch
↓ | Detail

↑ | Prototype
↓ | Tramway station

LIGHT AND SIGN

Matthias Berthold, Andreas Schön

↖↖ | **Shower head**
↑↑ | **The shower,** next to the village pond
↖ | **Base**
↑ | **Start button**

Bargteheide Voice Shower
Bargteheide

Positioned purely as a sculpture in a park or public square, this shower may be initially puzzling, yet it is much more than meets the eye. The shower head does not release water; instead, it has a loudspeaker installed inside. With the push of a button, the shower presents texts and sound recordings on the topic of water by residents of Bargteheide. They were collected and created during various interactions initiated by the artists. On the platform underneath the shower, glistening metal letters are chaotically displayed, looking like drops left over from the last use. Playing with the shower becomes a spectacle for everyone spending time at the park.

PROJECT FACTS
Address: Rathausstraße / Mittelweg, 22941 Bargteheide, Germany. **Client:** City of Bargteheide. **Completion:** 2008. **Production:** single piece. **Design:** individual design. **Functions:** art project. **Main materials:** audio electronic, high-grade steel, concrete.

Kramer Design Associates (KDA) / Jeremy Kramer

↑↑ | **Pedestrian wayfinding**, map directory
↗↗ | **Pedestrian wayfinding**, finger blades
↑ | **Vehicular wayfinding**, parking or building ID
↗ | **Vehicular wayfinding**, destination

York University Coordinated Signage and Wayfinding Program
Toronto

KDA was responsible for designing a new vehicular and pedestrian wayfinding program and a comprehensive interior sign program for the 55-acre university that was clear and easy to use, communicated the university's new brand identity, respected the architecture of the campus, and presented a consistent and timeless esthetic. KDA's design addressed safety concerns, provided more navigational night routes, and reflected the tradition of innovation and green-space openness of this contemporary learning and research institution.

PROJECT FACTS
Address: 4700 Keele Street, Toronto, ON M3J 1P3, Canada. **Client:** York University. **Completion:** 2003. **Production:** serial production. **Design:** individual design. **Functions:** signs. **Main materials:** powder coated steel poles, cast connectors, screen printed messaging.

LIGHT AND SIGN

Rainer Schmidt Landschaftsarchitekten

Welcome!
Munich

↖ | **Side view**, welcome sign in springtime
↑↑ | **Chinese photo session**
↑ | **School excursion**, the large seating area
↓ | **Photo montage**, design sketch

An exhibition sign was conceived within short notice for the exhibition of the Bayerisches Nationalmuseum entitled "The House of Wittelsbach and the Middle Kingdom – 400 years of China and Bavaria". It consists of the word "Welcome!" in Chinese characters. The oversized characters were erected on the lawn-covered ground floor of the museum's front yard, which was also designed by Rainer Schmidt Landschaftsarchitekten and completed in 2005. The characters consist of 3-dimensional wooden elements mounted on a steel base. In addition to its use as a popular photo motif for Chinese visitors, the construct is popular among children and adolescents who enjoy playing and sitting on it.

PROJECT FACTS
Address: Prinzregentenstraße 3, 80538 Munich, Germany. **Planning partner:** Atelier Seitz. **Client:** Bayerisches Nationalmuseum. **Completion:** 2009. **Production:** single piece. **Design:** individual design. **Functions:** sign. **Main materials:** steel, wood.

Michel Dallaire Design
Industriel – MDDI

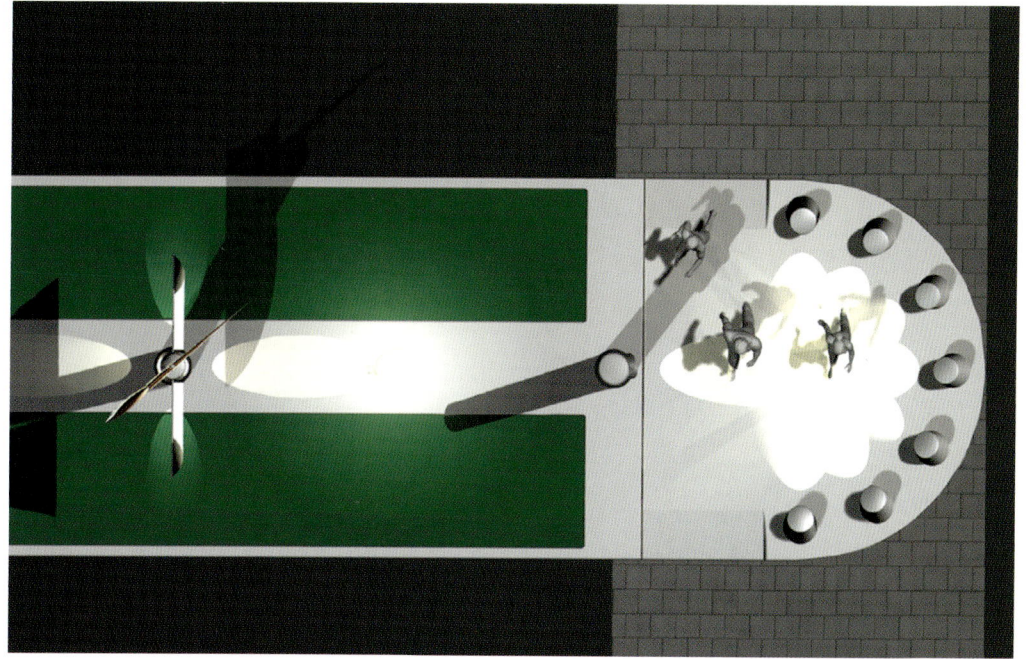

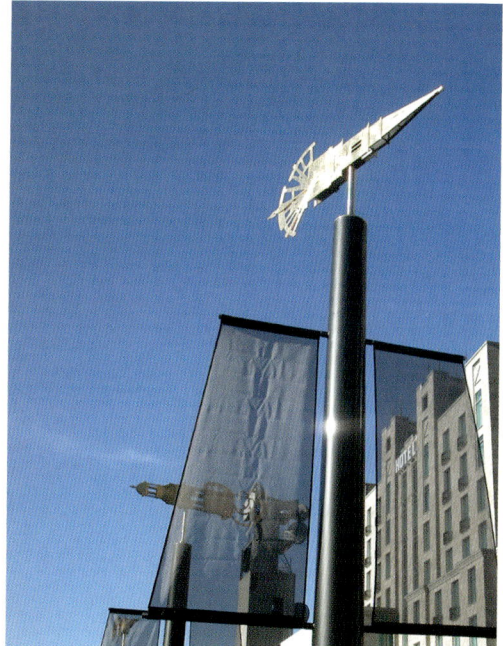

↑↑ | **Bird's-eye view,** rendering
↗↗ | **Top decorations**
↑ | **Perspective,** rendering
↗ | **General view,** impression of a sailing ship

Avenue Honore-Mercier
Quebec City

The purpose of this project was the transformation of the former Dufferin-Montmorency highway access to Quebec city into a more accessible and friendly boulevard for visitors, while respecting the historical status of the city as designated by UNESCO. The conceptual approach was intended to express the military, historical and maritime character of Quebec. The boundary stones in black granite evoke cannon barrels while the wind vanes masts recall the 3-mast vessel that is the symbol of Quebec city.

PROJECT FACTS
Address: Avenue Honore-Mercier, Quebec City, Canada. **Planning partner:** WAA – william asselin ackaoui. **Client:** City of Quebec. **Completion:** 2005. **Production:** serial production. **Design:** product line. **Functions:** illumination, bollard. **Main materials:** granite, stainless steel, fiberglass.

LIGHT AND SIGN

West 8 urban design & landscape architecture

↑ | **First OliviO,** Bridges Kanaaleiland Bruggen, Belgium
→ | **OliviO,** Town Square Middlesborough, UK

OliviO

The OliviO range of luminaries and poles was developed in collaboration with the German manufacturer Se'lux and has been installed for several West 8 projects throughout the world. OliviO was born out of a desire for an energy efficient, timeless, universal outdoor source of illumination. OliviO is now available in a full range of sizes, pole or wall mounted and in various colors. The conical shape combined with a spherical top gives the element a rotund and happy appearance. The lamp can be rotated by means of a structurally adjustable hinge in which the power supply cables have been integrated invisibly.

PROJECT FACTS

Planning partner: Se'lux. **Client:** different governmental and private organizations. **Completion:** 2000-current. **Production:** serial production. **Design:** set of parts. **Functions:** illumination. **Main materials:** aluminum.

↑ | **Artist impression OliviO,** Jubilee Gardens, London, UK

↗ | **Artist impression OliviO** for Noorderpark, Amsterdam, The Netherlands

↑ | **OliviO,** Town Square Middlesborough, UK

LIGHT AND SIGN | West 8 urban design & landscape architecture

↖ | Dragonlight at night
↑↑ | Dragonlight during the day
↑ | Detail paw

Dragonlight
Copenhagen

Dragonlight was designed as part of the Amerika Plads neighborhood. The inspiration of the existing dragon lighting columns led West 8 to design a more abstract version, hence creating a unique version, which helps to give the quarter a strong and evocative atmosphere. The light fitting, which allows the light to come out of the beak of the Dragon, is produced by Se'Lux, who is also responsible for the specially dirmensioned poles. In total there will be around 25 Dragonlights located at Amerika Plads.

PROJECT FACTS
Address: Amerika Plads, 2100 Copenhagen, Denmark. **Planning partner:** Metaalgieterij Bruijs in Bergen op Zoom and Se'Lux. **Client:** City & Port of Copenhagen. **Completion:** 2007. **Production:** serial production. **Design:** product line. **Functions:** illumination. **Main materials:** aluminum, magnesium, steel.

Freitag Weidenart, Bureau Baubotanik

↑↑ | Top of the lamp
↑ | General view
↗ | Detail
↓ | Sketch

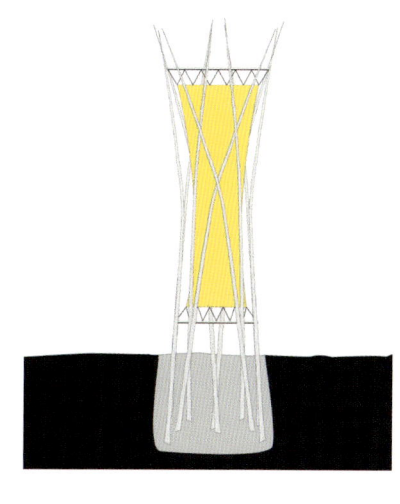

Weidenprinz Light Tree
Hartenholm

The light tree is a botanically structured light sculpture made of living plants. In terms of function, the light tree combines a conventional street lamp with any kind of city tree. It is equally suitable for decorating public squares as well as other public venues in which conventional illuminants are difficult to integrate in the natural context. A light tree is planted, grows roots and thus makes any type of foundation superfluous. In the course of the years, the plants interweave and the membrane's mounting rings grow inside the plants.

PROJECT FACTS

Address: private garden, 24628 Hartenholm, Germany. **Planning partner:** Ferdinand Ludwig, Bauer Membranbau. **Client:** private. **Completion:** 2006. **Production:** serial production. **Design:** individual design. **Functions:** illumination. **Main materials:** living wooden plants, stainless steel rings, PVC membrane, high-voltage neon tube.

LIGHT AND SIGN | Gonzalo Milà Valcárcel

↖ | Lights
↑↑ | Sketch
↑ | Detail
↓ | Plan

LITA

These light installations can be used as street furniture to illuminate open spaces and parks but they can also serve for private gardens to illuminate the path to the entrance or the sitting area on the terrace. This peculiar lighting "milestone" results in a very pleasing effect thanks to its marble screen that projects a light which is both unobtrusive and gentle. These traits liken it to a domestic beacon. The lights are also especially appropriate for natural spaces because with their neutral color and their inconspicuous design they do not disrupt the natural appeal of the surroundings. As they are available in different sizes they can be individually adapted to the environment.

PROJECT FACTS

Client: Macaedis. **Completion:** 2003. **Production:** serial production. **Design:** individual design. **Functions:** illumination. **Main materials:** Blanco Macael's marble.

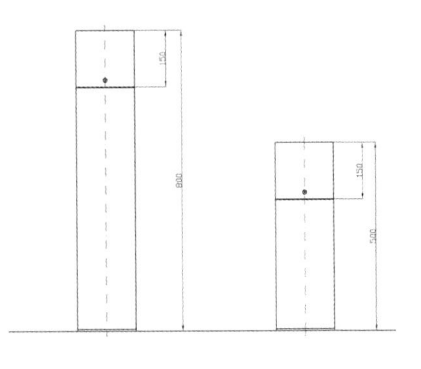

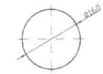

| West 8 urban design & landscape architecture

↑↑ | **Peak at Lippenplein**, Knokke, Belgium, 2007
↗ | Detail
↑ | Street view

Peak

The Peak is a light fixture for the outdoor illumination of parks, squares and other urban settings. The design consists of both a pole and a luminairy at a total height of 5.7 meters. The main material of the luminairy is cast aluminum and galvanized steel for the pole. The glass is made out of translucent or semi-translucent plastic. The first Peak was designed for Park JB Lebas in Lille, France and has been used subsequently in several West 8 projects.

PROJECT FACTS
Client: different governmental and private organizations. **Completion:** 2000. **Production:** serial production. **Design:** product line. **Functions:** illumination. **Main materials:** cast aluminum, galvanized steel and (semi-)translucent plastic.

LIGHT AND SIGN | Artadi Arquitectos / Javier Artadi

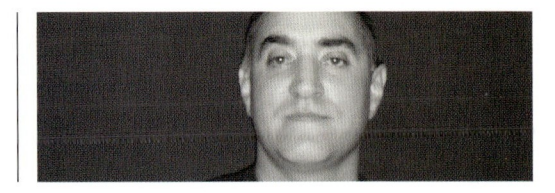

↑ | Green column

Miguel Dasso Boulevard
Lima

Miguel Dasso Boulevard is one of the most traditional streets of San Isidro. Its urban structure is divided into three sections with controlled perspectives at both ends; next to its popular cafés and bookstores these create an urban area that is unique to the district. The design proposal can be summarized in two basic interventions of great impact: a paving design which unifies both fronts of the urban space, and the incorporation of a "green columns" chain, which would act as the new symbols constituting the boulevard's spine.

PROJECT FACTS

Address: Miguel Dasso Street, San Isidro, Lima, Peru. **Client:** Municipality of San Isidro. **Completion:** 2007. **Production:** single piece. **Design:** individual design. **Functions:** illumination, pavement. **Main materials:** concrete bricks, marble, steel structures, acrylic.

199

↑ | Site plan
↓ | Colored pavement

↑ | Green columns, at night

LIGHT AND SIGN | töpfer.bertuleit.architekten

↑ | **Various lamps,** Mittlerer Ring Leipzig

Linea

Linea is distinguished by simple elegance and törsatile application possibilities. It is based on the reduction of the appearance to the key elements: pole and extension. Its clear and abstract shape allows its application in various urban situations. The lamp can be used in different variations. With light point heights located at four and a half, six, and eight meters, it can be used as street lighting in all standard situations. The light casing consists of aluminum, while the pole is made of galvanized painted steel, and the light cover, which can be opened without tools, is made of single-pane tempered safety glass.

PROJECT FACTS

Client: hess AG. **Completion:** 2006. **Production:** serial production. **Design:** product line. **Functions:** illumination. **Main materials:** aluminum, steel, glass.

↑ | Mittlerer Ring Leipzig
↓ | Linea variations

↑ | Detail

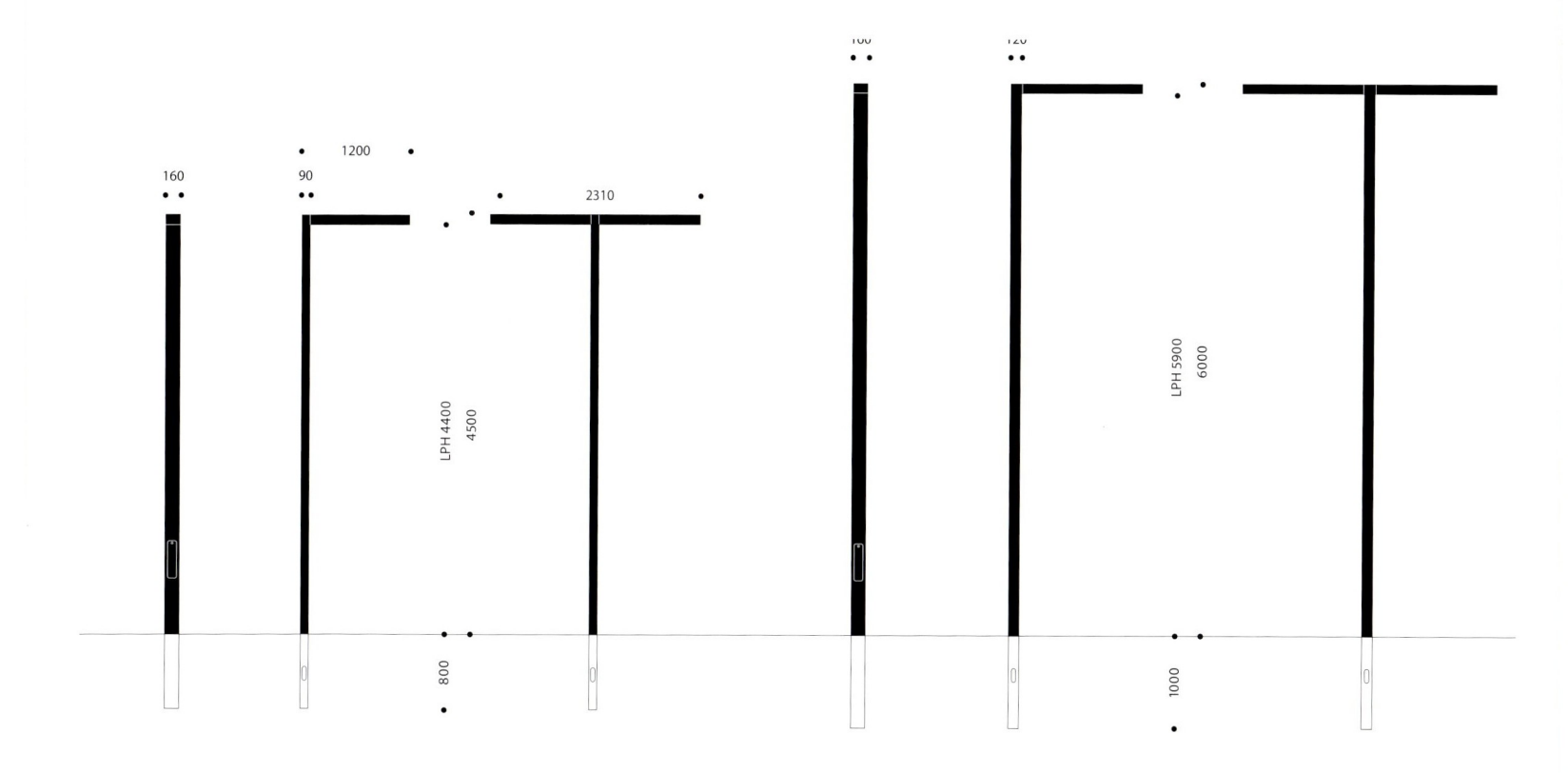

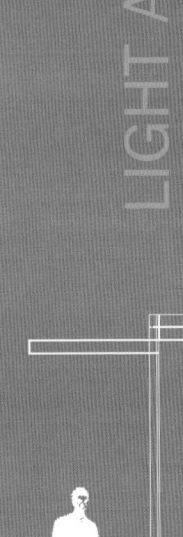

LIGHT AND SIGN

GARBAGE

BOUNDARY

BIKE AND PLAY

SEATING

ENSEMBLE **PAVEMENT** PRODUCT LINE PLANTS AND WATER SHELTER

PAVEMENT

Biuro Projektów Lewicki
Łatak / Piotr Lewicki,
Kazimierz Łatak

↑ | General view of the square

Nowy Square
Krakow

The identity of a place consists of forms, materials and views, as well as people's memories. The matrix of identity of Nowy Square is an attempt to record those memories. Bass relief – a stamp and an engraved picture initiates a projection from past times. There will be a sign-board of "Ziarno" company and the logo of the now non-existent Youth Culture House, personages of councilors and dodgy legends of the local underworld. Some signs will be pressed in horizontal and vertical plains of the surface during construction, others will appear later. The material of the images will fade in time and there will be new ones appearing in their place instead.

PROJECT FACTS **Address:** pl. Nowy, 31-056 Krakow, Poland. **Client:** City of Krakow. **Completion:** 2011. **Production:** single piece. **Design:** product line. **Functions:** seating, illumination, shelters, bicycle stand, garbage can, clocks, signs, pavement, temporary vending stands. **Main materials:** concrete with basalt gravel.

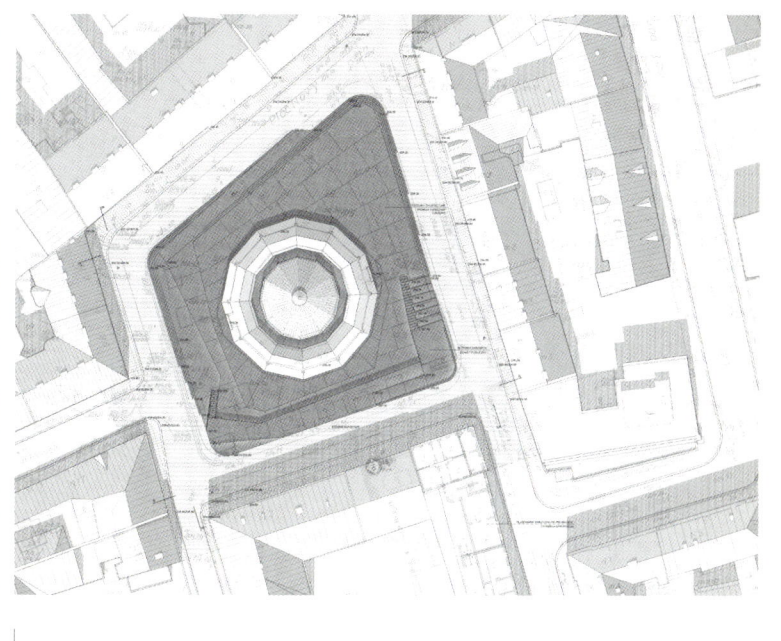

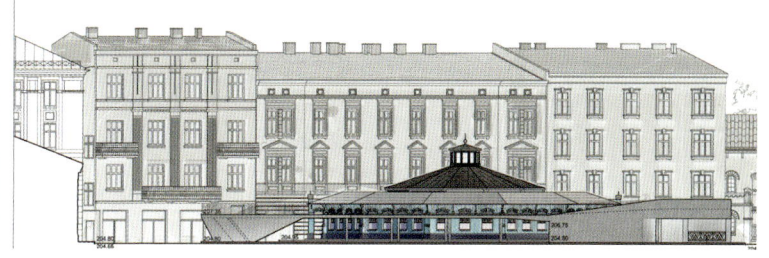

↑ | Concrete pavement
↓ | Studying the past

↑↑ | Square plan
↑ | Cross section, view of the south façades

PAVEMENT | Will Nettleship

↖↖ | **Courtyard**
↑↑ | **Central post**, a geometric version of ivy leaves
↖ | **Walkway to lake**
↑ | **Ivy circle**
↓ | **Sketch**, seating area

Centuries in turn
Fulton

This project for the center of a university campus reshapes the land forms and creates a central courtyard for a new art building plus an entrance plaza for an old theater and 244 meters of walkway. The university has an "Ivy Ceremony" for entering students dating back to the nineteenth century. The project represents the ivy ceremony with ivy expressed in geometric paving patterns, abstract sculptures, and literal images stamped in the walkways.

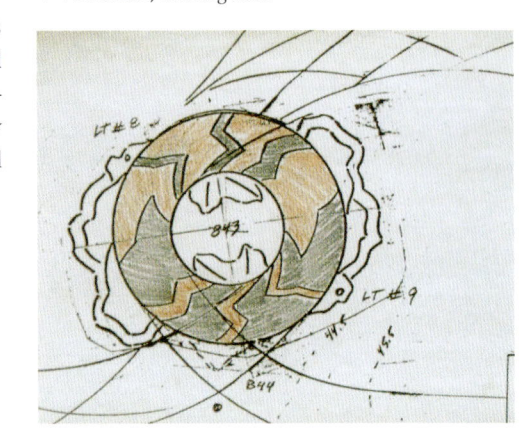

PROJECT FACTS
Address: William Woods University, Fulton, MO 65251, USA. **Client:** William Woods University. **Completion:** 1999. **Production:** single piece. **Design:** individual design. **Functions:** seating, pavement. **Main materials:** paving brick, concrete, earth forms.

Biuro Projektów Lewicki
Łatak / Piotr Lewicki,
Kazimierz Łatak

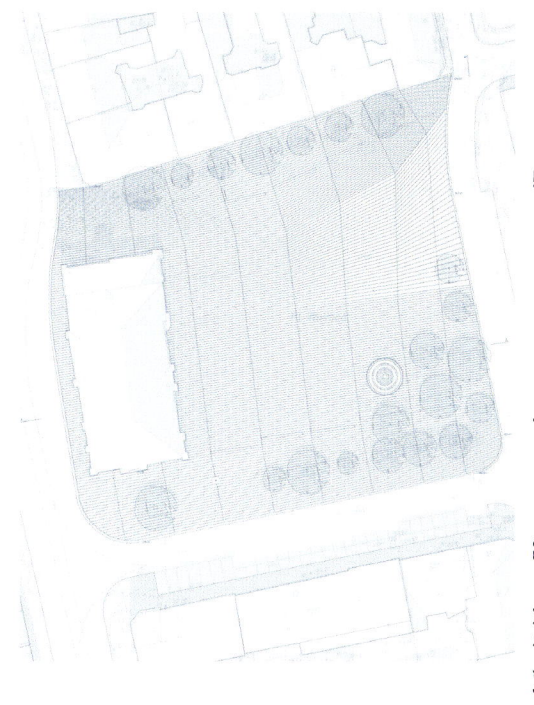

↑↑ | **Square plan**
↑ | **Place for exhibitions, concerts, meetings**
↗ | **General view**
↓ | **Sculpture-fountain**, with seatings on the base

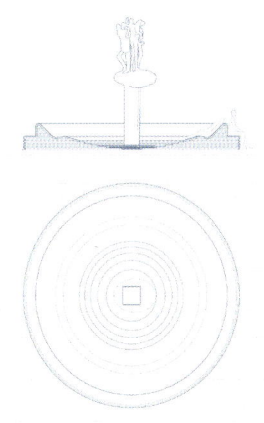

Wolnica Square
Krakow

The most suitable flooring material for this setting, given its attraction to users, history and quality, is exotic teak hardwood. The wood will be prepared in the form of untreated large-sized slabs, roughened at the surface to prevent slipping. The basic element will be a bench – a pile of planks stapled together that transforms into a glass lamppost. On its length the bench will change the angle of the seat and the back, offering various seating possibilities. A stand for bikes and the pedestal for the fountain with a Bronisław Chromy sculpture will be constructed on the same basis.

PROJECT FACTS
Address: pl. Wolnica, 31-060 Krakow, Poland. **Client:** City of Krakow. **Completion:** ongoing. **Production:** single piece. **Design:** set of parts. **Functions:** seating, illumination, shelters, plant tub, bicycle stand, fountain, garbage can, pavement. **Main materials:** exotic wood, glass.

PAVEMENT | JJR | Floor / Kristina Floor, FASLA

↑ | **Cactus flower plaza**
↗ | **Cantilevered stage,** at public amphitheater
→ | **Donald Lipski's "The Doors" sculpture,** aligns with Cactus

Arizona Canal at Scottsdale Waterfront

Scottsdale, AZ

Scottsdale Waterfront is a high density mixed use development comprised of a series of public plazas that link retail and residential components with public art installations along a linear park in front of the Arizona Canal in the heart of downtown Scottsdale, Arizona. The design uses the bold forms and colors of native cactus flowers such as saguaro, prickly pear, barrel cactus, and ocotillos within the hardscape patterns to unify the site and create dynamic spaces. These abstracted flowers define plazas, courtyards and gathering areas where forms are cast into vibrantly colored concrete paving, seat walls and fountains.

PROJECT FACTS **Address:** Scottsdale, AZ 85251, USA. **Production:** Weitz Construction. **Client:** Golub & Company, City of Scottsdale, Opus West Architects. **Completion:** 2007. **Production:** single piece. **Design:** individual design. **Functions:** hardscape plazas. **Main materials:** colored concrete.

PAVEMENT   JJR | FLOOR

PRICKLY PEAR BLOSSOM PLAZA

PRICKLY PEAR BLOSSOM
ENTRY PLAZA

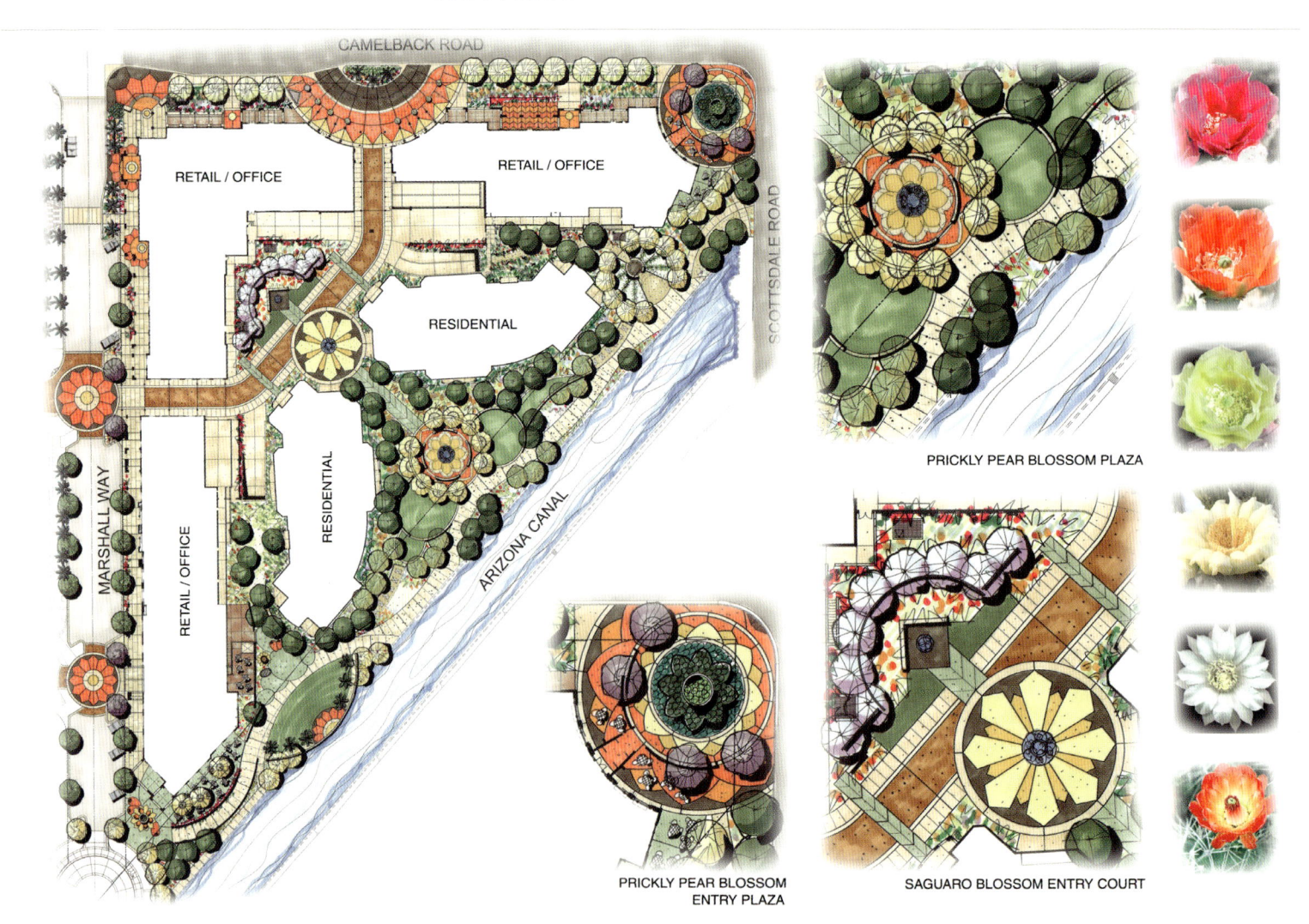

SAGUARO BLOSSOM ENTRY COURT

↑ | Conceptual site plan
← | Stylized prickly pear blossom

ARIZONA CANAL AT SCOTTSDALE WATERFRONT

211

← | **Sandblasted thorn paving**, detail
↓ | **Prickly Pear Plaza and Amphitheater**

PAVEMENT | Stacy Levy

↑ | Bench detail
→ | Watermap with kid

Watermap
Wynnewood

Watermap details a section of the Delaware River watershed surrounding the Friends' Central School. Tributaries of the Delaware and Schuylkill Rivers are deeply sandblasted into bluestone pavers. The names of the waterways and surrounding towns and cities are blasted into the stone. The terrace is sloped slightly so that rainwater will run into the runnels of the tributaries and then into the largest runnel of the Delaware River. Freshwater microorganisms found in local waterways are blasted into the bench tops, with brackish and marine organisms blasted on the teaching bench. This way the outdoor classroom and gathering space contains two views of the local watershed – one miniaturized and one greatly enlarged.

PROJECT FACTS **Address:** Fannie Cox Center for Science, Math and Technology, Friends' Central School, Wynnewood, PA 19096, USA. **Building Architect:** Graham Grund. **Client:** Friends' Central School. **Completion:** 2003. **Production:** single piece. **Design:** individual design. **Functions:** seating, fountain. **Main materials:** sandblasted Pennsylvania Bluestone.

PAVEMENT   STACY LEVY

↑ | Girl sitting on bench
← | Bench detail

WATERMAP

← | Bird's-eye view
↙ | Map detail
↓ | Drawing of Watermap

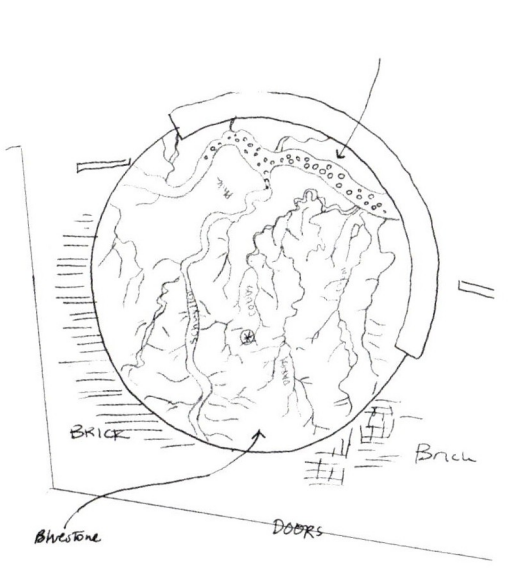

PAVEMENT Stacy Levy

↑ | **Overall view**, dry

Ridge and Valley
Pennsylvania

The local Spring Creek Watershed of the Ridge and Valley region is recreated in a bluestone terrace, punctuated by three boulder 'ridges' that rise from the terrace and create seating walls. All local streams and waterways are depicted with runnels carved six millimeter deep into the stone. When it is dry, this terrace is a scale map of the geology and watershed of this area. But when it rains the visitors' pavilion roof drains onto the terrace and the rainfall flows across the carved waterways, creating a miniature watershed. The artwork is both a sculptural object and an engineering system, allowing visitors to celebrate the hydrological cycle.

PROJECT FACTS

Address: The Arboretum at The Pennsylvania State University, University Park, Pennsylvania, PA 16802, USA. **Planning partners:** Philip Hawk & Co Stone Masons, MTR Landscape Architects. **Client:** The Pennsylvania State University. **Completion:** 2009. **Production:** single piece. **Design:** individual design. **Functions:** seating, fountain. **Main materials:** sandblasted Pennsylvania bluestone.

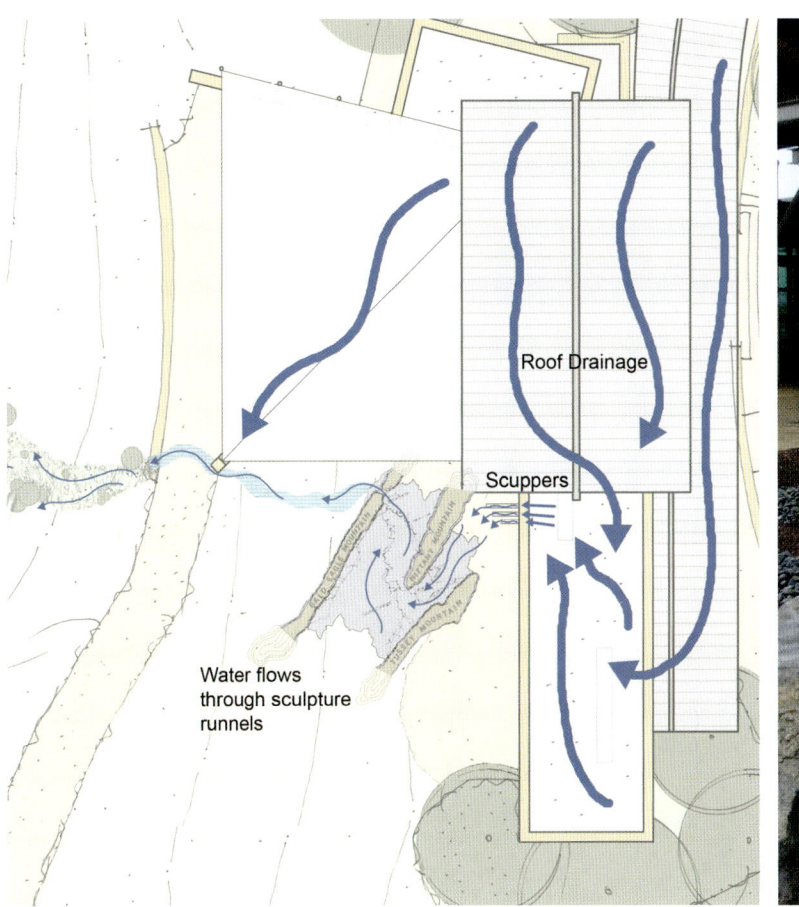

↑ | **Ridge and Valley plan,** with waterflow
↓ | **Seating detail**

↑ | **Just after a rainstorm**

PAVEMENT | BASE

↑ | **Wooden deck,** facing south

Solarium, Parc des Prés de Lyon
La Chapelle-Saint-Luc

The task was to restore the public park, which was originally created in the 1970s. For this purpose, the paths, entrance areas, most of the plants and the recreational facilities, which are primarily aimed at young people, were renovated and expanded. In addition, a skating park, more playgrounds, a miniature golf course, a fitness trail and much more was designed and added to render the entire setting more attractive and diverse. On an unused section at the center of the park, a 170 squaremeter solarium with a relaxation zone was created, turning the park into the setting for an overall exciting but also relaxing experience.

PROJECT FACTS **Address:** Parc des Prés de Lyon, 10600 La Chapelle-Saint-Luc, France. **Planning partner:** AAVP + ON. **Client:** Community d'Agglomération Troyenne. **Completion:** 2007. **Production:** single piece. **Design:** individual design. **Functions:** sun deck. **Main materials:** wood.

↑ | **Wooden pathway**
↓ | **Relaxing zone**, with lightings

↑ | **Detail**, backside

PAVEMENT

Tom Leader Studio

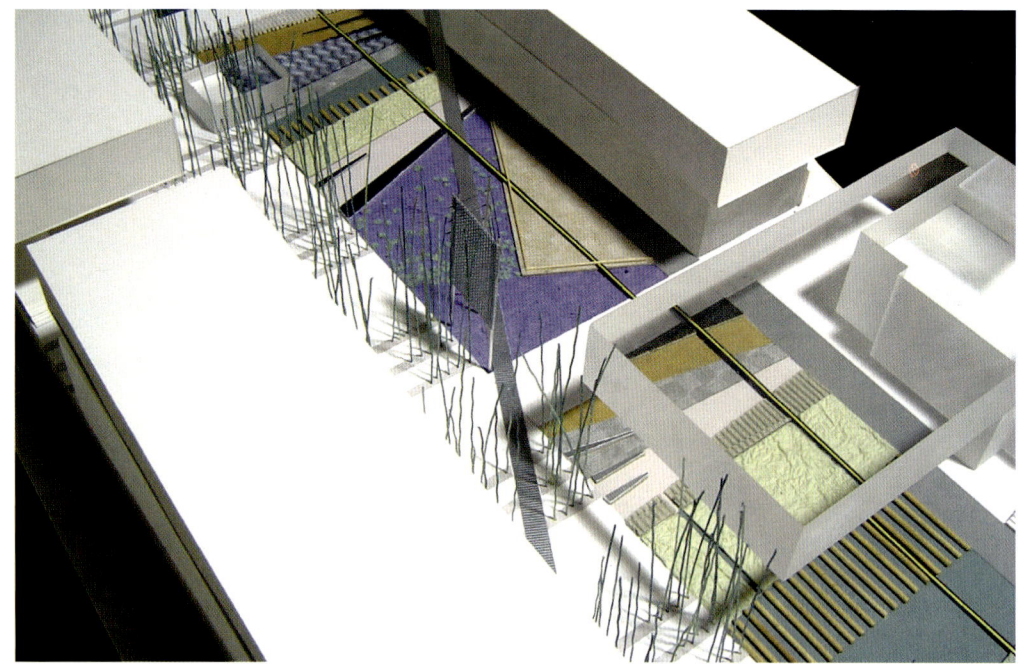

↖↖ | **Model**, detail
↑ | **View of "data stream"**
↖ | **Car parking**, model detail
↓ | **Section**, tower plaza

Shanghai Carpet
Shanghai

The design focuses on the contrasts between state-of-the-art digital media and the humble materials of daily life. Most of the new outdoor spaces are located as an "excavation" five meters below street level. Overhung by SOM's crystalline boxes, the design of the ground involves digging to uncover a new place rich with historic, rustic and recycled materials, such as metal, stone, brick, and timbers. Organizing the center is a very compressed version of this idea, a graphic "carpet" of these materials carved as a 200-meter bas-relief and flanked by a Timber Bamboo forest.

PROJECT FACTS
Address: Shanghai University District, Shanghai 200444, China. **Architects:** SOM San Francisco. **Client:** Shui On Properties. **Completion:** ongoing. **Production:** single piece. **Design:** individual design. **Functions:** pavement. **Main materials:** stone, brick, bamboo, stainless steel.

Agence APS, paysagistes dplg associés

↑↑ | Bird's-eye view
↗↗ | Bollards
↑ | Square view
↗ | Wooden deck, detail
↓ | Section

Place Aristide Briand
Valence

Facing south and the setting sun, protected from the Mistral, the place Aristide Briand enjoys a privileged location in the town center of Valence. The project reveals the typical nature of such a place by installing a palm grove on a "carpet of wood" as a way of evoking the "Mediterranean" spirit of Valence. Under twenty-six Chinese palms, several comfortable seats are arranged in groups of two or three, inviting the passer-by to bask in the rays of the sun as it sets behind the mountains of the Ardèche in complete tranquility while still in the center of town. In the middle of the square a small stream evokes the city's cultural heritage.

PROJECT FACTS
Address: Place Aristide Briand, 26000 Valence, France. **Planning partner:** Atelier Lumière, Cap Vert Ingenierie. **Client:** City of Valence. **Completion:** 2007. **Production:** single piece. **Design:** individual design. **Functions:** seating, fountain, pavement, bollards.

PAVEMENT | Sitetectonix Private Limited

↑ | **Intersection of Paving "Rays"**, with circular band

ITE College East
Singapore

The paving design originates from the social and interactive Central Forum gathering space at the heart of the site. Flanked by three buildings, the "Tropical Sun" icon generates rays on the pavement that radiate out along the three landscape concourses, each with its own character. The outwardly radiating intent strongly presents the holistic identity of the site, pulling one's attention towards the major central gathering space. This paving slides down the seats and steps of the amphitheater around the Forum Stage. Above, a roof garden is created with the same "Sun Ray" patterning originating from the skylight which directly overlooks the origins of the paving on the ground level.

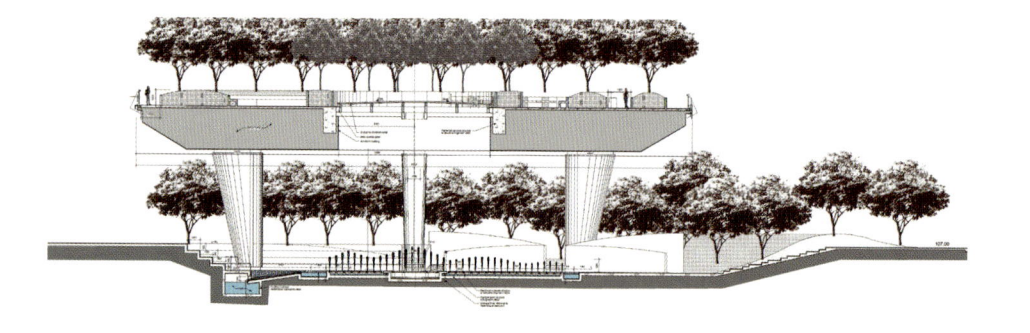

PROJECT FACTS

Address: 10 Simei Avenue, Singapore 486047, Republic of Singapore. **Architect:** RSP Architects, Singapore. **Client:** Institute of Technical Education. **Completion:** 2005. **Production:** single piece. **Design:** individual design. **Functions:** paving, seating. **Main materials:** natural stones: granites, pebbles, limestone, slate, stainless steel.

↑ | **Urban forest walk,** towards the central forum
↙ | **Section**

↑ | **Paving and planting pattern**
↓ | **Central forum amphitheater**

LIGHT AND SIGN

GARBAGE

BOUNDARY

BIKE AND PLAY

SEATING

ENSEMBLE   PAVEMENT   **PRODUCT LINE**   PLANTS AND WATER   SHELTER

PRODUCT LINE

Street and Garden Furniture Company / David Shaw

↑ | **Surfboard setting,** including a table and two benches

Burleigh – Surfboard Series
Burleigh Heads, QLD

Australia's Gold Coast is an iconic tourist location and home to some of the world's most famous surfing beaches. In developing the site for Burleigh Heads it was the intention to design a series of furniture items that reflect elements of the surfing culture. The overall forms make direct reference to surfboards, with the choice of colored timbers reflecting the 1950's board designs that were prevalent during the period when the site emerged as a major surfing destination. The support frames for the seats and tables are references to aquatic forms, and are manufactured from stainless steel for maximum protection against the corrosive nature of the environment.

PROJECT FACTS **Address:** Burleigh Heads, Gold Coast, QLD 4220, Australia. **Client:** Gold Coast City Council. **Completion:** 2003. **Production:** serial production. **Design:** product line. **Functions:** seating. **Main materials:** stainless steel, timber wood.

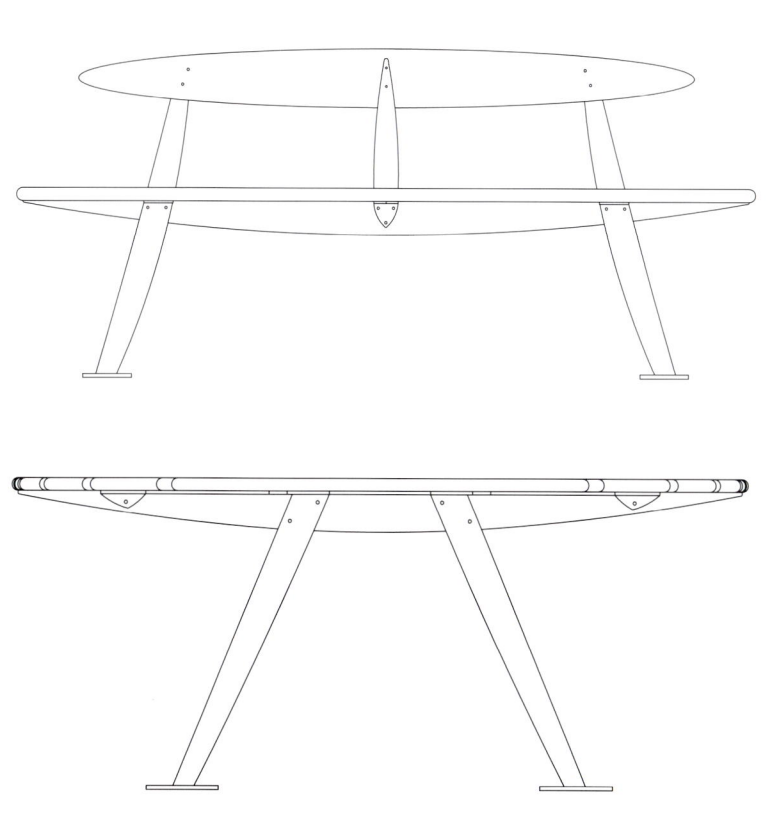

↑ | **Sections** of a bench with backrest and a table
↓ | **Rear view** of bench with backrest

↑ | **Side elevation** of bench with backrest

PRODUCT LINE | Lifschutz Davidson Sandilands

↑ | **New tram station,** on Avenue de la Liberté, Luxembourg

Luxtram
Luxembourg

This scheme for the revival of Luxembourg's tram system is inspired by the city's topography and transport heritage. It is based on three simple ideas: first to remove unnecessary clutter, second to install high-quality paving with street furniture and finally to configure the boulevards and public spaces to respond to the surrounding buildings rather than to motor traffic. Restoring simplicity and sensitivity to the streets will activate the public realm with cafés and shops. The architects of the line had the further opportunity to rethink the city's squares, working alongside the City of Luxembourg to create a new standard of urban space for Europe.

PROJECT FACTS **Address:** City of Luxembourg, Luxembourg. **Client:** Luxtram. **Completion:** 2014. **Production:** serial production. **Design:** product line. **Functions:** seating, illumination, shelters, garbage can, signs, tram shelters, digital displays, catenary system. **Main materials:** bronze, stainless steel, stone.

229

↑ | **Totem display unit,** with real time information display
↓ | **Exploded tram shelter,** showing the modular elements

↑↑ | **Elevation of the new tram station,** at Place de Paris, Luxembourg
↑ | **Seat design,** using stainless steel and formed natural stone seats

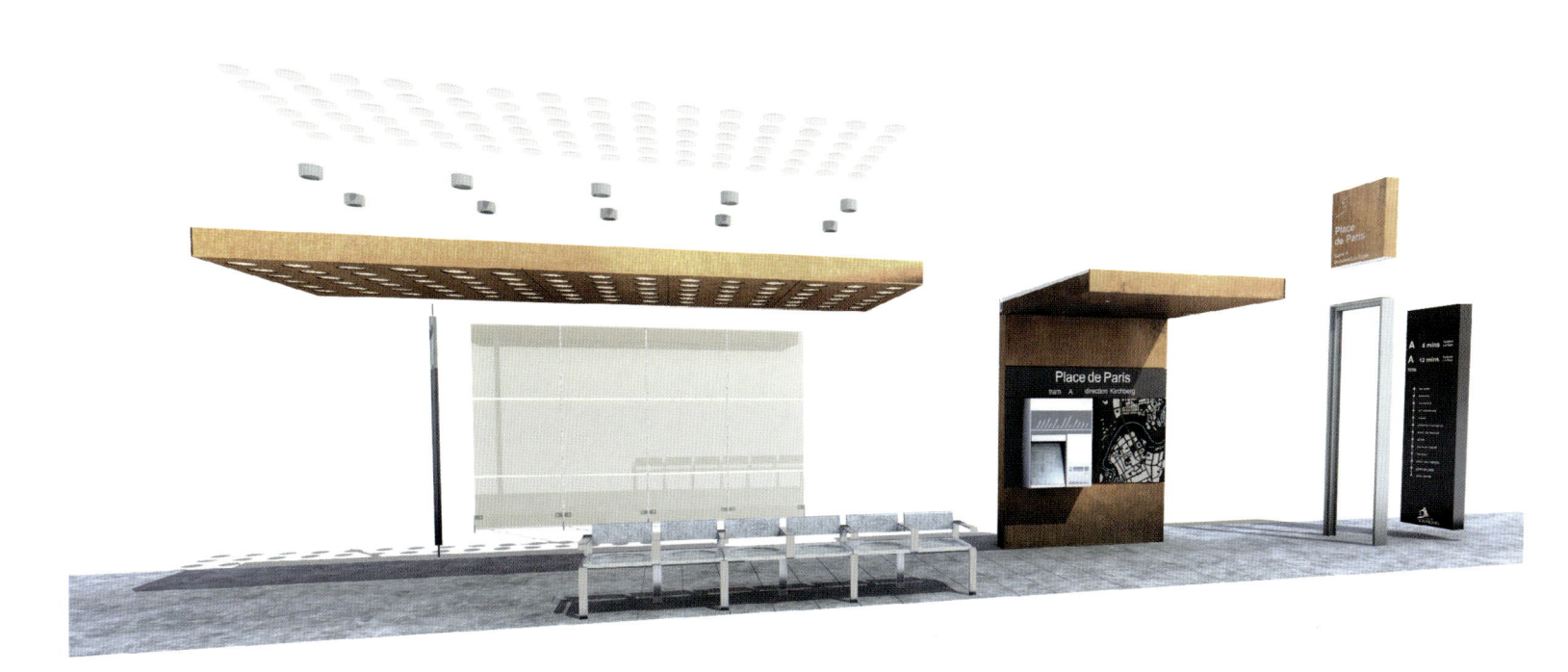

PRODUCT LINE | Lifschutz Davidson Sandilands

↑ | **Benches of the Geo system,** simple forms
↓ | **Elevations,** showing some of the elements

Geo

Geo is a coordinated street furniture system that provides a coherent and elegant way of servicing public space; opposed to the usual visual pollution of urban streetscapes. Geo is a modular, post-based system comprising three technically and aesthetically integrated categories of lighting, furniture and signage. The design is easy to maintain, minimal and durable and maximizes the potential of each element to accommodate existing requirements and emerging technologies. Each element is also designed for easy maintenance, security and cleaning. The range includes lighting, bus stops, bus shelters, seating, bollards, cycle racks, telephone boxes and cans.

PROJECT FACTS

Manufacturer: Woodhouse plc. **Completion:** ongoing. **Production:** serial production. **Design:** product line. **Functions:** seating, garbage can, illumination, bicycle stand, sign, shelter, bollard. **Main materials:** stainless steel, wood.

↑ | **Garbage can**
↓ | **Detail view,** illuminated bollard

↑ | **Finger post and bollards**

PRODUCT LINE

Kramer Design Associates
(KDA) / Jeremy Kramer

↑ | Bus shelter and waste receptacle
→ | Bus shelter

City of Toronto coordinated Street Furniture Program

Toronto

With its street furniture design, KDA contributed to the evolution of city streetscapes. This comprehensive design was selected for the city of Toronto's first-ever, 20-year street furniture contract. KDA's powerful designs included transit shelters, waste receptacles, benches, public washrooms, bike racks, information columns, public posting columns and multi-publication structures. More than 26,000 individual pieces of furniture will be deployed over the next twenty years. Additionally, KDA has designed a program of coordinated street furniture amenities for the City of Toronto including bollards, tree grates, railing systems, wayfinding signs, street lamps, planter boxes, and kiosks.

PROJECT FACTS **Address:** Toronto, ON, Canada. **Client:** City of Toronto. **Completion:** 2008. **Production:** serial production. **Design:** product line. **Functions:** transit shelters, waste receptacles, benches, public washrooms, bike racks, information columns, public posting columns and multi-publication structures. **Main materials:** TPO composite plastic, aluminum cast pedal (waste receptacle), polycarbonate, aluminum, safety glass (shelters).

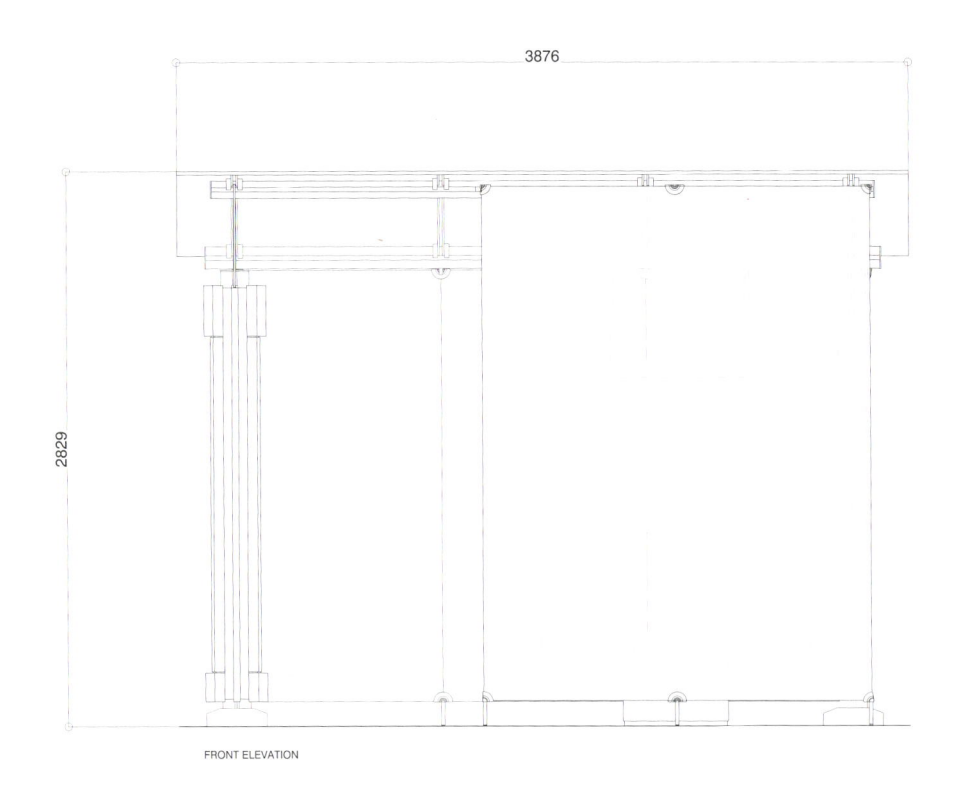

PRODUCT LINE   KRAMER DESIGN ASSOCIATES (KDA)

3876 | 2829

2071 | 2829

FRONT ELEVATION

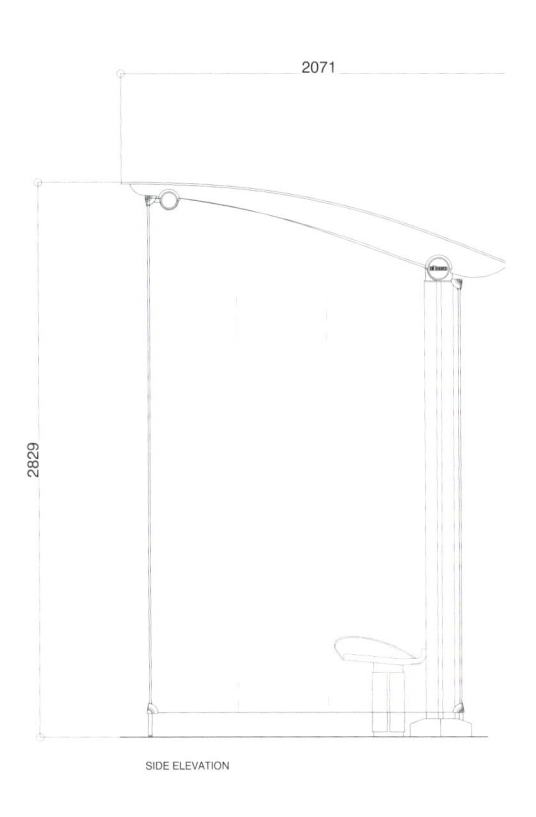

SIDE ELEVATION

↑ | Shelter elevations
← | Waste receptacle

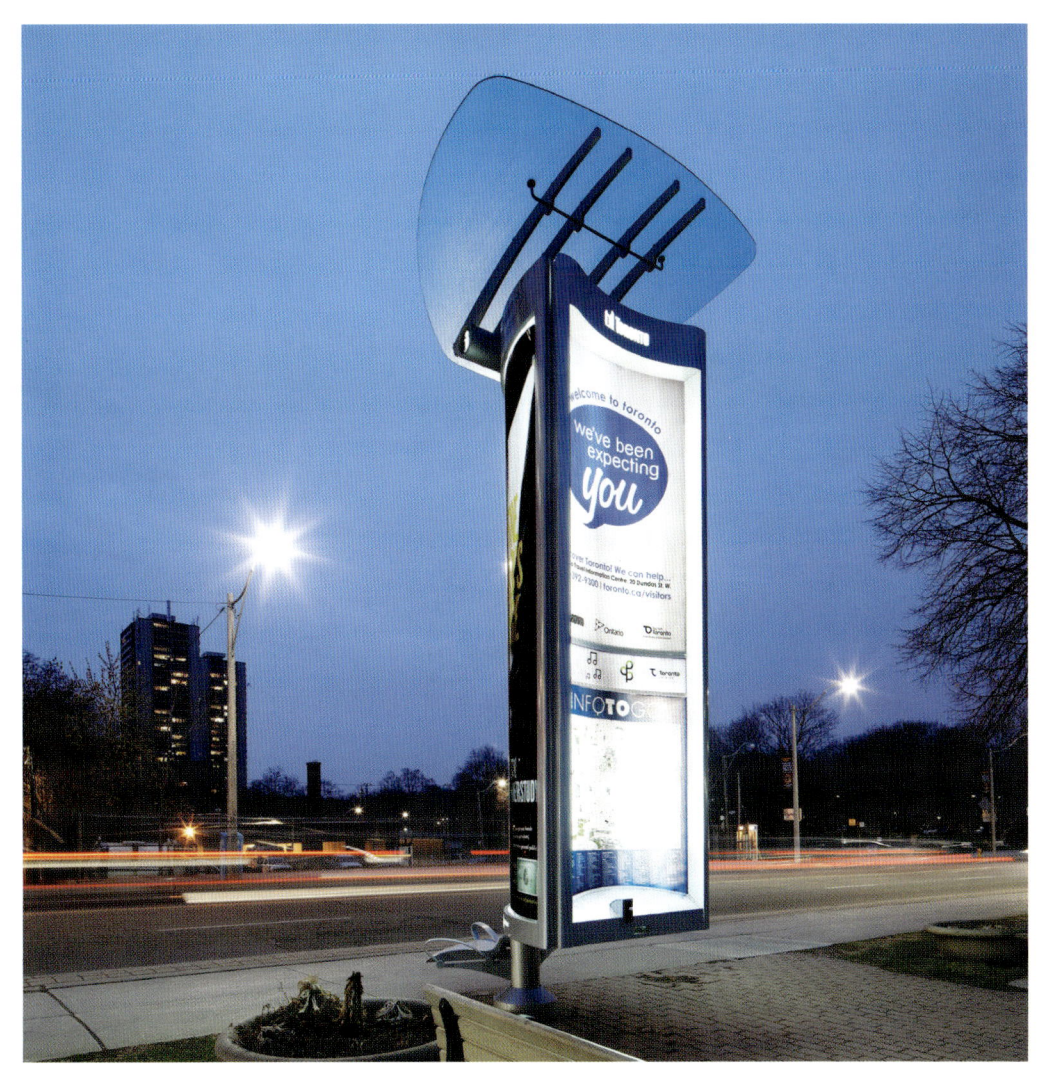

TORONTO COORDINATED STREET FURNITURE PROGRAM

← | Information column
↓ | Transit shelter

PRODUCT LINE | EBD architects ApS

↑ | **Table and benches** of the Mobilia line
↘ | **Sections of the bench**

Mobilia

Mobilia is urban space inventory developed as a building set of components that unite the quality of industrial production with the opportunity for individual layout in relevance to the actual project. The bench is a component that by itself or added to a course of lines and curves becomes an integrated part of the urban space. The bench is produced in modules of two meters length in straight or curved sequences with the smallest diameter of four meters. This provides entirely new geometric options related to industrially produced inventory for urban spaces. The dustbin is developed with a focus on simplified expression while simultaneously giving the product functionality.

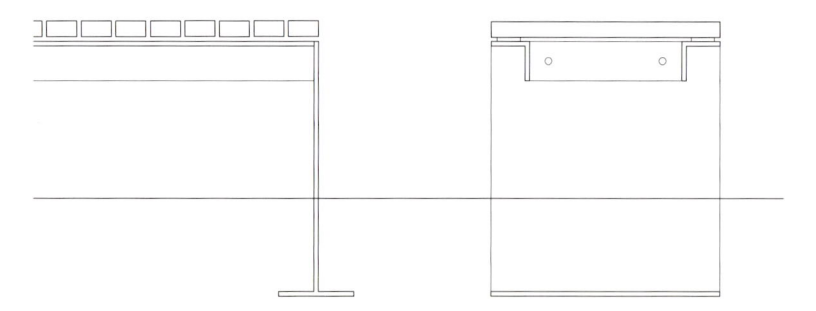

PROJECT FACTS   **Client:** GH form. **Completion:** 2002. **Production:** serial production. **Design:** product line. **Functions:** seating, table, garbage can, toilets, signs. **Main materials:** cast iron, steel, wood.

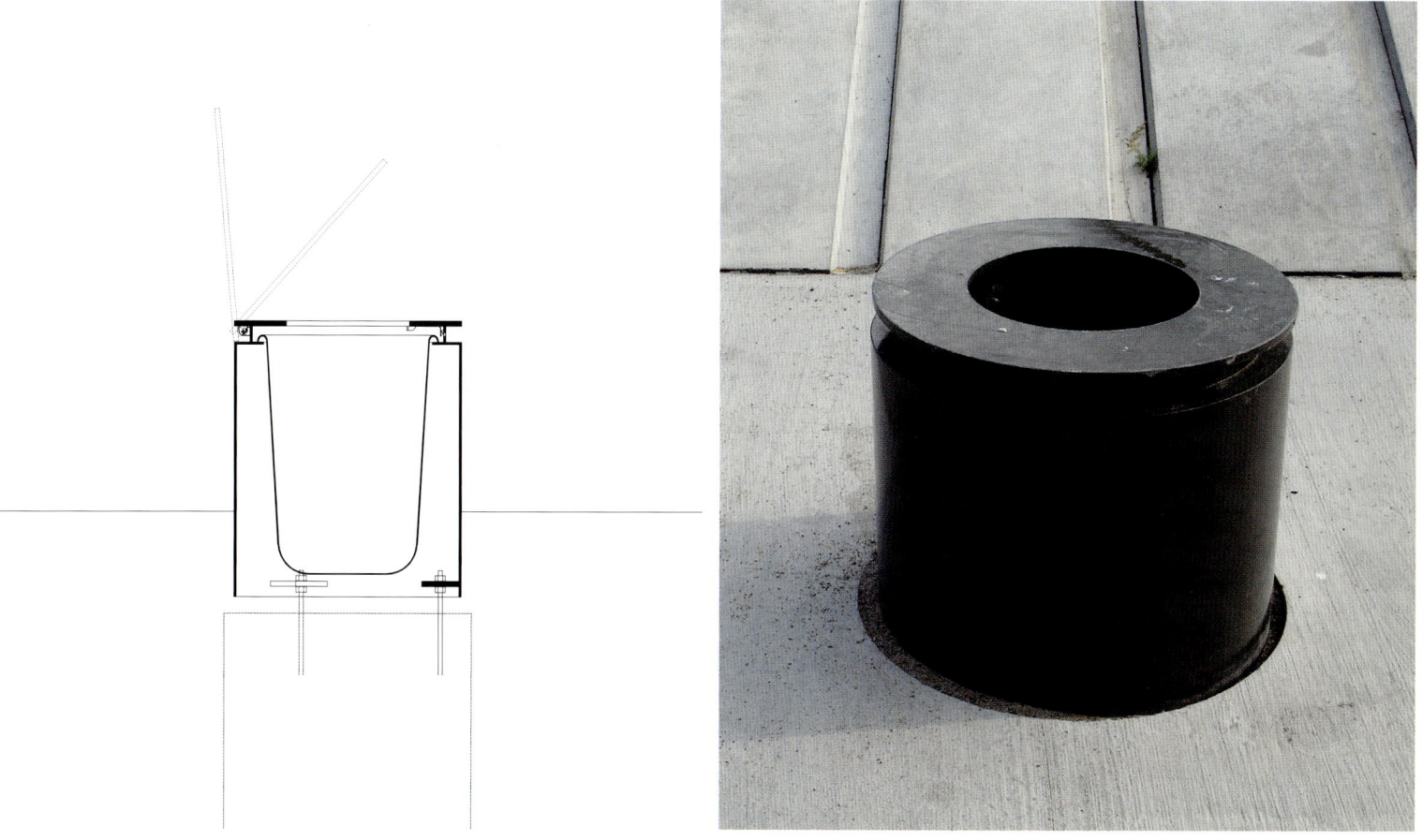

237

↑ | **Dustbin**
↘ | **Mobilia bench**

↑ | **Dustbin**, detail view

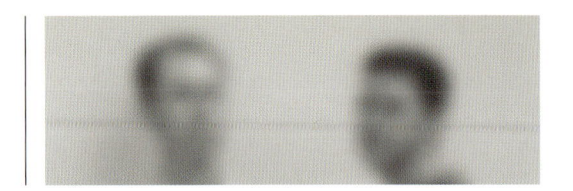

PRODUCT LINE   díez+díez diseño

↑ | **Infographic of the total program,** currently in development

Zen

Zen appears like a piece of urban furniture, used like an individual bench or architectural border, coupled with a totally innovative character. It exhibits a calm spirit and balance that could be defined as essentialist. This element has been created from a process of abstraction referring to the idea of rock as a natural shape. It can be easily integrated into natural and architectural spaces. Its geometry differs from the prevailing rationality and minimalism, and can even be considered organic. Zen establishes a fluid communion between the environments where it is installed and the potential user. Since it is based on a circle, Zen has no predefined orientation.

PROJECT FACTS Client: mago:URBAN. Completion: 2010. Production: serial production. Design: product line. Functions: seating, plant tub, boards. Main materials: concrete.

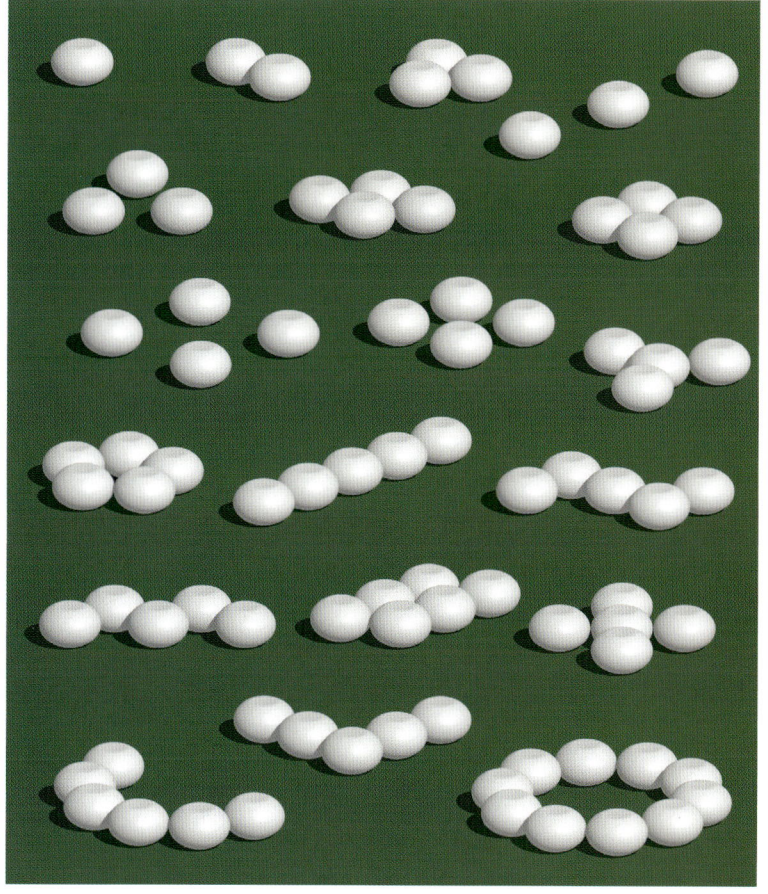

239

↑ | Placement scheme
↓ | Individual banks

↑ | Individual bank, detail

PRODUCT LINE | mmcité a.s. / David Karásek, Radek Hegmon

↑ | **Radium Bench,** with wooden backrest and seating
↘ | **Plans** of the models LR130 and LR160

Park Bench Radium

The key element and highlight of the design of this park bench is the basic frame molded out of a single sheet of metal. Seen from the front, this gives the bench a very delicate and slim appearance. The metal basic frame can also be equipped with wooden seats and backrests. In addition, there are various surface structures available that allow matching the bench to a variety of settings. The series includes benches with and without back rests as well as stools in simple yet exciting designs.

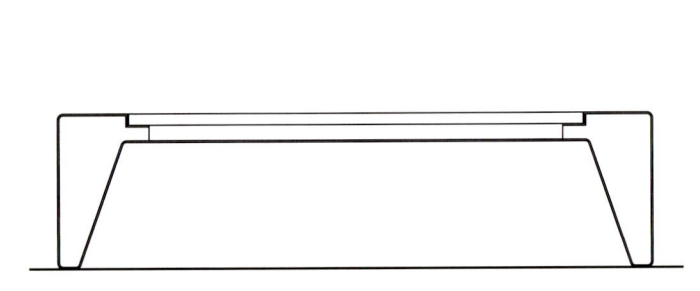

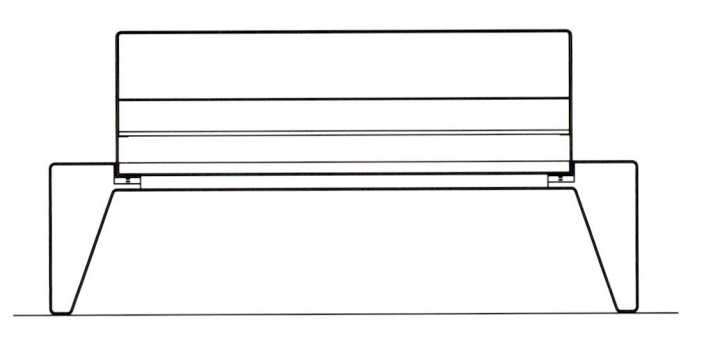

PROJECT FACTS

Client: mmcité a.s., Prague Airport, City of Pecs. **Completion:** 2005. **Production:** serial production. **Design:** product line. **Functions:** seating. **Main materials:** galvanized steel, metal sheet or solid wooden boards.

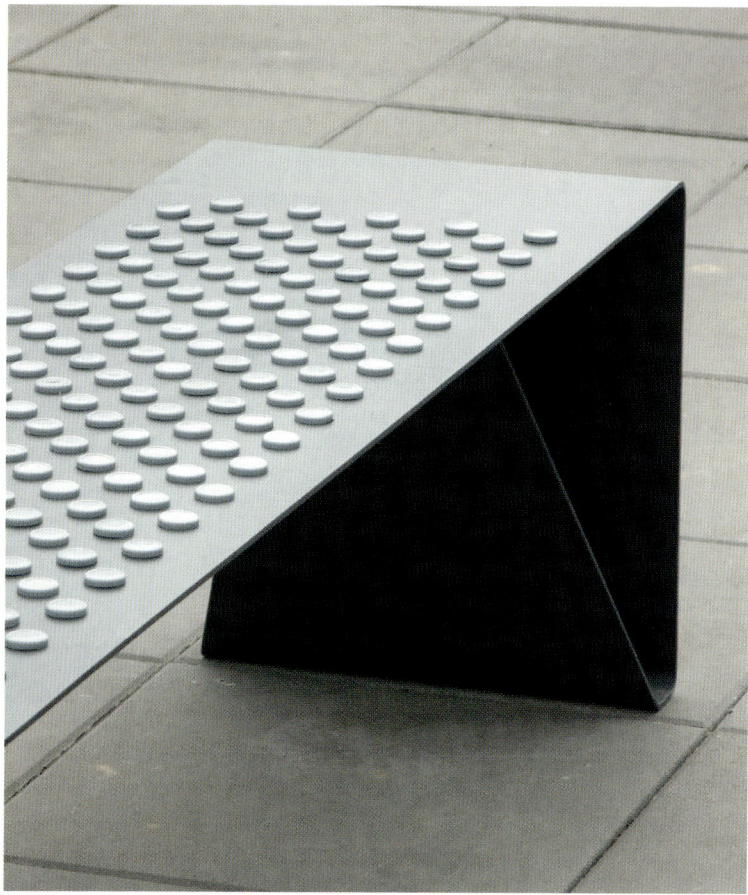

↑ | **Stools,** also part of the Radium line
↓ | **Radium bench** in a park area

↑ | **Detail view,** different surfaces are used

PRODUCT LINE | Agence Elizabeth de Portzamparc / Elizabeth de Portzamparc

↑ | Shelter

Tramway de Bordeaux
Bordeaux

Elisabeth de Portzamparc designed a complete product line for the new Tramway de Bordeaux. The first development phase included a 44.6-network of 124 stations. It reflects contemporary public traffic with an elegant and modern design. With gentle, thin forms and generous use of glass it stays modestly in the background, drawing attention only on the second glimpse. Made of milled and welded steel sheet as well as cast aluminum, the slim, discrete and feminine shape is sturdy enough for everyday use.

PROJECT FACTS **Address:** Bordeaux, France. **Client:** CUB (Communauté Urbaine de Bordeaux). **Completion:** 2004. **Production:** serial production. **Design:** product line. **Functions:** seating, illumination, shelters, garbage can, boards, sidewalk barriers. **Main materials:** cast iron, glass, wood.

↑ | Shelter, lights and garbage can
↓ | Product line

↑ | Lights and shelter by night

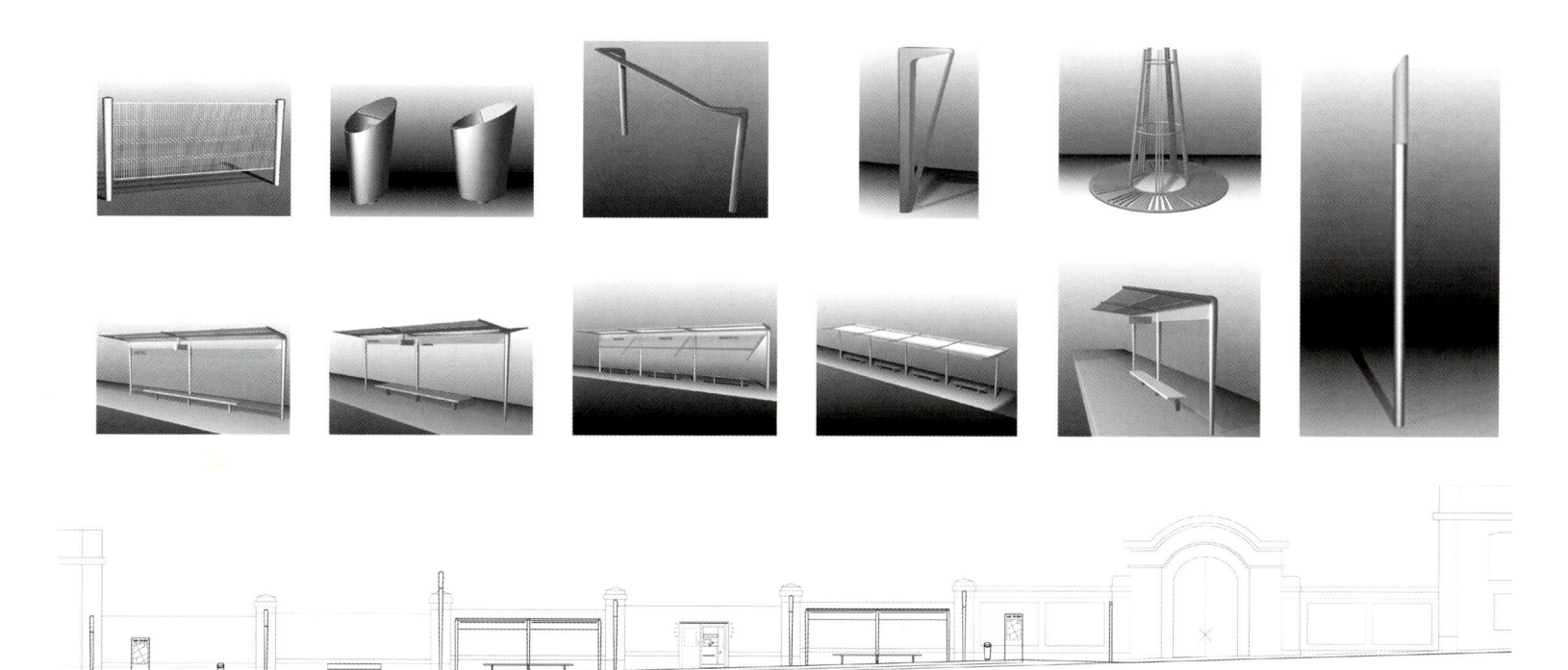

LIGHT AND SIGN

GARBAGE

BOUNDARY

BIKE AND PLAY

SEATING

ENSEMBLE   PAVEMENT   PRODUCT LINE   PLANTS AND WATER   SHELTER

SEATING | Mitzi Bollani

↖ | **Sketch**, seating
↑↑ | **Red chanterelles**, in Bibbiena
↑ | **People at a bus stop**, in Poggibonsi

Finferlo

Finferlo is a small, colorful low seat, which "pops up" to meet a variety of seating requirements. Finferlo takes up very little space and thus can provide an amusing rest at bus stops or shelters. It offers a resting place for weary travelers in areas where there are no benches. A number of seats can be arranged together to create an informal relaxation place.

PROJECT FACTS
Client: MODO srl. **Completion:** 2005. **Production:** serial production. **Design:** individual design. **Functions:** seating. **Main materials:** iron.

Anouk Vogel landscape architecture

↑↑ | Sparrow bench
↑ | Lime bench
↗ | Pairs of bench profiles

Vondel Verses

Amsterdam

The final step in the renovation of the Vondelpark is the replacement of the park furniture, which today consists of an agglomeration of standard elements from different periods. Vondel Verses takes its inspiration from the original ideas of the Vondelpark, which is designed in a romantic English landscape style. The park contains a medley of different characters that come together as a whole. This variation is reflected in the application of different motifs in the frames of the benches, inspired by the flora and fauna of the location. The vegetal motifs are continued in the design of the lamp post, which subtly mimics a daffodil bud, and the kiosk, which is covered by a pattern of ivy.

PROJECT FACTS

Address: Vondelpark, Oud Zuid, Amsterdam, The Netherlands. **Planning partner:** Johan Selbing. **Client:** City of Amsterdam. **Completion:** 2011. **Production:** serial production. **Design:** individual design. **Functions:** seating. **Main materials:** cast iron, coated wood.

SEATING | Studio Makkink & Bey BV

↖↖ | **Main elevation**
↑↑ | **Detail,** integrated dining table and chair
↖ | **Production process**
↑ | **Side elevation**

Tokyo City Bench
Tokyo

Day-tripper is based on a study of the different postures people assume on the street during a day, while learning, sitting, or squatting. Seven postures were fixed and shaped in the wave-like form of this work. More formal pieces of "furniture" were integrated in this wave – like a dining table or chairs. Working initially from an appreciation of European scale and culture, in this case the designers have chosen to fabricate the works using a skin of fiberglass, printed with a white flower pattern on pink-colored polyester.

PROJECT FACTS
Address: Tokyo, Japan. **Planning partners:** Silvijn v/d Velden, Christiaan Oppewal. **Client:** Droog Design. **Completion:** 2002. **Production:** single piece. **Design:** individual design. **Functions:** seating. **Main materials:** wood, fiberglass, polyester.

sandellsandberg /
Thomas Sandell

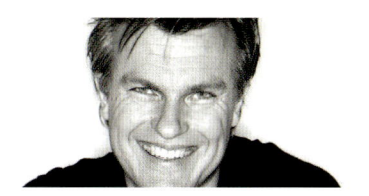

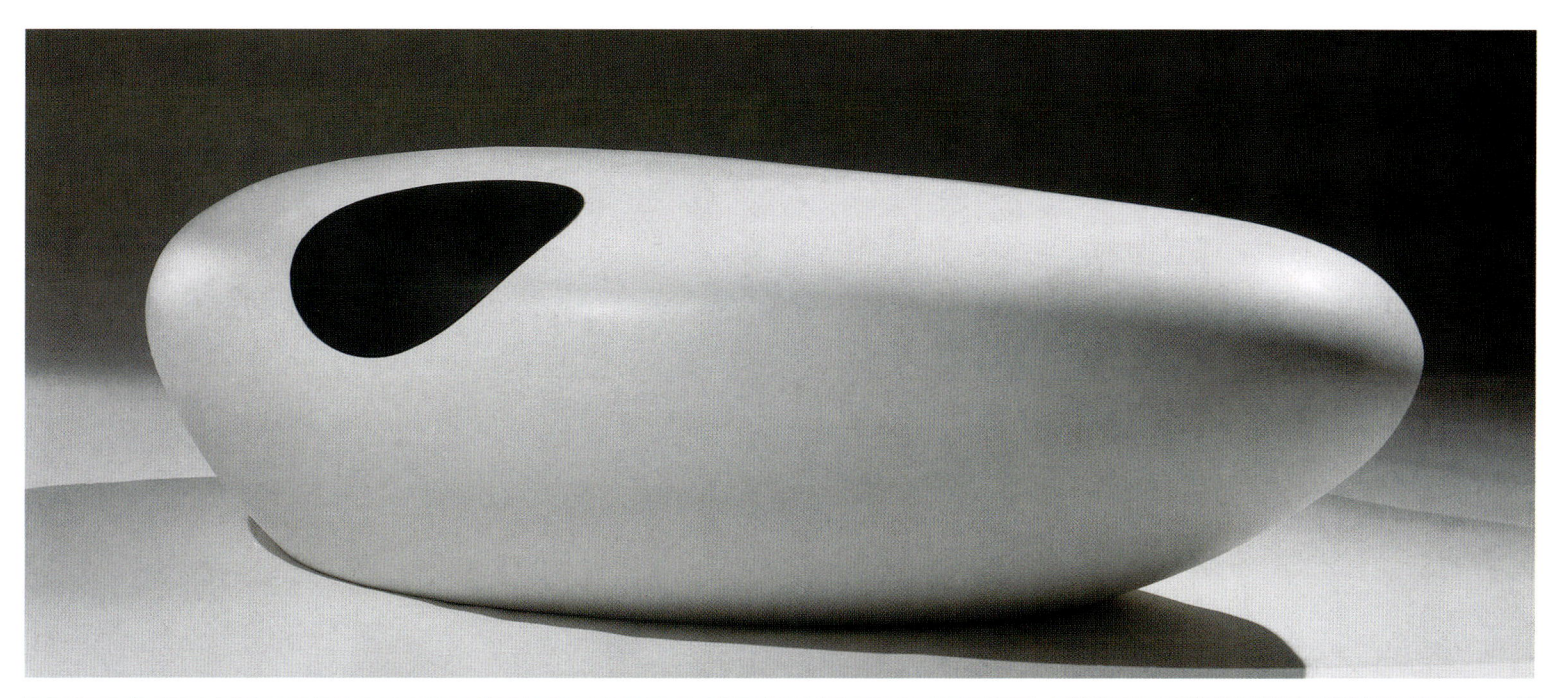

↑↑ | **Total view**
↑ | **Site image,** with people
↗ | **Detail**
↓ | **Sketch**

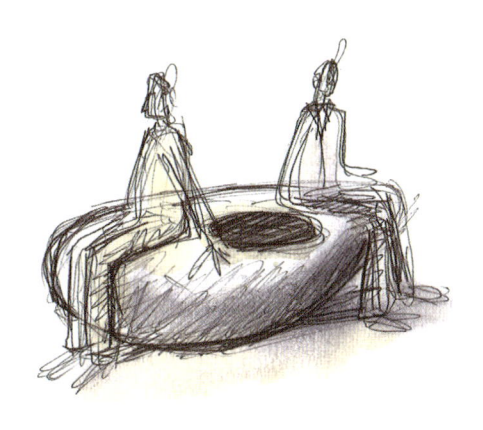

Streetscape Furniture
Tokyo

Roppongi hills, one of Japans largest integrated property developments, stemmed from the concept of living, working and shopping in close proximity to eliminate commuting time. Thomas Sandell and sandellsandberg were commissioned to design an installation for one of the outdoor spaces and decided to create a seating arrangement with a shape and material that correspond to the modern, playful and inviting feel of the urban streetscape.

PROJECT FACTS
Address: Roppongi Hills, Tokyo, Japan. **Client:** Mori Building Society. **Completion:** 2003. **Production:** single piece. **Design:** individual design. **Functions:** seating. **Main materials:** thermoformed Corian, with injected polyuretan foam.

SEATING | Buro Poppinga

↑ | **The Big Bench,** perspective view

The Big Bench

The Big Bench by Buro Poppinga was developed for Grijsen park & straatdesign as a durable product for contemporary public spaces. Great effort was exerted to make it look good from the front as well as the back. It is meant to be a modern version of the classic park bench made from castings and shelves. It has an H-shaped profile and consists of 90- to 120-mm boards. A particular distinguishing detail of the bench is that not all of its wood is trapped between the castings. The front shelf of the seat and the top shelf of the back continue across the entire length of the bench. These free boards are attached to the bench via other boards, the seat and backrest, which in turn are connected to the castings.

PROJECT FACTS **Client:** Grijsen park & straatdesign. **Completion:** 2007. **Production:** serial production. **Design:** individual design. **Functions:** seating. **Main materials:** coated cast aliminum, hardwood.

251

↑ | **Side elevation**
↘ | **Looking beautiful** from the back as well as from the front

↑ | **Isometric drawing**

SEATING | NL Architects

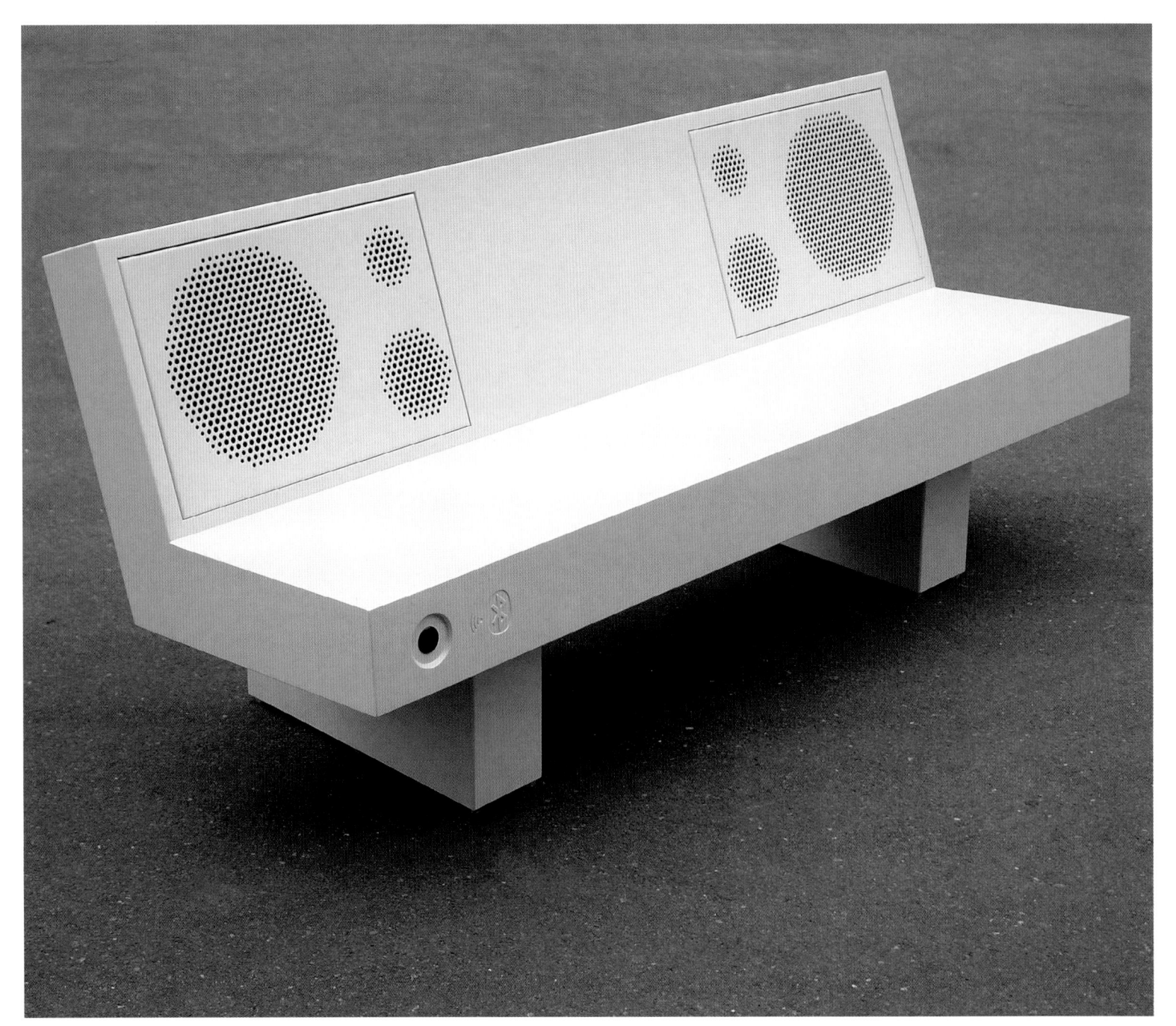

↑ | **Boom Bench** with integrated hi-fi system

Boom Bench

This extraordinary street object is a crossover of a hi-fi unit and a bench and caters to the desire to enjoy one's own music in public. It especially appeals to the younger generation who like to share their music. The Boom Bench features eight 60-watt co-axial speakers and two subwoofers that can be accessed through Bluetooth. The Boom Bench is a type of super-sized docking station. Everyone can connect his/her player or cell phone to the amplifier to play his/her music with 95 dB high-quality sound. It is a new kind of street furniture that will not only shape the public visually but also acoustically.

PROJECT FACTS

Planning partner: Scott Burnham. **Client:** Droog Design. **Completion:** 2008. **Production:** serial production. **Design:** individual design. **Functions:** seating, hi-fi unit, docking station. **Main materials:** plywood, stainless steel.

↑ | **Group of kids** enjoying the acoustic bench
↓ | **Front view**

↑ | **Bench in use**

SEATING | Estudio Cabeza / Diana Cabeza

↑ | Area version and row lay out

Topografico Bench

Sinuous, unsymmetrical and irregular, this bench's undulating surface slides like the earth, glides like wet sand and draws watermarks like on a still damp surface. Its topographic expression evokes subtle ergonomic qualities, while its concrete materiality is user-friendly. Consisting of a basic module 1.80 x 0.70 x 0.40 meters with or without a backrest, it can be configured in numerous and varied ways, for example matched side-to-side, back-to-back or in combinations of both with chemical or mechanical anchors.

PROJECT FACTS

Client: Government of Buenos Aires and private clients. **Development team:** Diana Cabeza, Martín Wolfson, Diego Jarczak. **Completion:** 2003. **Production:** serial production. **Design:** individual design. **Functions:** seating. **Main materials:** pre-cast concrete with color aggregate, natural finishing.

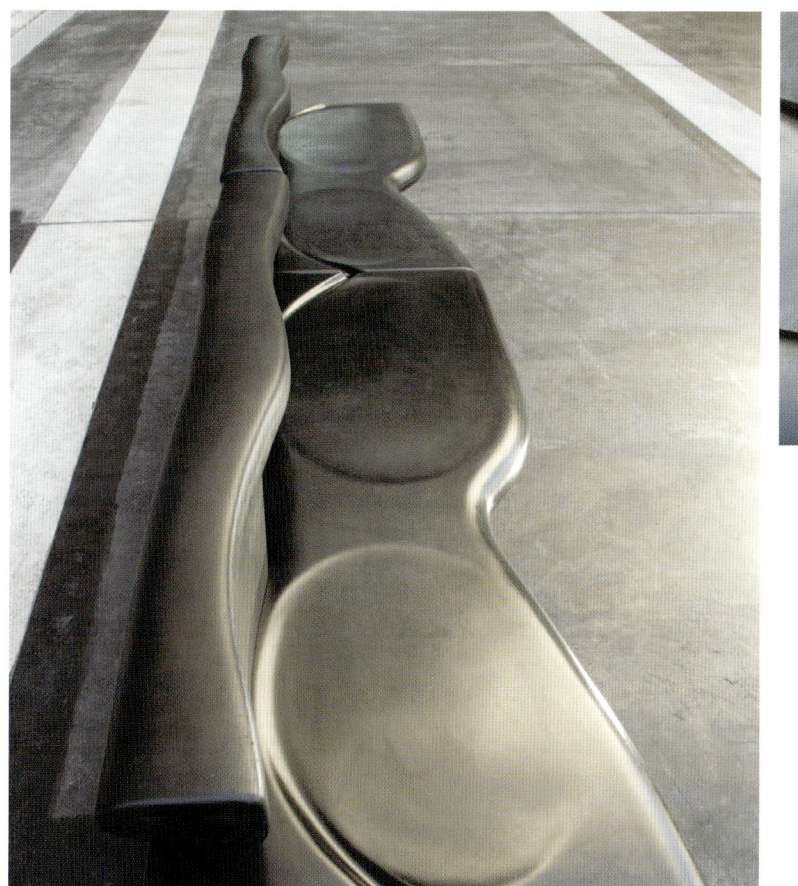

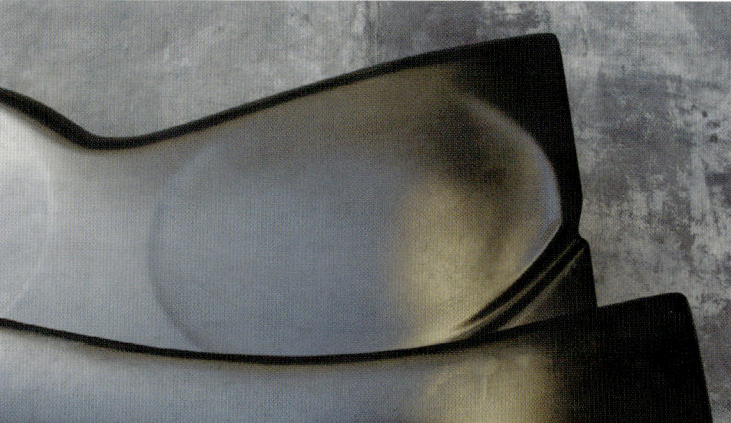

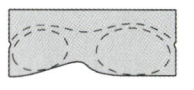

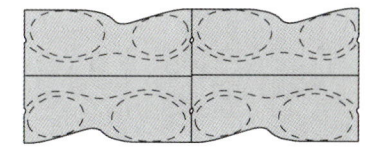

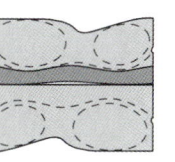

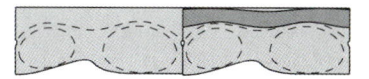

255

↑ | **Bench,** with backrest row
↓ | **Bench,** without backrest row

↑↑ | **Close up**
↑ | **Layouts**

SEATING | Estudio Cabeza / Diana Cabeza

↑ | **Bench,** with and without backrest row
→ | **Use situation**

Patrimonial Bench
Buenos Aires

This bench was especially designed for the historical center of Buenos Aires. It is made of pre-cast concrete with an incorporated off-white color aggregate, typical of turn-of-the-century Buenos Aires façades. With or without a backrest and a base unit measuring 1.40 meters in length, it can be installed in individual units or assembled into a long continuous row of benches. Furthermore, as benches with or without backrests can also be combined to be approached from either side, very singular configurations may be obtained. The bench is fixed to an on-site concrete base.

PROJECT FACTS **Address:** Historical center of the City of Buenos Aires, Argentina. **Development team:** Diana Cabeza, Alejandro Venturotti, Diego Jarczak. **Client:** Government of the City of Buenos Aires. **Completion:** 2008. **Production:** serial production. **Design:** individual design. **Functions:** seating. **Main materials:** pre-cast concrete with color aggregate, natural finishing.

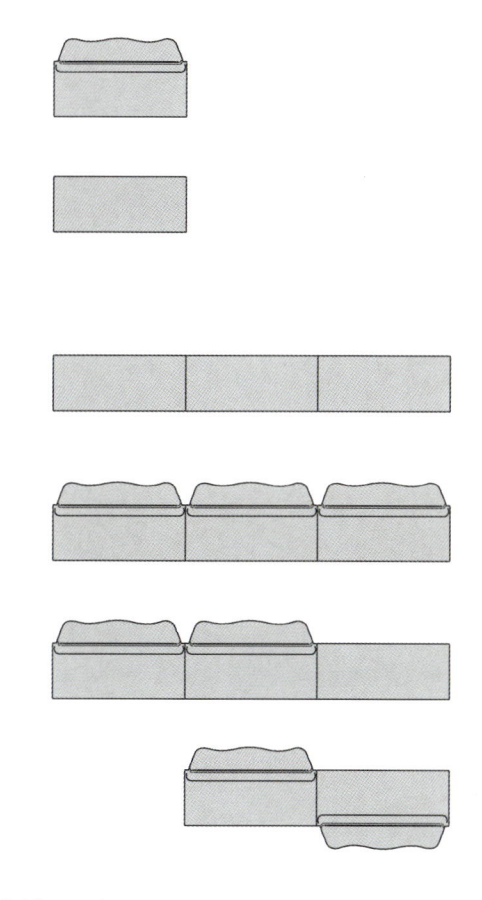

↑ | Layouts
↓ | Close Up

SEATING | Estudio Cabeza / Diana Cabeza

↑ | **Different compositions**
→ | **Detail,** red and brown granite
↑ | **Singel, double and tripple seats**

Encuentros

Buenos Aires

"Encuentros" is inspired by the rocks of "Playa Negra", a black South Atlantic beach on the coast of Tierra del Fuego. It pays homage to the end of the world and acts as a bridge to join distant places of the earth, celebrating the encounter with nature and the feeling of acknowledgement and delight. "Encuentros" proposes an evocative encounter place, to wait, to rest, to see and be seen and eventually to come in touch with oneself and nature.

PROJECT FACTS
Address: Tribuna Plaza, Casa Foa 2009 Edition, City of Buenos Aires, Argentina.
Development team: Diana Cabeza, Alejandro Venturotti. **Client:** City of Buenos Aires.
Completion: 2009. **Production:** single piece. **Design:** individual design. **Functions:** seating. **Main materials:** red and brown Sierra Chica Argentine granite.

díez+díez diseño

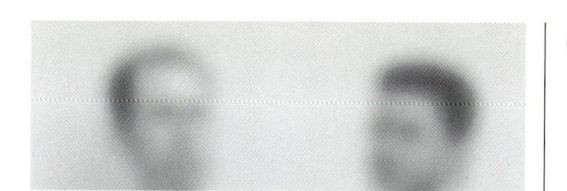

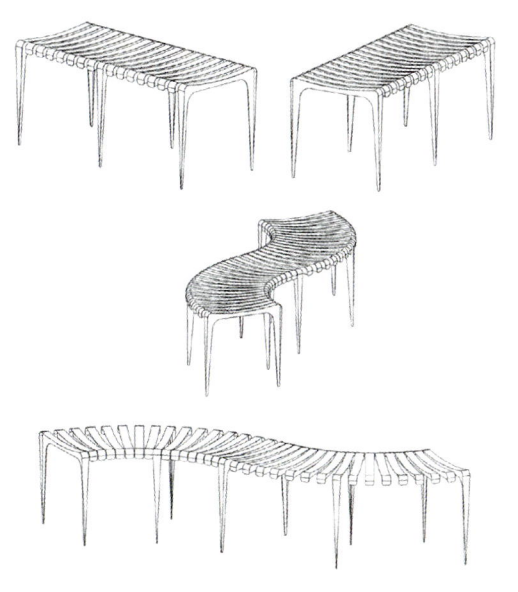

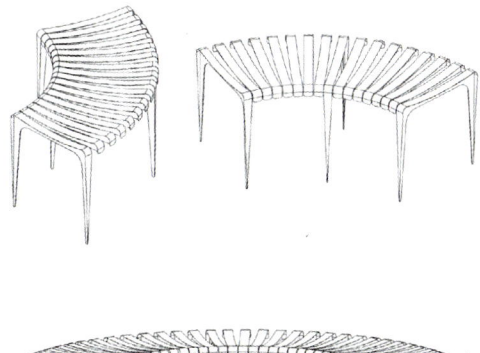

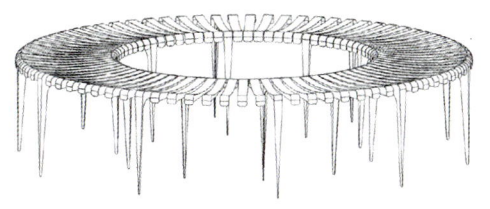

↑↑ | **Bench,** with backrest
↑ | **Infographic,** different possibilities of compositions
↗ | **Detail**

Miriápodo

The bench was created as a potentially infinite seat element that, in a lateral way, travels across spaces, cities and fields, squares and buildings, accommodating people with different needs, allowing diverse uses while being in a continuous metamorphosis. The versatility of its composition and function lies in the completely free modulation of the two basic elements that form the initial program, which are the leg and the slat. Both elements articulate and fix around a joint once the desired position is set. This allows the layout from a basic seat of 50 cm to seats of any length, adopting curved, straight, mixed, etc.

PROJECT FACTS

Planning partner: Trem diseño industrial. **Client:** Tecnología & Diseño Cabanes. **Completion:** 2005. **Production:** serial production. **Design:** product line. **Functions:** seating. **Main materials:** cast aluminum.

SEATING | Owen Song

Solar Bench
Seoul

Solar Bench frees itself from the design concepts of traditional benches. It is a new approach to the concept of a bench. While serving the traditional function, this bench becomes a Wi-fi hot-spot also offering nightly illumination through its thin-film solar battery. Eco-friendly, it is made of aluminum and recycled plastics in addition to the solar battery. It offers the public utilization of natural electricity charged by sunlight. Eventually, it is an element of an "Eco City".

PROJECT FACTS
Address: Nonhyun-dong, 70-7, 135-010, Seoul, South Korea. **Planning partner:** Byungmin Woo, Seonkeun Park. **Client:** Samsung Electronics. **Completion:** 2008. **Production:** single piece. **Design:** individual design. **Functions:** seating, Wi-Fi, lighting. **Main materials:** plastic, solar panel.

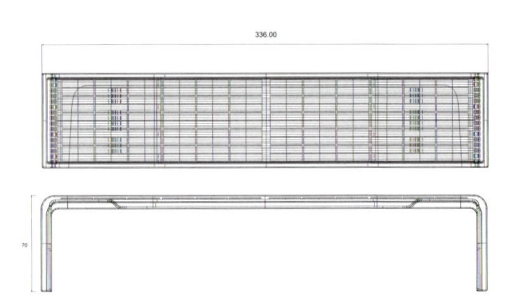

↖ | Solar benches
↑↑ | Variations in colors
↑ | Detail, Wi-Fi spot
↓ | Plan

Foreign Office Architects
(FOA) / Farshid Moussavi,
Alejandro Zaera-Polo

261

↑↑ | Row of seats
↑ | In use
↑ | Single element

cuc

The bench cuc can be constructed at any desired length by assembling the modular elements in a row. The curved silhouette of the seating area is convexly/concavely interlinked, also enabling a change of adirection within the row. cuc was designed for the Parc dels Auditoris de Barcelona as part of the Forum de les Cultures Barcelona 2004. The individual concrete elements, weighing 229 kilos each, are available in light grey or sand yellow.

PROJECT FACTS
Manufacturer: mago:group. **Client:** Barcelona Park. **Completion:** 2005. **Production:** serial production. **Design:** individual design. **Functions:** seating. **Main materials:** concrete.

SEATING

Nea Studio /
Nina Edwards Anker

↑ | Bird bed in use
↘ | Plan and section

→ | Bed of alminum wings, different versions

Bird Bed

The Bird Bed, a piece from the Arctic Furniture Line, is a daybed for two. Its durable surfaces make it ideal for relaxing in urban streets and parks. The daybed flexes comfortably under the body's weight. Its profile resembles a bird in flight whose 'wings' carry the user so that he seems to be hovering in mid-air. There are two different versions of the seating object available. The garden version is dug into the ground (preferably medium hard soil or a sidewalk), while the version with a base can be bolted into the ground. Fabricated of 2.5 millimeter-thick high gloss painted aluminum, it appears slender and light.

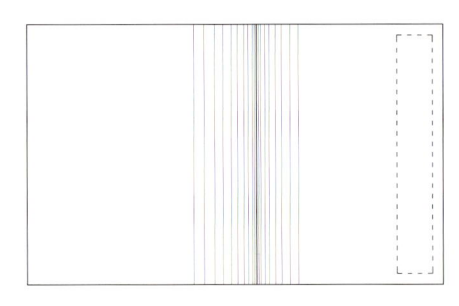

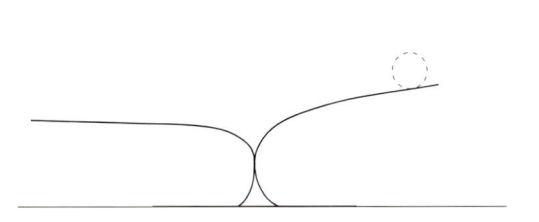

PROJECT FACTS   **Client:** private. **Completion:** 2006. **Production:** serial production. **Design:** product line. **Functions:** seating. **Main materials:** aluminum.

SEATING | Architektin Mag. arch. Silja Tillner

↑ | **Park bench "Swinger"** in the city of Vienna

Park Bench Swinger

The bench "Swinger" was developed as part of the revitalization of the Gürtel ring road of Vienna. Its dynamically curves correspond to the new spirit and image of the central ring road area, while its ergonomic shape invites passers-by to sit down and relax. The battens of its ergonomically rounded back and seat are made of cedar wood, while the basic frame is made of flat bar steel. Whether standing on its own or as part of a group, the bench is a wonderful addition to the appearance of the city. Its mix of esthetics and sturdiness makes it an ideal city furniture item.

PROJECT FACTS **Client:** City of Vienna. **Completion:** 1998. **Production:** serial production. **Design:** individual design. **Functions:** seating. **Main materials:** wood, steel.

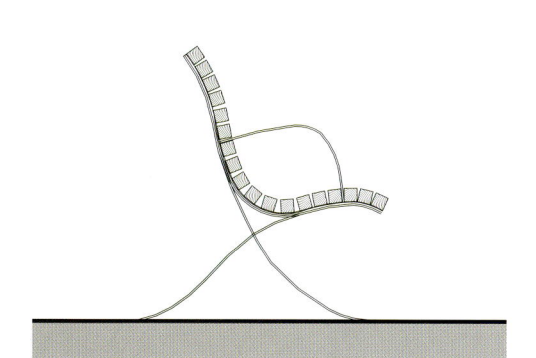

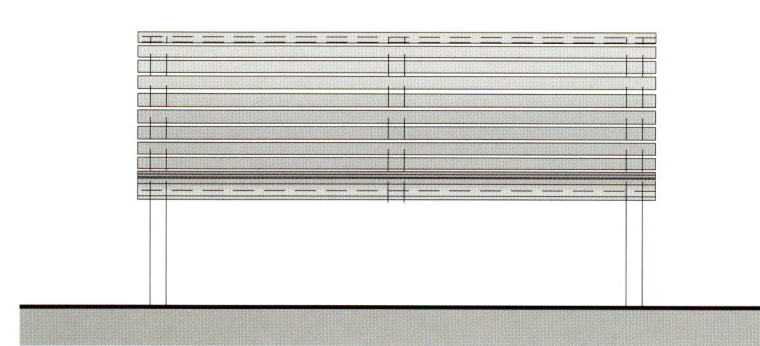

↑ | Elevations
↓ | Close-up view

↑ | Delicate and simple form

SEATING

Caesarea Landscape
Design Ltd.

↖ | Side elevation
↑↑ | Perspective
↑ | Detail

Bench Castle 717

The bench with an elegant and unique look fits into a dynamic context. Legs and arm rests are made of high-quality cast iron GGG-40 in the colors gray, black and blue. Eight boards available in different kinds of wood connect the cast-iron sides. It is available in various sizes: 1.40, 1.10 or 0.70 meters.

PROJECT FACTS
Client: Park in Ceasaria. **Completion:** 2010. **Production:** serial production. **Design:** product line. **Functions:** seating. **Main materials:** cast iron, wooden beams.

Diego Fortunato

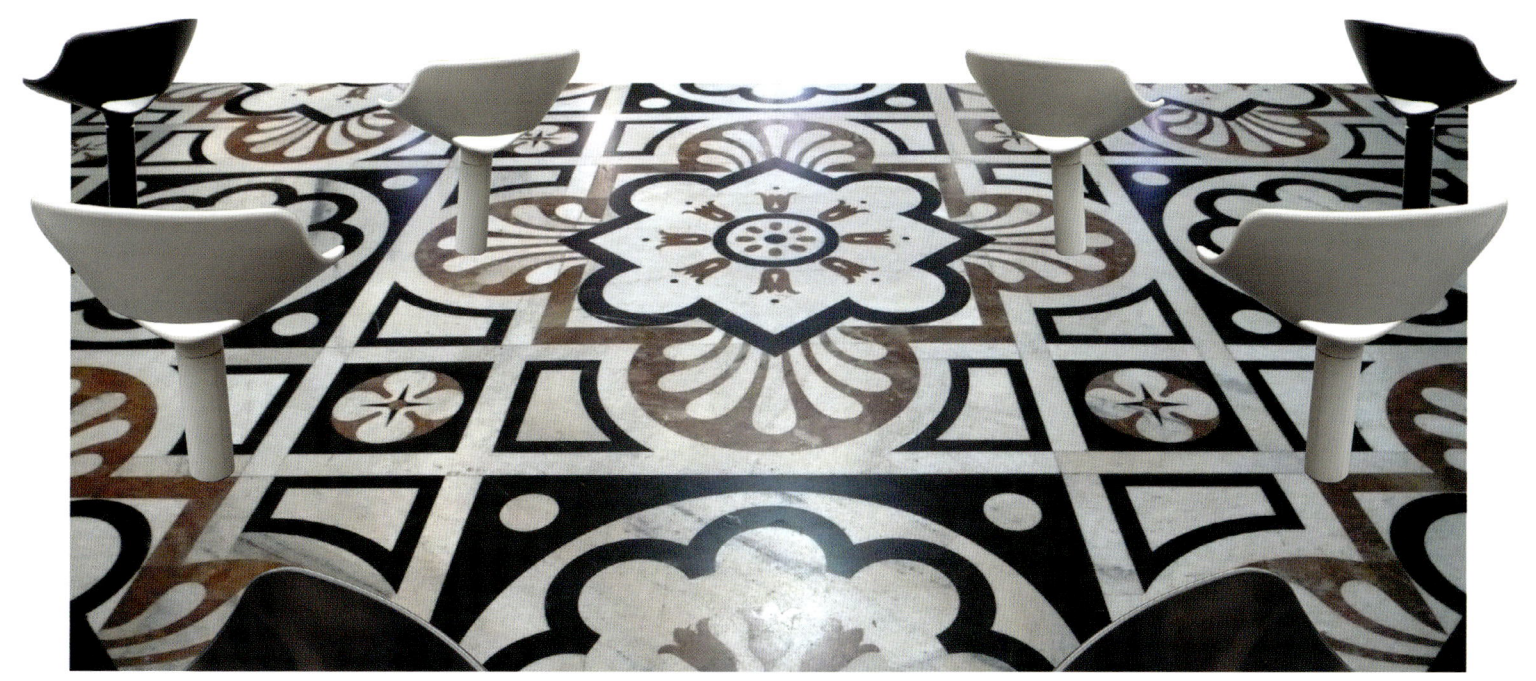

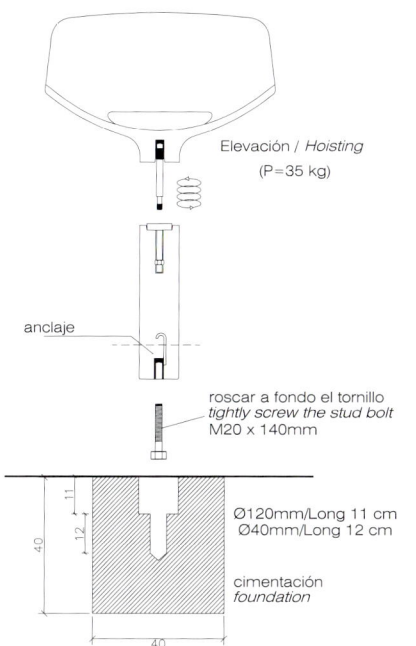

↑↑ | **Urban chair SOL**
↑ | **Plan,** seat
↗ | **Garbage can NET,** in combination with chair SOL

SOL and NET

SOL consists of a 35-kg chair made of UHPC, high performance concrete. The seat bucket is placed on a single narrow tube structure, which is bolted to the ground. It has has a mechanism that allows the chair to turn arround like an office chair. Available in black and white, it is acid treated and water repellant. The waste basket/ashtray NET with the same surface structure is made of reinforced cast stone.

PROJECT FACTS
Client: ESCOFET 1886. **Completion:** 2005. **Production:** serial production. **Design:** product line. **Functions:** seating, garbage can. **Main materials:** polymer concrete (chair), reinforced cast stone (garbage can).

SEATING

Caesarea Landscape
Design Ltd.

Benches Martelo

↖↖ | **Bench Martelo 791** and garbage can Caesarion 958BM
↑↑ | **Benches Martelo 792**
↖ | **Benches Martelo 791**
↑ | **Bench Martelo 746**

The modern-looking, smooth-lined metal bench and the wavy, comfortable bench without back support have a square seat perforation pattern. It is galvanized and enameled in pure polyester and matches the RAL color key. Available in different combinations, the different options include anchoring to the pavement, rubber footings, and solid cement legs with a rough texture in white or gray as well as handles.

PROJECT FACTS
Client: Gold Internet, municipality of Afula, shopping center in Carmiel. **Completion:** 2008. **Production:** serial production. **Design:** product line. **Functions:** seating. **Main materials:** perforated metal, decorated stone base in different shades.

Estudio Cabeza /
Diana Cabeza

↑ | **Sets of tables and seats**
↗↗ | **Table,** with chess board
↗ | **Sets and singel seats**

Alfil Set

The built-in chess board is ideal for parks and other recreational areas where users can indulge in games, such as chess, checkers, cards, etc. Its color combination renders this pre-cast reinforced unit flexible applicable for a number of different uses and context options while requiring very little maintenance. Embedding bases are included to cater for two, three or four seats. Without the base, the elements can be embedded into in-situ built-in concrete. When an adequate base is provided they can also be embedded into the ground on a suitable substratum.

PROJECT FACTS
Development team: Diana Cabeza, Mario Celi, Diego Jarczak. **Client:** public and private clients. **Completion:** 2000. **Production:** serial production. **Design:** product line. **Functions:** Set of table and seats, drinking fountain. **Main materials:** precast reinforced concrete with black color aggregate, natural finishing.

SEATING | West 8 urban design & landscape architecture

↑ | **Timber seat at Lippensplein**, Knokke, Belgium, 2006

West 8 Timber Seat

Today, 20 years after the long linear timber seat was constructed on the Schouwburgplein in Rotterdam, the bench concept as an outdoor meeting place continues to be a success. The monumentality of the seat relates well to the scale of its environment, while its welcoming character invites passersby to linger. Ergonomically, it provides comfort and protection. The design principles have stood 'the test of time' and are now eagerly copied by manufacturers of street furniture. The specific form and the scale of seat and backrest constitute the basis of a family of benches, regularly used in other West 8 projects. They are all remarkable outdoor objects and readily relate to their varying contexts.

PROJECT FACTS

271

Client: different governmental and private organizations. **Completion:** first version 1993. **Production:** serial production. **Design:** product line. **Functions:** seating. **Main materials:** wood, steel.

↑ | **Long linear Timber seat at Schouwburgplein,** Rotterdam, The Netherlands, 1993
↓ | **Timber seat at Leidsche Rijn Park,** The Netherlands, 1993

↑ | **Timber seat at Neude,** Utrecht, The Netherlands, 1998

SEATING | West 8 urban design & landscape architecture

↑ | **Swirl-bench,** Library University of Utrecht

West 8 Swirl Bench

Swirl-bench's generous circular shape, made up of different segments, can be easily placed in a variety of locations. Due to its size it can accommodate quite a few people at once. The hole in the middle allows people to sit down facing either inwards or outwards, providing either a little intimacy or the possibility to turn away from the others and take in the surroundings. The seat is relatively low and wide and therefore comfortable to sit on. The bench's "belly buttons" act as little drainage holes. Each segment is made out of two cast parts that are joined together and that are available in various colors and textures. In addition to the donut shape, other configurations are also possible.

PROJECT FACTS

Client: various. **Completion:** first version 2005. **Production:** serial production. **Design:** set of parts. **Functions:** Seating. **Main materials:** polyester concrete.

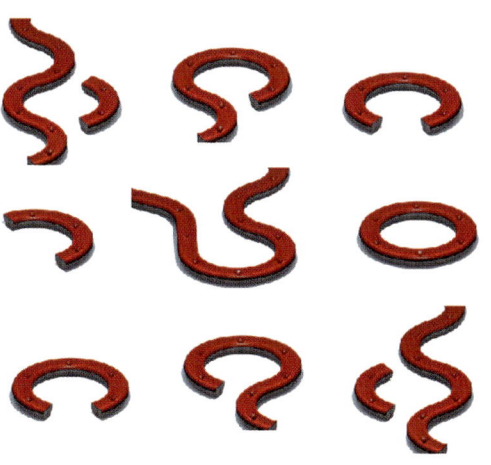

273

↑ | **Segment of swirl-bench,** different configuration
↓ | **Artits Impression Swirl-bench,** Library University of Utrecht

↑↑ | **Swirl-bench in Luxury village,** Moscow, 1995
↑ | **Different configurations**

SEATING | ASPECT Studios (Sydney Office)

↑ | **Robust park bench** of timber and concrete

Benches at Pirrama Park

Sydney, NSW

The brief for the Pirrama Park was to develop a new public park for a post-industrial piece of land on the Pyrmont peninsula. The prime location of the site on Sydney's waterfront offered the opportunity to create a memorable public park area for local residents and the wider community. The brief also required appropriately scaled community facilities and public realm elements including shade canopies, benches, a kiosk and toilets to be included within the design. The custom-designed benches are part of a suite of furniture designed for the site. The bench features recycled timber as the seat and backrest, fixed to a solid but elegant piece of concrete that wraps around to become a 'mat' for the users' feet.

PROJECT FACTS **Address:** Pirrama Rd, Pyrmont, Sydney NSW 2009, Australia. **Planning partner:** Hill Thalis Architecture, Urban Projects, CAB Consulting. **Client:** City of Sydney Council. **Completion:** 2009. **Production:** single piece. **Design:** individual design. **Functions:** seating. **Main materials:** concrete, timber.

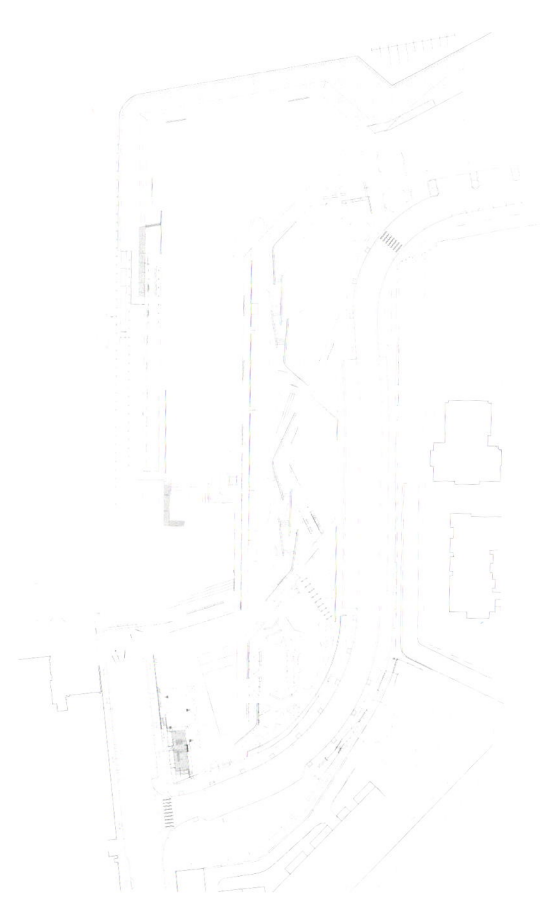

↑ | Site plan of Pirrama Park
↓ | View at twilight

↑ | Side perspective

SEATING | Zaha Hadid Architects

↑ | General view

Wirl

Hong Kong

Wirl is a typical piece of art that functions as street furniture. It was conceived to reflect the intensity of a hyper-acceleratory force within an elastic tactile form. As the curvature of the surface dynamically and seamlessly twists and turns, dynamic form and functional furnishings are seamlessly integrated. Swells provide areas for seating while stretches in the form furnish opportunities to recline. A generous upward sweep provides shade and frames present views of the surroundings. Different-sized voids allow for a variety of experiential possibilities of entering into and interacting with the sculpture for visitors of all sizes, who are always surrounded by a cloud of swirling forces lifting off the ground.

PROJECT FACTS **Address:** City Art Square, 1 Yuen Wo Road, Sha Tin, N.T. Hong Kong, China. **Planning partner:** Patrik Schumacher. **Client:** Sun Hung Kai Properties Ltd. **Completion:** 2008. **Production:** single piece. **Design:** individual design. **Functions:** seating, sculpture. **Main materials:** EPS foam reinforced with fiberglass shell.

↑ | **Sculpture,** usable as a bench
↓ | **Side view,** center part

↑ | **Back side**

SEATING

Broadbent / Stephen Broadbent

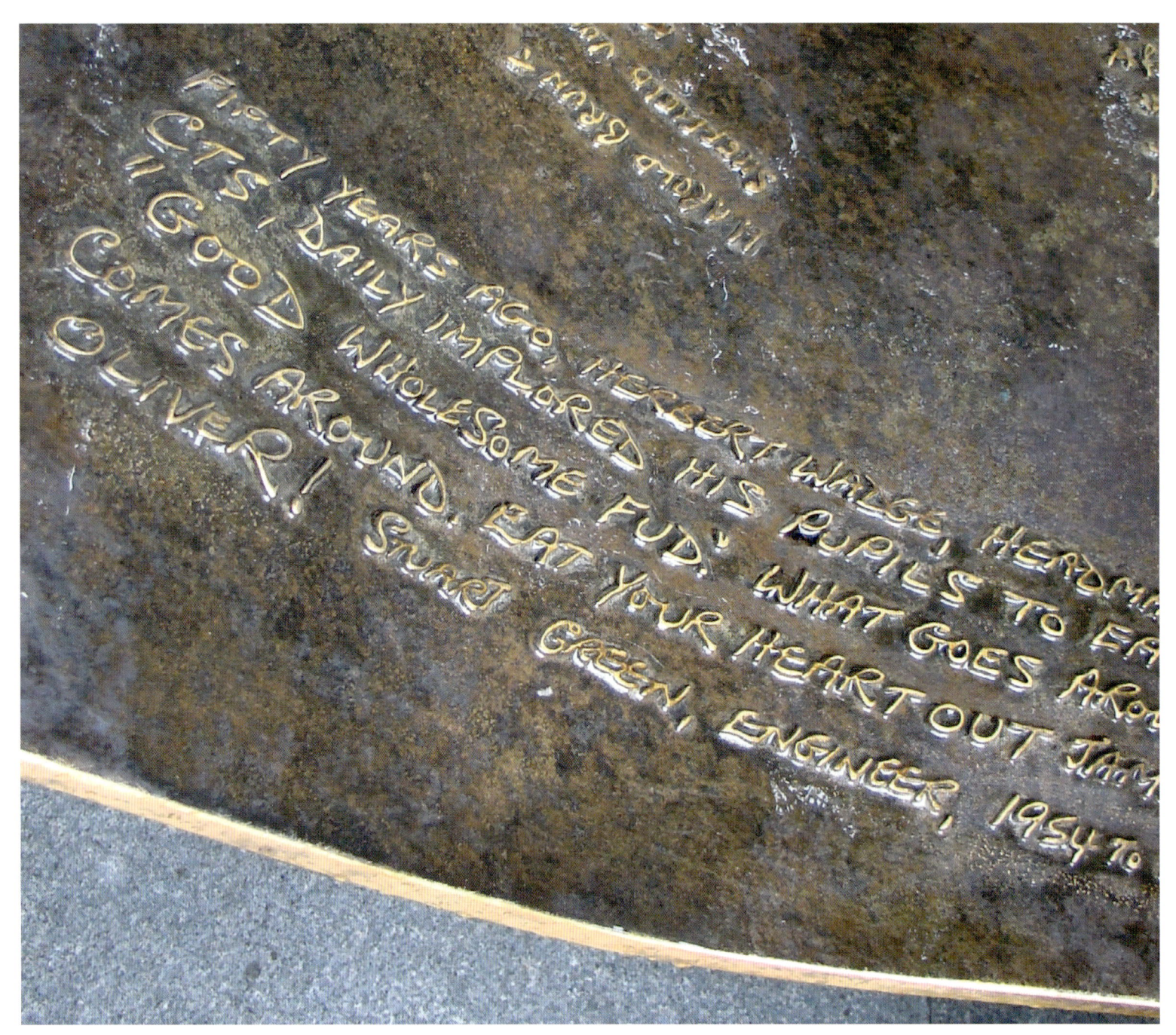

↑ | Detail of typography

Leopold Square
Sheffield

A stunning collection of grade II landmarked Victorian school buildings in Sheffield, England, were carefully renovated and contemporary new buildings added to this mixed-use development, with a new public square at its heart. Broadbent was commissioned through the landscape architects Planit-ie to produce sculptural seating units for the public square, which would celebrate some of the life and history of the old Sheffield Central School. Broadbent engaged former pupils who provided personal memories, either as written statements or drawings. These were modeled and cast into the bronze seating units.

PROJECT FACTS

Address: Leopold Square, Sheffield S1 1RG, United Kingdom. **Landscape Architects:** Planit-ie. **Client:** Ask Property Developments. **Completion:** 2007. **Production:** single piece. **Design:** individual design. **Functions:** seating. **Main materials:** bronze.

↑ | Graffiti proposal
↓ | Leopold seats and fountain

↑ | Overview of Leopold Square and seats

SEATING | Street and Garden Furniture Company / Surya Graf

↑ | **View at sunrise,** showing the right bench
↓ | **Plan**

The Wave
Alexandra Headland

While having an obvious function, the brief for the Wave bench was to be a focal point along the boardwalk while fitting harmoniously into the foreshore landscape. The design took direct inspiration from its coastal location, reflecting many aspects of this environment and lifestyle. The overall form, the shaping details in the timber, and the curved metal leg details are all references to aspects of the ocean. In addition, the design allows various users to individually decide how they wish to use the seat. Relying on CAD technology to produce a quality product in a quick and cost effective manner, the design uses timber and metal components, which are durable and easy to maintain.

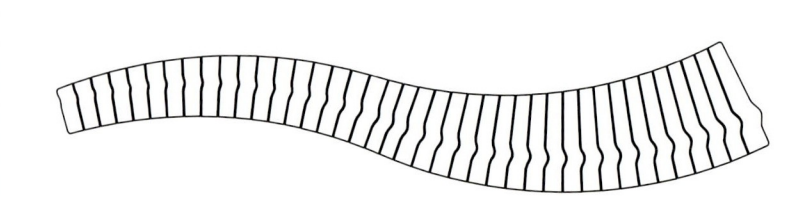

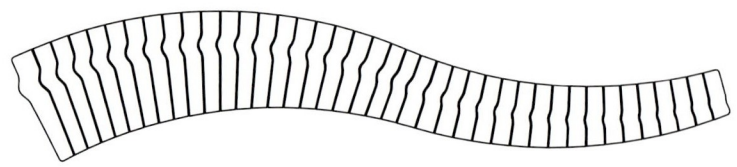

PROJECT FACTS **Address:** Pinch Point, Alexandra Headland, QLD, Australia. **Client:** Sunshine Coast Regional Council. **Completion:** 2007. **Production:** single piece. **Design:** individual design. **Functions:** seating. **Main materials:** timber, steel.

↑ | Timber shaping detail
↓ | **The Wave** at Boardwalk Lookout

↑ | Steel leg and curved framing

SEATING | Street and Garden Furniture Company /
Miranda Lockhart

↑ | **View of the bench** against sunset

Mollymook
Mollymook Beach

Aspects of the coastal location along with functional considerations became the key elements used to develop the Mollymook designs. The platform seats allow for a variety of seating positions for users to enjoy views, breezes and the sun as conditions change throughout the day. The laser-cut pattern details in the steel backrests resemble the shapes left by wave action in sand. This effect is enhanced by the back to back seating arrangement, which plays with light and shadow effects that change according to the viewers' position. Just as wave action continually changes patterns in the sand, this sense of change is emphasized with the movement of the sun creating shadow effects when light passes through the pattern.

PROJECT FACTS **Address:** Mollymook Beach, Mollymook, NSW 2539, Australia. **Client:** Shoalhaven City Council. **Completion:** 2006. **Production:** serial production. **Design:** product line. **Functions:** seating. **Main materials:** stainless steel, timber wood.

↑ | **Reflections and patterns** in the backrest
↓ | **Elevations**

↓ | **Backrest detail**

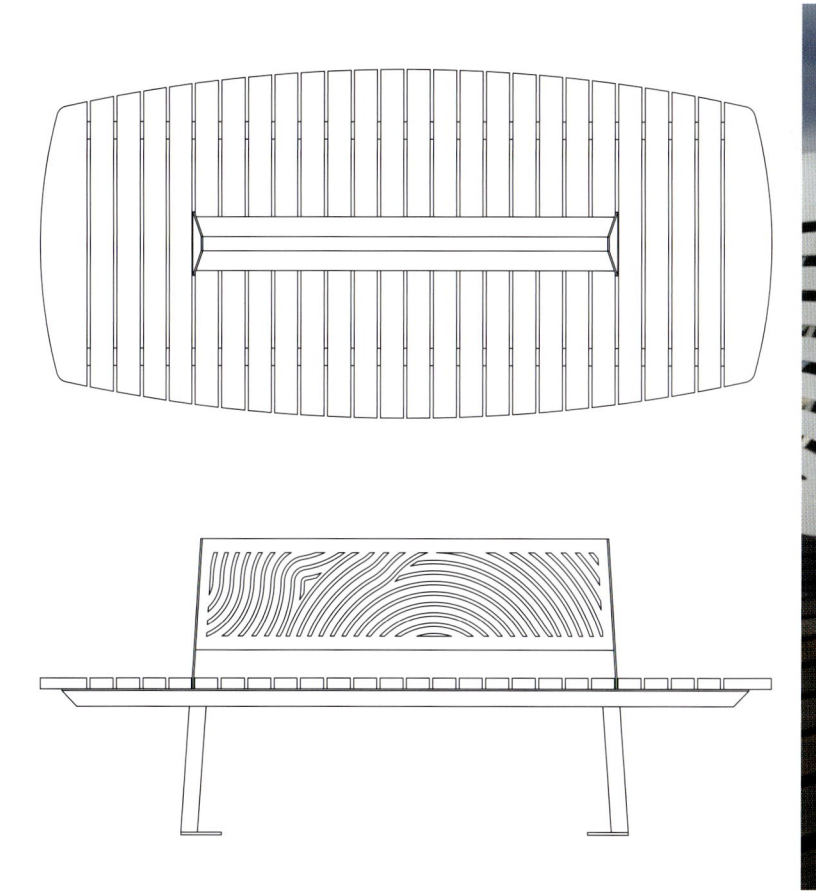

SEATING | Street and Garden Furniture Company / Alexander Lotersztain

↑ | **The Twig**, robust and appealing

Twig
Brisbane

Twig is a modular seating system designed for public spaces that encourages diversification and interaction among people. The single component modular design allows for a variety of positional combinations, and the creation of "conversation pockets" throughout the chosen landscape. The design is extremely robust and easily maintained, which makes it well suited to high-wear outdoor environments. While the Twig is manufactured from precast concrete, the roundness of the form suggests a visual softness. Twig is a very sculptural element that blurs the boundaries between the built form and external space, and suggests new ways of formal and informal outdoor living.

PROJECT FACTS

Address: Southbank Institute of Technology, 66 Ernest Street, South Brisbane, QLD 4101, Australia. **Client:** Southbank Institute of Technology, Cox Rayner Architects, Gamble McKinnon Green Landscape Architects. **Distribution:** Street and Garden Furniture (North America, Oceania), Escofet (EU, middle East, Asia). **Completion:** 2007. **Production:** serial production. **Design:** individual design. **Functions:** seating, plant tub. **Main materials:** concrete.

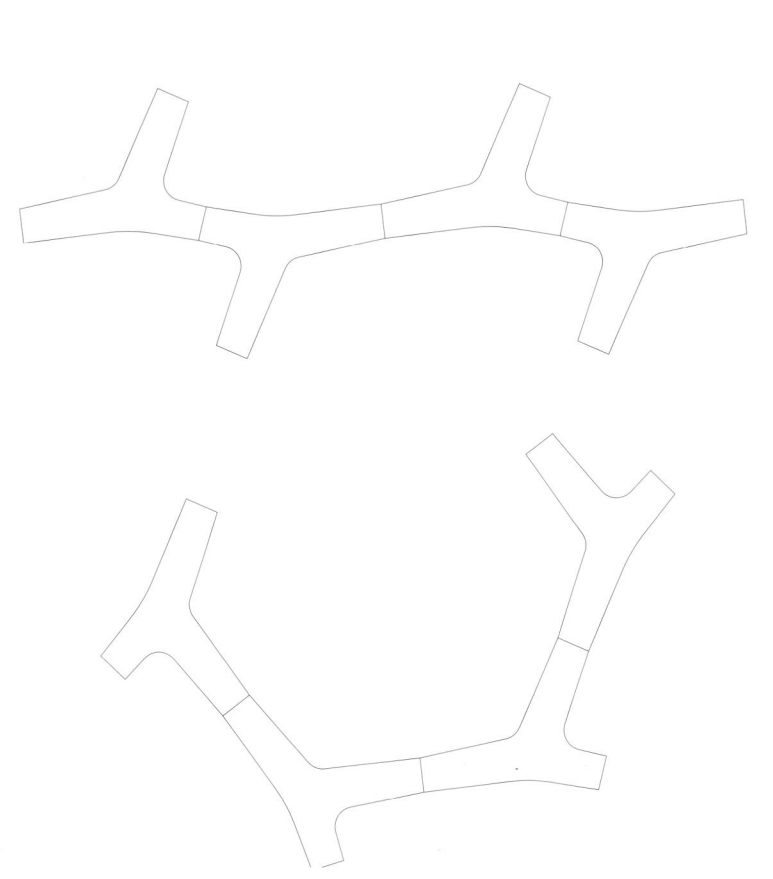

↑ | **Possible layout plans**
↓ | **Double function** as planter and seating unit

↑ | **Detail view**

SEATING | Michel Dallaire Design Industriel – MDDI

↑ | **Seating,** view from back

QIM
Montreal

The main objective of this project was to design a complete family of urban furniture that clearly identifies, distinguishes and valorizes the Quartier international de Montreal. Advanced material technologies were used, with aluminum as the MDDI material in a variety of transformation processes, such as extrusion, sand-casting, pressurizing, die-casting, and numerical machining. The thematic visual vocabulary was inspired by the contrast of the circle with the absolute vertical rectitude. The project includes a variety of elements – tandem lighting fixtures and posts, street and park benches, bicycle holders, trash-bins, road sign supports, and special hardware components.

PROJECT FACTS **Address:** Daoust Lestage Inc, 3575 St Laurent, Montreal, QC H2X 2T7, Canada. **Client:** QIM. **Completion:** 2003. **Production:** serial production. **Design:** individual design. **Functions:** seating, illumination, bicycle stand, garbage can, signs. **Main materials:** aluminum, IPE wood.

↑ | **Seating,** side view
↓ | **Seatings,** overview

↑ | **Seating backside,** lamp and garbage can

SEATING | Lucile Soufflet

↑ | **Soft Bench**, view from above
↗ | **Sketch**
→ | **Soft Bench**, with undulating seat

Soft Bench

Soft Bench is a street object with a familiar line which suddenly undulates and twists to offer flexible and relaxed seating on a half of its length. Used for seating in the classical position or for a casual horizontal position, its design allows users to take the time to enter into the object and its functionalities. It raises the issue of public and private spaces, in the shape of appropriate urban furniture that allows relaxing and contemplating the space and the landscape. Its simple but unusual form and its delicate frame constitute the special character of this bench.

PROJECT FACTS **Planning partner:** TF France. **Client:** TF France. **Completion:** 2008. **Production:** serial production. **Design:** individual design. **Functions:** seating. **Main materials:** steel.

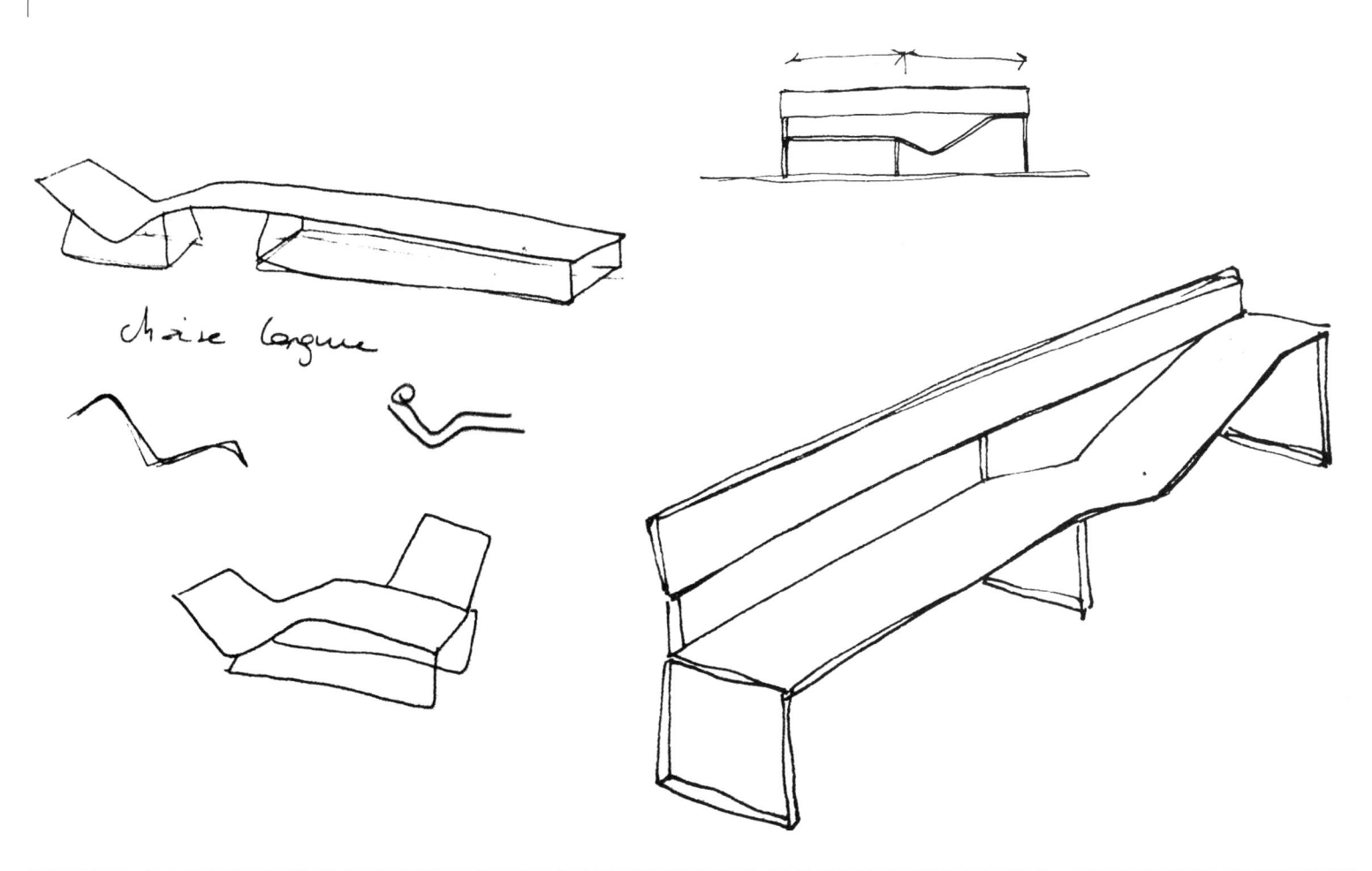

289

SEATING | Lucile Soufflet

↑ | **Circular benches** on Grand Place, Mons
↘ | **Sections** of different parts of the bench

Bancs Circulaires

The first bench was commissioned by the Brussels city council in 2003 for a little square in the center of Brussels. The city council required a metallic railing around a tree in the middle of the square that could also function as a bench. The designer proposed to enlarge the railing and simply to maintain the theme of sitting around a tree. This bench unfolds in a circle, extends itself and returns around the tree. Part of the concept was to play with the making process and produce a circular shaped element in the bench. At each end, the profiles gradually deform themselves and back rests slowly appear to create seats facing each other. Different models of the bench based on the same principle were created later.

PROJECT FACTS **Client:** Cities of Brussels, Mons, Luxembourg. **Completion:** 2003. **Production:** single piece. **Design:** individual design. **Functions:** seating. **Main materials:** steel.

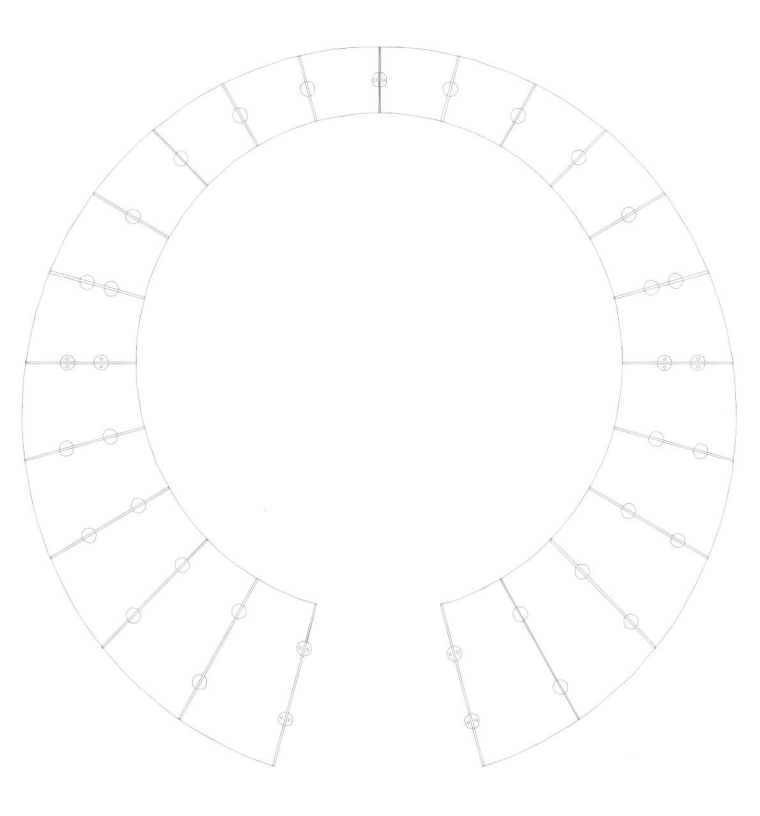

↑ | **Plan**
↓ | **Grand Place**, different perspective

↑ | **Different arrangement** of the bench

SEATING

Jangir Maddadi
Design Bureau AB

↑ | **Union Bench 8-seater** with plant tub
↘ | **Plans**

Union Bench Collection

Designer Jangir Maddadi knew that to create a piece of public furniture would require a study of the public itself. After three years of intensive research into seating behavior, Maddadi melted the need for individualism and the desire for social contact in a product that heralds a revolution in the traditional street bench by changing its physicality altogether. The subtle simplicity of this piece of urban furniture constitutes an elegant contrast to the robust concrete and wood construction. The island-like arrangement of up to three semi-spherical seats gives users a 360-degree view no matter where they choose to sit. A widespread seating area creates comfort when sharing the bench with strangers or friends.

| **PROJECT FACTS**
Completion: ongoing. **Production:** serial production. **Design:** product line. **Functions:** seating, plant tub. **Main materials:** concrete, wood.

↑ | **The black collection,** scattered on a public square
↓ | **12-seater**, in orthogonal arrangement

↑ | **12-seater,** arranged around a tree

SEATING | Benjamin Mills

↑ | **Tree Guard Bench,** seating position at daytime
↘ | **Day to night transformation**

Tree Guard Bench

Tree Guard Bench is designed to provide both tree protection as well as an elegant seating solution. The unexpected appeal of the design lies in its ability to transform. Tree Guard Bench is intended to change intuitively with the needs of the space in which it occupies, seamlessly shifting form to coincide with the rising and setting of the sun. This provides extra tree protection at night and enhances the use of its surroundings in the day. The role of street furniture is considered in a holistic manner here, resulting in a mesmerizing and sculptural design that aims to challenge our perceptions of how public seating should look and perform.

PROJECT FACTS **Completion:** 2009. **Production:** single piece. **Design:** individual design. **Functions:** seating, tree guard. **Main materials:** aluminum.

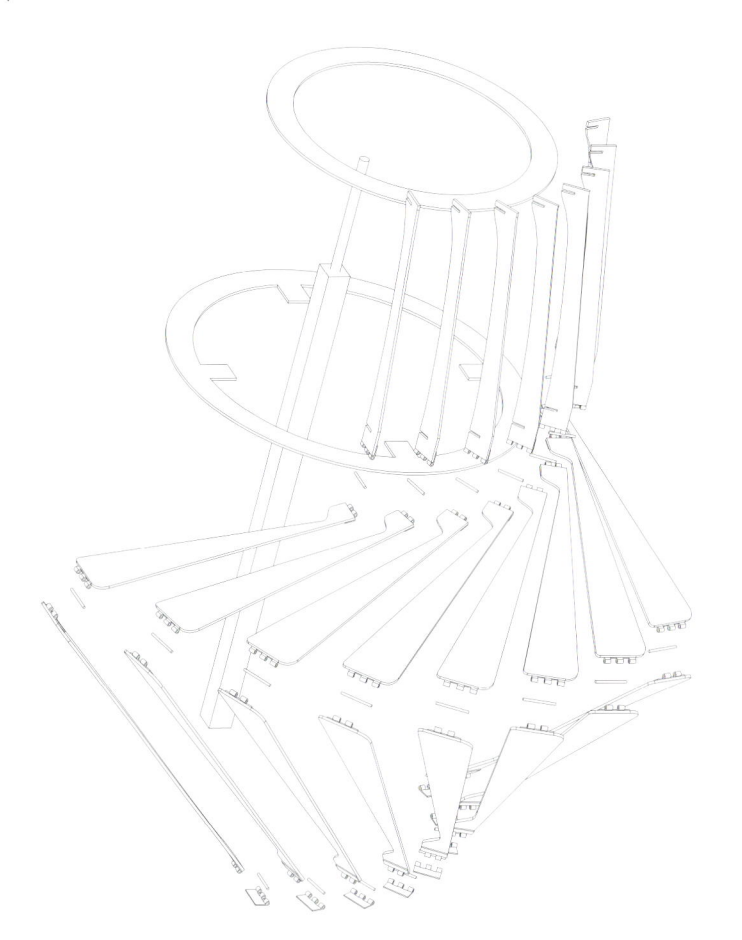

295

↑ | **Exploded section**
↓ | **Transformation sequence**

↑ | **Tree Guard Bench** in a public square

SEATING | díez+díez diseño

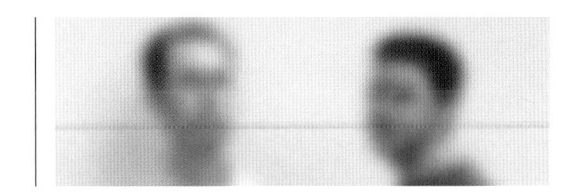

↑ | **Elevation,** robust concrete bench

Pleamar Bench

The idea of this bench model was inspired by a rock, for recovering of "the natural" in the urban environment. It combines the heavy charateristic of rock with a fluid pattern in the surface – bringing two different elements together in one body. The bench has a modular structure and consists of two main elements. The first element is straight, measuring two meters in length and 80 centimeters in width. The second element is curved and covers 45 degrees. In combining both elements the most different bench forms can be arranged – from circular via curved to linear compositions. The single elements weigh approximately 1,500 and 1,000 kilograms. They are placed immediately on the floor.

PROJECT FACTS **Client:** GITMA. **Completion:** 2006. **Production:** serial production. **Design:** individual design. **Functions:** seating. **Main materials:** concrete.

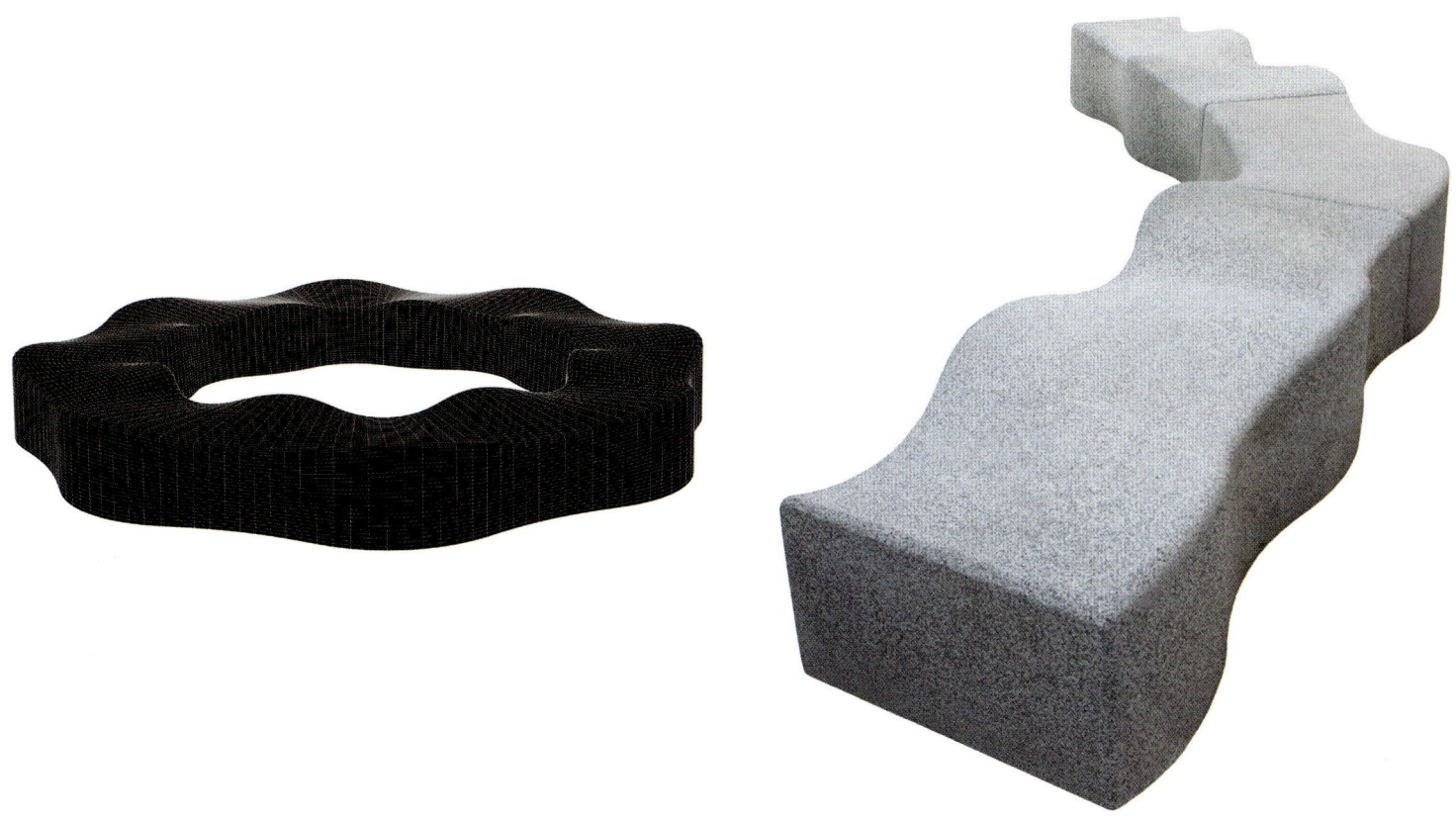

297

↑ | **Scheme,** possible arrangement
↓ | **Modular structure,** the bench can be adjusted to its environment

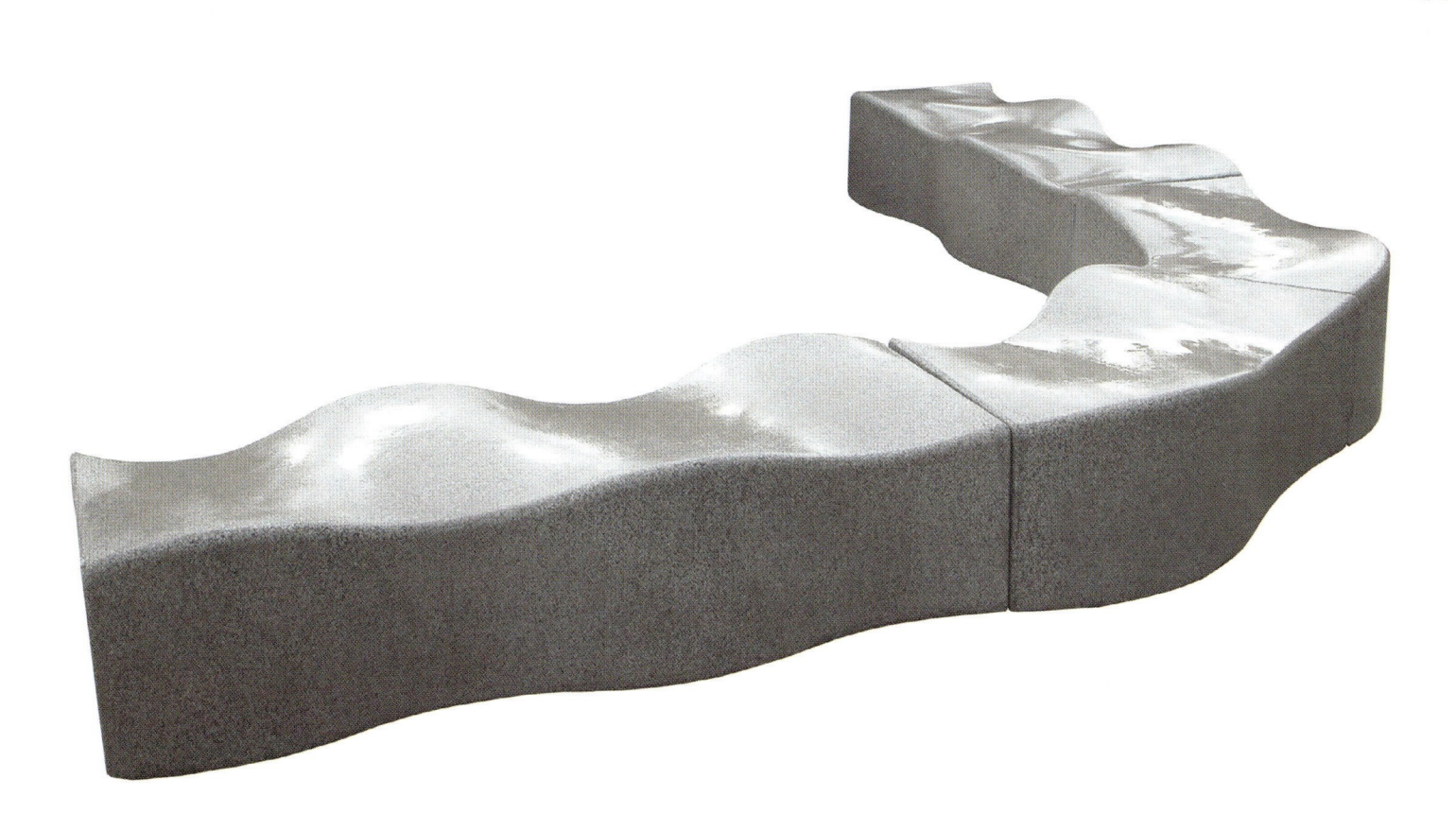

↑ | **Elevation**

SEATING | díez+díez diseño

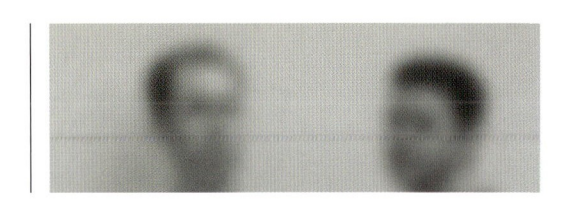

↑ | Long bench

Ponte

Ponte managed to create a precise balance in developing a bench with contemporary forms. Refined with a touch of classicism, it can be easily integrated into areas such as traditional urban centers, historical sites, parks and gardens, where the placing of more innovative concepts would be problematic. Its longitudinal curvature coupled with the downward inclination of the seat that is shaped like a drainage duct facilitates the removal of water trapped in the seating area. As a result, the bank contains areas with seat heights that differ by three centimeters from its middle towards the ends, allowing people with different heights to find their ideal seat.

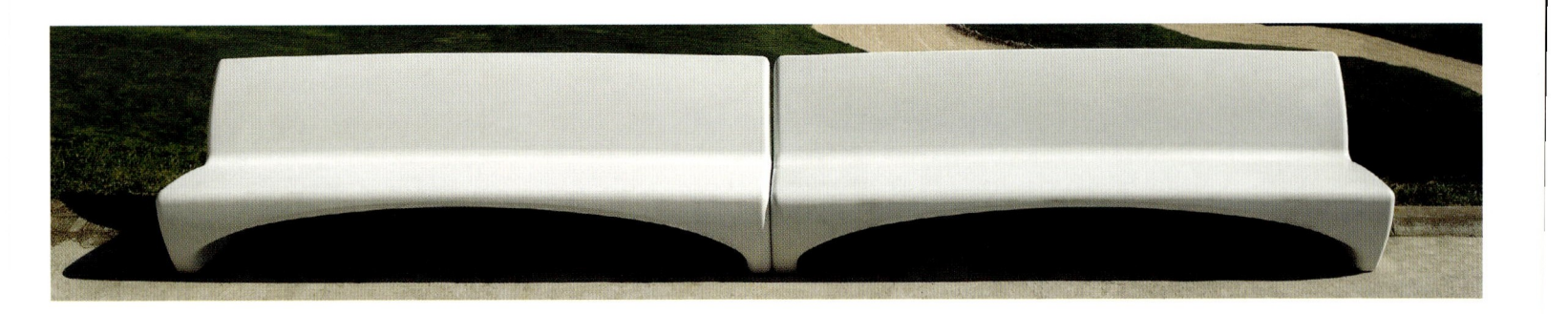

PROJECT FACTS **Client:** Paviments MATA. **Completion:** 2009. **Production:** serial production. **Design:** individual design. **Functions:** seating. **Main materials:** concrete.

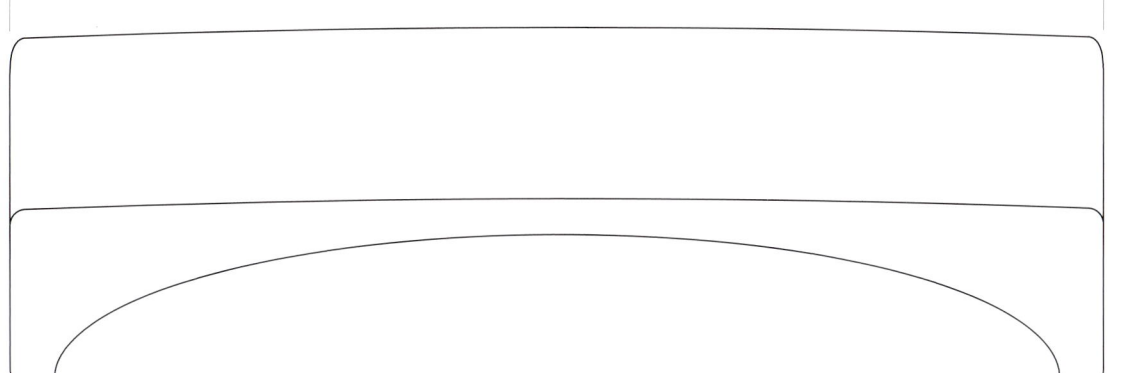

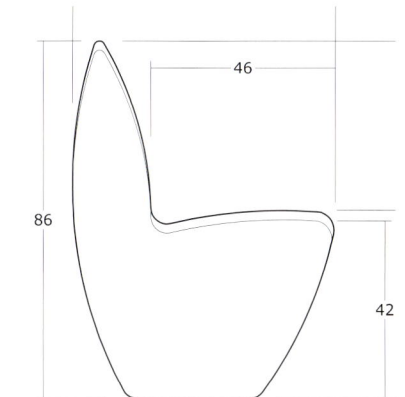

↑↑ | Plan
↑ | Small bench
↙ | Combination of two long benches

↑ | Chairs
↓ | Perspective

SEATING | díez+díez diseño

↑ | Row of concave and convex seats

Dove

The Dove program consists of two seating elements with attachments, one concave and the other convex, and a third flat piece that functions in both of the other two positions. It can be said that Dove is a family of benches with the same genetic profile. These three elements have an incredible versatile composition and can be placed individually or in groups, as well as in curved rectilinear or mixed, opened or closed formations. It is an esthetic element with smooth and pleasant surfaces that invites to stop and rest, to meditate or simply to relax. The elements are made of concrete and can be combined by simply placing them side by side.

PROJECT FACTS

Client: Paviments MATA. **Completion:** 2007. **Production:** serial production. **Design:** individual design. **Functions:** seating. **Main materials:** concrete.

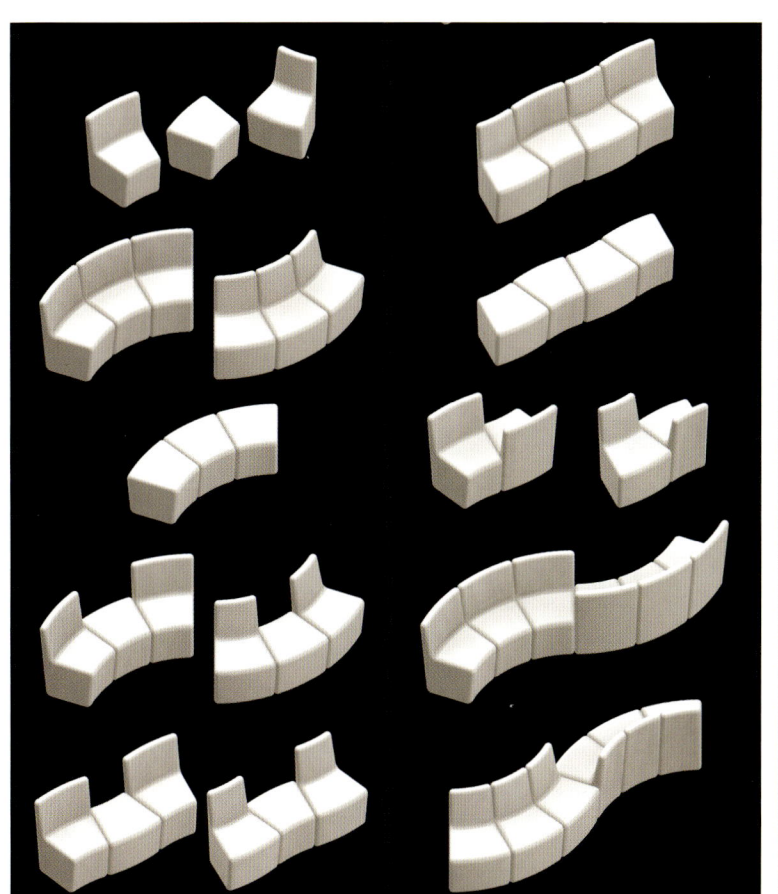

↑ | Placement scheme
↓ | Curve of seats

↑ | Linear composition

SEATING | Diego Fortunato

↑ | **SIT Collection** at Maison de Quartier in Sédan, France

SIT Collection

The SIT Collection is a modular system of concrete seating elements that are special not only in their rounded surfaces but also in the way they are combined. It consists of cubic seating elements of different length that form benches or stools. Backrests of different length can join the seating elements. They are shaped to be simply placed behind the benches or stools and provide a comfortable public seating accommodation. The rounded shape of the bodies not only gives them a beautiful countenance but also prevents the urban furniture from getting soiled, as rainwater can easily drain off.

PROJECT FACTS Client: ESCOFET 1886. **Completion:** 2005. **Production:** serial production. **Design:** product line. **Functions:** seating. **Main materials:** concrete.

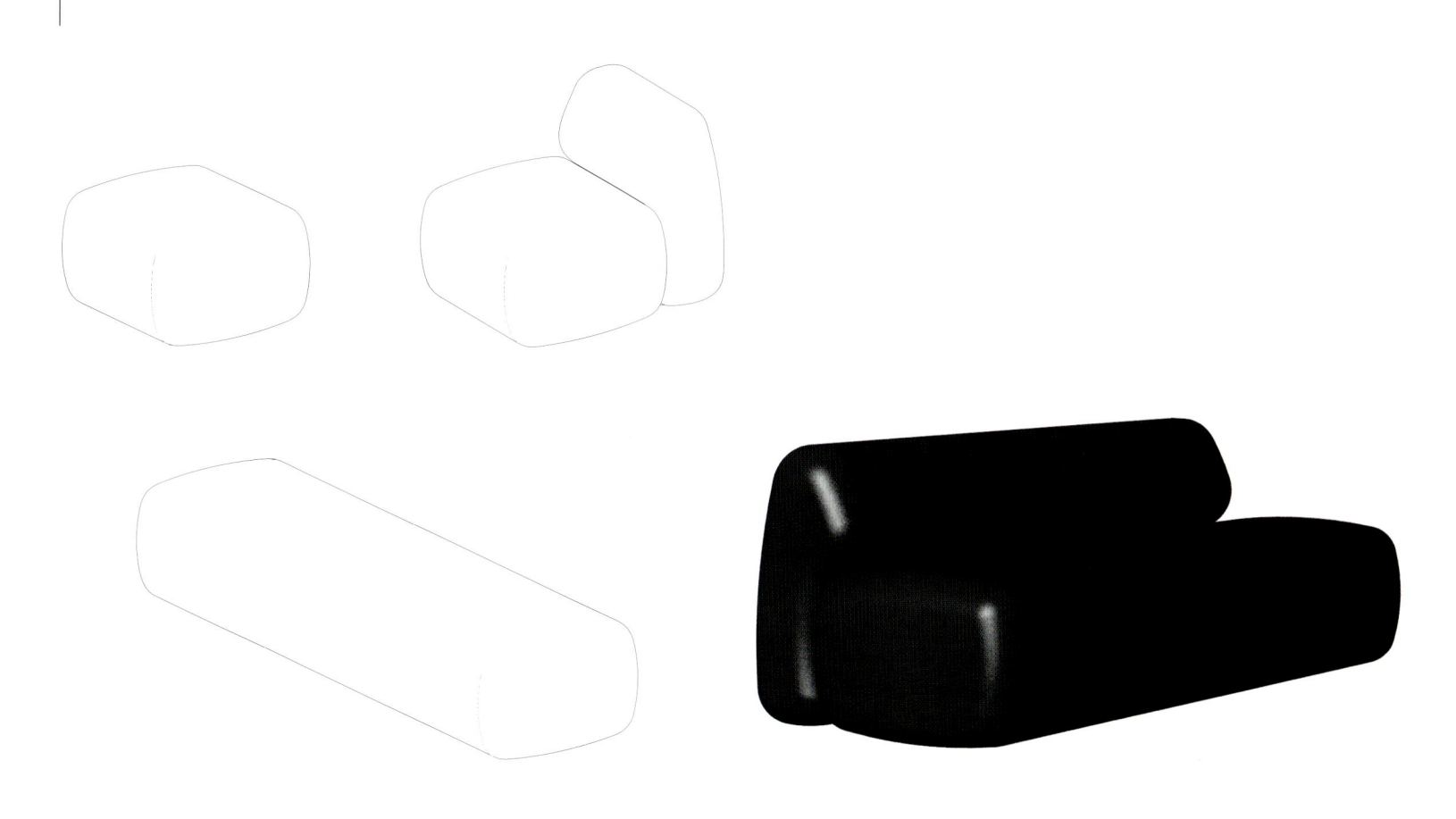

↑ | **Elevations**
↓ | **SIT Collection** in Sant Pere Pescador, Girona

↑ | **Long backrest and bench** in black

SEATING | nahtrang / Ester Pujol, Daniel Vila

↑ | **Bamboo wood stool,** placed indoors
↗ | **Perspective view,** bamboo wood bench and stool
→ | **Bamboo wood bench and stool**

LINK

The LINK bench is an extremely light, urban-style seating element, with a high formal content. Its structure, recalling the essence of the popular classic folding stool, is simple, attractive and balanced, with echoes of the East. A modest little gem whose proportions make it easy to integrate into the environment. LINK's subtlety of form and smart combination of materials – steel and concrete or steel and bamboo wood – make it a balanced element in the urban landscape or for contract furnishing. The series includes the LINK bench, LINK stool, LINK table and LINK wall seat models, all with two seat options, made of concrete or bamboo.

PROJECT FACTS

Client: ESCOFET 1886. Completion: 2009. Production: serial production. Design: product line. Functions: seating. Main materials: steel, concrete, bamboo wood.

305

SEATING   NAHTRANG

↑ | **Frontal view of the set**
← | **Concrete bench and stool,** perspective view

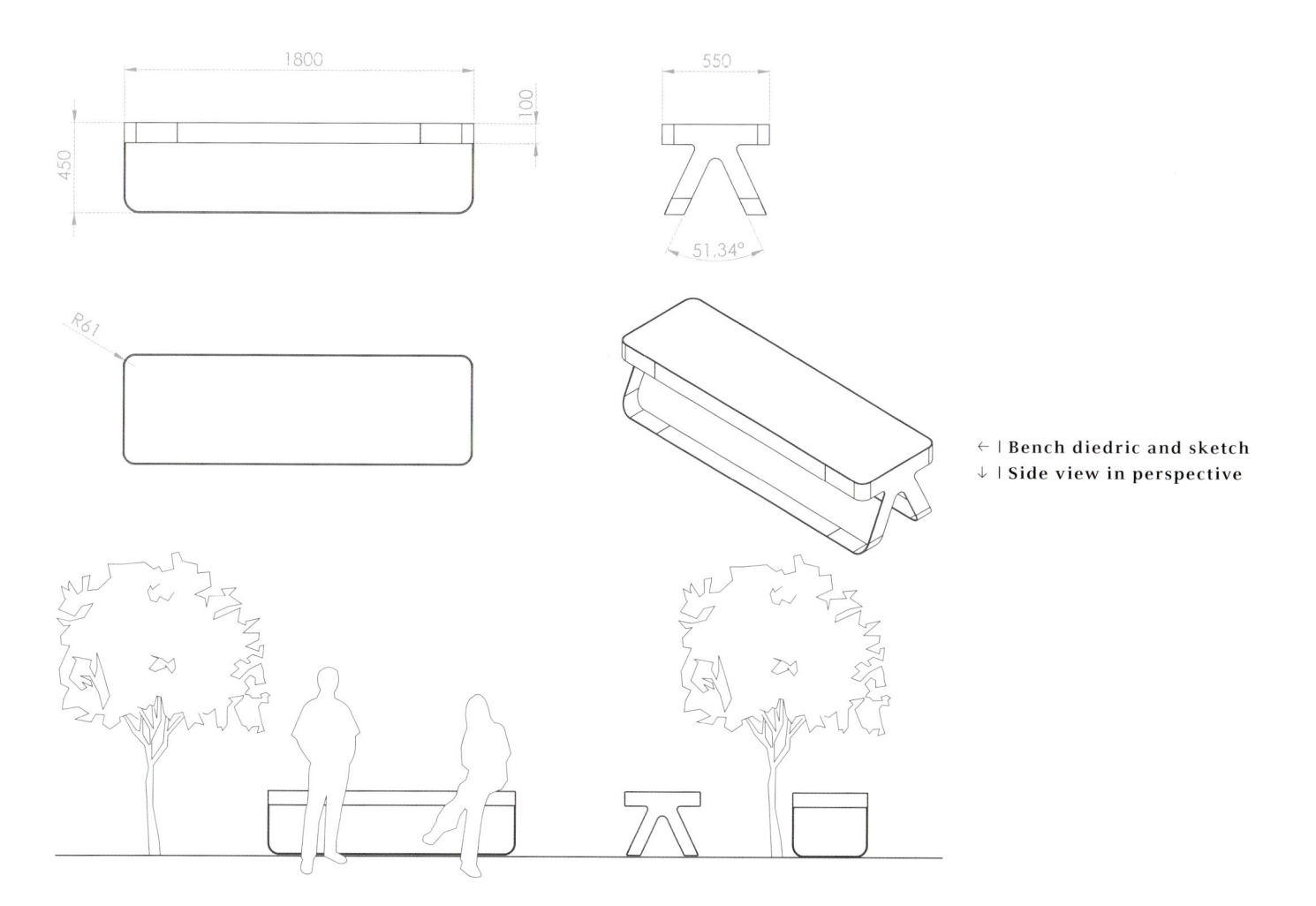

LINK

← | Bench diedric and sketch
↓ | Side view in perspective

SEATING | Juan Carlos Ines Bertolin, Gonzalo Milà Valcárcel

↑ | **Benches,** Forum, Barcelona

SILLARGA / SICURTA

This urban chaise longue is made of steel-reinforced reconstituted stone, which was specifically designed for this project. The object is destined for gardens, promenades, rest areas and parks for comfortable sitting and enjoying the surrounding nature. The ergonomic design features an inclined backrest and slightly inclined leg support. Both of these functions are intended to improve the blood circulation, for example after exercise. Sillarga provides a decent and definitely laid-back way of sitting in public spaces.

PROJECT FACTS

Client: ESCOFET 1886. **Completion:** 1996. **Production:** serial production. **Design:** product line. **Functions:** seating. **Main materials:** steel-reinforced reconstituted stone.

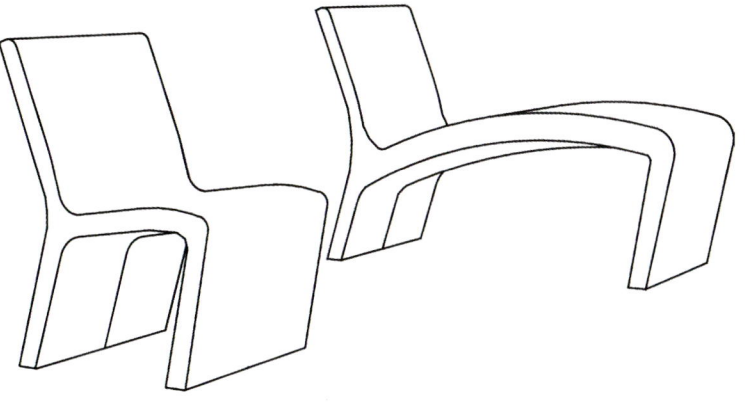

↑ | **La Marbella beach,** Barcelona
↓ | **Barceloneta beach,** Barcelona

↑↑ | **La Marbella beach,** Barcelona
↑ | **Sketch**

SEATING

Street and Park Furniture / Michelle Herbut

↑ | View of Botanic Bench
↘ | Different elevations

Botanic Bench

The Botanic Bench was designed to suit a specific site in South Australia. Inspired by the growth and organic nature of the plants at the Botanical Gardens, the aim was to simulate the bench 'growing' out of the ground and to take advantage of the resulting curve. This adds another possibility to the ways the bench is utilized, by using it as the much sought backrest that nature so often omits. The resulting bench is unique in its appearance, with its round and organic forms it blends harmoniously into the background of a park landscape. The design company of Street and Park Furniture was asked to help the designer with production and manufacturing issues.

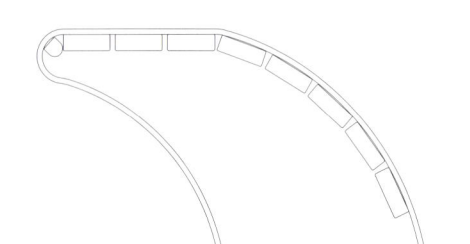

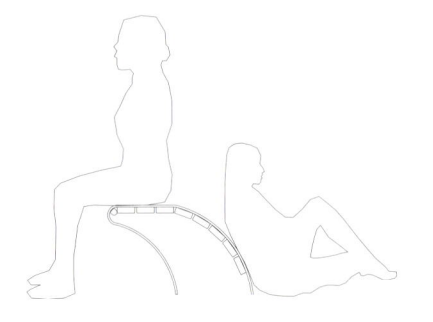

PROJECT FACTS

Client: University Project. **Completion:** 2004. **Production:** single piece. **Design:** individual design. **Functions:** seating. **Main materials:** aluminum, timber, stainless steel.

311

↑ | Deatil view
↓ | Perspective view

SEATING | Street and Park Furniture

↑ | **Seat** with curved supporting frame

Tea Tree Gully Seat
Modbury

The City of Tea Tree Gully is moving forward with dynamic developments. One of these developments was to create a visual impact with a uniquely designed range of street furniture, introducing modern and innovative techniques into local construction and design. Street and Park Furniture worked in collaboration with a design firm to create a range of exciting urban furniture, including seats, tree guards, bins, bollards, fencing and banner poles. The Tea Tree Gully Seat displays an astonishing curved frame structure that creates a light and vivid countenance despite the robustness of the materials.

PROJECT FACTS   **Address:** 571 Montague Road, Modbury, SA 5092, Australia. **Planning partner:** Arketype. **Client:** City of Tea Tree Gully. **Completion:** 2004. **Production:** serial production. **Design:** product line. **Functions:** seating. **Main materials:** hardwood timber, aluminum, galvanized mild steel.

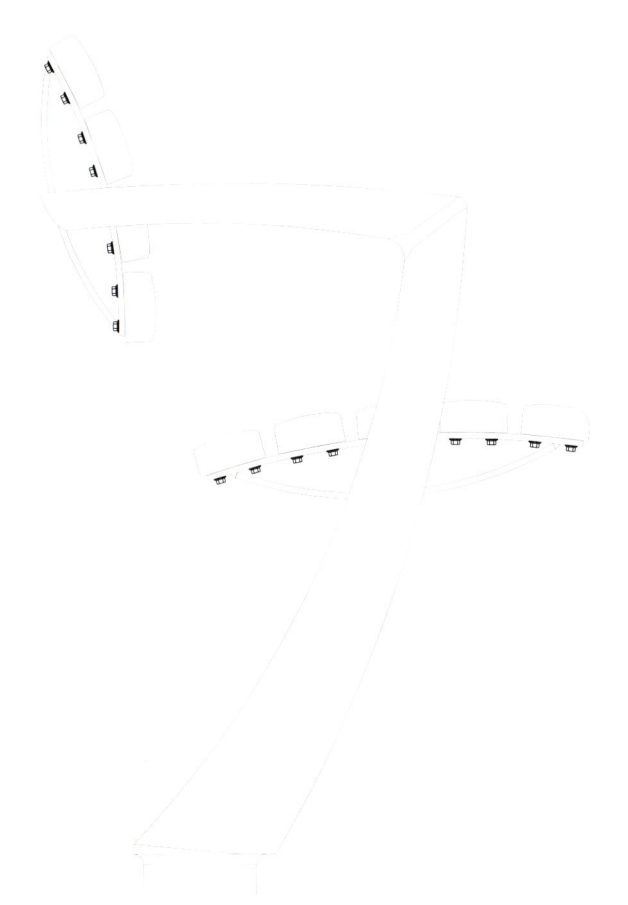

313

↑ | **Side elevation**
↓ | **Front view**

↑ | **Side view** of the seat

SEATING | Baena Casamor Arquitectes BCQ S.L.P. / Toni Casamor, David Baena

↑ | **SO-FFA elements,** fit together to allow any combinations

SO-FFA
El Prat de Llobregat

SO-FFA benches were originally designed as neutral pieces of furniture for any location where the designers thought a few blocks of black basalt would fit. In non-urban areas, anything can be used to sit, a low wall, a trunk tree or a rock. Since there weree no properly sized stones for the project, they were built taking care with angles toni how they could fit together to allow any combination. The designers were also interested in the way young people use a bench; for example when sitting on the back with their feet on the seat. So the group of 'stones' was supposed to accommodate all these positions and any others. These urban elements were built with simple geometries and of solid concrete, so they could be used as free-standing elements.

PROJECT FACTS **Address:** Illa 10 urban development in Sant Cosme, Carrer Anoia, Cardener, Ronda Sud, Avgda. Onze de Setembre, 08820 El Prat de Llobregat, Barcelona, Spain. **Manufacturer:** ESCOFET 1886 SA. **Client:** Incasòl. **Completion:** 2007. **Production:** serial production. **Design:** product line. **Functions:** seating. **Main materials:** cast stone.

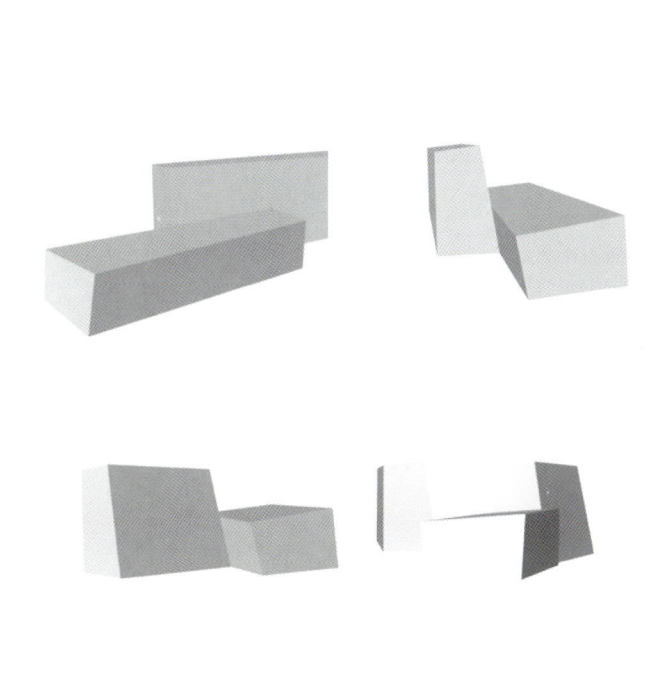

↑ | **Elevations**
↓ | **Flexible arrangement of the space,** adapts to the users habits

↑ | **Furnitures,** like a few blocks of black basalt

SEATING | Toyo Ito and Associates, Architects

↑ | Benches in urban context

Modular Bench Naguisa

This furniture made of concrete was designed Toyo serve as a bench that can adapt to the spirit of towns or large parks. It can have soft curves like the flow of the river, with an appealing dignity that arouses people's imagination. For the design of this furniture, circular arc pieces of about four meters in length are used as modules. The curved surface where they are gouged serves as the seating side and the organically consecutive shape functions as a backrest allowing users to lean their backs or rest their arms to find their own favorite seating position.

| **PROJECT FACTS** | **Client:** Escofet. **Completion:** 2005. **Production:** serial production. **Design:** individual design. **Functions:** seating. **Main materials:** reinforced cast stone.

↑ | **Benches in park context**
↓ | **Plans**

↑↑ | **Bench,** completely closed like a ring
↑ | **Bench,** soft curves like the flow of the river

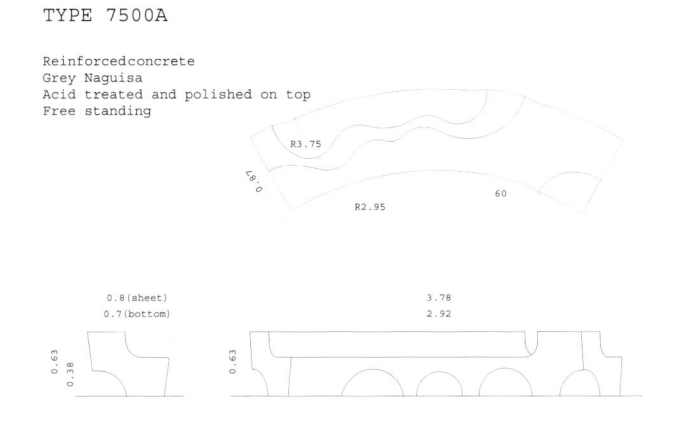

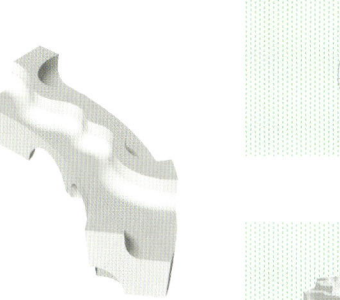

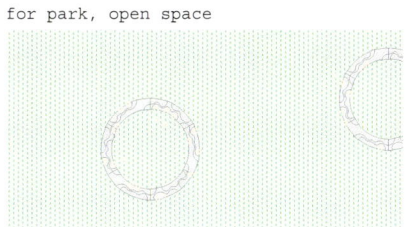

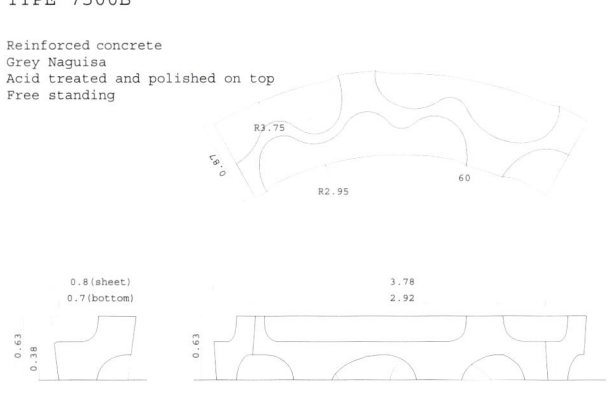

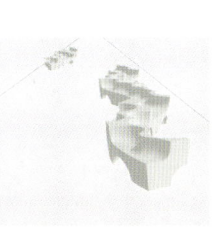

TYPE 7500A

Reinforced concrete
Grey Naguisa
Acid treated and polished on top
Free standing

for park, open space

TYPE 7500B

Reinforced concrete
Grey Naguisa
Acid treated and polished on top
Free standing

for street

SEATING | Alexandre Moronnoz

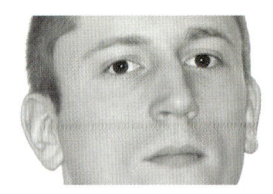

↑ | Detail

Y

"Y" is a design for scalable park and garden furniture: its length can be defined freely and its base width is also variable. This unconventional outdoor seating idea consists of a series of vertical slats of laser-cut wood. They are linked together by adjustable assembly fixings, offering a wide range of configuration options. The quality of the "retified", (thermally treated) wood allows the furniture to withstand outdoor weather conditions. "Y" is named for the geometric shape of its basic module, which is thus transformed from a visual motif into a functional form.

PROJECT FACTS

Production: Prototype Concept. **Technical partner:** RETItech. **Client:** VIA, prototype. **Completion:** 2006. **Production:** single piece. **Design:** individual design. **Functions:** seating. **Main materials:** laser-cut retified wood, mechanical assembly.

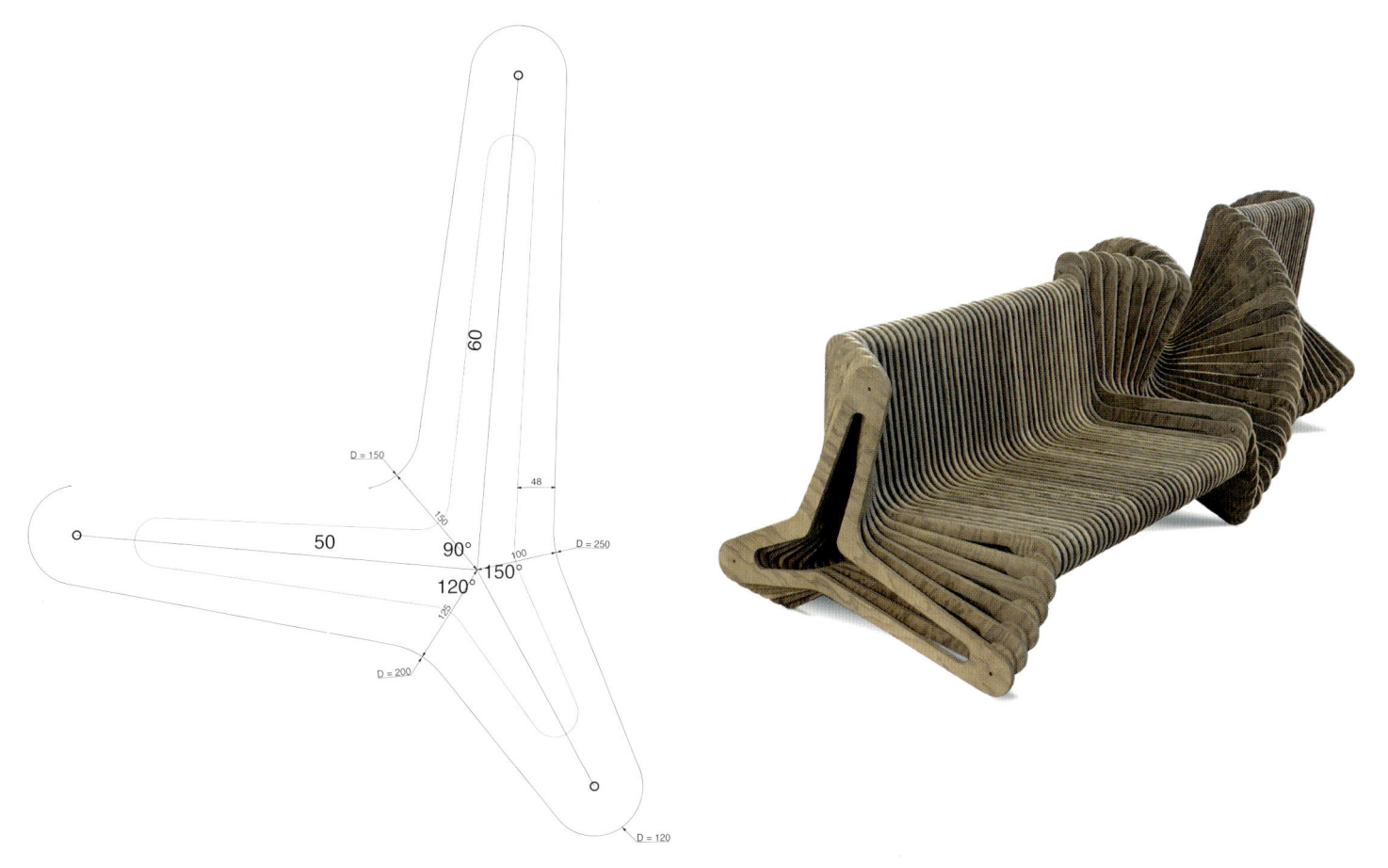

319

↑ | Plan
↓ | Detail

↑ | Scalable park and garden furniture

SEATING | Alexandre Moronnoz

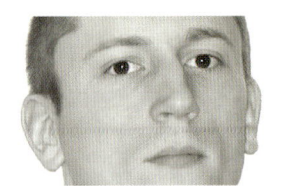

↑ | **Inside**, detail

Interferences
Brussels

The unique urban park bench, installed in Les Jardins du Fleuriste, has a calm and organic exterior and a frenetic, moving, exposed interior. A balance between order and disorder, movement and stability characterizes the volume. Equally at home amidst urban bustle or swaying grasses, Interference is an eye-catching addition to any landscape. The dimensions may be extended to suit each setting. At once urban and organic, reflective of its environment (a public space marked by constant movement), this park bench balances order with chaos in a spirit conducive to friendly encounters.

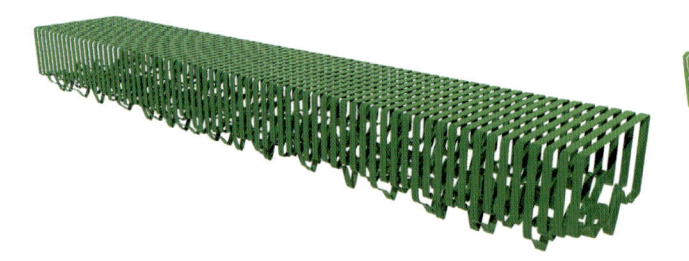

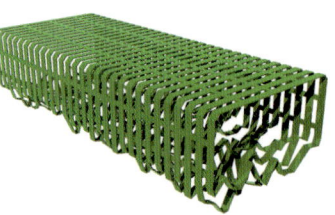

PROJECT FACTS **Address:** Les Jardins du Fleuriste, Av. Sobieskilaan and Av. de Robiniers, 1020 Brussels, Belgium. **Planning partner:** Parkdesign / Pro Materia. **Client:** BGE-Brussels-Environnement. **Completion:** 2007. **Production:** serial production. **Design:** individual design. **Functions:** seating. **Main materials:** laser-cut bent and soldered steel, electroplated zinc, epoxy paint.

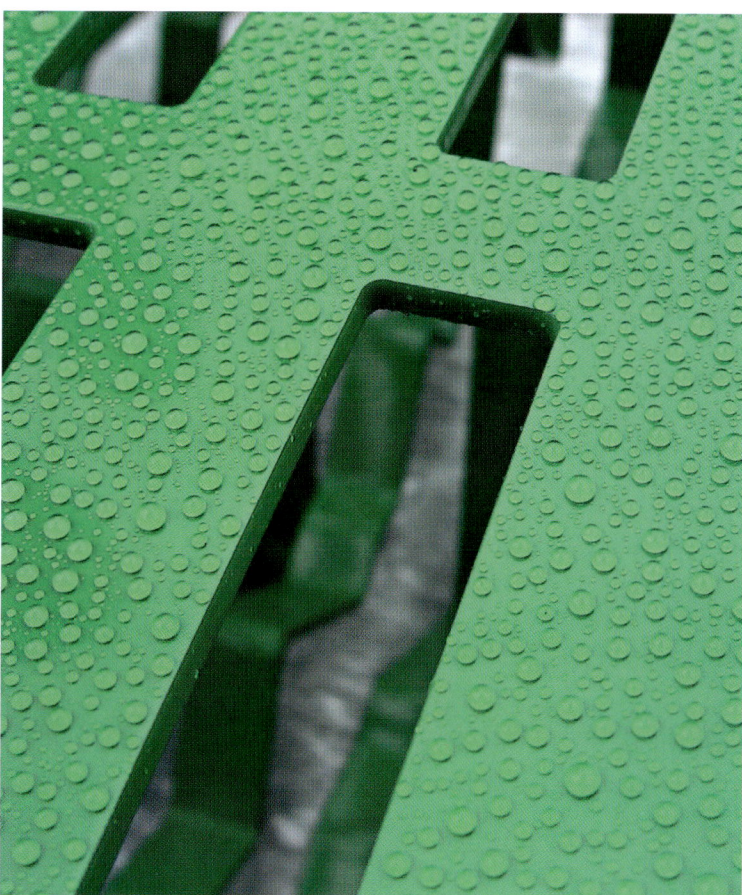

321

↑ | Plan
↙ | Design studies

↑ | Detail
↓ | Bench

SEATING | Alexandre Moronnoz

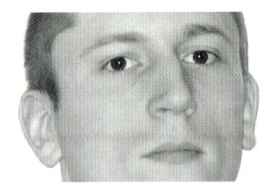

↑ | Bench

Muscle
St-Etienne

As spectacular to gaze at as it is comfortable to rest on, Muscle is a counterproposal to traditional stiff and motionless street furniture thanks to its dynamic forms and purified lines. It is a piece that compliments both contemporary architectural structures and modern landscape designs. The bench offers the possibility of sitting or lying down in response to the surface's relief. Like the fibrous structure of a muscle, the cut metal sheets work with compression and tension to maintain the rigidity of the resting platform. The smooth gun metal gray epoxy finish reflects the light and adds to the sense of lightness. As the sun passes through the metal bars, the shadows mix with the actual piece, adding yet another dimension.

PROJECT FACTS

Address: Cité du Design, 42000 St-Etienne France. **Completion:** 2008. **Production:** serial production. **Design:** individual design. **Functions:** seating. **Main materials:** steel, primary zinc epoxy powder coating.

323

↑ | Detail
↓ | Design sketch

↑ | Making of

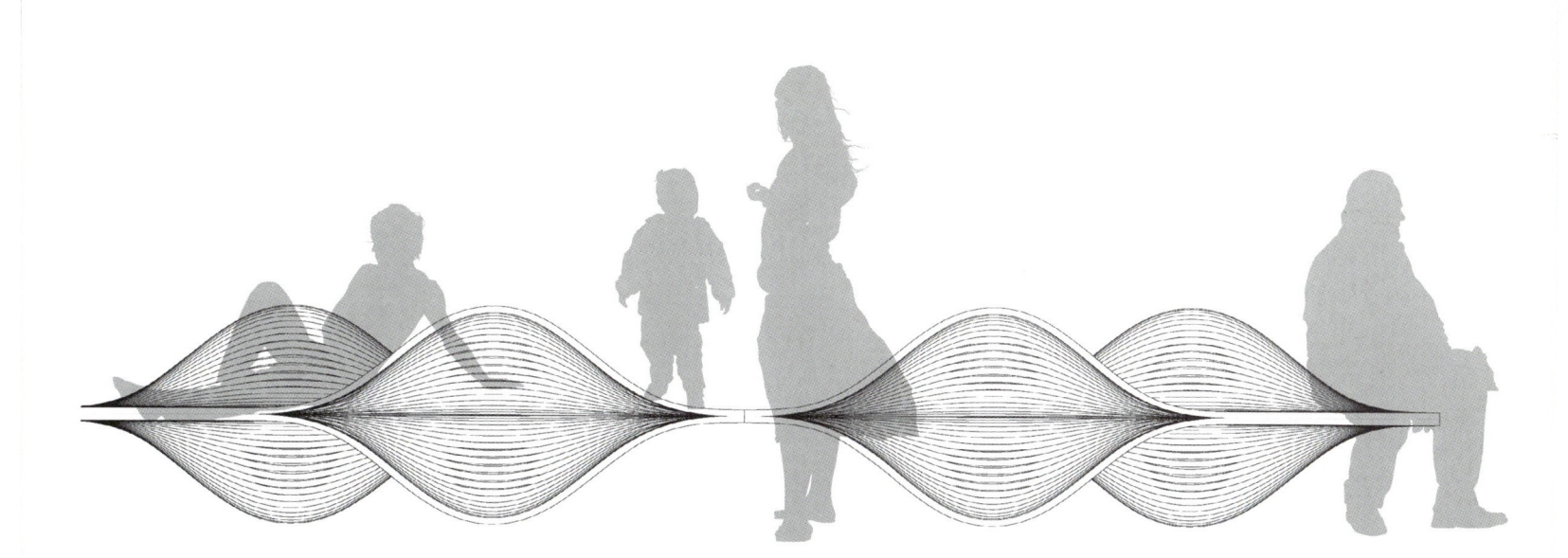

SEATING | Mitzi Bollani

↑ | **Trottola,** as part of a public playground

Trottola Spinning Top

This unusually shaped furniture resembles a spinning top, whose soft and playful shape blends in intriguingly with parks or playgrounds and invites older dwellers to rest and use it as a seat whereas children are encouraged to use it as toy. Its biomorphic design offers different possibilities for sitting or lying down as people like, it can be a flexible, fixed or rotating seat where a number of children can play together, discovering how the way they move directly affects the movements of the top. It is a street object which not only combines different uses but also unites different age groups.

PROJECT FACTS

Client: MODO srl. **Completion:** 2005. **Production:** serial production. **Design:** individual design. **Functions:** seating, play. **Main materials:** fiber glass.

325

↑ | **Sketches**
↓ | **Organic form** blends perfect with green spaces

↑ | **View of Trottola** within a backyard

SEATING | Aziz Sariyer

↑ | **liquirizia,** modular seating furniture

liquirizia

liquirizia is a multi-unit bench that can be combined in a modular manner to create a variety of different forms. It can be adapted to the location in which it is used, regardless of whether it is an open plaza or a narrow courtyard. The cross-section of each element displays a horizontal and a vertical axis melting into a cross with soft and rounded shapes. The horizontal axis forms the seating whereas the vertical axis constitutes both the backrest and the foot. The curvature of the whole structure does not only prevent the bench from overturning but also gives the object a slender and playful appearance. liquirizia is made of aluminum and can be delivered in different colors and finishes.

| **PROJECT FACTS** | Client and manufacturer: altreforme. Completion: 2008. Production: serial production (limited edition). Design: product line. Functions: seating. Main materials: aluminum.

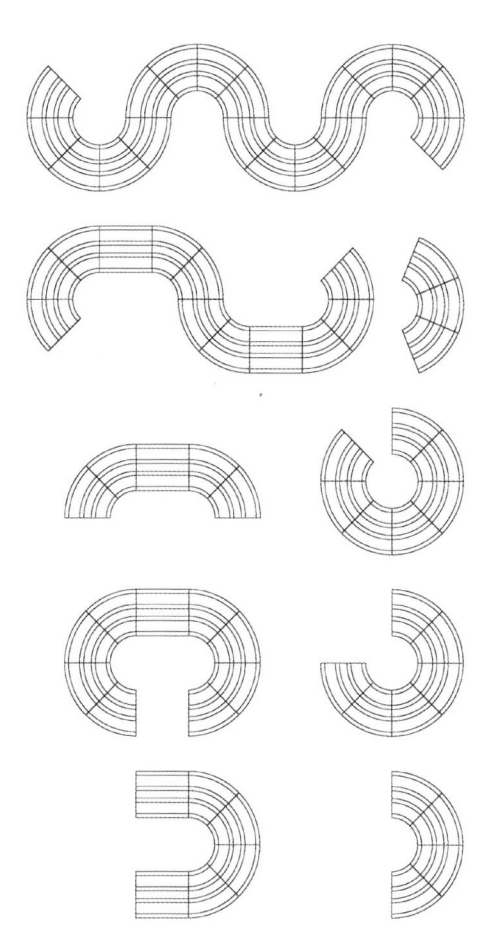

↑ | **Possible arrangements**
↓ | **Front elevation**

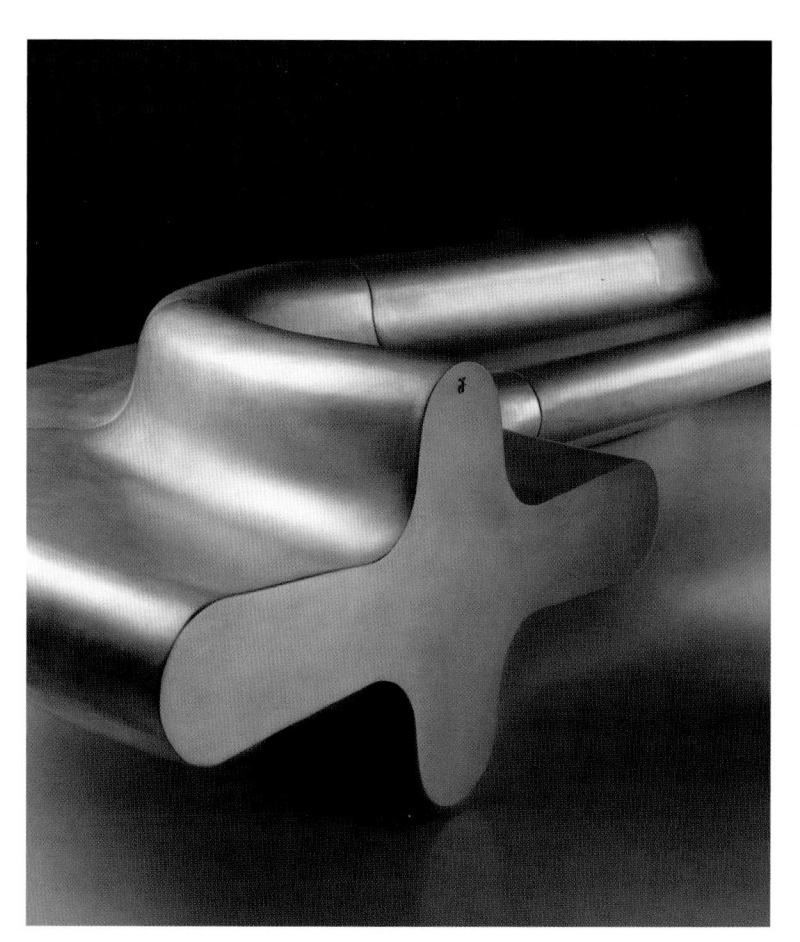

↑ | **Detail view,** section

SEATING | Aziz Sariyer

↑ | Perspective view

mariù

mariù is a console table with a stately size and surprising soft and elegant shapes. Its slender curved shape gives the structure a warm and feminine appearance. However, stability is also gained from this geometry – a sinuous curve providing balance and enabling the structure to rest on a very small foot surface. Visually, the table surprises the perceiver with changing looks according to the viewer's position and angle. mariù is made of aluminum and is well balanced, self-supporting its wide figure with harmony on only one centimeter thick S-shaped line. It is a harmonious designed piece of public furniture that offers robustness while being esthetically appealing at the same time. mariù can be delivered in different colors and finishes.

PROJECT FACTS Client and manufacturer: altreforme. Completion: 2008. Production: serial production (limited edition). Design: individual design. Functions: console table. Main materials: aluminum.

↑ | **Detail view,** sharp edge and emblem
↓ | **Concept rendering**

↑ | **Slender countenance,** side elevation

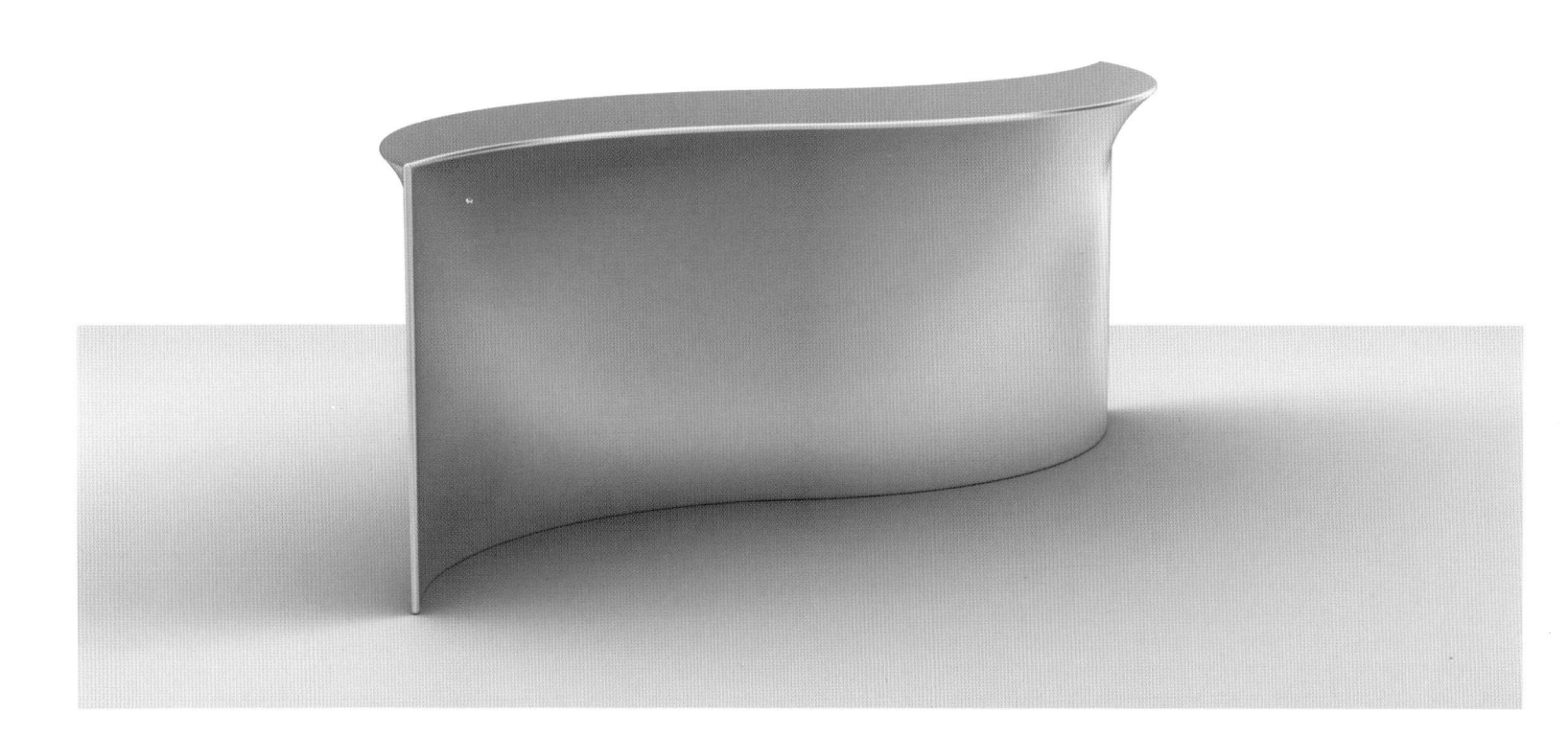

SEATING

Esrawe Studio / Hector Esrawe

↑ | The form of the bench evokes a nest symbol

Nido Bench
Mexico City

This bench was developed based on an invitation to artists, architects and designers to develop an urban bench is placed at the Paseo de la Reforma. The proposal was for an element that would "embrace" the user, generating a rather intimate space in relation to the outside. Based on sketches and models, a random structure was approached that evokes a "nest" as a symbol of protection and isolation. The exhibition 'Diálogo de Bancas' at the Paseo de la Reforma was a success. When this urban furniture was placed there, the citizens made regular use of it to rest their feet, to meet someone, or just to sit there for a while.

PROJECT FACTS

Address: Paseo de la Reforma avenue, C.P. 06600 Mexico City, Mexico. **Client:** City of Mexico City. **Completion:** 2007. **Production:** single piece. **Design:** individual design. **Functions:** seating. **Main materials:** coated metal.

↑ | Sketch
↓ | Perpective view

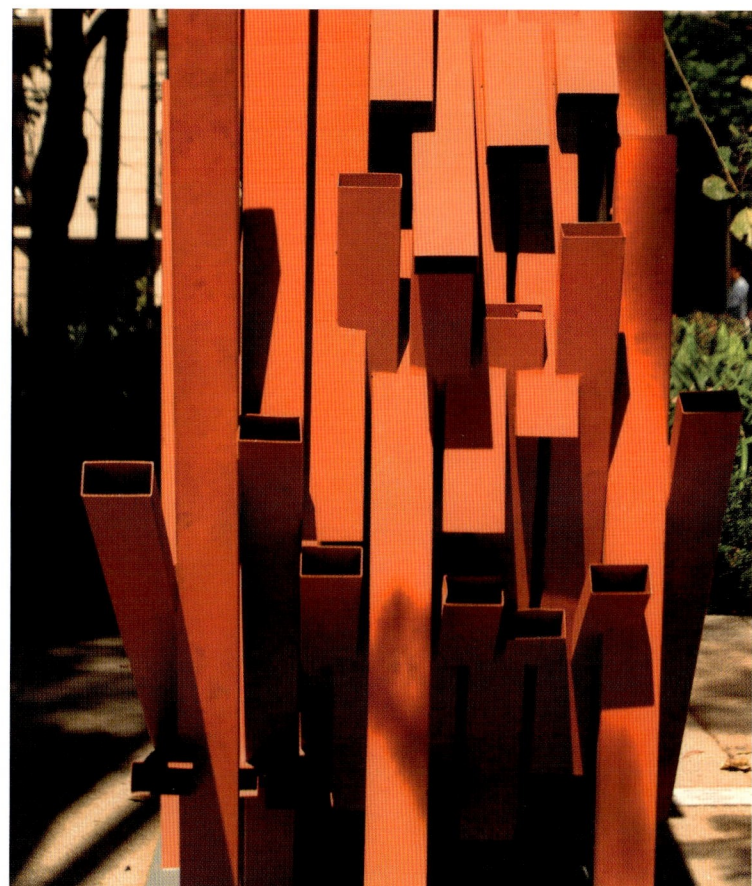

↑ | Bench in use
↓ | Detail

SEATING | Brodie Neill

↑ | Highly reflective surface

Reverb Chair

The bold, emerging geometry of the Reverb Chair is the striking new edition of the ever-expressive furniture forms by Brodie Neill. Hand-formed neid mirror-polished from sheet aluminum, the single inverted skin is functional, yet poised in a sculpturally dynamic pose. The highly reflective surface amplifies the tapering typology through a transition from curvaceous seat into the elliptical vortex of the back stabilizer. Inspired by the reverberation of sound, the Reverb Chair's membrane flows outward before returning back onto itself. Born from the pursuit to push materials to their limits, the fluting form is both seamless in structure and in surface.

PROJECT FACTS

Client: The Apartment Gallery. **Completion:** 2009. **Production:** single piece. **Design:** individual design. **Functions:** seating. **Main materials:** nickel plated aluminum.

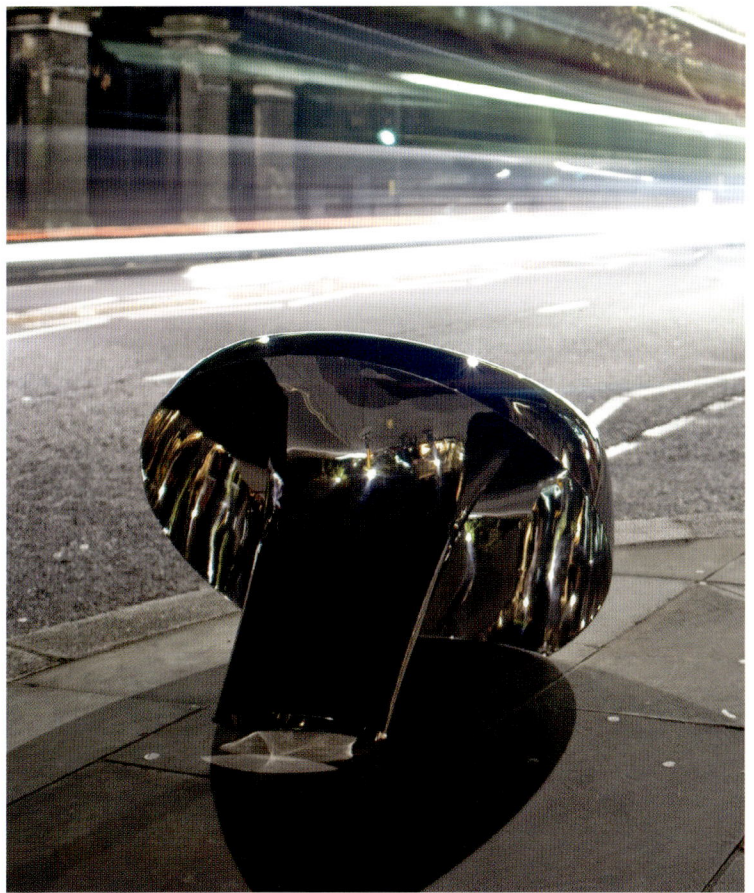

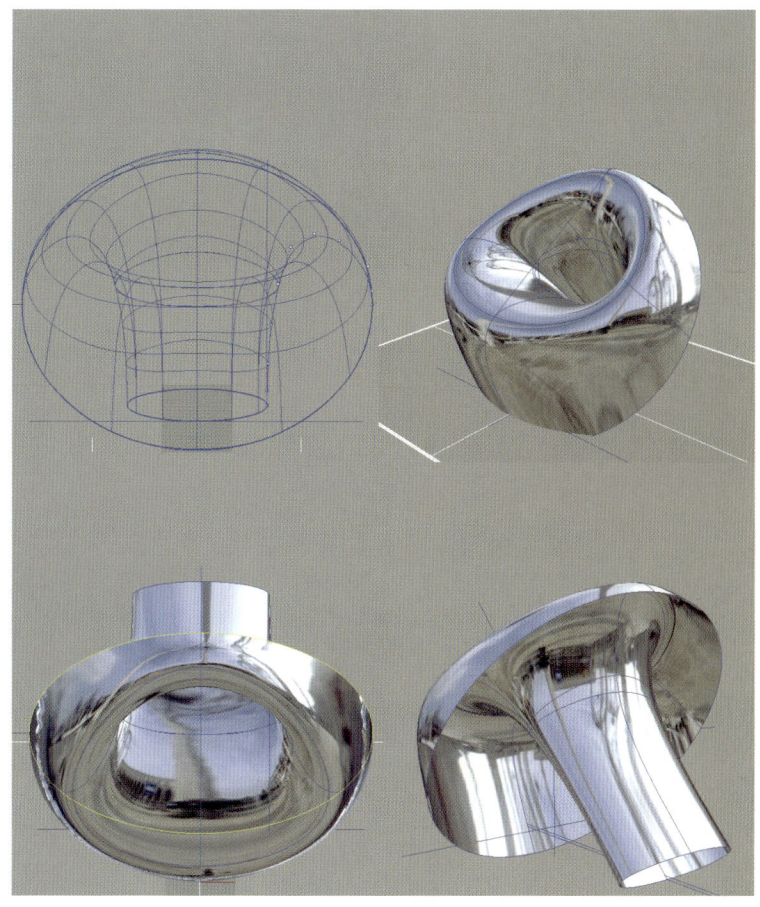

333

↑ | **View from back**
↓ | **Side view**

↑ | **Design sketches**, screen shots
↓ | **Detail**

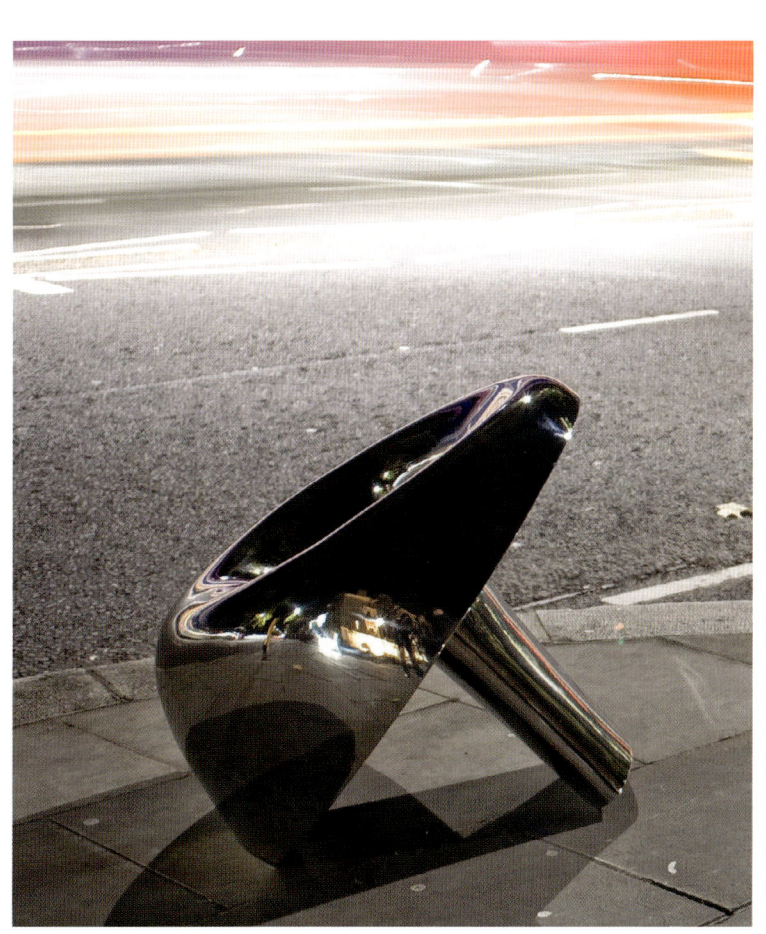

SEATING | Julian Mayor

↑ | Sculpture and seating furniture

Regency Benches
London

The benches at Regency Apartments can be seen as a mixture of seating furniture and sculpture. Their form was developed as a reaction to the site, a fluid series of volumes inspired by their position near the water and to the layers of history contained within. The surfaces are made up of a complex series of planes that act as angled mirrors to the ambient light, allowing the shapes to react to light conditions and the color and brightness of the sky. The artwork on the benches was created by students at the nearby Millbank Primary School as part of a series of workshops exploring the history of the area. Art, design, education and public use are melted in this well-thought out project.

PROJECT FACTS **Address:** Regency Apartments, Regency Street, Pimlico, London SW1P 4AD, UK. **Client:** Westminster City Council, London. **Completion:** 2006. **Production:** single piece. **Design:** individual design. **Functions:** seating, sculpture. **Main materials:** stainless steel.

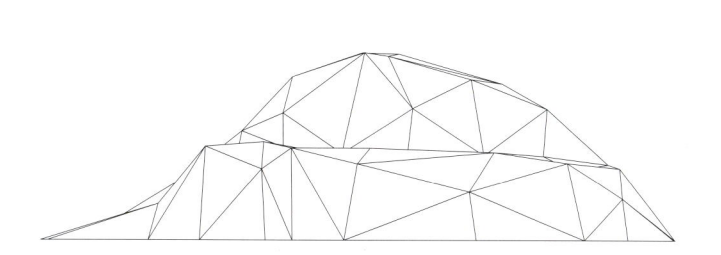

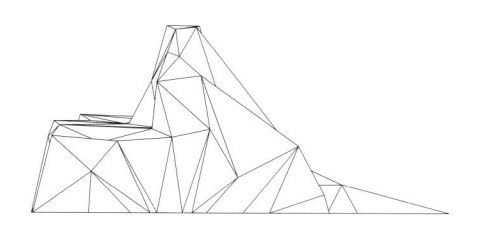

↑ | **Elevations**
↓ | **Perspective view**

↑ | **Deatil view,** artwork on the planes

SEATING | Gitta Gschwendtner

↖ | River view
↑↑ | White Bag Stool
↑ | Tank view

Bag Stools
London

The task was to investigate the tangible link between design and the city in an installation for the Design Museum Tank exploring the theme "Consume". In reference to material consumption, Gitta Gschwendtner created Woodcrete stools cast from moulds based on paper shopping bags. Their individual, irregular form evolves during the casting process and the Woodcrete is made up from a mixture of concrete and wood fibers which make it a light and environmentally-friendly material. The stools provide the visitor with a place to enjoy the view of London, taking in its sights and sounds and presenting an alternative to the materialistic consumption prevalent in our lives today.

PROJECT FACTS
Address: temporary installation at the Design Museum Tank, Shad Thames, London SE1 2YD, United Kingdom. **Client:** Design Museum. **Completion:** 2008. **Production:** single piece. **Design:** individual design. **Functions:** seating. **Main materials:** woodcrete.

Tokujin Yoshioka Design

↑ | **Seat**, in use
↗↗ | **Perspective view**
↗ | **Piece of glass**

Chair that disappears in the Rain
Tokyo

The "Streetscape Project" – to which 11 designers were commissioned to design open-air furniture – has been completed in 2003 in the Roppongi Hills in Roppongi, Tokyo. "Chair that disappears in the rain" was designed as part of that project by Tokujin Yoshioka. In the rain this chair exhibits a similar effect as shards of glass that are dropped into water with their outlines gradually disappearing. The chair is made from a massive block of glass that is crafted by special techniques, the same cutting reflex plate material used in giant observatory telescopes.

PROJECT FACTS
Address: Roppongi 6 chome (Keyakizaka St.) Tokyo 106-0032, Japan. **Client:** Mori Building. **Completion:** 2002. **Production:** single piece. **Design:** individual design. **Functions:** seating. **Main materials:** glass.

SEATING | BRUTO d.o.o. / Matej Kučina

↑ | Wooden bench and garbage can

Šentvid Urban Park
Ljubljana

The framework of the park is based on a pattern of cycle tracks, pedestrian paths and transverse concrete walls that constitute the ribs of the configuration. The individual expansions along the communication axis create flat areas in form of tectonic interruptions of the basic construction that can be used for different urban programs. This arrangement gives the impression of visually broadening the space and at the same time constitutes an element of articulation for creating the inner program-areas. Due to its spatial concept and roadside position, the park definitely has an urban character which is reflected in the use of street graphics, bright colors, urban street equipment, and lighting elements.

PROJECT FACTS

Address: 1000 Ljubljana, Slovenia. **Tunnel and bridge architecture:** Elea iC. **Client:** DARS. **Completion:** 2010. **Production:** single piece. **Design:** product line. **Functions:** seating, garbage can. **Main materials:** wood (seating), steel, plastic, concrete (garbage can).

↑ | Promenade with passage
↓ | Wood bench detail plans

↑ | Benches on the promenade

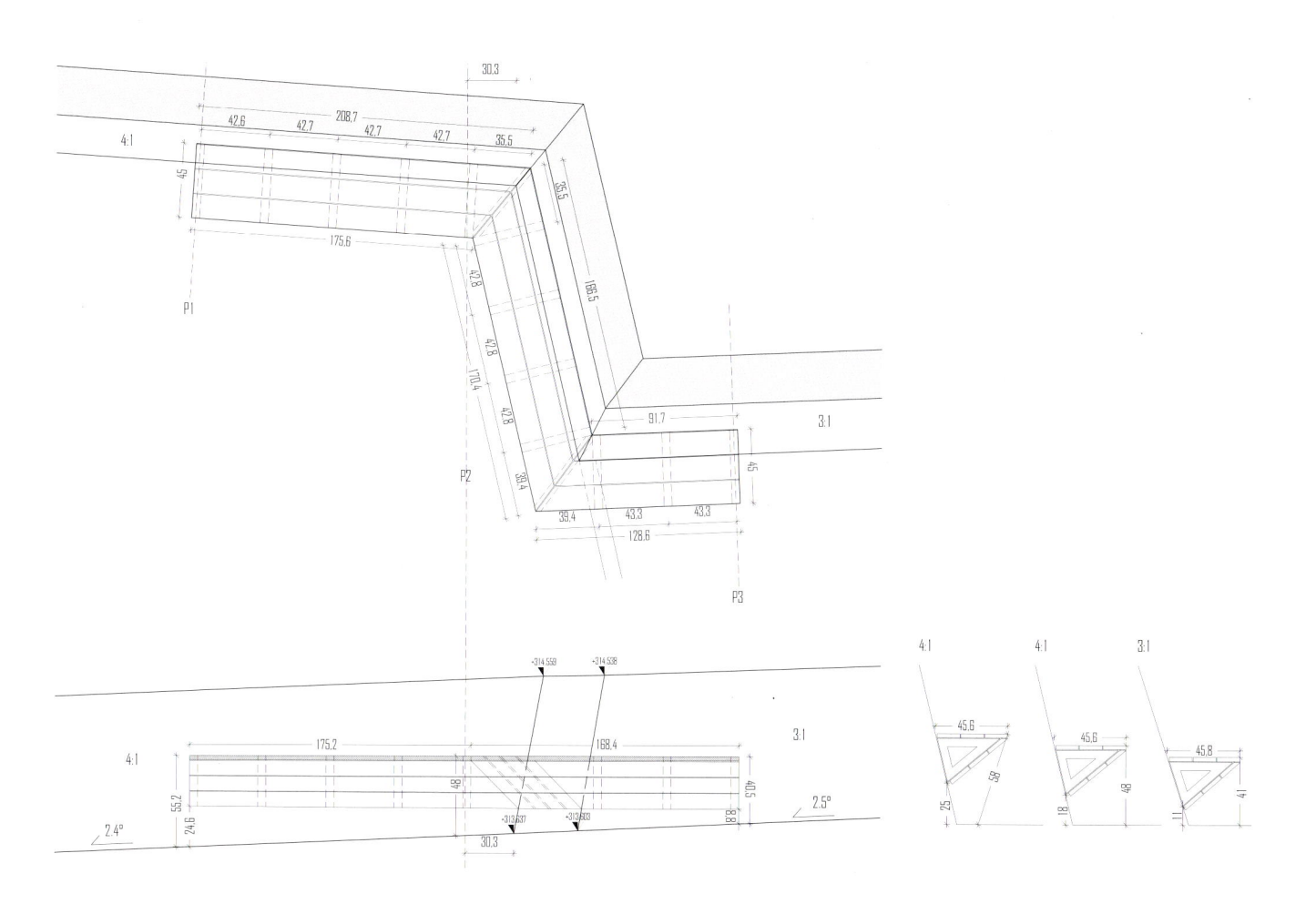

SEATING | Earthscape

↑ | **Steps with flowers**

Marunouchi Oazo North Building
Tokyo

The goal of this project was to inscribe memories into the land and make a connection with the future. The rectangles etched into the exterior and the first floor entrance are floor plans of two of the previous uses of this location, a Hosokawa Family Samurai House, and the Transit Authority Building, recreated in their original positions. Sceneries from each of these two time periods were engraved above them. The objects positioned on the landscape (such as benches) were intended to remind people of the memories of history and the land, such as grasslands, forests, and fields of flowers, while also evoking the future, as well as the present, allowing them to once again recognize the connections between the past and the future.

PROJECT FACTS

Address: 1-6-5 Marunouchi Chiyoda-ku Tokyo, Japan 100-0005. **Architects:** Mitsubishi Jisho Sekkei Inc., Nikken Sekkei Ltd., Yamashita Sekkei Co. Ltd. **Client:** Mitsubishi Estate Co. Ltd., Marunouchi Hotel, Nippon Life Insurance Company. **Completion:** 2004. **Production:** single piece. **Design:** individual design. **Functions:** seating, signs. **Main materials:** black granite.

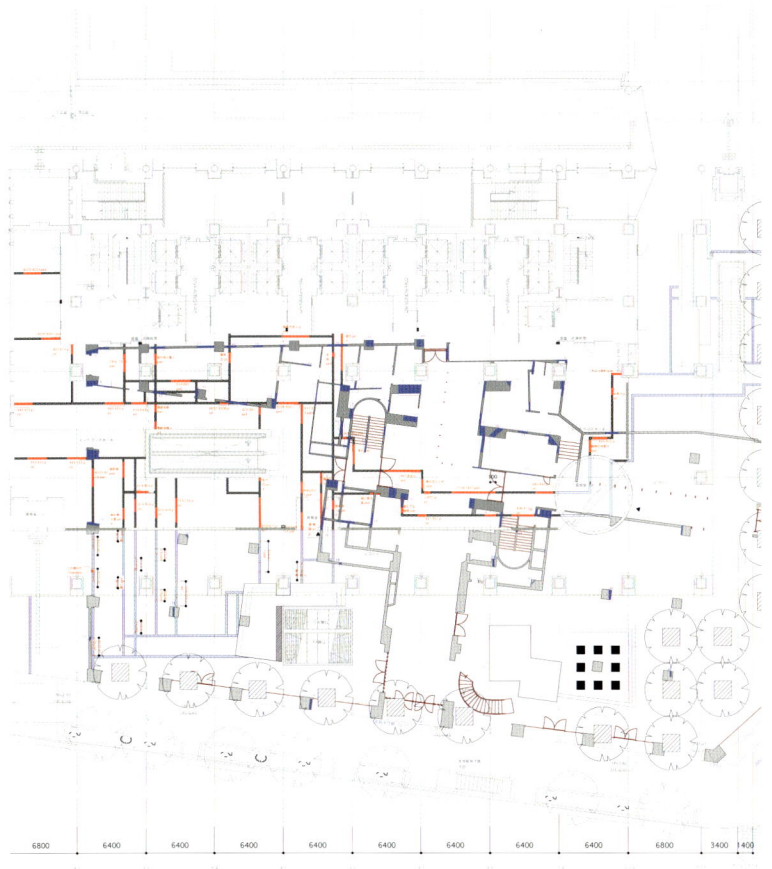

341

↑ | Site plan
↓ | Steps with leaves

↑ | Bird's-eye view

SEATING | Earthscape

↑ | **Seating bench,** around an old cherry tree

Two Generations of Cherry Blossoms

Kawasaki

The four cherry trees that used to blossom in the Toshiba Horikawa-cho factory site were transplanted to the entrance of Lazona Kawasaki, and now serve to greet people as they enter the facility. The black, ring-shaped bench positioned around one of those trees is engraved with the history of the factory, and the old factory landscape. Additionally, a piece from this bench is located on the far side of the river. It has been engraved with a scene of cherry blossoms in full bloom, while a cherry blossom sapling was planted here to help people imagine the future landscape.

PROJECT FACTS **Address:** Lazona Kawasaki, 72-1 Horikawa-cho Saiwai-ku Kawasaki city Kanagawa, Japan 212-0013. **Client:** Toshiba / Mitsui Fudosan Group Ltd. **Completion:** 2006. **Production:** single piece. **Design:** individual design. **Functions:** seating. **Main materials:** black granite.

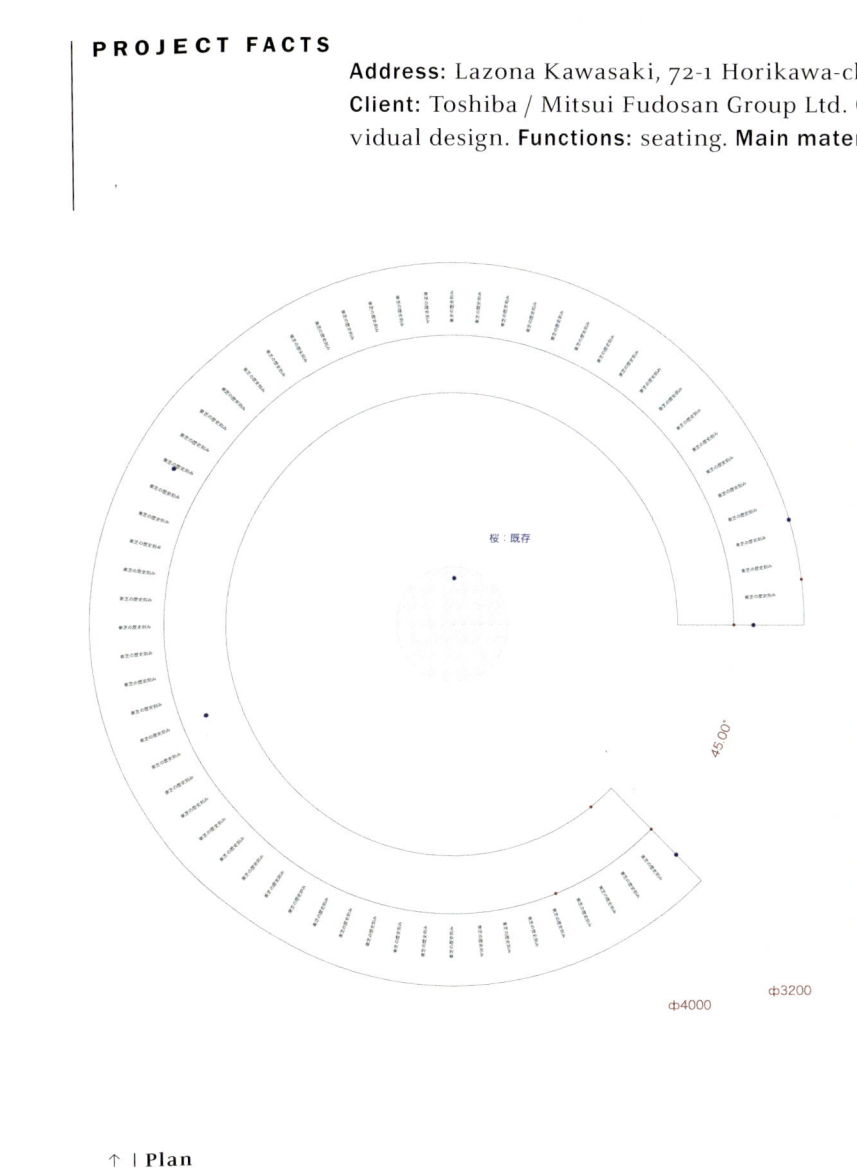

↑ | Plan
↓ | Bird's-eye view

↑ | **Black granite,** engraved with the history of the factory, and the old factory landscape

SEATING | Earthscape

↑ | **Lazona Kawasaki,** nature benches (left) and city benches (right)

Nature and City Bench
Kawasaki

The two kinds of benches constitute part of "the axis of the city" and "the axis of nature" of the Kawasaki plaza. The city bench was decorated with urban motifs, while the nature bench was decorated with natural motifs. For this purpose, the colors of the urban landscapes of Kawasaki city and the surrounding nature were analyzed and applied to the pieces, which have either a geometric or an organic profile.

PROJECT FACTS **Address:** Lazona Kawasaki, 72-1 Horikawa-cho Saiwai-ku Kawasaki city Kanagawa, Japan 212-0013. **Architect:** Ricardo Bofill Leví and Yamashita Sekkei Inc. **Illumination:** Sola associates. **Client:** Toshiba / Mitsui Fudosan Group Ltd. **Completion:** 2006. **Production:** single piece. **Design:** product line. **Functions:** seating. **Main materials:** DuPont Corian.

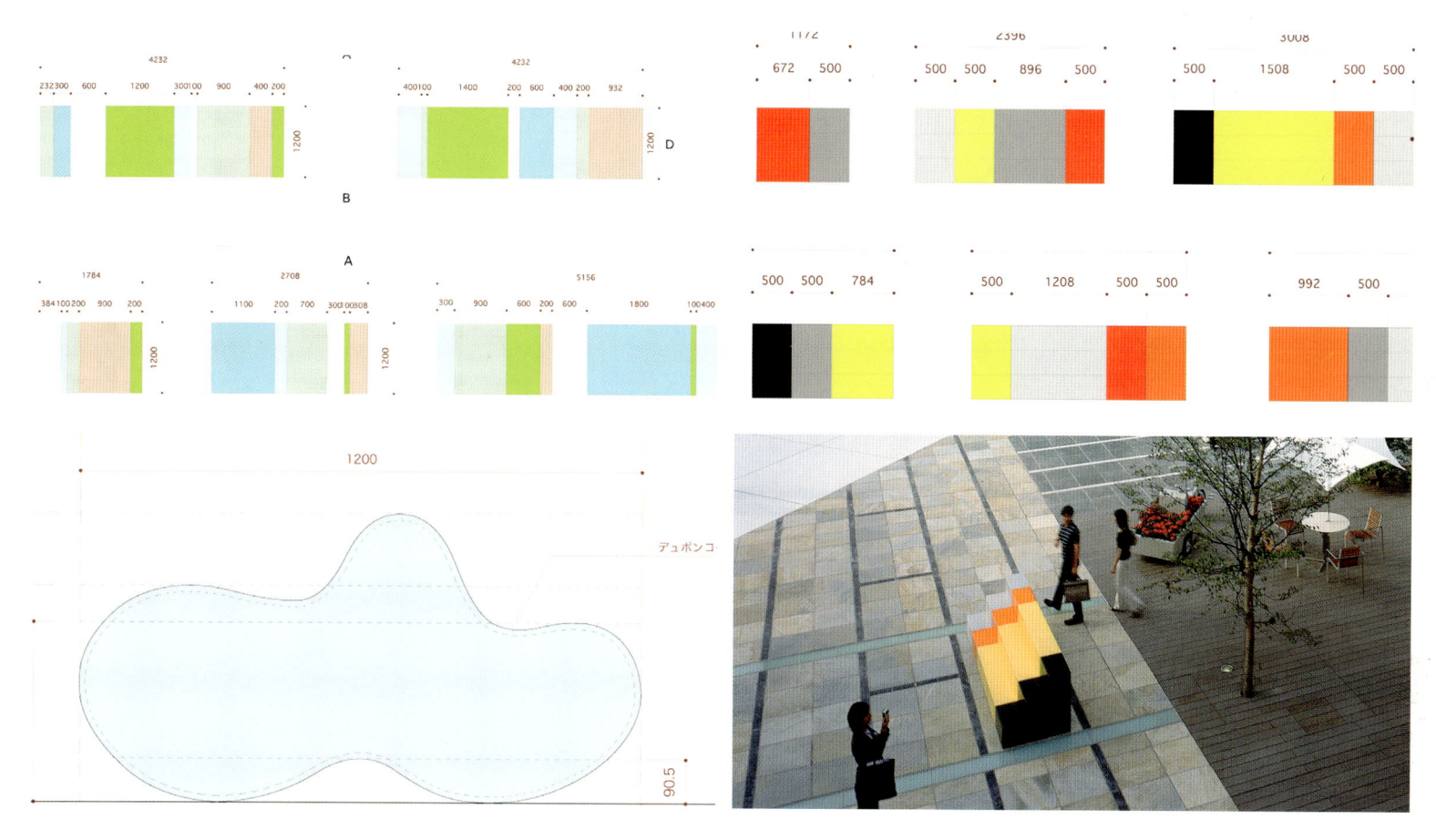

↑↑ | **Color conept,** nature bench
↑ | **Cross section,** nature bench
↓ | **Nature bench**

↑↑ | **Color conept,** city bench
↑ | **City bench**
↓ | **Nature bench,** by night with light sculpture

SEATING | Earthscape

↑ | **Black cubes,** symbolizing winter
→ | **Earth thermometer,** experience by sitting on and touching the stones with different colors

Earth Thermometer
Tokyo

By sitting on and touching this chair, you can experience the temperature (seasonal and global-warming) of the earth. The bench, which is a minimalist cube made from stones in the gray scale between white and black, reveals the minute differences between each stone's reflexivity and absorptive capacities, and demonstrates the relationships between light and color, and the heat energy that light possesses. In summer, the white cubes completely reflect light waves, and are pleasingly cool to touch. In winter, the black cubes absorb plenty of light, providing warmth to people who sit on them. In this way, people can have their own conversations with the sun through the personal experience of sitting on the cubes.

| PROJECT FACTS **Address:** Central Gov't Bldg. No.7, 2-2-3 Kasumigaseki Chiyoda-ku Tokyo, Japan 100-8959. **Architect:** Kume Sekkei, Taisei Corporation, Nippon Steel Corporation. **Landscape:** Ohtori Consultants. **Client:** Kasumigaseki No.7 PFI. **Completion:** 2007. **Production:** single piece. **Design:** individual design. **Functions:** seating. **Main materials:** various stone.

↑ | **Bird's-eye view**
↑↑ | **Detail**

↑ | **White cubes,** symbolizing summer

SEATING | Earthscape

↑ | **Shadow of the buildings and plants,** from July 11th, 2003, 1:47 PM and 15 seconds

Memory Chair
Tokyo

The Memory Chair preserves the shadow of the former Ministry of Education Building and its plants as it stood on July 11th, 2003, 1:47 PM and 15 seconds, the moment it was knocked down. This engraved shadow overlaps with the shadow of the new Central Government Building and plants, and brings to mind memories of the location and the flow of time.

| **PROJECT FACTS** | **Address:** Central Gov't Bldg. No.7, 2-2-3 Kasumigaseki Chiyoda-ku Tokyo, Japan 100-8959. **Architect:** Kume Sekkei, Taisei Corporation, Nippon Steel Corporation. **Landscape:** Ohtori Consultants. **Client:** Kasumigaseki No.7 PFI. **Completion:** 2007. **Production:** single piece. **Design:** individual design. **Functions:** seating. **Main materials:** black granite.

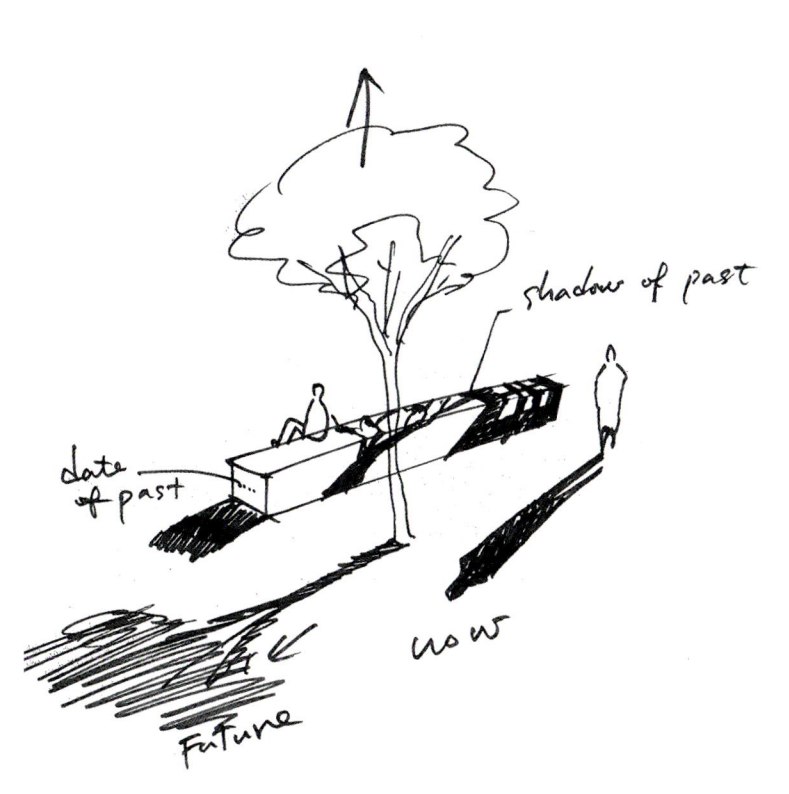

↑ | Sketch
↓ | General view

↑ | **The engraved shadow,** overlapped with the shadow of the current buildings and plants

SEATING | Earthscape

↑ | **Slits of the light**

Fukuoka Bank
Fukuoka

These benches are installed in the main branch of the Fukuoka Bank, in the Hakata Region of the Fukuoka prefecture. For the benches, panels based on silk and Hakata-style textiles that are traditionally produced in this region were used. Lights are built into the benches, which illuminate the traditional patterns at night.

PROJECT FACTS **Address:** 2-13-1 Tenjin Chuo-ku Fukuoka, Japan. **Architect:** MHS Planners, Architects & Engineers. **Client:** Fukuoka Bank. **Completion:** 2008. **Production:** single piece. **Design:** individual design. **Functions:** seating. **Main materials:** black granite.

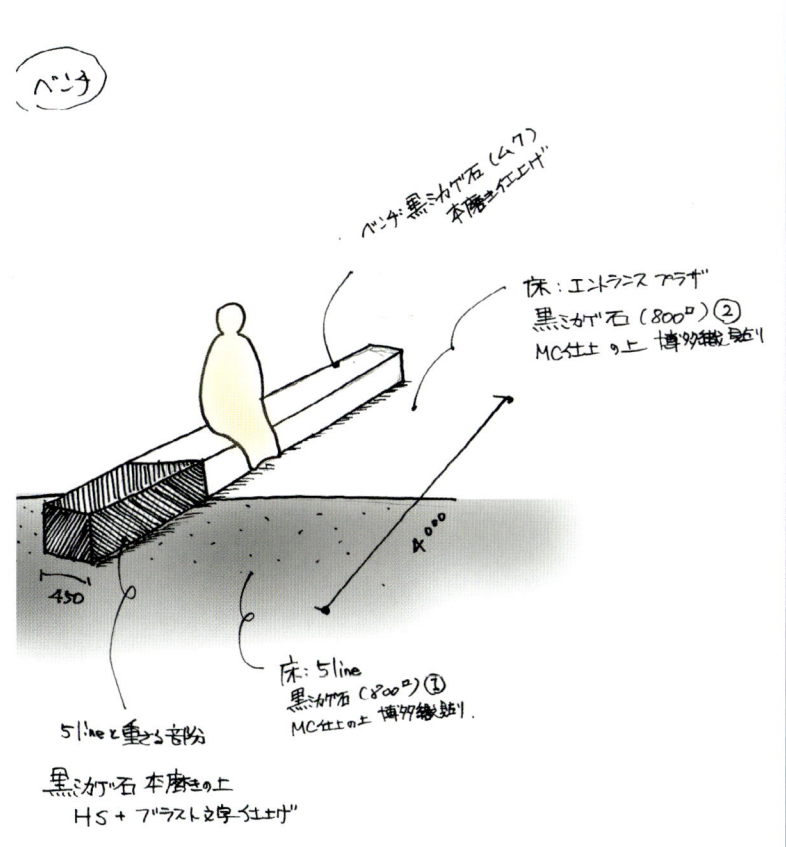

↑ | Sketch
↓ | The five benches

↑ | **Detail of the panels,** based on the silk and Hakata-style textiles

SEATING | City Mall Alliance – Isthmus, Reset, Christchurch City Council and Downer EDI

↑ | **Stewart Plaza Seat,** with integrated illumination
→ | **Hack Circle Seats,** placed along the tram line

City Mall
Christchurch

The Christchurch City Mall redevelopment is an upgrade of the central city pedestrian mall into a shared street. Conceptually the project draws on the rich garden city history of Christchurch and the broader alluvial plane landscape. A collection of custom-designed furniture elements was developed using local stone materials along with stainless steel and hardwood timber. Lighting was included to create visual highlights and meet safety requirements. The streetscape design contains a number of coordinated elements including the Stewart Plaza Seats, Hack Circle Seats, Cashel Mall Seats, Planter Boxes, a Stage, and Lightpole Climbers.

PROJECT FACTS **Address:** 222-282 High Street, 76-166 Cashel Street, Christchurch, New Zealand 8011. **Client:** Christchurch City Council. **Completion:** 2009. **Production:** single piece. **Design:** individual design. **Functions:** seating, illumination, plant tub, barrier. **Main materials:** granite, hardwood timber, stainless steel.

SEATING   CITY MALL ALLIANCE

↑ | **Drawing** of the Stewart Plaza Seat
← | **Deatil view** of the Hack Circle Seat

CITY MALL

← | **Detail of natural stone** used for the Hack Circle Stage
↓ | **Perspective view** of Cashel Street

SEATING

Isthmus / Evan Williams

↑ | **Night view** towards seaside
↘ | **Sketch** of Boat Seat

Boat Seat
North Shore City

The Boat Seat is inspired by the small timber boats often found pulled ashore in clusters along Auckland's harbour edge. Rather than mimic the boats forms the seats have a distinctively modern aesthetic distinguished by a 'wandering' stainless steel channel. This unifying element forms part of the mounting frame that the 'vitex' hardwood timber boards are fixed upon. Slatted timber closing panels to the ends of the seating elements allow access to the mounting points on the concrete plinths. The dynamic arrangement of the seating allows for informal seating and for groups to gather within the plaza spaces.

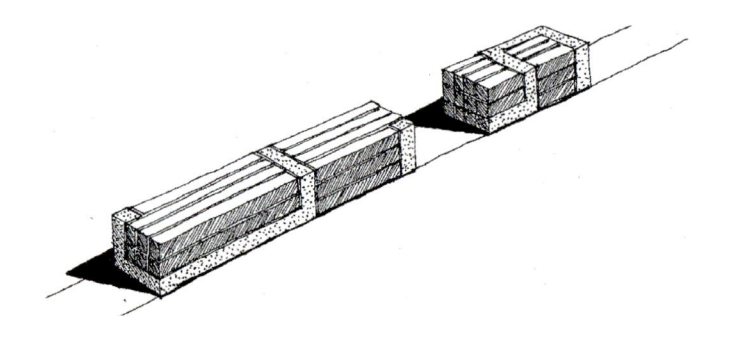

PROJECT FACTS **Address:** Beach Front Lane, Browns Bay, North Shore City, Auckland 0630, New Zealand. **Client:** North Shore City Council. **Completion:** 2008. **Production:** single piece. **Design:** individual design. **Functions:** seating. **Main materials:** hardwood timber, stainless steel.

357

↑ | **Boat Seat perspective**
↓ | **Night view** over the plaza

↑ | **Detail,** Boat Seat

SEATING | Earthworks Landscape Architects

↑ | **Sculpture,** seated on a curved bench

Pier Place Square
Cape Town

The foreshore area of Cape Town was built on land claimed from the sea. The concept for Pier Place Square was to design a space that is didactic in its reflection of history while at the same time commenting on the current users and inner city life in Cape Town. Charcoal cobbles were used in a sea of white to resemble tiny bits of marine and other debris left after the waves pull back and lines in underwater sand ripples, debris-cobbles will also accumulate around the sculptures like energy particles. The sculptures resemble life in the surrounding buildings and people living on the streets of the foreshore. The benches refer to sand dunes floating above the ground plain.

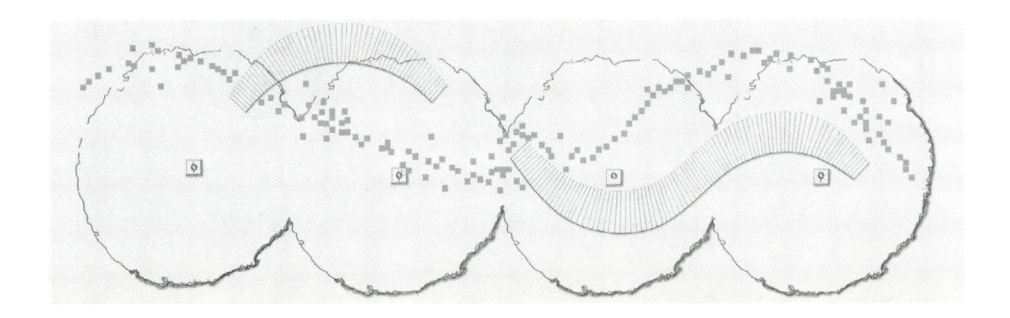

PROJECT FACTS

Address: Pier Place Square, Heerengracht Street, Cape Town, South Africa. **Artists:** Egon Tania (sculptures), Andrew Phillips (benches). **Client:** City of Cape Town. **Completion:** 2008. **Production:** single piece. **Design:** individual design. **Functions:** seating, illumination, sculpture. **Main materials:** galvanized steel, wood.

↑ | **Perspective drawing**
↓ | **Arrangement of benches**

↑ | **Curved bench,** viewed from above

SEATING | PLEIDEL ARCHITEKTI s.r.o.

↑ | **Pillars,** representing the three prehistorical epochs

Pedestrian Zone Sala
Sala

This pedestrian zone was created as a part of the larger town center of Sala. The main purpose of the architectural work was to solve an inconvenient transport situation concerning transit in the direction of the town center. The aim was also to create new public spaces for citizens and visitors. The public spaces are fitted with special equipment for different public activities, e.g. a podium with a water surface and street furniture. The entire space is interlaced with greenery.

PROJECT FACTS

Address: main square and main street, City of Sala, Slovak Republic. **Client:** City of Sala. **Completion:** 2007. **Production:** serial production (seating, garbage cans, lights), single piece (sculpture "3 Epochs", fountain, podium). **Design:** product line (by mmcité a.s.), individual design (by Imrich and Ondrej Pleidel). **Functions:** seating, illumination, garbage cans, bicycle tracks, information boards and columns, drinking fountain, sculptures, fountain with podium. **Main materials:** stone, concret, metal, wood.

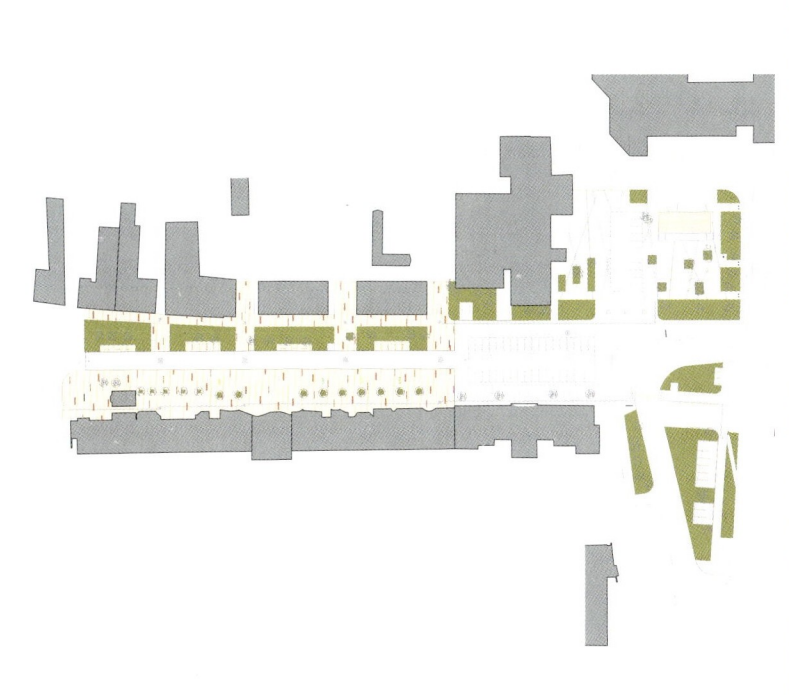

↑ | Site plan
↓ | Benches in line

↑ | Garbage can and benches
↓ | Benches on the square

SEATING | Smedsvig Landskaps-arkitekter AS / Arne Smedsvig

↑ | Wood bench

Benches at Indre Kai
Haugesund

Haugesund is a small west-coast town of 30,000 inhabitants. The inner quay is situated close to the town center, and is frequented by ferries with several departures a day. The quay with its restaurants and workshops is also a popular harbor for private yachts along the coast. The improvement of the quay was built in four sequences, the remaining stages consisting of a playground and an amphitheater connecting the southern parts with the town main street. The new design includes an outdoor floor of granite, cobblestones and wood, as well as new furniture such as wooden benches, lighting, and facilities for private yachting.

PROJECT FACTS

Address: Indre kai, 5525 Haugesund, Norway. **Planning partner:** Prosjektkonsult AS, Cowi AS. **Client:** Municipality of Haugesund. **Completion:** 2008. **Production:** single piece. **Design:** individual design. **Functions:** seating with lighting inside. **Main materials:** Norwegian oak.

↑ | **Bird's-eye view**
↓ | **Site plan**, detail

↑ | **Detail bench**

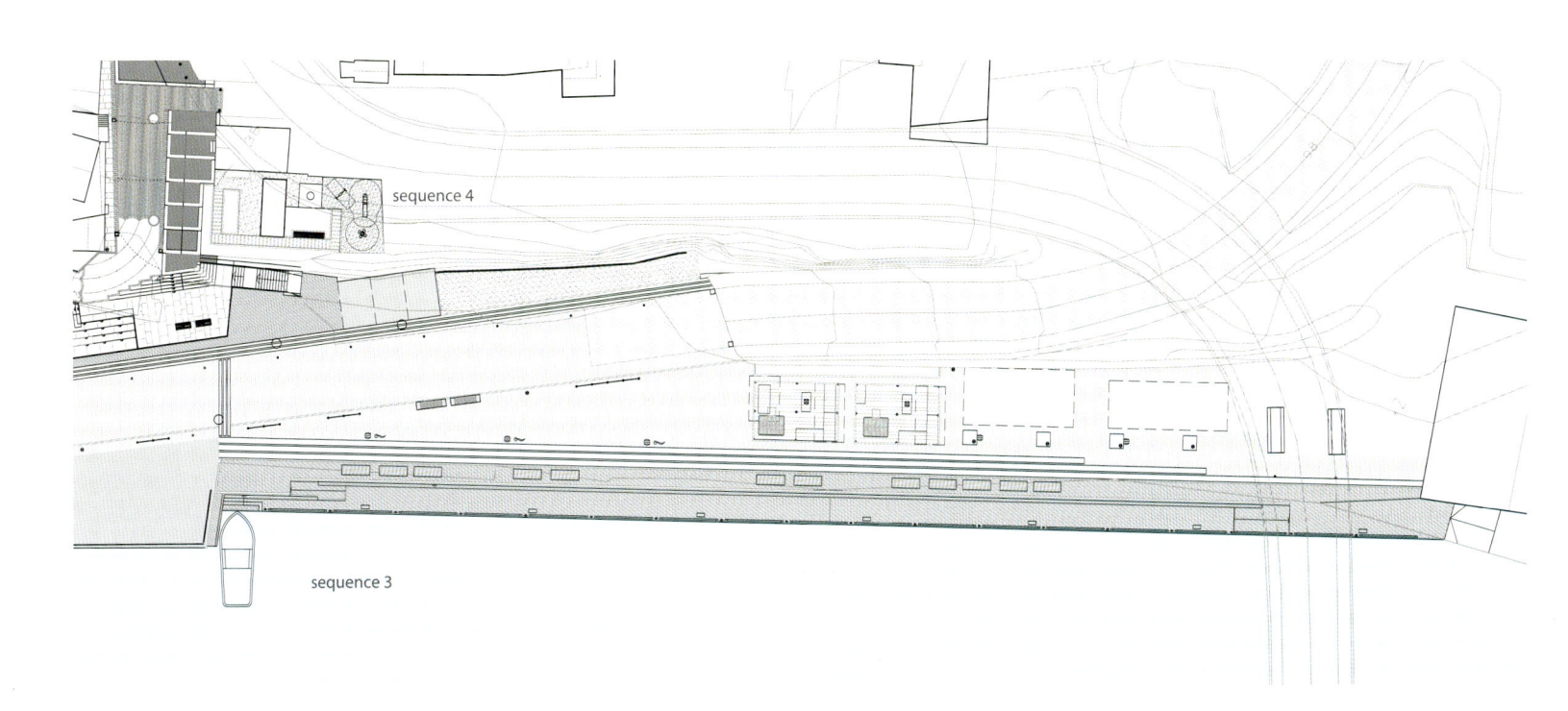

sequence 4

sequence 3

SEATING | Turenscape / Kongjian Yu

↑ | **The red ribbon runs across a former garbage dump** and has a strong contrast with the native wolf tail grass.
→ | **Running through the grove** and bending with the terrain

The Red Ribbon
Qinhuangdao City

A "red ribbon" spanning five hundred meters extends against a background of natural terrain and vegetation, which integrates the functions of lighting, seating, environmental interpretation, and orientation. While preserving as much of the natural river corridor as possible during the process of urbanization, this project demonstrates how a minimal design solution can achieve a dramatic improvement to the landscape.

PROJECT FACTS **Address:** east bank of Tanghe river between Gangcheng street and Beihuan street, Qinhuangdao City, China. **Planning partner:** Lin Shihong. **Client:** The Landscape Bureau, Qinghuangdao City, Hebei Province, China. **Completion:** 2008. **Production:** single piece. **Design:** individual design. **Functions:** seating, illumination. **Main materials:** fiber steel.

SEATING   TURENSCAPE

↑ | Site plan
← | Sunset

THE RED RIBBON

367

← | The red ribbon in snow
↓ | Concept sketch

SEATING

Ryo Yamada & Ayako Yamada

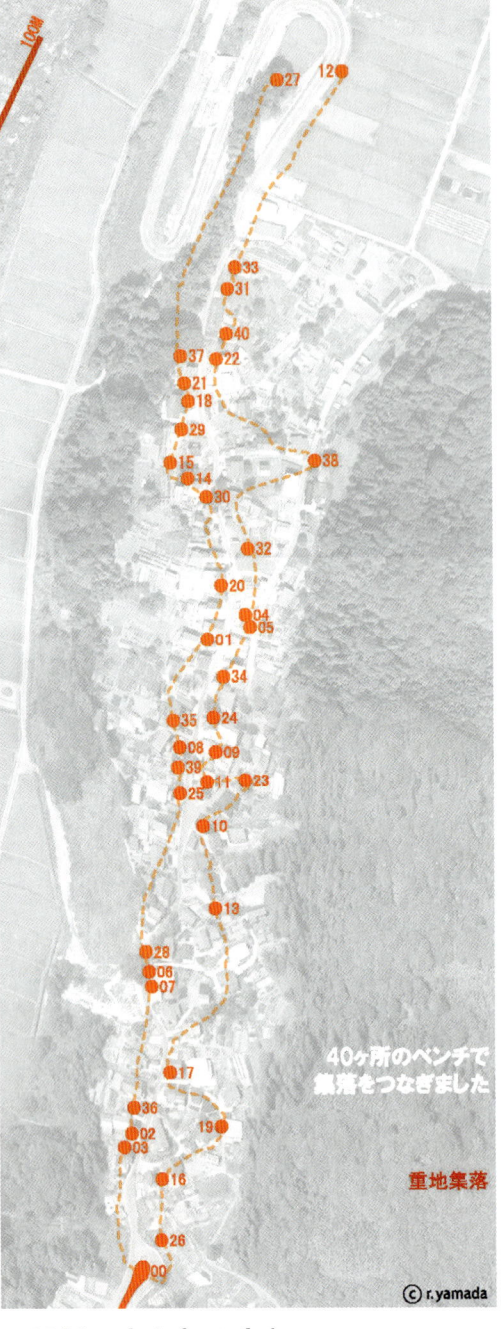

↖↖ | **Bench,** in front of a house
↖ | **Seating,** next to a memorial
↑ | **Layout plan**
↖ | **Combination of seatings**

Nakasato Juji Project

Tokamachi-city, Niigata

The project created a roadside public park in an agricultural region. The site had previously been occupied by an old house that was demolished as a part of road extension construction. Thematically, the architects sought to memorialize the character and spirit of the demolished home and other traditional homes in the area, and to capture the essence of the community. Much of the material used was drawn from what was left of the demolished house, while space has been provided for local residents to plant flowers and grass.

PROJECT FACTS
Address: Juji Nakasato Tokamachi-city Niigata, Japan. **Client:** Art Front Gallery & Niigata Prefacture. **Completion:** 2006. **Production:** serial production. **Design:** product line. **Functions:** seating, table. **Main materials:** scrapped woods.

Caesarea Landscape Design Ltd.

↑↑ | **Benches Rhodes 756,** with waste baskets Ceasarion BM958 and pergola Marquess 439/1
↗↗ | Seats Rhodes 767
↑ | Benches Rhodes 756
↗ | Seats Rhodes 767

Benches and Seats Rhodes

The densely perforated seats of the Rhodes series generate a transparent look. The seat perforation pattern has a metal thickness of two or three millimeters and forms rhomboid holes. The bench is carried by 2.5" tubular legs in variations with rubber foot bases or anchored on cement in gross texture. All reinforcements and components are made of six-millimeter-thick metal. Galvanized and oven-painted in pure polyester, the bench matches the RAL color key.

PROJECT FACTS
Client: City of Ramat Hasharon, Capital Jerusalem. **Completion:** 2009. **Production:** serial production. **Design:** product line. **Functions:** seating. **Main materials:** perforated metal, decorated stone base in different shades.

SEATING | Ryo Yamada & Ayako Yamada

↑ | Several seatings

Anonymous Garden
Sapporo

This welcoming outdoor space can be utilized not only by one person, but by a whole group. Like the sense of freedom provided by park benches, the flexibility of these arrangements offers a sense of peace and can be pleasantly shared by many people. Repeated simple patterns allow this arrangement to adapt to future changes as the design concept took into consideration the inclusion of additional pieces of furniture and simple modifications. Mass-produced wood materials were used to allow easy maintenance and simple application in other areas. All the works including planning, designing and construction were completed by the architect Ryo Yamada.

PROJECT FACTS **Address:** Shower Street Sapporo, Japan. **Client:** Sapporo City. **Completion:** 2008. **Production:** serial production. **Design:** individual design. **Functions:** seating, boards, table. **Main materials:** wood.

↑ | **Seating**
↓ | **Plan and plan detail**

↓ | **Different levels,** creating seatings and tables

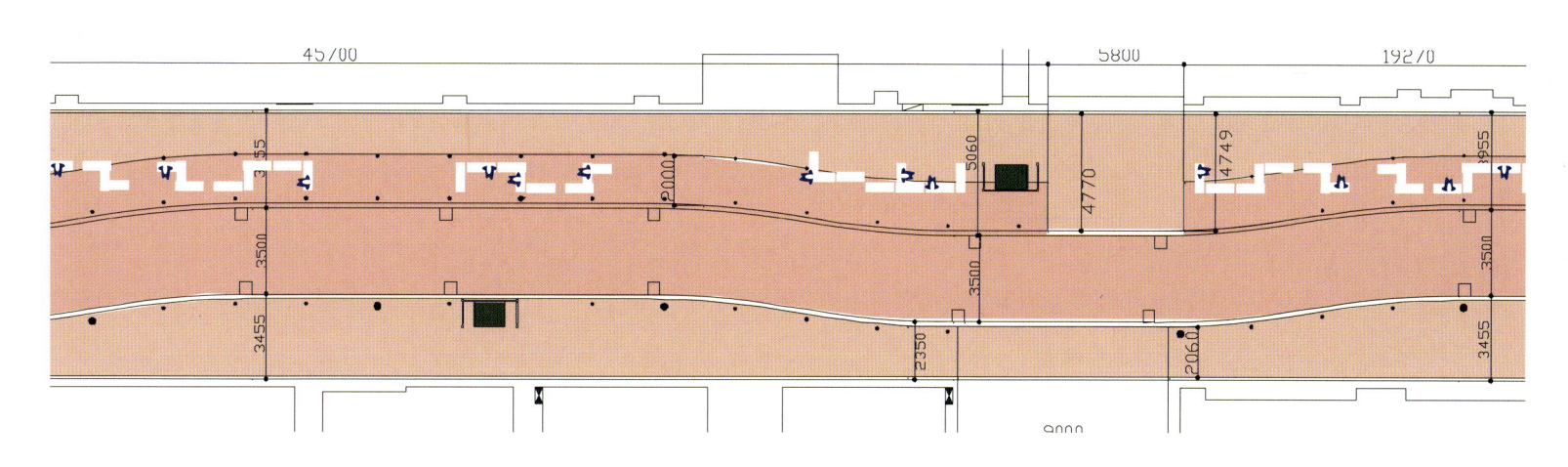

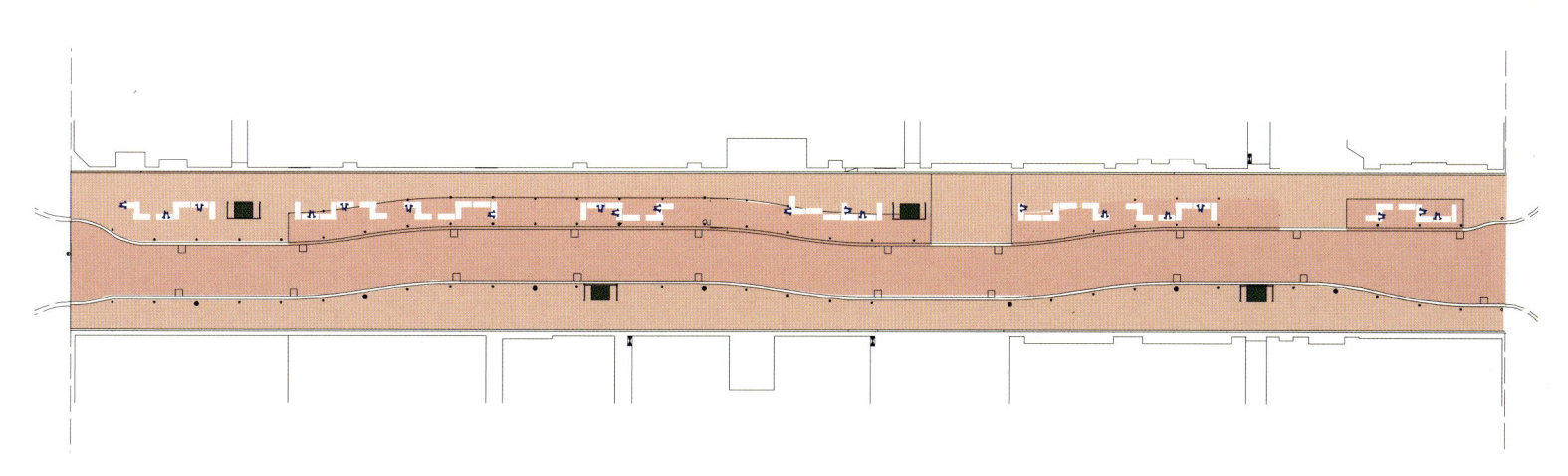

SEATING | OLIN / Richard Roark

↑ | **Bubble Bench in use,** comfortable for lying and sitting

Bubble Bench
Camana Bay

Camana Bay is a vibrant community on Grand Cayman with a sustainable, urban mission. The Bubble Bench, designed by OLIN specifically for the project, contributes to the aquatic fantasy theme of its downtown Gardenia Cinema Courtyard. Azure blue, glowing orange and deep sea green colors recall the plants and corals found in the dramatic reefs surrounding Grand Cayman. At night, the Bubble Benches have an iridescent glow, with rings reminiscent of water ripples and spheres at varying heights like air bubbles rising from the deep. The effect celebrates the otherworldly beauty of the sea, which so many come to Grand Cayman to experience. The Bubble Benches provide playful, unique seating directly inspired by natural beauty.

PROJECT FACTS

Planning partner: Epoch Product Design. **Client:** Cayman Shores Development Ltd. **Completion:** 2009. **Production:** single piece. **Design:** individual design. **Functions:** seating, illumination. **Main materials:** thermo-formed acrylic, stainless steel.

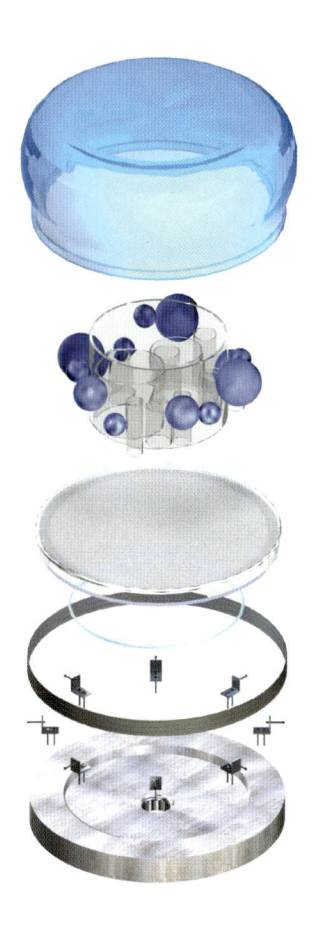

↑ | **Bubble Bench assembly**
↓ | **Benches and illuminated fountain**

↑ | **View at dusk,** illuminated bench

SEATING | OLIN / Lucinda R. Sanders

↑ | Curved Glass Bench

Glass Bench
New York City

Being only blocks from Ground Zero, the Museum of Jewish Heritage required a perimeter, including an entry plaza, to secure the landscape around the building while simultaneously welcoming and complementing its institutional mission. The solution was an inherent contradiction: glass benches as security. Generous translucent benches made of recycled glass were designed to be welcoming, delicate and ephemeral, masking the internal structure which functions as an impenetrable security barrier. Set deep into the concrete below, imperceptible steel posts within the benches perform like bollards, preventing vehicular access. At night the benches are illuminated and create a hauntingly beautiful and memorable blue glow.

PROJECT FACTS **Address:** 36 Battery Place, New York, NY 10280, USA. **Planning partner:** Domingo Gonzalez Architectural Lighting Design, Joel Berman Glass Studios, Dewhurst Macfarlane & Partners. **Client:** Museum of Jewish Heritage. **Completion:** 2007. **Production:** single piece. **Design:** individual design. **Functions:** seating, illumination, barrier. **Main materials:** ipe wood, stainless steel, textured cast glass, concrete.

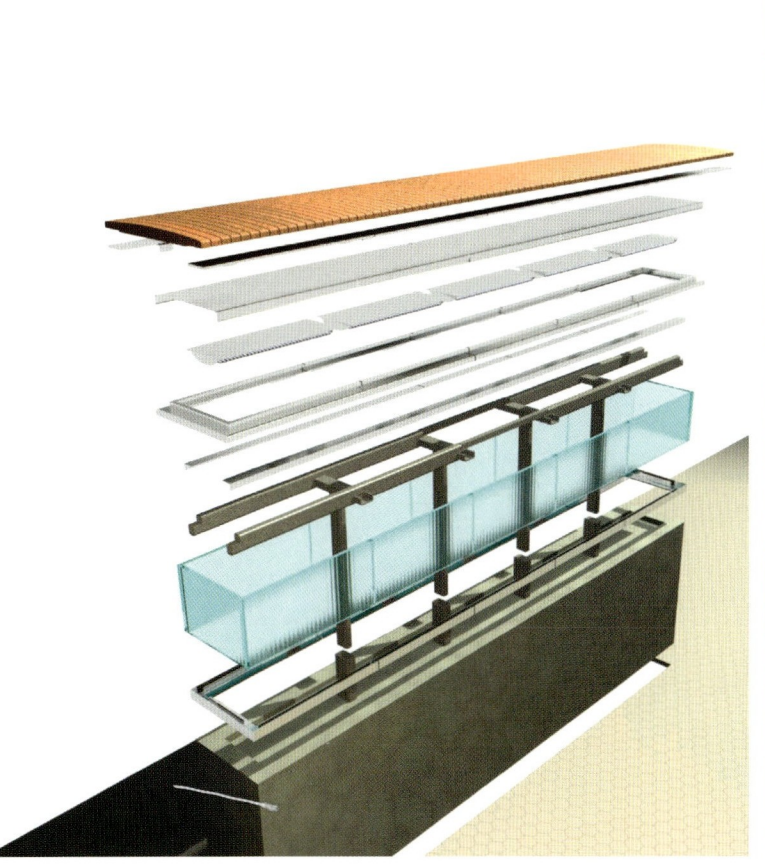

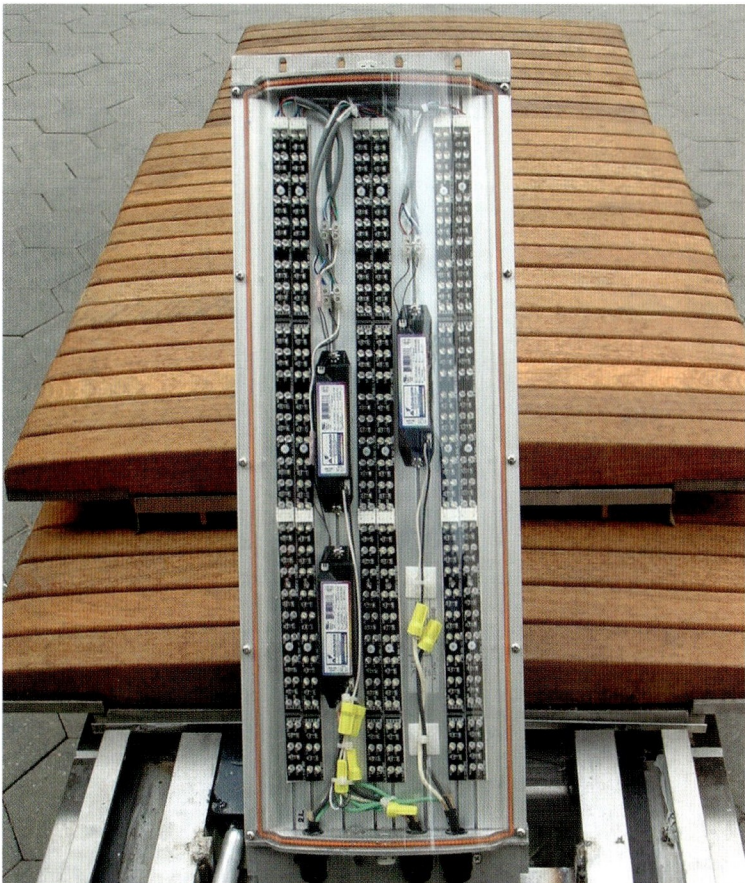

375

↑ | **Glass Bench assembly**
↓ | **Night view,** Glass Bench spreads blue light

↑ | **Light fixtures** resting below the wood top

SEATING | KOMPLOT Design / Boris Berlin, Poul Christiansen

↑ | **Chairs and tables,** in front of fair ground of CODE 09, Copenhagen
→ | **Close up view**

Concrete Things
Copenhagen

Concrete Things is a series of outdoor concrete furniture dealing with the relation between the individual and the collective in public space. They consist of simple geometric shapes with a pavement-inspired grid that takes on the shape of the user, keeping the memory of somebody once seated in them. Draining holes in the bottom of the cavity on the intersections of the grid pattern of "channels" keep the seating surface dry. Drawn in the air by thin lines of steel rods it becomes a weightless "wireframe" ghost-image of the heavy, very "material" concrete chair.

PROJECT FACTS **Address:** Rigshospitalet, Copenhagen University Hospital, Blegdamsvej 9, 2100 Copenhagen, Denmark. **Planning partner:** Danish Technological Institute. **Client:** NOLA Industrier AB, Sweden. **Completion:** 2009. **Production:** serial production. **Design:** individual design. **Functions:** seating, plant tub, space organizing, façade protection. **Main materials:** self tightening concrete, powder coated stainless steel rod.

SEATING　　　　　　　　　　　　　KOMPLOT DESIGN

↑ | **Waiting area,** at the Copenhagen University Hospital
← | **Concrete chair**
↓ | **Wireframe,** ghost version of Concrete chair

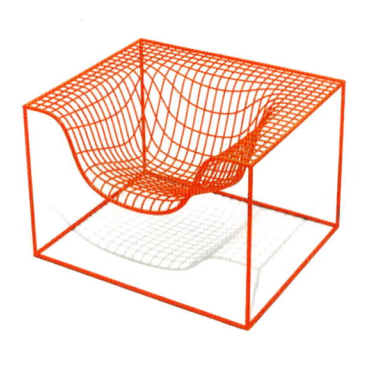

CONCRETE THINGS

← | Chairs and tables
↓ | Close up view

LIGHT AND SIGN

GARBAGE

BOUNDARY

BIKE AND PLAY

SEATING

ENSEMBLE PAVEMENT PRODUCT LINE PLANTS AND WATER SHELTER

SHELTER | Buro North / Soren Luckins

↑ | **Solar shades** from kid's perspective, showing visual feeadback LEDs
↗ | **Solar shade** can be easily rotated towards the sun
→ | **Detail view**

Veil Solar Shade

The Veil Solar Shade is a concept for Australian primary school yards to integrate solar energy harvesting in a both pragmatic and evocative form. Utilizing information about consumption and energy as an educational tool, this interactive concept explores the visual connection between energy and the environment. It features a broad solar panel surface that is rotated throughout the day by children to best suit the position of the sun. The underside of the shade provides visual feedback to instantly indicate the quantity of energy being collected. Correct solar orientation will generate a positive visual message, incorrect orientation will indicate a low amount of power collection.

PROJECT FACTS **Client:** Victorian Eco – Innovation Laboratory. **Completion:** ongoing. **Production:** serial production. **Design:** individual design. **Functions:** shelter, solar collection, education. **Main materials:** aluminum, membrane

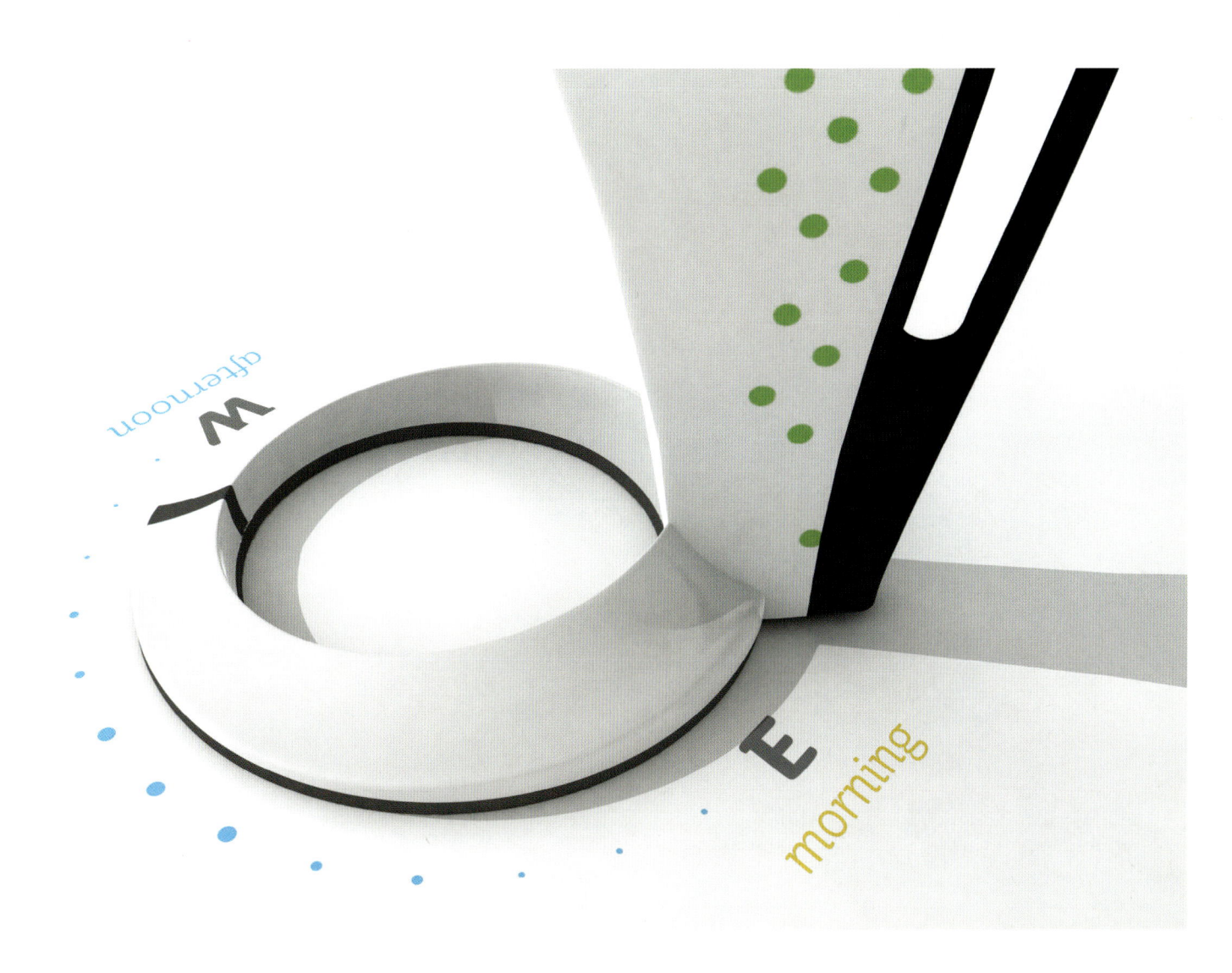

383

SHELTER   BURO NORTH

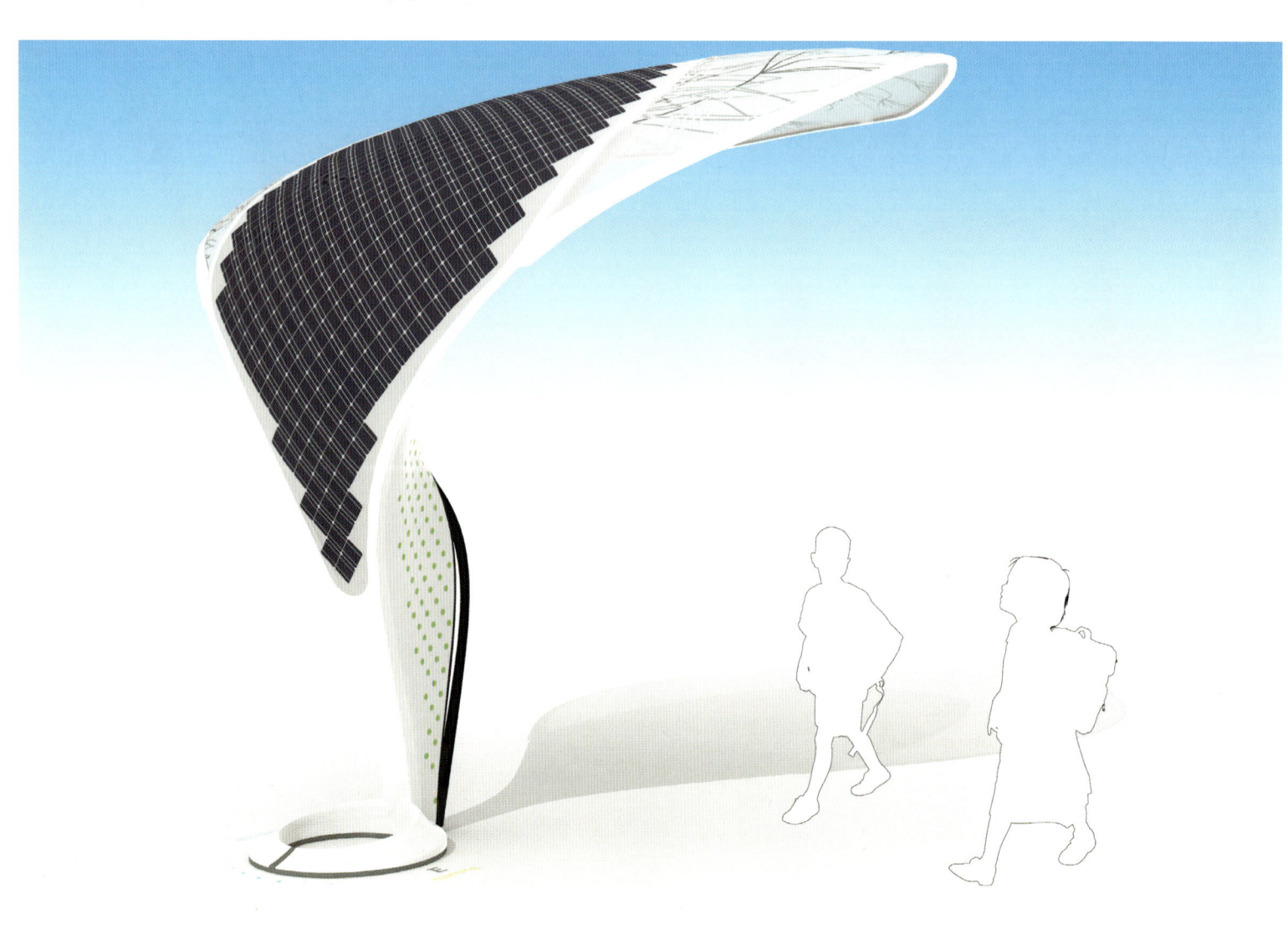

← | **Sketch**
↓ | **Elevation**
→ | **Solar shades** in a school yard

VEIL SOLAR SHADE

SHELTER | Grimshaw / Nicholas Grimshaw

↑ | **Bus Shelter,** perspective view
→ | **Newsstand,** perspective view

Street Furniture Franchise
New York

Grimshaw worked with Cemusa on an exclusive range of street furniture to be installed and operated in New York City over the next 20 years. The range comprises a bus shelter, newsstand, and automatic public toilet. Robustness and durability were key design drivers, in order to allow the furniture to endure an unremitting street environment. Constructed from recyclable components, including high-resistance tempered laminated glass and stainless steel, the high quality furniture is made of self-finishing materials which will withstand heavy use. Contextually, the design needed to be distinctive whilst blending into the urban landscape with minimal visual or spatial intervention.

PROJECT FACTS   **Planning partner:** Grimshaw Industrial Design, Billlings Jackson Design, STV. **Client:** Cemusa Inc. **Completion:** 2007. **Production:** serial production. **Design:** product line. **Functions:** seating, toilet, shelter, newsstand. **Main materials:** steel, glass.

SHELTER GRIMSHAW

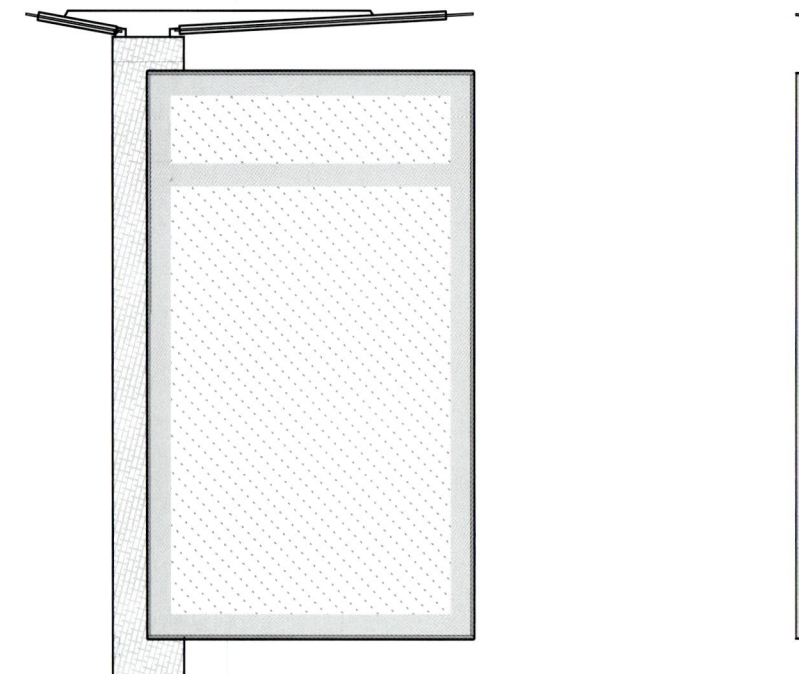

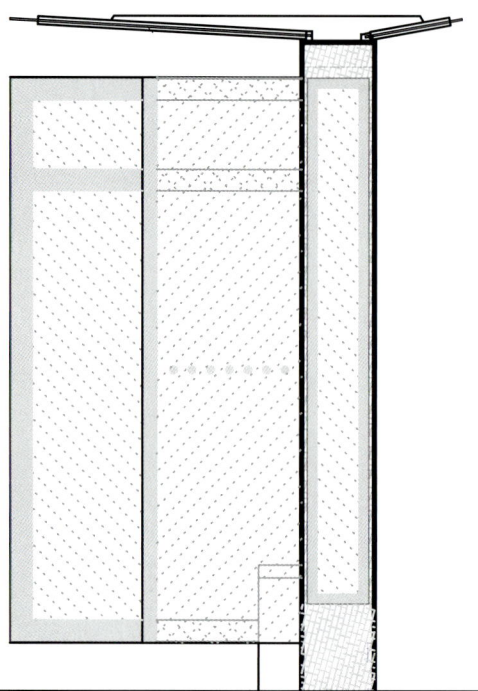

↑ | **Side elevations,** bus shelter
← | **Bus shelter,** perspective view

STREET FURNITURE FRANCHISE

← | **Toilet**
↓ | **Bus shelter**, front view

SHELTER

Pedro Silva Dias

↑ | **Nicho telephone column** at Lisbon Expo'98

Nicho PT

This public telephone column was first conceived for the 1998 Lisbon World Fair (Expo'98), and later applied all across Portugal. Initially, the project consisted of a triangular plan column with rounded faces. The glass shelter is a geometrical development of the basic plan. An interior steel structure supports a modular system of stainless steel panels. The structure develops in three vertical modules and three horizontal modules reaching a total of nine. The horizontal module development permits the application of one, two or three telephones to the central panels. The signage elements are applied on the superior panels, while the inferior panels allow access to the interior of the column.

| PROJECT FACTS

Client: Portugal Telecom. **Completion:** 1998. **Production:** serial production. **Design:** individual design. **Functions:** telephone column. **Main materials:** stainless steel.

391

↑ | **Detail view**
↓ | **Exploded perspective,** different models

↑ | **Public telephone** in use

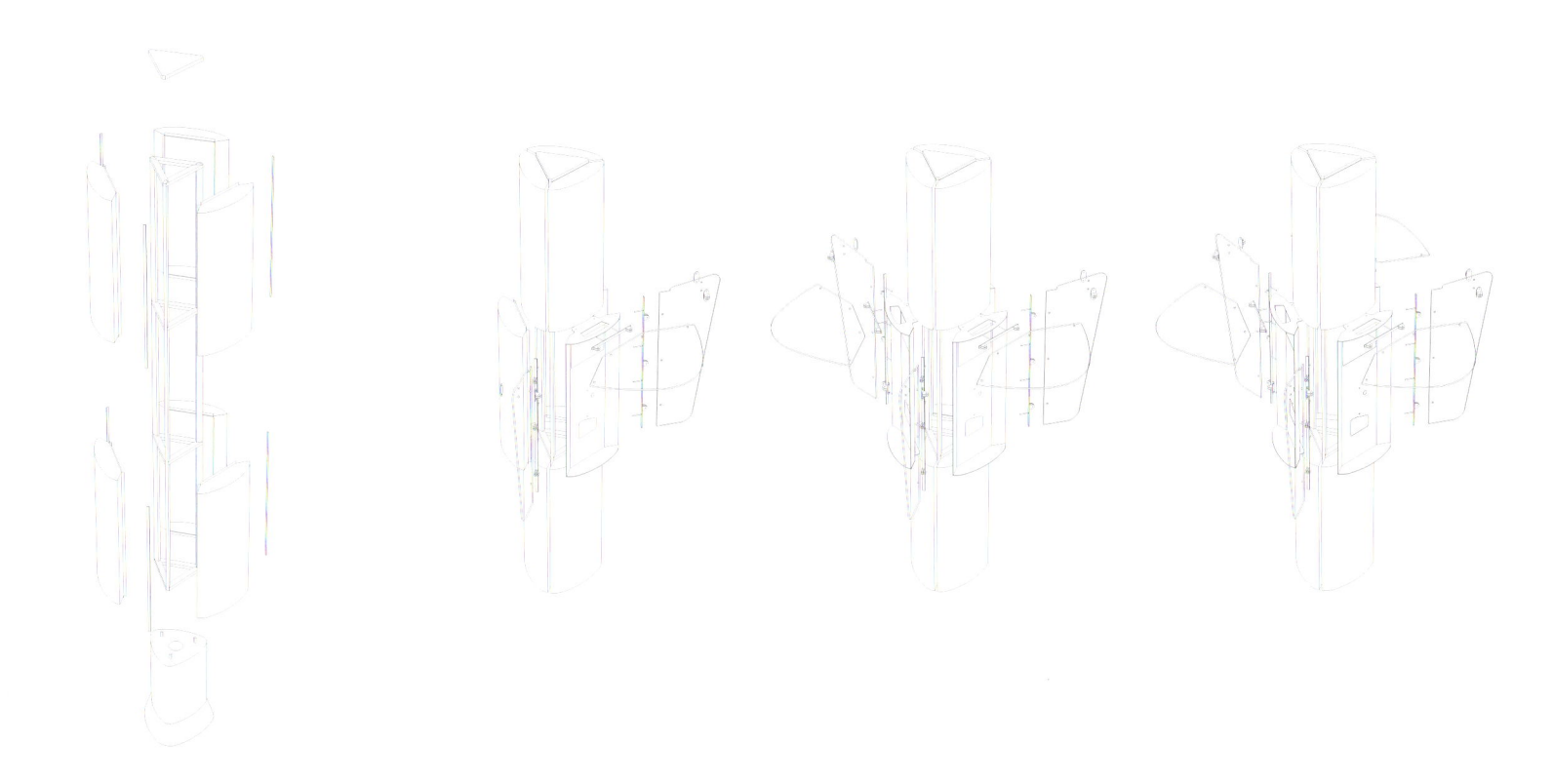

SHELTER | Pedro Silva Dias

↑ | **Steel column,** framed by curved glass wings

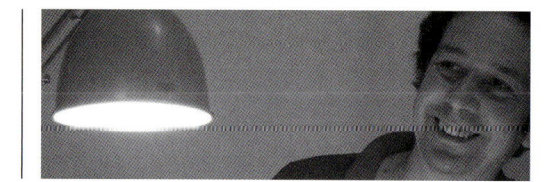

Cabine PT

Maintaining the morphological line and materials used on the public telephone column previously created for the same company, the aim of this project was to design an object of great transparency that can fit into any urban typology. The plan, based on a triangle, was therefore adapted to the functional needs of a small interior space. Putting the telephone in one of the triangle corners reduced the residual space needed for the standard quadrangular plan equipment. The body of the telephone booth consists of the two glass panels involving the stainless steel column. The curved outline visually reduces its dimensions, while allowing more versatile orientation in public spaces.

PROJECT FACTS

Client: Portugal Telecom. **Completion:** 2007. **Production:** serial production. **Design:** individual design. **Functions:** telephone booth. **Main materials:** steel, glass.

393

↑ | **Exploded perspective**
↓ | **Detail view,** glass wings mounting

↑ | **Cabine PT,** perspective view

SHELTER | Heatherwick studio

↑ | Newspaper kiosk closed
→ | Rear view

Newspaper Kiosks
Kensington & Chelsea

The new kiosks designed for selling newspapers at a number of locations throughout the Borough of Kensington & Chelsea will replace the dull rectangular boxes with roller shutters that render them dead and unwelcoming by night and with flat surfaces that make them a target for graffiti. The aim was to design a kiosk without flat surfaces on the outside that looks good at night as well as during the day, with a different kind of opening and closing mechanism to make the vendor's life easier. The new kiosk thus has a distinctive form – the result of a more ergonomic arrangement of magazine shelves which also renders the outside a less obvious target for vandalism.

PROJECT FACTS **Client:** Royal Borough of Kensington & Chelsea. **Completion:** 2007. **Production:** serial production. **Design:** individual design. **Functions:** kiosk. **Main materials:** wood, glass, patinated brass.

SHELTER HEATHERWICK STUDIO

↑ | Detail view
← | Stepping-outward form

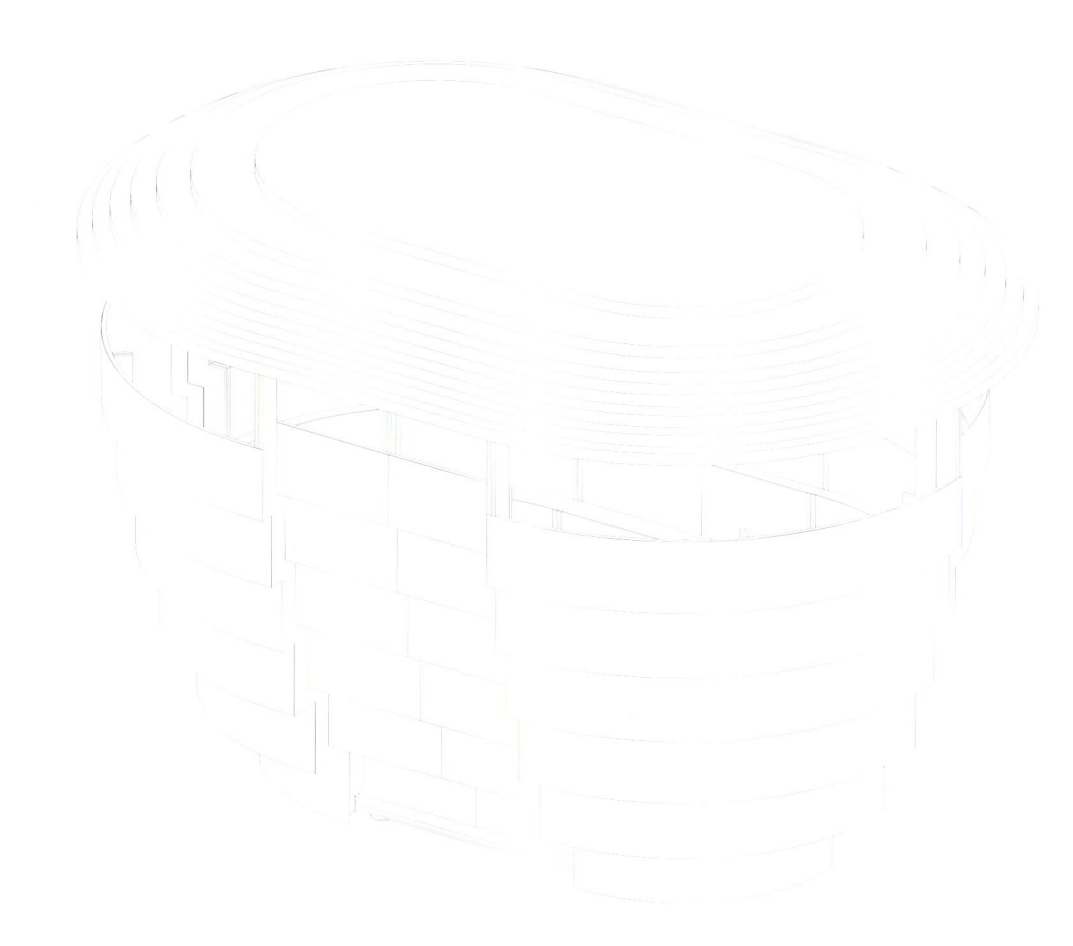

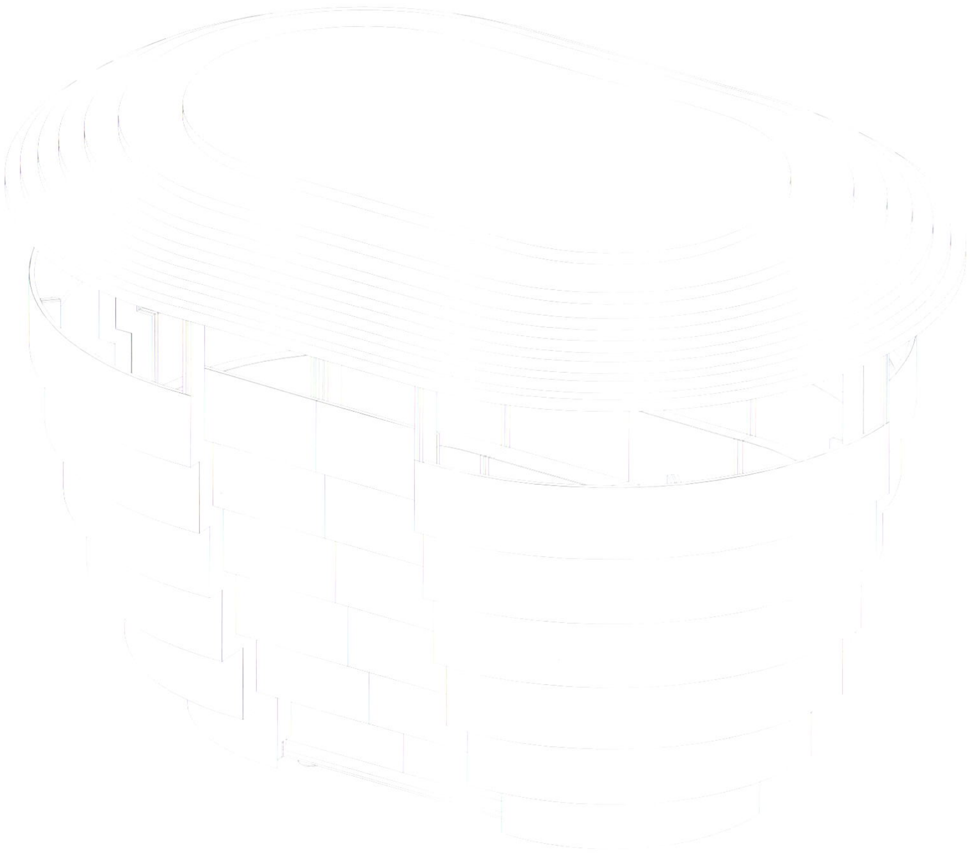

NEWSPAPER KIOSKS

397

← | **Isometric view**
↓ | **Front elevation,** showing kiosk half opened

SHELTER | Estudio Cabeza / Diana Cabeza, Leandro Hcinc, Martín Wolfson

↑ | Bus shelter

Urban Furniture and Equipment
Buenos Aires

Urban elements must respond to the geographical and cultural environments that surround them and be able to blend with its general disposition and particularities. These elements are intended to be placed on sidewalks. Endowed with a front and a back part, they allow people to walk throughout their perimeter and use them in different ways and from different directions. This creates continuity between the private realm and the open public space and confers a more dynamic perception of the city while avoiding the urban pathways that these elements usually generate. The project focuses on preserving the historical heritage of the city, while providing modern urban elements for everyday life. The whole system of urban elements was created with the idea of accessibility.

PROJECT FACTS

Address: City of Buenos Aires, Argentina. **Graphic design:** Osvaldo Ortiz, Gabriela Falgione, Pablo Cosgaya, Marcela Romero. **Client:** Government of Buenos Aires. **Completion:** 2005. **Production:** serial production. **Design:** product line. **Functions:** shelters, signs. **Main materials:** cast iron, painted steel, steel structure, laminated green glass with translucid PVB.

Bus shelter | B Type

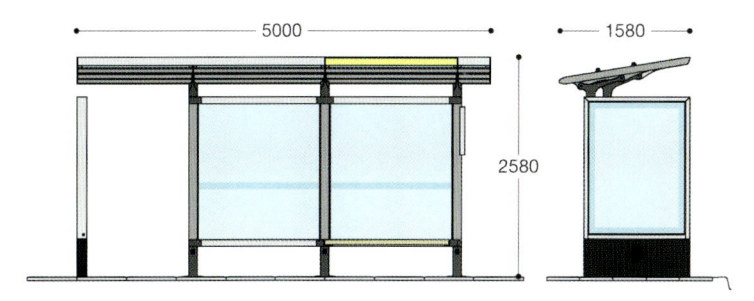

Street signage | 5B Type

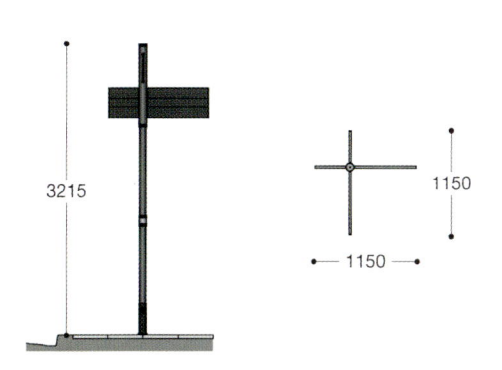

↑ | Plans and views
↓ | Bus shelter

↑ | Signage system

SHELTER | Architektin Mag. arch. Silja Tillner, Prof. Valie Export

↑ | **Glass structure** below the bridge
→ | **Transparent glass cube**

Kubus EXPORT – The transparent Room
Vienna

"The Glass Room" is an independent transparent room which was inserted under a bridge of the Gürtel main ring road in Vienna. It is artended for use by art exhibitions in the broadest sense. On the side facing the ring road, a door has been installed. The permeability of the bridge towards both ring road sides is emphasized by the absolute transparency of the glass construction. The bearing elements are four glass frames, which consist of two struts and a binding beam located on top. The glass panes made of laminated safety glass are fixed in between. For the cube to appear to "float", it is illuminated from the inside by a light strip positioned on the floor.

PROJECT FACTS

Address: Gürtel Boulevard, Brücke Friedmanngasse 3, 1160 Vienna, Austria. **Planning partner:** Ingenieurbüro Vasko & Partner, F&A Fenster-Glas-Sonderkonstruktionsbau GmbH. **Client:** MA 57, Frauenbüro. **Completion:** 2000. **Production:** single piece. **Design:** individual design. **Functions:** artwork, exhibition space, stage. **Main materials:** glass.

401

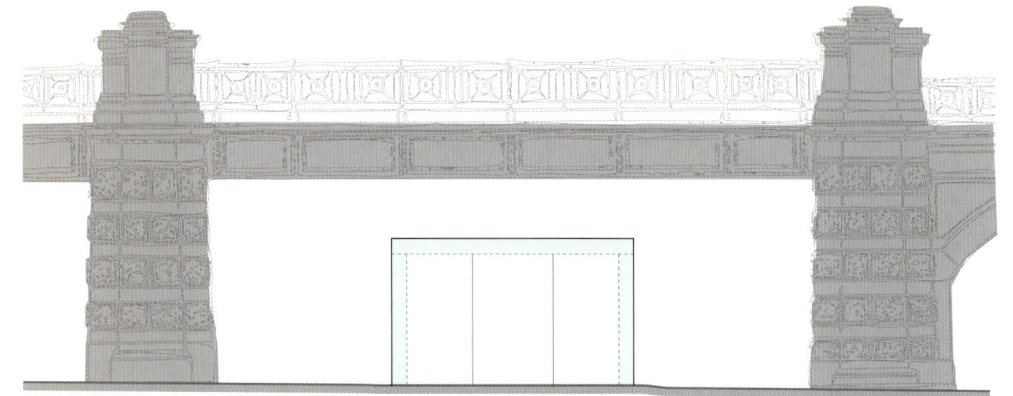

SHELTER   ARCHITEKTIN MAG. ARCH. SILJA TILLNER, PROF. VALIE EXPORT

↑ | **Night view,** the cube is illuminated from ground level
← | **Section and plan**
→ | **Night view,** the structure seems to hover weightlessly

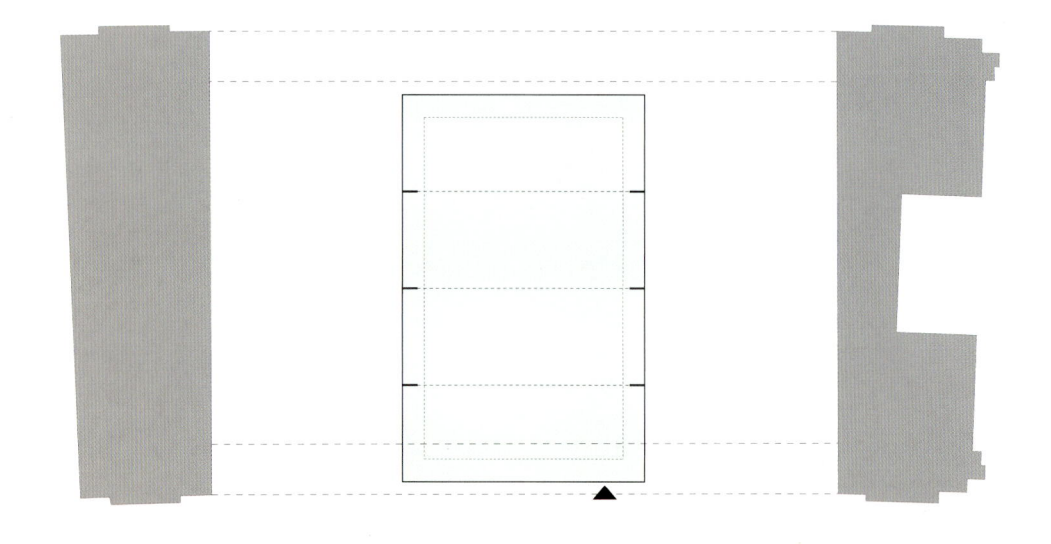

KUBUS EXPORT

SHELTER

mmcité a.s. /
David Karásek,
Radek Hegmon

↑ | **Regio bus shelter,** total view
↘ | **Plans of Regio Rg210b**

Regio Shelters

The Regio bus shelters with their glazed exteriors only minimally impact the appearance of the urban landscape. Curved bearing structures provide them with a modern and rather delicate style. The Regio series includes several models, which are all made of wood, glass and steel. From an open system without side walls to shelters enclosed from three sides, all public transportation requirements can be fulfilled. The structure of the roof varies also within the system from plan flat roofs, via tilted roof structures, to wing-like variations. As a modern piece of urban furniture, Regio combines esthetics with simplicity and durability.

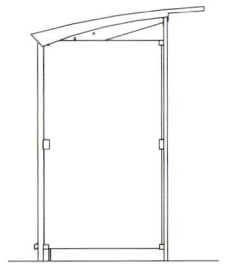

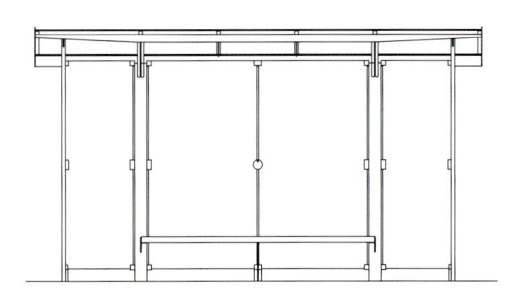

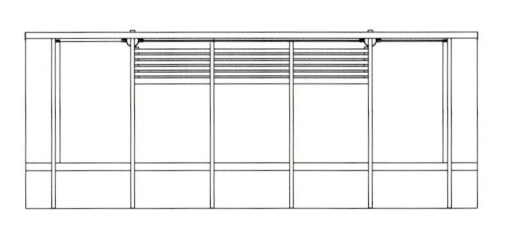

PROJECT FACTS

Client: mmcité a.s., TEC Gembloux. **Completion:** 1998. **Production:** serial production. **Design:** product line. **Functions:** shelter. **Main materials:** steel, glass, wood.

↑ | **Detail view,** frame and glazing
↓ | **Detail view,** wooden bench and glazing

↓ | **Deatil view,** glazing fixture

SHELTER | Bacco Arquitetos Associados / Jupira Corbucci, Marcelo Consiglio Barbosa

↑ | José Maria Lisboa stop

Transfer Stations
São Paulo

The design of the transfer stations emerged from the synthesis between the problems posed by the municipal administration and a project idea that sought to change some pre-established concepts. It was proposed that the stations should not "have a façade" to minimize interference with the neighborhood. Working with the longitudinal section solves the problem of modules and interference with the neighborhood with a different perspective and another way to offer shelter. The portico is designed with two curves in its extremities, creating continuity between floor and roof and defining the concept of a closed and aerodynamic object – automotive aesthetics coupled with image technology.

PROJECT FACTS

Address: Av.9 de Julho, Av. Rebouças and others, São Paulo, SP, Brasil. **Client:** SPTrans. **Completion:** 2004. **Production:** serial production. **Design:** product line. **Functions:** bus stop shelters. **Main materials:** steel.

407

↑ | **Getúlio Vargas stop,** detail
↓ | **Bird's-eye view,** station on 9 de Julho avenue

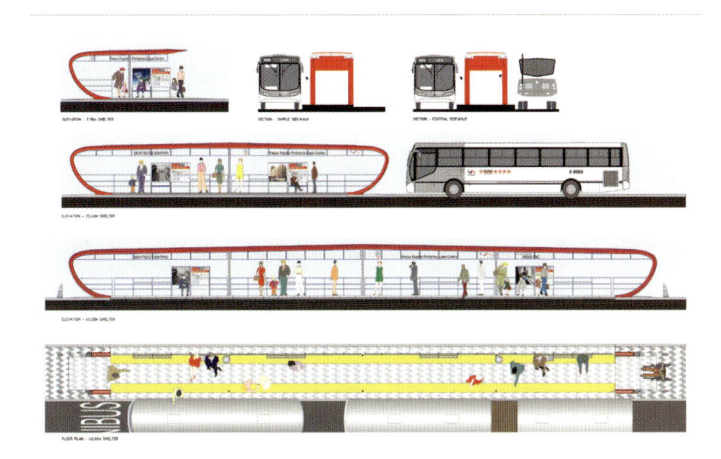

↑↑ | **Types of arrengements of the primary module**
↑ | **Designed curve**

SHELTER | Miró Rivera Architects / Juan Miró, Miguel Rivera

↑ | Side elevation

Texas Cowboys Pavilion
Austin

This addition to the alumni center grounds extends the uses of the facility by creating an outdoor pavilion amidst the trees. Flanking the football stadium, it offers a location for pre-game events and post-game parties, lectures and presentations. The speakers, A/V connections and moveable spotlights provide flexibility for various events, which thanks to integral fans, indirect lighting and roll-down sunshades, can occur all year round and at any time of day. The expressive structure of the pavilion takes its roots from the existing alumni center trellises. The beams, trusses and glass roof form a system balanced upon two brick columns and stabilized by post-tensioned stainless steel cables.

PROJECT FACTS **Address:** The University of Texas at Austin, Austin, TX, USA. **Client:** The Texas Exes. **Completion:** 2004. **Production:** single piece. **Design:** individual design. **Functions:** multi-function outdoor pavilion. **Main materials:** steel, glass and brick.

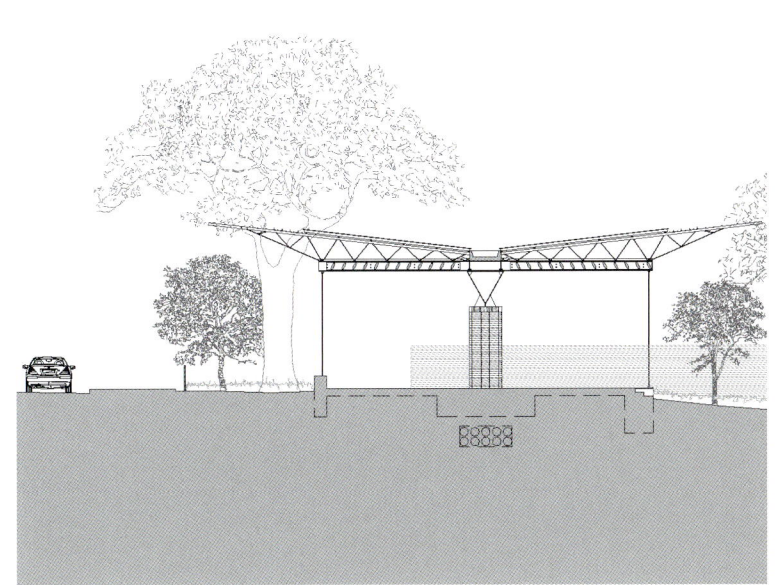

↑ | **Section**
↓ | **Side elevation at night,** with the shades down

↑ | **Close up view of the steel structure**
↓ | **Pavilion at night,** with the University of Texas football stadium in the background

SHELTER

Rainer Schmidt
Landschaftsarchitekten

↑ | **View along the main axle of the central park**
→ | **View of the pergola,** near the forest garden

Central Park, Parkstadt Schwabing
Munich

The central park of Parkstadt Schwabing is framed by six to ten-floor service buildings. To create human proportions, large pergolas measuring 10 x 10 x 10 meters structure the park. Allocated to the pergolas, thematic gardens create small-scale leisure areas in the open park space. The thematic gardens reflect the vicinity and visual connection to the Alps. The themes include a rock garden, a forest garden, a mountain lake garden, or an Alpine foothills garden.

PROJECT FACTS
Address: Oskar-Schlemmer-Straße, 80807 Munich, Germany. **Planning partner:** André Perret Architekt, Munich. **Client:** City Tec, Munich. **Completion:** 2002. **Production:** single piece. **Design:** individual design. **Functions:** pavilion. **Main materials:** steel.

SHELTER RAINER SCHMIDT LANDSCHAFTSARCHITEKTEN

↑ | Draft sketches
← | Layout

CENTRAL PARK, PARKSTADT SCHWABING

← | Overview plan
↙ | Perspective view of the mountain lake garden

SHELTER | BRUTO d.o.o. with Urban Švegl / Matej Kucina

↑ | **Steel cube in green,** small structure unit
↗ | **Big structure unit**
→ | **Pavilion interior,** big structure unit

Pavilions for Smokers
Ljubljana

With new restricted indoor non smoking rules it became necessary to design a smoking pavilion for a big Telecom company. Series of mobile modular units were designed, which can be combined on different structures. All units are made of 3 x 3 x 3 meter steel cube structures and they have various membranes and details. They can be joined together and combined in several ways and sizes to build a modular pavilion structure.

PROJECT FACTS **Address:** Vojkova 78, 1000 Ljubljana, Slovenia. **Client:** Mobitel d.d. **Completion:** 2008. **Production:** single piece. **Design:** individual design. **Functions:** shelters, seating. **Main materials:** steel construction, composite decking, polycarbonate plates.

SHELTER BRUTO D.O.O. WITH URBAN ŠVEGL

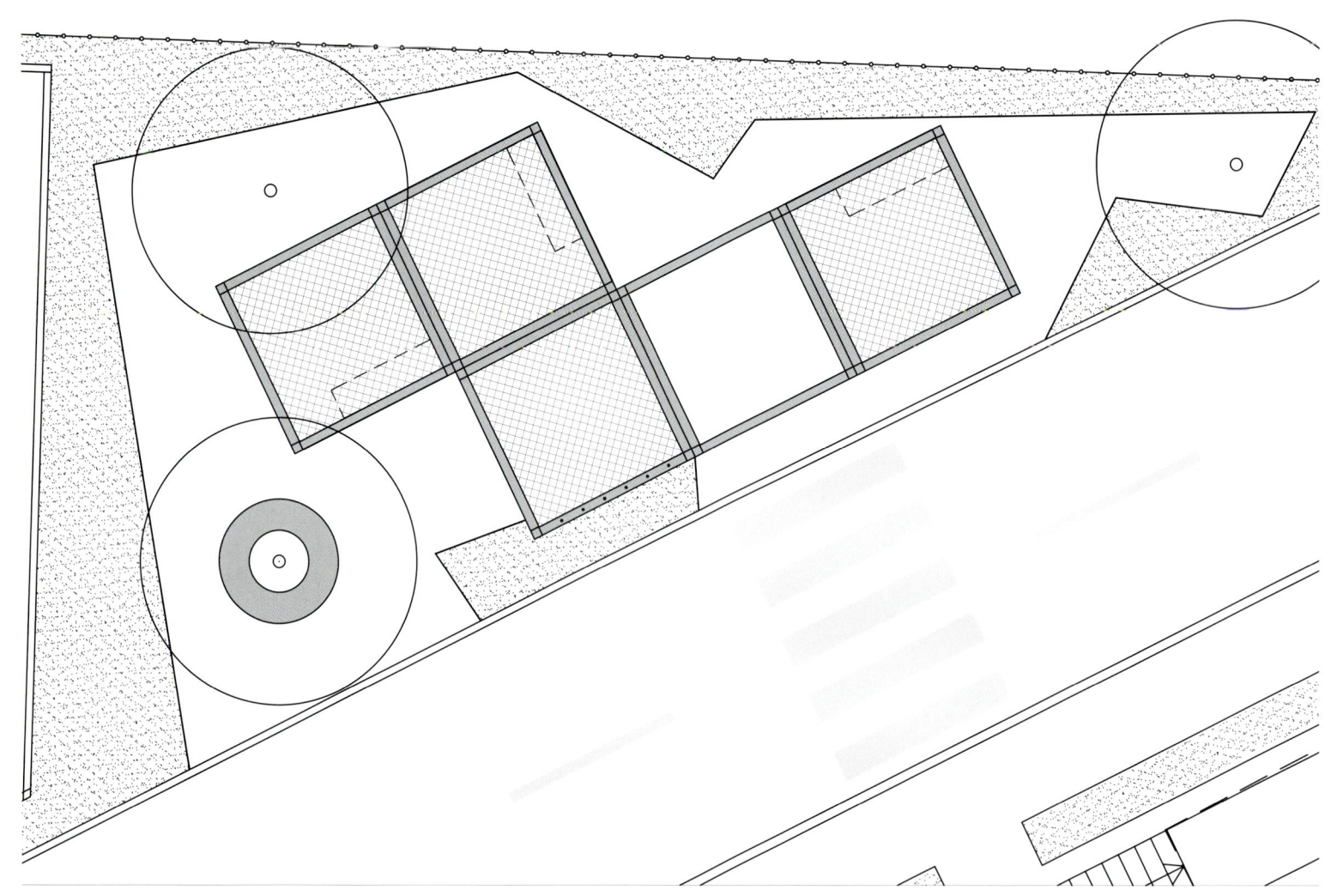

↑ | Site plan
← | View through the pavilion

PAVILIONS FOR SMOKERS

← | Single unit
↓ | Design sketch

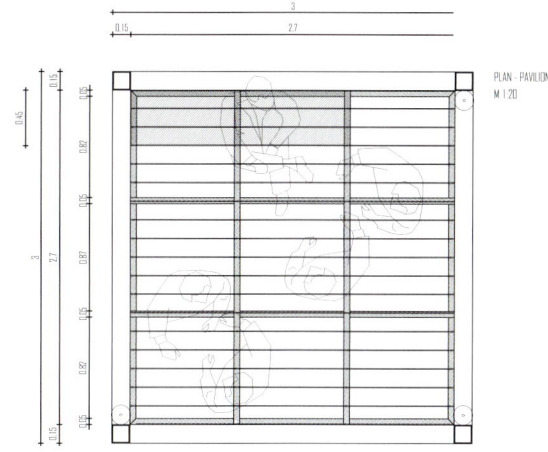

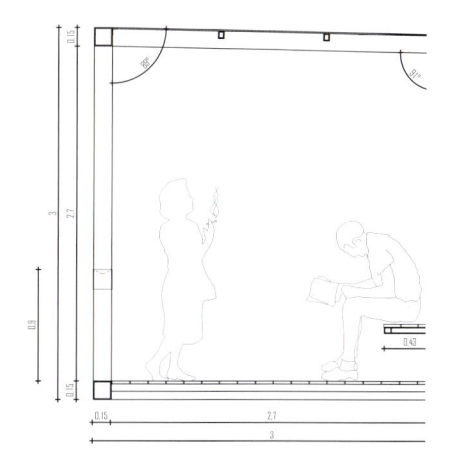

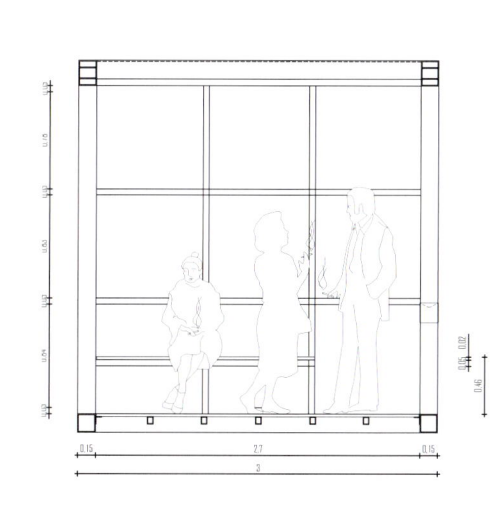

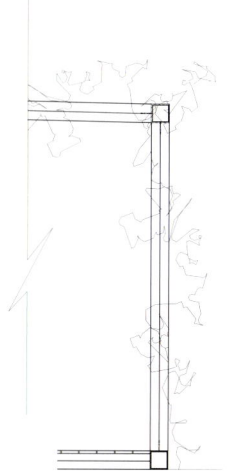

SHELTER | Corbeil + Bertrand
Architecture de paysage

↑ | **Front view,** with the board walk transformed in bench at the rear

Hortus urbanus
Montréal

Unlike a hortus conclusus (cloistered garden), this proposal more closely resembles a hortus apertus (open garden) or hortus urbanus (city garden), anchored in a resolutely contemporary setting – a significant indicator of which is the residual land that is its foundation. Hortus urbanus experiments with vegetation and common place materials, juxtaposing them in a creative collection and diverting them from their intended vocation to reconstruct their meaning. Wood, galvanized steel, recycled polymer, translucent synthetic fabric, remnants of slate, and birch trees come together to form a whole.

PROJECT FACTS **Address:** Old Montreal, Montreal, Canada. **Graphic design:** FEED. **Landscape designer:** Stéphane Bertrand, Jasmin Corbeil. **Designer "Tête-à-tête" black furniture:** Ineke Hans. **Client:** Flora International Montréal. **Completion:** 2007. **Production:** single piece. **Design:** individual design. **Functions:** shelter. **Main materials:** galvanised steel, recycled polymer, translucent synthetic fabric, remnants of slate, Canadian hemlock lumbers.

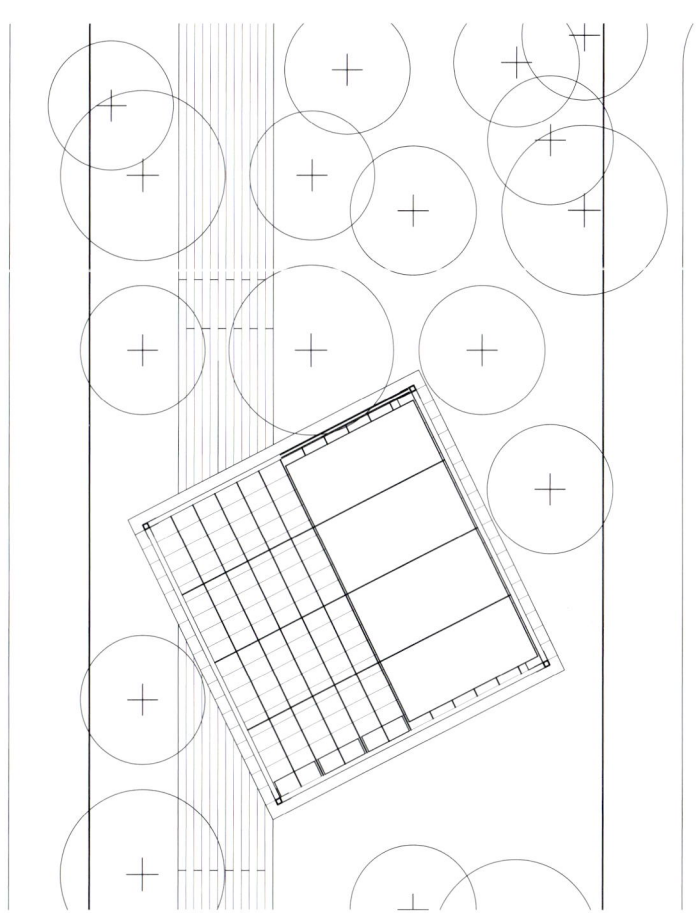

↑ | **General site plan**
↓ | **View from the back,** with hemlock board walk

↑ | **Inside view,** with Humulus japonicus (Hop) wall
↓ | **Side view,** with printed screen

SHELTER | Della Valle + Bernheimer Design, LLP

↑ | View through laser-cut steel skin

Butterfly Pavilion
Tulsa

Della Valle Bernheimer's design for a garden structure at the Philbrook Museum of Art is based on the spirit and etymology of the word "pavilion", which is derived from the French papillon, meaning butterfly. The cocoon-like Butterfly Pavilion is also inspired by the entomological transformation of the silkworm into the butterfly. During metamorphosis, the silkworm pupates, spinning itself an intricate chamber. The Butterfly Pavilion resembles a cocoon, not spun of silk but etched and cut from plate steel. Using laser cutting technology, a diminutive 8' x 16' pavilion was fabricated from wood decking and steel tubes.

PROJECT FACTS

421

Address: Philbrook Museum of Art, 2727 South Rockford Road, Tulsa, OK 74114, USA. **Client:** Philbrook Museum of Art. **Completion:** 2005. **Production:** single piece. **Design:** individual design. **Functions:** shelter. **Main materials:** steel.

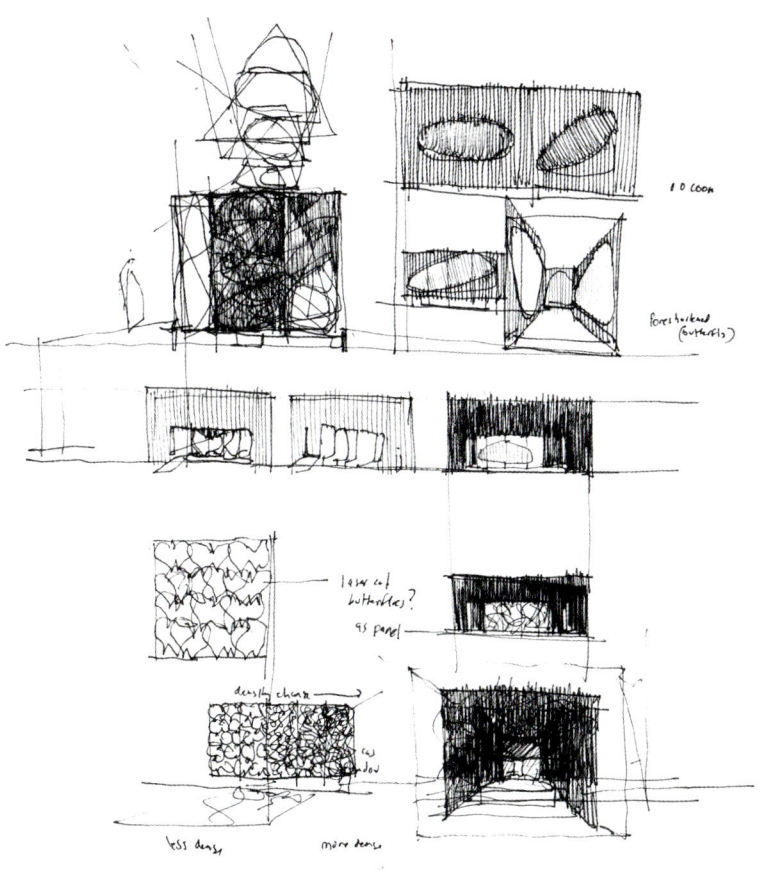

↑ | Sketch
↓ | General view

↑ | Interior
↓ | View of trees through laser-cut steel skin

SHELTER | NIO architecten

↑ | Sitting area

The Amazing Whale Jaw
Hoofddorp

At the beginning of the year 2003, a bus station was built on the forecourt of Hoofddorp's Spaarne Hospital. Located in the middle of a square, this facility block is a public area in the form of an island that serves as a junction for the local bus service. The design of this kind of building is generally neutral, but here the aim was to create a strong, individual image that was less austere and generic. Hence, the building was designed in the tradition of Oscar Niemeyer as a cross between white Modernism and black Baroque. The building is completely made of polystyrene foam and polyester and constitutes the world's largest structure made of synthetic materials (50 x 10 x 5 meters).

PROJECT FACTS **Address:** Voorplein Spaarne Ziekenhuis, 2130 AT Hoofddorp, The Netherlands. **Client:** Schiphol Project Consult. **Completion:** 2003. **Production:** single piece. **Design:** individual design. **Functions:** bus stop. **Main materials:** polystyrene foam, polyester.

↑ | The shelter is giving a frame to the adjacent buildings
↓ | Plan and elevations

↑ | Bird's-eye view

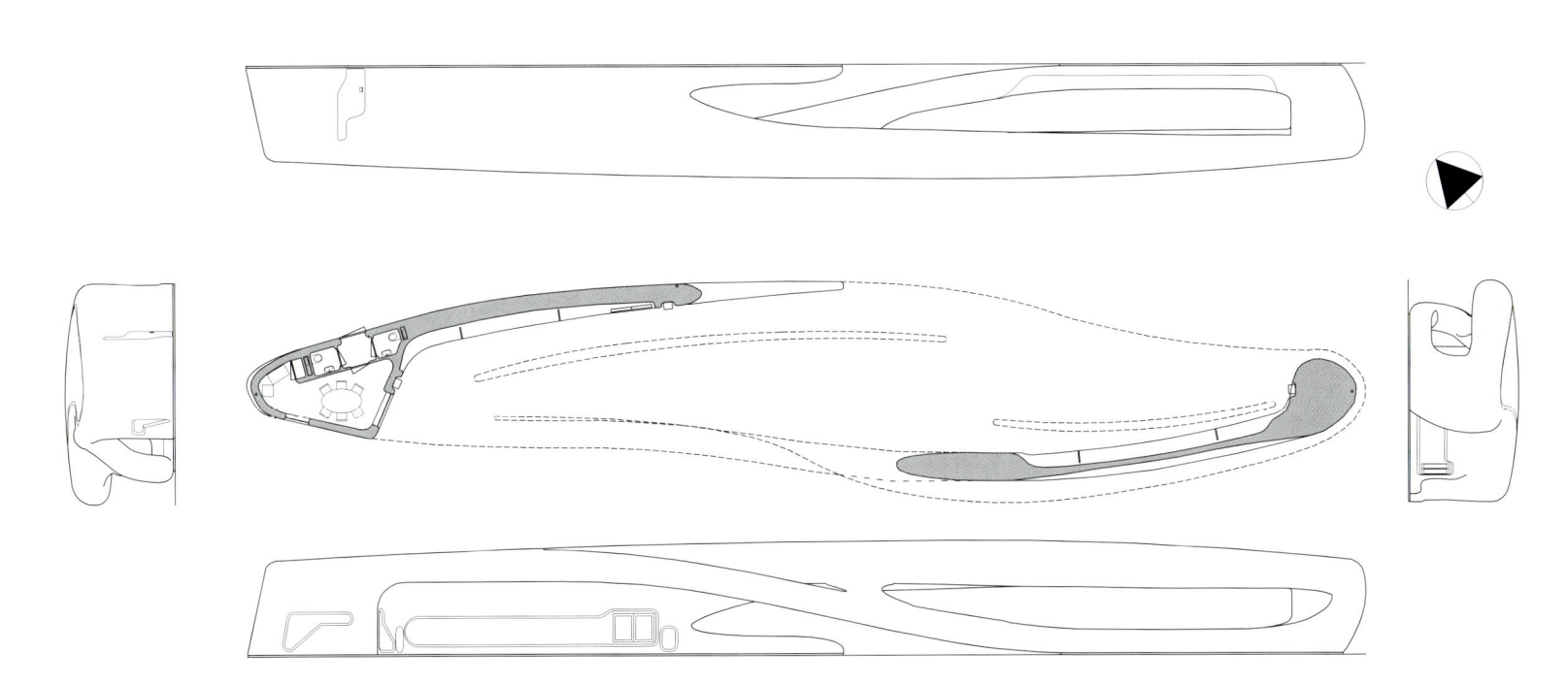

SHELTER | Claude Cormier architectes paysagistes inc.

↑ | **The Grand Pergola,** in front of the City Hall (by Auguste Perret, 1957)

Pergola
Le Havre

For the inaugural year of Le Havre's Contemporary Art Biennale, Claude Cormier designed a pop art piece for the City Hall's grand pergola. Pergola is a tribute to Le Havre-born artist Monet, forefather of impressionism: 90,000 plastic balls are arranged into an image of the wisteria blooms that figure in many of the artist's oeuvres. The balls come in five vivid colors – an abstracted impressionist palette – and climb towards the abundant sunlight, creating an exuberant play of color, light and shadows underneath. As with many of the designers' projects, the deliberate insertion of the artificial shakes up preconceived ideas – but the installation also aims, more simply, to delight visitors.

PROJECT FACTS **Address:** City Hall, 76084 Le Havre, France. **Curator:** Claude Gosselin, Centre Internationale d'art contemporain de Montréal. **Client:** Le Havre Biennale d'art contemporain. **Completion:** 2006. **Production:** single piece. **Design:** individual design. **Functions:** pergola. **Main materials:** plastic Christmas balls.

↑ | **Making of**
↓ | **Swarms of pink, purple, green, blue balls,** bluring with the existing flourish of climbing leaves

↑ | **Interior view**

SHELTER | Brähmig, Ströer / Lutz Brähmig, Udo Müller

↑ | **Discrete esthetics,** appearance of the City Toilet
→ | **Interior view,** one of two toilets

City Toilet

The City Toilet was developed in compliance with the highest safety and hygienic requirements. It is equipped with a separate cleaning unit in which the entire WC bowl is cleaned and dried after every use. The handicap-accessible facility features two toilet bowls that are cleaned alternately, always keeping one available for use. A separate cabinet also contains two urinals, allowing the city toilet to be used by three persons simultaneously. The floor of both cabins is cleaned and dried automatically in adjustable cycles. Prior to every cleaning process, sensors ensure that no one is inside the facility.

PROJECT FACTS
Client: Ströer Out-of-Home Media AG. **Completion:** 2008. **Production:** serial production. **Design:** individual design. **Functions:** toilet. **Main materials:** stainless steel, polycarbonate.

↖ | **Floor cleaning**
↑ | **Toilet bowl cleaning**
← | **Section**

CITY TOILET

← | **Interior view**
↓ | **Detail view**, urinals

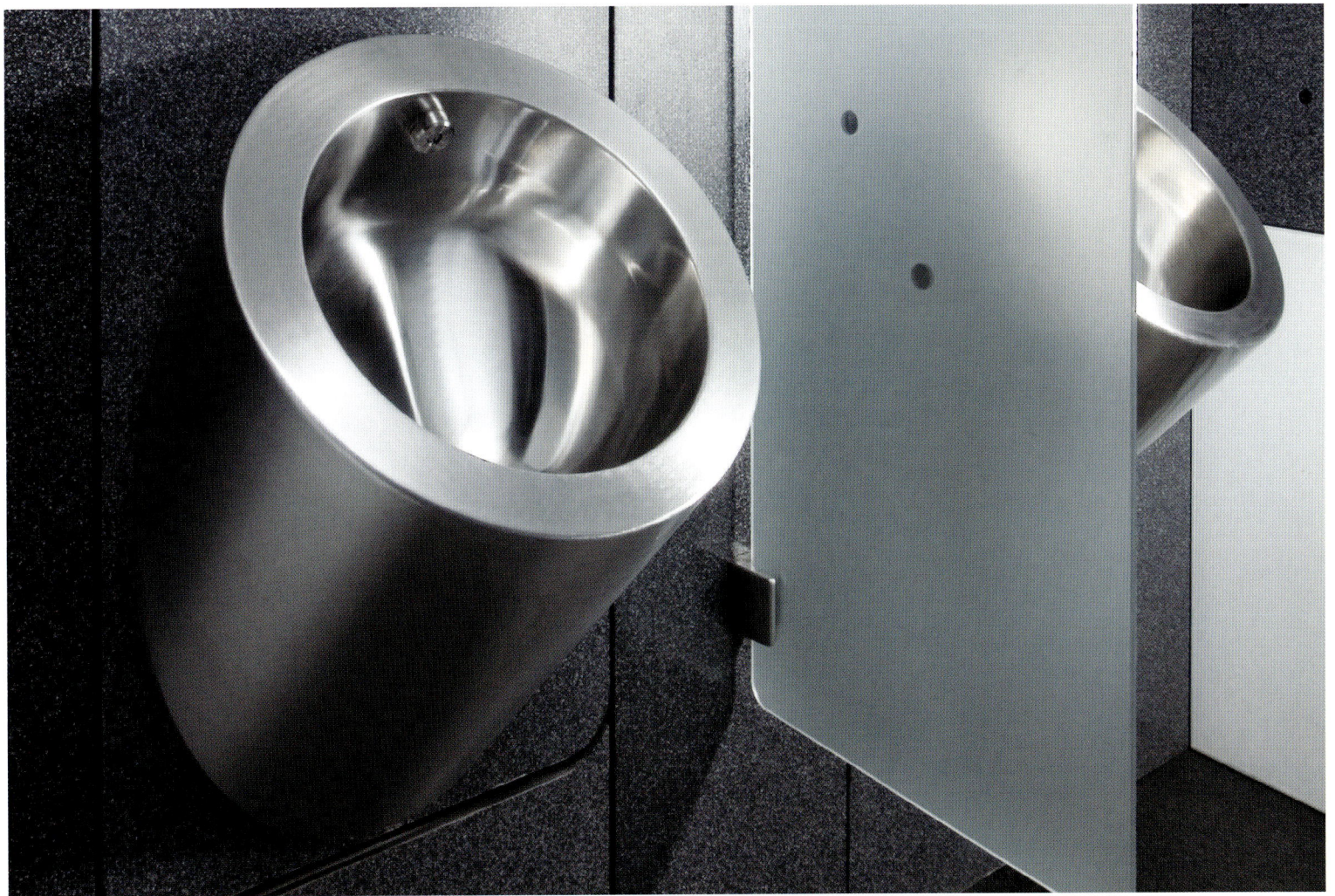

SHELTER

Miró Rivera Architects / Juan Miró, Miguel Rivera

↑ | **View looking down on restroom**

Trail Restroom
Austin

The restroom was conceived as a sculpture in a park, a dynamic object along the active trails. It consists of vertical Corten steel plates whose width and height vary in size. The panels form a spine that coils at one end to form the restroom walls. The plates are staggered in plan to control views and to allow penetrating light and fresh air. Door and roof were fabricated from steel plates as well. The restroom is handicap-accessible and, in addition to a chest of drawers, urinal, sink and bench inside, it includes a drinking fountain and shower outside. The plumbing fixtures are made of heavy duty stainless steel and there is no need for artificial light or mechanical ventilation inside.

PROJECT FACTS **Address:** Lady Bird Lake Trail, Austin, TX, USA. **Client:** The Trail Foundation. **Completion:** 2008.
Production: single piece. **Design:** individual design. **Functions:** toilets. **Main materials:** Corten steel.

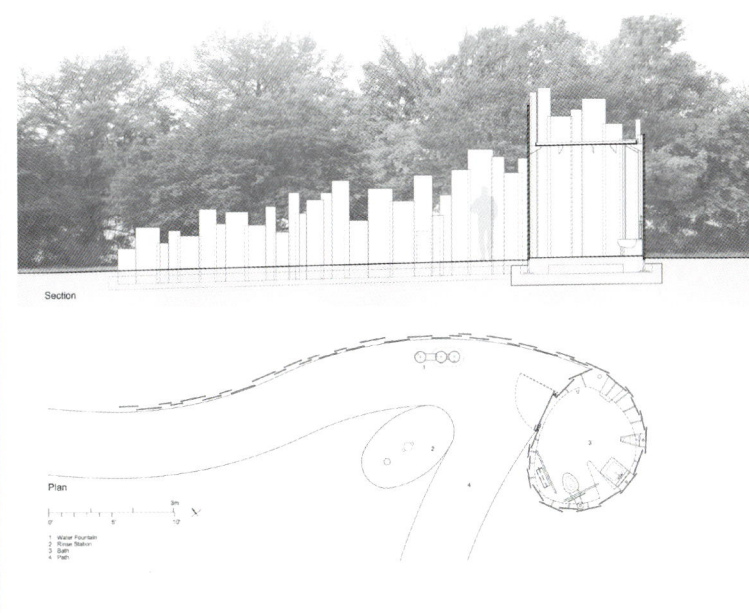

↑ | Interior
↓ | Entrance area

↑ | Elevation and restroom plan
↓ | Close up of Corten steel panels

Index

Ar

Architects, Designers and Manufacturers

ARCHITECTS INDEX

3GATTI

via de' Ciancaleoni 34
00184 Rome (Italy)
T +39.0645.2213589
F +39.178.2299321
mail@3gatti.com
www.3gatti.com

→ 116, 118

3LHD architects

N. Bozidarevica 13/4
Zagreb, HR-10000 (Croatia)
T +385.1.2320200
F +385.1.2320100
info@3lhd.com
www.3lhd.com

→ 148

Bjarne Aasen Landskapsarkitekt MNLA

Hoffsveien 1a
0275 Oslo (Norway)
T +47.21.586341
bjarne.aasen@linklandskap.no

→ 72

Rovero Adrien Studio

Chemin des roses 11
1020 Renens (Switzerland)
T +41.21.6343435
mail@adrienrovero.com
www.adrienrovero.com

→ 14

altreforme

viale Alcide de Gasperi, 16
23801 Calolziocorte (Italy)
T +39.0341.6381
F +39.0341.630239
info@altreforme.com
www.fontana-group.com

→ 326, 328

Agence APS, paysagistes dplg associés

31, Grande rue
2600 Valence (France)
T +33.4.75785353
F +33.4.75785350
agence.aps@wanadoo.fr

→ 221

Arriola & Fiol arquitectes

Carrer Mallorca 289
8037 Barcelona (Spain)
T +34.93.4570357
F +34.93.2080459
arriolafiol@arriolafiol.com
www.arriolafiol.com

→ 87, 89

Artadi Arquitectos

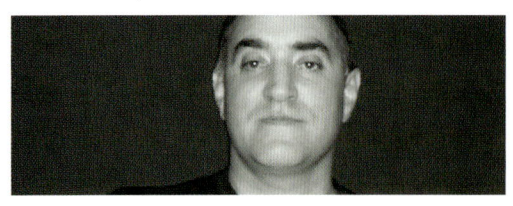

Camino Real 111
Of 701 San Isidro Lima (Peru)
T +511.2226261
info@javierartadi.com
www.javierartadi.com

→ 198

ASPECT Studios (Melbourne Office)

Level 1, 30–32 Easey Street
Collingwood, VIC, 3066 (Australia)
T +61.3.94176844
F +61.3.94176855
aspectmelbourne@aspect.net.au
www.aspect.net.au

→ 82

ASPECT Studios (Sydney Office)

Studio 61, Level 6, 61 Marlborough Street
Surry Hills, NSW, 2010 (Australia)
T +61.2.96997182
F +61.2.96997192
aspectsydney@aspect.net.au
www.aspect.net.au

→ 274

Bacco Arquitetos Associados

Rua General Jardim 645, cj 21
São Paulo, SP (Brasil)
T +55.11.32585961
bacco@bacco.com.br
www.bacco.com.br

→ 406

Baena Casamor Arquitectes BCQ S.L.P.

C.Sant Magí 11–13, 1r
08006 Barcelona (Spain)
T +34.93.2372721
F +34.93.2373218
mail@bcq.es
www.bcq.es

→ 314

LODEWIJK BALJON landscape architects

Cruquiusweg 10
1019 AT Amsterdam (The Netherlands)
T +31.20.6258835
F +31.20.4206534
landscape@baljon.nl
www.baljon.nl

→ 102

BAM Vastgoed

Runnenburg 9
3981 AZ Bunnik (The Netherlands)
T +31.30.6598988
info@bam.nl
www.bam.nl

→ 102

BASE

259, rue Saint-Martin
75003 Paris (France)
T +33.1.42778181
F +33.1.42778198
baseland@free.fr
www.baseland.fr

→ 218

Bureau Baubotanik, Storz Schwertfeger GbR

Innerer Nordbahnhof 1
70191 Stuttgart (Germany)
T +49.711.9335770
info@baubotanik.de
www.baubotanik.de

→ 195

Bauer Membranbau

Neulandstraße 19
85354 Freising (Germany)
T +49.8161.4965565
F +49.8161.92281
info@bauermembranbau.de
www.bauermembranbau.de

→ 195

Matthias Berthold, Andreas Schön

Palmaille 28
22767 Hamburg (Germany)
mail@allermoeher-wand.de
www.allermoeher-wand.de

→ 58, 188

Mitzi Bollani

Via D. Vitali, 3
29121 Piacenza (Italy)
T +39.0523.757086
F +39.0523.071924
studio@mitzibollani.com
www.mitzibollani.com

→ 13, 324, 246

BRÄHMIG GmbH

Robert-Bosch-Straße 10
01454 Radeberg (Germany)
T +49.3528.4197900
F +49.3528.419790
info@braehmig-media.de
www.braehmig-media.de

→ 426

Broadbent

Droppingstone Farm, New Lane, Harthill
Chester CH3 9LG (United Kingdom)
T +44.1829.782822
F +44.1829.782820
enquiries@sbal.co.uk
www.sbal.co.uk

→ 278

BRUTO d.o.o.

Mesarska 4d
1000 Ljubljana (Slovenia)
T +386.1.2322195
F +386.1.2322197
info@bruto.si
www.bruto.si

→ 110, 114, 338, 414

ARCHITECTS INDEX

Buro North

Level 1, 35 Little Bourke Street
Melbourne, VIC 3000 (Australia)
T +61.3.96543259
F +61.3.94459042
buronorth@buronorth.com
www.buronorth.com

→ 382

Estudio Cabeza

Serrano 1249
C1414DEY Buenos Aires (Argentina)
T +54.11.47726183
F +54.11.47770811
info@estudiocabeza.com
www.estudiocabeza.com

→ 160, 254, 256, 258, 269, 398

Caesarea Landscape Design Ltd.

PO Box 70
Caesarea 30889 (Israel)
T +972.4.6263006
F +972.4.6263062
info@caesarion.co.il
www.caesarion.co.il

→ 172, 173, 266, 268, 369

CCM Architects

PO Box 2182
Wellington (New Zealand)
T +64.4.4729354
F +64.4.4725945
Guy.Cleverley@ccm.co.nz
www.ccm.co.nz

→ 122

Corbeil + Bertrand Architecture de paysage

T +1.514.2296490
info@stephane-bertrand.ca
www.stephane-bertrand.ca

→ 418

Claude Cormier architectes paysagistes inc.

5600, De Normanville
Montreal, QC H2S 2B2 (Canada)
T +1.514.8498262
F +1.514.2798076
info@claudecormier.com
www.claudecormier.com

→ 138, 424

CSP Pacific

306 Neilson St, Onehunga
Auckland 1642 (New Zealand)
T +64.9.6341239
F +64.9.6344525
www.csppacific.co.nz

→ 126

d e signstudio regina dahmen-ingenhoven

Plange Mühle 1
40221 Düsseldorf (Germany)
T +49.211.30101200
F +49.211.3010142225
drdi@ingenhovenarchitekten.eu
www.drdi.de

→ 42

Michel Dallaire Design Industriel – MDDI

322, Peel Street
Montreal, QC H3C 2G8 (Canada)
T +1.514.2829262
F +1.514.2829975
info@dallairedesign.com
www.dallairedesign.com

→ 191, 286

Della Valle + Bernheimer Design, LLP

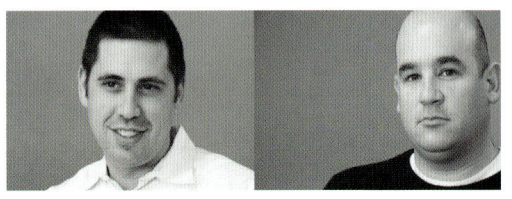

20 Jay Street, Suite 1003
Brooklyn, NY 11201 (USA)
T +1.718.2228155
F +1.718.2228157
info@dbny.com
www.d-bd.com

→ 420

Despang Architekten

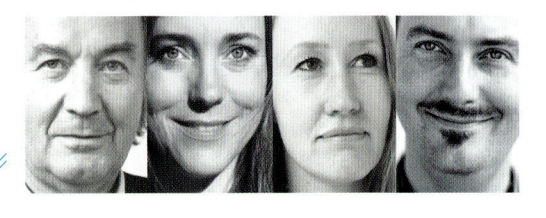

Am Graswege 5
30169 Hanover (Germany)
T +49.511.882840
F +49.511.887985
info@despangarchitekten.de
www.despangarchitekten.de

→ 186

díez+díez diseño

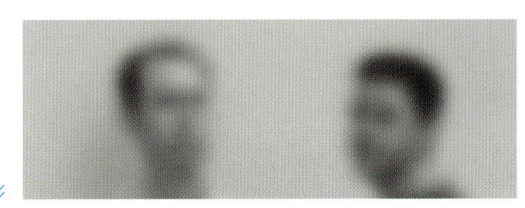

C/ José de Cadalso, 68, 2ºD
28044 Madris (Spain)
T +34.91.7069695
F +34.91.7069695
diezmasdiez@terra.as
www.diezmasdiez.com

→ 34, 41, 154, 238, 259, 296, 298, 300

Droog Design

Staalstraat 7a/b
1011 JJ Amsterdam (The Netherlands)
T +31.20.5235050
F +31.20.3201710
info@droog.com
www.droog.com

→ 248, 252

Earthscape

2-14-6 Ebisu Shibuya-ku
Tokyo, 150-0013 (Japan)
T +81.3.62773970
F +81.3.62773970
info@earthscape.co.jp
info@earthscape.co.jp

→ 120, 156, 158. 164, 340, 342, 344, 346, 348, 350

Earthworks Landscape Architects

Po box 48205, Kommetjie
Cape Town 7976 (South Africa)
T +27.21.828708517
earthworks@tiscali.co.za
www.earthworkslandscapearchitects.com

→ 358

EBD architects ApS

Struenseegade 15A, 2
2200 Copenhagen N (Denmark)
T +45.32.965700
F +49.541.572660
www.info@ebd.dk
www.ebd.dk

→ 174, 236

ENVAC AB

Fleminggatan 7, 3 tr
112 26 Stockholm (Sweden)
T +46.8.7850010
www.envacgroup.com

→ 175

Epoch Product Design

810 NW Wallula Ave.
Gresham, OR 97030 (USA)
T +1.503.6674100
F +1.707.4437797
ideas@epochdesign.com
www.epochdesign.com

→ 372

ESCOFET 1886 SA

Ronda Universitat 20
08007 Barcelona (Spain)
T +34.93.3185050
F +34.93.4124465
informacion@escofet.com
www.escofet.com

→ 154, 267, 284. 302, 304, 308, 314, 316

Esrawe Studio

Culiacan 123 Piso 5
Colonia Hipódromo Condesa (Mexico)
T +52.55.55539611
info@esrawe.com
www.esrawe.com

→ 330

Prof. Valie Export

www.valieexport.at

→ 400

Foreign Office Architects (FOA)

55 Curtain Road
London EC2A 3PT (United Kingdom)
T +44.207.0339800
F +44.207.0339801
london@f-o-a.net
www.f-o-a.net

→ 261

Diego Fortunato

Rosselló 255
08008 Barcelona (Spain)
T +34.629.778107
F +34.933.686865
mail@diegofortunato.com
www.diegofortunato.com

→ 267, 302

Freitag Weidenart

Gartenstraße 21
85354 Freising (Germany)
T +49.8161.91576
F +49.8161.7495
freitag-weidenart@arcor.de
www.freitag-weidenart.com

→ 195

GH form

Bækgaardsvej 64
4140 Borup (Denmark)
T +45.59.450780
sus@ghform.dk
www.ghform.dk

→ 236

GITMA

Sangroniz 2
48150 Sondika (Spain)
T +34.94.4710613
F +34.94.4536121
www.gitma.es

→ 296

ARCHITECTS INDEX

Grijsen park & straatdesign

Lorentzstraat 13
7102 JH Winterswijk (The Netherlands)
T +31.543.516950
F +31.543.513050
info@grijsen.nl
www.grijsen.nl

→ 250

Grimshaw

100 Reade Street
New York, NY, 10013 (USA)
T +1.212.7912501
F +1.212.7912173
info@grimshaw-architects.com
www.grimshaw-architects.com

→ 18, 386

Grupo de Diseño Urbano

Fernando Montes de Oca 4, Col. Condesa
Mexico City, 06140 (Mexico)
T +52.55.55531248
F +52.55.52861013
anaschjetnan@gdu.com.mx
www.gdu.com.mx

→ 144

Gitta Gschwendtner

Unit F1, 2-4 Southgate Road
London N1 3JJ (United Kingdom)
T +44.2.072492021
mail@gittagschwendtner.com
www.gittagschwendtner.com

→ 61, 336

GTL Landschaftsarchitekten

Grüber Weg 21
34117 Kassel (Germany)
T +49.561.789460
F +49.561.7894611
kontakt@gtl-kassel.de
www.gtl-kassel.de

→ 169

Zaha Hadid Architects

Studio 9, 10 Bowling Green Lane
London EC1R 0BQ (United Kingdom)
T +44.20.72535147
F +44.20.72518322
mail@zaha-hadid.com
www.zaha-hadid.com

→ 276

Heatherwick studio

364 Gray's Inn Road
London WC1X 8BH (United Kingdom)
T +44.20.78338800
F +44.20.78338400
studio@heatherwick.com
www.heatherwick.com

→ 394

Heijmans N.V.

Graafsebaan 65
5248 JT Rosmalen (The Netherlands)
T +31.73.5435111
F +31.73.5435220
www.heijmans.nl

→ 102

hess AG

Lantwattenstraße 22
78050 Villingen-Schwenningen (Germany)
T +49.7721.9200
F +49.7721.920250
hess@hess.eu
www.hess.eu

→ 200

Isthmus

PO Box 90366
Auckland 1142 (New Zealand)
T +64.9.3099442
F +.64.9.3099060
akl@isthmus.co.nz
www.isthmus.co.nz

→ 126, 130, 352, 356

Toyo Ito and Associates, Architects

Fujiya Building, 1-19-4,Shibuya, Shibuya-ku
Tokyo, 150-0002 (Japan)
T +81.3.34095822
F +81.3.34095969
www.toyo-ito.co.jp

→ 140, 316

JCDecaux SA

17, rue Soyer
92523 Neuilly-sur-Seine (France)
T +33.1.30797979
info_ventes@jcdecaux.fr
www.jcdecaux.fr

→ 20

JJR | Floor

1425 N. First Street, 2nd Floor
Phoenix, AZ 85004 (USA)
T +1.602.4621425
F +1.602.4621427
design@floorassociates.com
www.floorassociates.com

→ 208

Agence Patrick Jouin

8, Passage de la Bonne Graine
75011 Paris (France)
T +33.1.55288920
F +33.1.58306070
agence@patrickjouin.com
www.patrickjouin.com

→ 20

Sungi Kim & Hozin Song

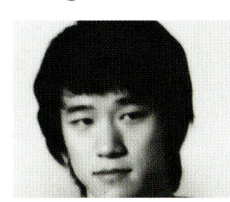

224-1010 Chungmu-APT, Jaegung-dong, Kunpo-si
Kyounggi-do [435-764] (Republic of Korea)
T +82.10.55955942
sungi.kim@gmail.com
www.sungikim.com

→ 60

KMA Creative Technology Ltd

12 St Denys Court
York, YO1 9PU (United Kingdom)
T +44.7973.190365
contact@kma.co.uk
www.kma.co.uk

→ 12

KOMPLOT Design

Amager Strandvej 50
2300 Copenhagen S (Denmark)
T +45.32.963255
F +45.32.963277
komplot@komplot.dk
www.komplot.dk

→ 376

KOSMOS

Rävala Pst. 8-808
Tallin 10143 (Estonia)
T +372.6.312050
F +372.6.312050
info@kosmoses.ee
www.kosmoses.ee

→ 70

Kramer Design Associates (KDA)

103 Dupont Street
Toronto, ON M5R-1V4 (Canada)
T +1.416.9211078
info@kramer-design.com
www.kramer-design.com

→ 189, 232

Tom Leader Studio

1015 Camelia Street
Berkeley, CA 94710 (USA)
T +1.510.5243363
F +1.510.5243863
mail@tomleader.com
www.tomleader.com

→ 220

LEURA srl.

Via Vitali, 3
29100 Piacenza (Italy)
T +39.0523.757086
leura@leura.it
www.leura.it

→ 13

Stacy Levy

576 Upper Georges Valley Rd,
Spring Mills, PA 16875 (USA)
T +1.814.3604346
stacy@stacylevy.com
www.stacylevy.com

→ 212, 216

Biuro Projektów Lewicki Łatak

ul. Dolnych Młynów 7/7
31-124 Krakow (Poland)
T +48.12.6335920, T +48.12.6338693
F +48.12.6337944
biuro@lewicki-latak.com.pl
www.lewicki-latak.com.pl

→ 104, 108, 204, 207

Lifschutz Davidson Sandilands

Island Studios, 22 St Peter's Square
London W6 9NW (United Kingdom)
T +44.208.6004800
F +44.208.6004700
mail@lds-uk.com
www.lds-uk.com

→ 228, 230

ARCHITECTS INDEX

Macaedis

Ctra Olula del Río, Macael, Km 1,7
04867 Macael (Spain)
T +34.950.126370
F +34.950.126078
info@macaedis.com
www.macaedis.com

→ 196

Machado and Silvetti Associates

560 Harrison Avenue, Suite 301
Boston, MA 02118 (USA)
T +1.617.4267070
F +1.617.4263604
info@machado-silvetti.com
www.machado-silvetti.com

→ 134

Jangir Maddadi Design Bureau AB

Södra Långgatan 38
Kalmar (Sweden)
T +46.8.41046066
hello@jangirmaddadi.se
hello@jangirmaddadi.se

→ 292

mago:group, mago:URBAN

Pol. Industrial Masia d'en Barreres, s/n - P.B. 25
08800 Vilanova (Spain)
T +34.93.8148661
info@magogroup.com
www.magogroup.com

→ 238, 261

Studio Makkink & Bey BV

Overschieseweg 52 a
3044 EG Rotterdam (The Netherlands)
T +31.10.4258792
F +31.10.4259437
studio@jurgenbey.nl
www.studiomakkinkbey.nl

→ 248

Marinaprojekt d.o.o.

M. Krleze 1
Zadar (Croatia)
T +385.23.333716
F +385.23.334866
marina-projekt@w.t-com.hr

→ 90

Julian Mayor

106 Sclater Street
London E1 6HR (United Kingdom)
T +44.7775.516005
info@julianmayor.com
www.julianmayor.com

→ 334

Gonzalo Milà Valcárcel

c/ Fusina 6, ent-1º
08002 Barcelona (Spain)
T +34.93.2681982
gonzalo@fusina6.com
www.fusina6.com

→ 178, 196, 308

Benjamin Mills

T +44.78.07567701
ben@ben-mills.com
www.ben-mills.com

→ 294

Miró Rivera Architects

505 Powell Street
Austin, TX 78703 (USA)
T +1.512.4777016
F +1.512.4767672
info@mirorivera.com
www.mirorivera.com

→ 408, 430

mmcité a.s.

Bílovice 519
687 12 Bílovice (Czech Republic)
T +420.572.434290
F +420.572.434283
obchod@mmcite.cz
www.mmcite.com

→ 36, 48, 176, 240, 360, 404

MODO srl.

S.S.Padana Superiore 11, n°28
20063 Cernusco sul Naviglio (Italy)
T +39.0292.592024
F +39.0292.591791
info@modomilano.it
www.modomilano.it

→ 15, 246, 324

Alexandre Moronnoz

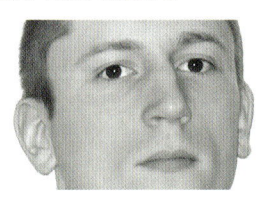

67, rue de Paris
93100 Montreuil (France)
T +33.6.63415834
contact@moronnoz.com
www.moronnoz.com

→ 318, 320, 322

nahtrang

c/ Arcs 8, 2n-1a c.p.
08002 Barcelona (Spain)
T +34.93.3427844
F +34.93.3022837
nahtrang@nahtrang.com
www.nahtrang.com

→ 304

Nea Studio

110 Bleecker Street, No 4 D
New York, NY 10012 (USA)
T +1.917.6905480
nina@neastudio.com
www.neastudio.com

→ 262

Brodie Neill

57-60 Charlotte Road
London EC2A 3QT (United Kingdom)
T +44.207.6133123
info@brodieneill.com
www.brodieneill.com

→ 332

Will Nettleship

526 Pinehurst Avenue
Placentia, CA 92870 (USA)
T +1.714.5793636
F +1.714.5791239
wnsculptor@aol.com
www.sculpture.org

→ 146, 206

NIO architecten

Schiedamse Vest 95a
3012 BG Rotterdam (The Netherlands)
T +31.10.4122318
F +31.10.4126075
nio@nio.nl
www.nio.nl

→ 422

NL Architects

Van Hallstraat 294
1051 HM Amsterdam (The Netherlands)
T +31.20.6207323
F +31.20.6386192
office@nlarchitects.nl
www.nlarchitects.nl

→ 252

NOLA Industrier AB

Repslagargatan 15b
118 46 Stockholm (Sweden)
T +46.8.7021960
F +46.8.7021962
headoffice@nola.se
www.nola.se

→ 376

Numen / For Use

Canisiusgasse 13/16
1090 Vienna (Austria)
T +43.664.2607447
info@architekci.info
www.foruse.info

→ 148

OKRA landschapsarchitecten bv

Oudegracht 23
3511 AB Utrecht (The Netherlands)
T +31.30.2734249
F +31.30.2735128
mail@okra.nl
www.okra.nl

→ 50, 86, 88, 168

OLIN

Public Ledger Building, Suite 1123,
150 South Independence Mall West
Philadelphia, PA 19106 (USA)
T +1.215.4400030
F +1.215.4400041
info@theolinstudio.com
www.theolinstudio.com

→ 166, 372, 374

Osterwold & Schmidt – Exp!ander Architekten

Brühl 22
99423 Weimar (Germany)
T +3643.7736580
F +3643.7736581
mail@osterwold-schmidt.de
www.osterwold-schmidt.de

→ 30

Studio Pacific Architecture

Level 2, 74 Cuba Street
Te Aro 6011 (New Zealand)
T +64.4.8025444
F +64.4.8025446
architects@studiopacific.co.nz
www.studiopacific.co.nz

→ 130

ARCHITECTS INDEX

Paviments MATA

Càntir, 1 Zona Industrial del Sud
08292 Esparreguera (Spain)
T +34.93.7771300
F +34.93.7771704
info@pmata.com
www.pavimentsmata.com

→ 34, 298, 300

PLEIDEL ARCHITEKTI s.r.o.

SNP 17
927 00 Sala (Slovak Republic)
T +421.31.7704913
pleidel@salamon.sk
www.pleidel-architekti.sk

→ 360

Atelier Boris Podrecca

Jörgerbadgasse 8
1170 Vienna (Austria)
T +43.1.427210
F +43.1.4272120
podrecca@podrecca.at
www.podrecca.at

→ 74

Buro Poppinga

Anjeliersstraat 145 hs
1015 NE Amsterdam (The Netherlands)
T +31.20.6811637
info@poppinga.nl
www.poppinga.nl

→ 250

Agence Elizabeth de Portzamparc

104 rue Oberkampf
75011 Paris (France)
T +33.1.53633232
info@elizabethdeportzamparc.com
www.elizabethdeportzamparc.com

→ 242

PWP Landscape Architecture, Inc.

739 Allston Way
Berkeley, CA 94710 (USA)
T +1.510.8499494
F +1.510.8499333
info@pwpla.com
www.pwpla.com

→ 161

RASTI GmbH

An der Mühle 21
49733 Haren (Germany)
T +49.05934.70350
F +49.05934.703510
info@rasti.eu
www.rasti.eu

→ 24

Tejo Remy & Rene Veenhuizen

Uraniumweg 17
3542 AK Utrecht (The Netherlands)
T +31.30.2944945
T +31.30.2944945
atelier@remyveenhuizen.nl
www.remyveenhuizen.nl

→ 46

Rios Clementi Hale Studios

639 N Larchmont Blvd.
Los Angeles, CA 90004 (USA)
T +1.323.7851800
F +1.323.7851801
info@rchstudios.com
www.rchstudios.com

→ 94, 98

Janet Rosenberg + Associates

148 Kenwood Avenue
Toronto, ON M6C 2S3 (Canada)
T +1.416.6566665
F +1.416.6565756
office@jrala.ca
www.jrala.ca

→ 138, 162

Adrien Rovero with Christophe Ponceau

Chemin des roses 11
1020 Renens (Switzerland)
T +41.21.6343435
mail@adrienrovero.com
www.adrienrovero.com

→ 62

Samsung Electronics

Samsung Main Building. 250,
Taepyeongno 2-ga, Jung-gu, Seoul (Republic of Korea)
T +11.82.2.7277114
F +11.82.2.7277985
www.samsung..com

→ 260

sandellsandberg

Östermalmsgatan 26A
114 26 Stockholm (Sweden)
T +46.8.50653100
F +46.8.50621707
info@sandellsandberg.se
www.sandellsandberg.se

→ 249

Santa & Cole

Parc de Belloch Ctra. C-251, Km. 5,6
08430 La Roca (Spain)
T +34.938.619100
F +34.938.711767
info@santacole.com
www.santacole.com

→ 178

Aziz Sariyer

Acisu Sk Cem Ap. No.11 D.3 34357 Besiktas
Istanbul (Turkey)
T +90.212.3271585
F +90.212.2588032

→ 326, 328

Sasaki Associates

64 Pleasant Street
Watertown, MA 02472 (USA)
T +1.617.9263300
F +1.617.9242748
info@sasaki.com
www.sasaki.com

→ 78, 182

Rainer Schmidt Landschafts-architekten

Klenzestraße 57c
80469 Munich (Germany)
T +49.89.2025350
F +49.89.20253530
mail@Schmidt-Landschaftsarchitekten.de
www.schmidt-landschaftsarchitekten.de

→ 169, 190, 410

Pedro Silva Dias

Travessa das Necessidades 9, 2°
135-220 Lisbon (Portugal)
T +351.962.574991
atelier@pedrosilvadias.com
www.pedrosilvadias.com

→ 40, 390, 392

Sitetectonix Private Limited

22 Cross Street, #02-52/54 China Square Central
Singapore 048421 (Singapore)
T +65.6327.4452
F +65.6327.8042
marinaong@sitetectonix.com
www.sitetectonix.com

→ 140, 222

Siteworks-Studio

826 C Hinton Avenue
Charlottesville, VA 22901 (USA)
T +1.434.9238100
F +1.434.2956611
wilson@siteworks-studio.com
www.siteworks-studio.com

→ 52

Smedsvig Landskapsarkitekter AS

Øvre Korskirkesmau 2b
5018 Bergen (Norway)
T +47.55.210470
F +47.55.210480
post@smedsvig-landskap.no
www.smedsvig-landskap.no

→ 362

Owen Song

2 College Street No. 2373
Providence, RI 02903 (USA)
T +1.401.3682922
msong@g.risd.edu
www.owensong.kr

→ 260

Lucile Soufflet

7 rue de la Hutte
1495 Sart-Dames-Avelines (Belgium)
T +32.71.954553
F +32.71.954553
info@lucile.be
www.lucile.be

→ 288, 290

ARCHITECTS INDEX

SQLA inc. LA

530 Molino Street No. 204
Los Angeles, CA 90013 (USA)
T +1.213.3831788
F +1.213.6130878
la@sqlainc.com
www.sqlainc.com

→ 136

STORE MUU design studio

3-25-1-211 Shinkoiwa katsushikaku
Tokyo 1240024 (Japan)
T +81.3.58799085
F +81.3.58799086
info@storemuu.com
www.storemuu.com

→ 16

Street and Garden Furniture Company

PO Box 3662
South Brisbane, QLD 4101 (Australia)
T +61.7.38441951
F +61.7.38449337
sales@streetandgarden.com.au
www.streetandgarden.com.au

→ 226, 280, 282, 284

Street and Park Furniture

Unit 13 / 19 Heath Street
Lonsdale 5160 South Australia (Australia)
T +61.8.83296750
F +61.8.83296799
sales@streetandpark.com.au
www.streetandpark.com.au

→ 310, 312

Ströer Out-of-Home Media AG

Ströer Allee 1
50999 Cologne (Germany)
T +49.2236.96450
F +49.2236.9645299
info@stroeer.com
www.stroeer.de

→ 426

Tecnología & Diseño Cabanes

Parque Industrial Avanzado Avenida de la Ciencia, 7
3005 Ciudad Real (Spain)
T +34.926.251354
F +34.926.221654
info@tdcabanes.com
www.tdcabanes.com

→ 41, 259

Architektin Mag. arch. Silja Tillner

Margaretenplatz 7/2/1
1050 Vienna (Austria)
T +43.1.3106859
F +43.1.310685915
tw@tw-arch.at
www.tw-arch.at

→ 264, 400

Tokujin Yoshioka Design

9-1 Daikanyama-cho, Shibuya-ku
Tokyo 150-0034 (Japan)
T +81.3.54280830
F +81.3.54280835
yoshioka@tokujin.com
www.tokujin.com

→ 337

töpfer.bertuleit.architekten

Am Friedrichshain 2
10407 Berlin
T +49.30.53214780
F +49.30.53214785
mail@tb-architekten.de
www.tb-architekten.de

→ 200

Turenscape

Zhong Guan Cun Fa Zhan Da Sha,
12 Shang Di Xin Xi Road, Haidian Dist
Beijing 100085 (China)
T +86.1.3801193799
F +86.10.62967511
kj@turenscape.com
www.turenscape.com

→ 364

Valentin Design

T +61.449.052599
valentin@valentindesign.com
www.valentindesign.com

→ 126

Anouk Vogel landscape architecture

Nieuwe Teertuinen 17-XI
1013 LV Amsterdam (The Netherlands)
T +31.20.6201595
info@anoukvogel.nl
www.anoukvogel.nl

→ 57, 247

Vulcanica Architettura

Piazza Matteotti 7
80133 Naples (Italy)
T +39.081.5515146
F +39.081.5515146
studio@vulcanicaarchitettura.it
www.vulcanicaarchitettura.it

→ 147

WAA – william asselin ackaoui

55 Mont-Royal Avenue West, Suite 805
Montreal, Quebec, H2T 2S6 (Canada)
T +1.514.9392106
F +1.514.9392107
waa@waa-ap.com
www.waa-ap.com

→ 191

Studio Weave

33 St. John's Church Road
London E9 6EJ (United Kingdom)
T +44.20.85103665
Hello@studioweave.com
www.studioweave.com

→ 66

West 8 urban design & landscape architecture

Schiehaven 13m
3024 EC Rotterdam (The Netherlands)
T +31.10.4855801
F +31.10.4856323
west8@west8.com
www.west8.com

→ 192, 194, 197, 270, 272

Woodhouse plc

Spa Park, Leamington Spa
Warwickshire CV31 3HL (United Kingdom)
T +44.1926.314313
F +44.1926.883778
enquire@woodhouse.co.uk
www.woodhouse.co.uk

→ 230

Ryo Yamada

2Jo- 9Chome, 5-1-202, Hiragishi Toyohira
Sapporo (Japan)
T +81.11.8879487
F +81.11.8879487
ryo@ryo-yamada.com

→ 56, 368, 370

YHY design international

Terenzio 12
Milan 20133 (Italy)
T +39.0349.732720
yoanndesign@gmail.com
www.yoanndesign.com

→ 28

ZonaUno

Via Mazzini, 7
20123 Milan (Italy)
T +39.0289.690231
F +39.0289.690231
info@zonauno.it
www.zonauno.it

→ 15

PICTURE CREDITS

Je Ahn, London	66–69
Shigeki Asanuma, Tokyo, Courtesy of Earthscape	157 a. r., 157 b., 158, 159 b., 160, 161 b., 164–165, 340–343, 346–349
Paul Bardagjy Photography, Austin (TX)	409 b. l., 409 r., 430
Valerie Bennett	261 (portrait)
S. Bertrand, Montreal	418–419
studio bisbee	288–289
Domagoj Blazevic, Split	149 a.
Tom Bonner, Los Angeles (CA)	94–97
Nicolas Borel	242–243
Chris Brown	208–211
Radek Brunecky	422 a. l., 422 a. r.
Dolores Cáceres	160
Lana Cavar, Zagreb	148 (portrait)
Cemusa Inc.	386–387
Chuck Choi, Cambridge	213, 215 a., 215 b. r.
Josep Codina, Toni Casamor	314–315
Julio Cunill, Barcelona	178, 179 b.
Mike Curtain, Brisbane	226–227
Dart Realty (Cayman) Ltd.	373 b.
Simon Devitt, Auckland	126–131, 352–357
Ryan Donnell	166 (portrait), 374 (portrait)
Steve Double	276 (portrait)
Epoch Product Design	372
Escofet	87 a. r., b. l., 316–317
Damir Fabijanic, Zagreb	74–77, 151 a.
Enrico Fantoni	254
Fillioux&Fillioux	319 a. r.
Neil Fox, Toronto	139-139, 162, 163 l.
Jeff Gahres / Grimshaw New York	19 b.
GH form	236–237
B. Gigounon	288 (portrait)
Glowfrog Studios, London	228
Francisco Gomez Sosa	144–145
Florian Groehn, Sydney	224 (portrait), 275 b., 280–285, 284 (portrait)
Iann Gross & Emilie Müller	14
Steffen Groß, Weimar	30–33
Jeppe Gudmundsen-Holmgreen, Copenhagen	376 (portrait), 378 b. l., 378 b. r.
V. Tony Hauser, Toronto	138 (portrait l.), 162 (portrait)
Philip Hawk, Lemont	217 b.
Luke Hayes, London	336
Olivier Helbert	218–219
Irena Herak	110 (portrait), 114 (portrait), 338 (portrait), 414 (portrait)
hess AG, Villingen-Schwenningen	200
Barrie Ho Architecture Interiors Ltd	276–277
Martin Hogenboom	422 (portrait)
Bjorn van Holstein	250–251
João Jacinto, Lisbon	40 (portrait), 390 (portrait), 392 (portrait)
Mario Jelavic, Split	148, 149 b., 150 a., 151 b.
Zoé Jobin	62 (portrait)
Richard Johnson, Toronto	232–233
Pernille Kaaber, New York (NY)	262–263
Ott Kadarik	70–71
Miran Kambič	110–115
Rik Klein Gotink, Harderwijk	103 a., 103 m., 103 b.
KMA Creative Technology Ltd	12 b. r.
Nelson Kon, São Paulo	406–407
Pawe_ Kubisztal, Krakow	105–109
Craig Kuhner, Arlington (TX)	78–79, 81
Alain Laforest	286–287
Stephan Lee	134–135
Andrew Lloyd, Melbourne	82–85
Soren Luckins, Melbourne	382 (portrait)
Björn Lux, Hamburg	58–59
Equipo Macaedis, Macael Almería	196
mago group	261
Dan Males, Isthmus, Wellington	132
Ezio Manciucca, Lecco	326–329
Beat Marugg, Barcelona	87 a. l.
Brian McCall, KDA	189
Paul Mccredie	122–125
Ana Mello, São Paulo	406 (portrait)
Peter Mitchell, SPA, Wellington	133
Mori Building	337 r. a., 337 r. b.
Ben ter Mull	51, 86 a. r.
Ramon Muntades	308, 309 a. l.
Robert Newald, Vienna	264 (portrait), 400 (portrait l.)
Adam van Nieuwenhuizen and Zeenat Johnstone	358–359
Monika Nikolic, Kassel	264–265
Lorena Noblecilla	198–199
North News & Pictures Ltd	12 a. l., b. l.
Mustafa Nuhoglu, Istanbul	326 (portrait), 328 (portrait)
Daniel Nytoft, Berlin/Copenhagen	379 a.
Markn Ogue	394 (portrait)
Masahiro Okamura	337 (portrait)
OKRA and Schul & CO Landskabsarkitekter	88
Koji Okumura / Forward Stroke, Tokyo, Courtesy of Earthscape	120–121, 156, 159 a. r., 161 a. r., 344–345
Andres Otero	62–63
Christobal Palma	394–397
Hans Pattist	422
Jacques Perron	424–425
Andrzej Pilichowski-Ragno, Krakow	104 (portrait)
Piston Design, Austin (TX)	408, 409 a. r., 431
Sabine Puche	318, 319 b., 320–323
Laia Puig, Barcelona	178 (portrait), 179 a., 196 (portrait), 308 (portrait), 309 a. r., 309 b.
Shen Qiang, Shanghai	116–119
Kiran Ridley	61
Mariela Rivas	398–399
Sabina Saritz, Vienna	400 (portrait r.)
Anne von Sarosdy, Düsseldorf	42 (portrait)
Michael Schoner	253 a.
Ryan Schude, Los Angeles (CA)	94 (portrait), 98 (portrait)
Se'lux	193 a. r., 193 b., 194 l., 194 r. a., 197
Scott Shigley, Chicago (IL)	98–101
Helen Smith-Yeo, Singapore, Sitetectonix	140–143, 222–223
Juliusz Sokołowski, Warsaw	104 (portrait), 108 (portrait), 204 (portrait), 207 (portrait)
Christian Spielmann, Hamburg	58 (portrait), 188
Rupert Steiner, Vienna	400–403
Stipe Surać	90–93
Urban Švegl	414–417
Daniel Swarovski & Co.	42–45
töpfer.bertuleit.architekten, Berlin	201
Roel van Tour	248
Chris van Uffelen, Stuttgart	8, 186, 187 b. l., 187 b. r.
visualhouse, London	229 a. l., 229 a. r., 229 b.
Matt Wain, London	228 (portrait), 230 (portrait)
David Walker, ©2002, PWP Landscape Architecture, Inc.	161
Herbert Wiggerman	46–47
Wilky Photography	332–333
Ed Wonsek, Arlington (MA)	80 b., 182–185
Woodhouse plc, Leamington Spa	230–231
Wright State University, Dayton (OH)	146
Casimir Zdanius / Grimshaw New York	18, 19 a., 388–389
Hernan Zenteno	255 a. l., 255 b., 256–258

All other pictures, especially portraits and plans, were made available by the architects.

Cover front from left to right, from above to below: mmcité a.s. | Piston Design / Austin, Texas | Se'lux | Richard Johnson, www.richardjohnson.ca | Richard Johnson, www.richardjohnson.ca | SIMON DEVITT / AUCKLAND | Richard Johnson, www.richardjohnson.ca | Woodhouse plc, Leamington Spa | Barrie Ho Architecture Interiors Ltd

Cover back: left: paul mccredie; right: Nelson Kon, São Paulo

IMPRINT

The Deutsche Nationalbibliothek lists this publication in the Deutsche Nationalbibliographie; detailed bibliographical data are available on the Internet at http://dnb.ddb.de

ISBN 978-3-03768-043-8

© 2010 by Braun Publishing AG
www.braun-publishing.ch

The work is copyright protected. Any use outside of the close boundaries of the copyright law, which has not been granted permission by the publisher, is unauthorized and liable for prosecution. This especially applies to duplications, translations, microfilming, and any saving or processing in electronic systems.

1st edition 2010

Editorial office: van Uffelen
Editorial staff: Marek Heinel, Anika Burger, Sarah Schkölzinger, Chris van Uffelen
Translation: Cosima Talhouni
Graphic concept: ON Grafik | Tom Wibberenz
Layout: Marek Heinel, Georgia van Uffelen
Reproduction: Bild1Druck GmbH, Berlin

All of the information in this volume has been compiled to the best of the editors' knowledge. It is based on the information provided to the publisher by the architects' and designers' offices and excludes any liability. The publisher assumes no responsibility for its accuracy or completeness as well as copyright discrepancies and refers to the specified sources (architects' and designers' offices). All rights to the photographs are property of the photographer (please refer to the picture).